The Modern Jewish Experience

This volume has been cosponsored by

THE JEWISH THEOLOGICAL SEMINARY OF AMERICA
and
THE INTERNATIONAL CENTER FOR UNIVERSITY TEACHING
OF JEWISH CIVILIZATION, JERUSALEM

Chancellor of the Jewish Theological Seminary:
Ismar Schorsch

Provost of the Jewish Theological Seminary:
Ivan G. Marcus

Academic Chairman of the International Center:
Moshe Davis

Project Director:
Jack Wertheimer

We gratefully acknowledge the continued support of
THE JOSEPH AND CEIL MAZER FOUNDATION OF NEW YORK
William Mazer, President
and
Daniel G. Ross, Vice President

THE MODERN JEWISH EXPERIENCE

A Reader's Guide

Edited by
JACK WERTHEIMER

NEW YORK UNIVERSITY PRESS
New York and London

NEW YORK UNIVERSITY PRESS
New York and London

Library of Congress Cataloging-in-Publication Data
The Modern Jewish experience : a reader's guide / edited by Jack Wertheimer.
    p.   cm.
Includes bibliographical references and index.
ISBN 0-8147-9261-8 — ISBN 0-8147-9262-6 (pbk.)
1. Jews—History—1789–1945—Study and teaching (Higher)   2. Jews—History—
1945– —Study and teaching (Higher)   3. Jews—Civilization—Study and teaching
(Higher)   4. Bibliography—Jews—History.   5. Jews—History—Bibliography.
6. Jews—History—Outlines, syllabi, etc.   I. Wertheimer, Jack.
DS115.95.M63 1993
909′.04924′00711—dc20   92–31668
                                                             CIP

New York University Press books are printed on acid-free paper,
and their binding materials are chosen for strength and durability.

Manufactured in the United States of America

c 10 9 8 7 6 5 4 3 2 1
p 10 9 8 7 6 5 4 3 2 1

Contents

Preface

Jack Wertheimer

The pace of scholarly research and academic publications in fields of Judaica has quickened dramatically in the second half of the twentieth century. Item: New scholarly journals in a variety of languages are now devoted to research on a broad array of specialized topics, ranging from rabbinic law to Zionism, from Biblical archaeology to modern Jewish literature. Over a half dozen scholarly periodicals deal exclusively with the Holocaust. Item: Institutions of higher learning around the globe sponsor academic conferences on Jewish history and civilization featuring an international cast of scholars. On the occasion of the five-hundredth anniversary of the expulsion of Jews from Spain, to cite one example, a dozen American universities mounted impressive conferences designed to assess the impact of 1492 on Jewish history. Few of these institutions had paid much attention to earlier anniversaries such as the tercentenary of Jewish settlement in the United States (1954). Item: In the middle decades of the century, the Jewish polymath, Professor Salo Baron, produced a multivolume history of the Jews which attempted to incorporate a vast bibliographical apparatus to acquaint readers with all the pertinent scholarly literature. Today, not even a team of scholars would dare embark on such a venture, given the explosion of new research in so many different languages.

The major consumers and producers of this new scholarship are found in Jewish Studies programs that have proliferated at institutions of higher learning around the world since the 1960s. From the vantage point of the nineties, it is difficult to fathom that until thirty years ago, Jewish Studies courses (as opposed to Hebrew language instruction) were mainly limited to a few elite universities, rabbinical seminaries, and Hebrew teachers' colleges. Today there are few colleges at public or private institutions of higher learning that do not sponsor at least some courses on aspects of Jewish study. Indeed, courses on the Holocaust, Jewish literature in translation, Modern Hebrew language, and sociology of the Jews abound — even at colleges under Christian auspices. The professors of these courses number some thousand individuals in North America alone, who are augmented by hundreds of colleagues in Israel, every West European country, former Eastern Bloc nations, Latin America, South Africa, and some Asian countries.

In order to establish an institutional link between these burgeoning Jewish Studies programs, Professor Moshe Davis established the International Center for the University Teaching of Jewish Civilization in Jerusalem. Among the major initiatives sponsored by the International Center has been a series of curricular guides which could serve as teaching aids. In light of the explosion of research on Jewish topics, nonspecialists can benefit from guidance through the thicket of new monographs, source anthologies, textbooks, and scholarly essays outside their own subfields of specialization.

The Modern Jewish Experience, the fruit of collaboration between the International Center and the Jewish Theological Seminary of America, aims to provide such guidance on a range of issues and research pertaining to modern Jewish history, culture, religion, and society. This book is intended primarily for an audience of college professors who teach courses on aspects of Jewish life in the modern world. Some have been trained as specialists in a field of Judaica, such as modern Jewish history, Yiddish or Hebrew literature, modern Jewish thought, or modern rabbinics. Others were trained as generalists and then developed an expertise on their own through research projects — such as American historians who write mainly on Jews in the United States, authorities on French literature who are particularly drawn to the work of Jewish writers, demographers who have a special interest in Jewish population patterns. And still others have been asked by their academic institutions to develop courses on an aspect of the modern Jewish experience based on their nonacademic interest in Jews or Judaism.

This book aims to provide teachers of the modern Jewish experience with a variety of resources. The first section offers twenty-nine essays by leading scholars who seek to orient their colleagues to the major interpretive and methodological issues in fields of modern Jewish studies. Each essay identifies the most helpful books and articles for the college professor who wishes to learn more about a topic for teaching, as opposed to research, purposes.*

*Throughout this volume, the author and title of each work cited is included in the text, with the facts of publication relegated to a footnote. Each work can then be cited (within any chapter) simply by its footnote number.

Most of these essays also recommend a means of structuring three class sessions to highlight key aspects of the topic; they also identify helpful reading assignments for students. The essays in Part 1 therefore provide a means for the college professor to diversify courses on the Modern Jewish Experience by adding class discussions on otherwise unremarked Jewish communities, social and political issues, religious and ideological movements, and disciplinary perspectives.

Part 2 offers several practical resources to expand the teaching repertoire for undergraduate courses on the Modern Jewish Experience. It opens with an annotated listing of bibliographies on specialized topics, catalogues to films, music, the arts, and periodicals, and guides to collections and databases pertaining to modern Jewry. Armed with these guides, the professor can easily uncover teaching material to enrich courses on modern Jewry. A concluding section provides sample syllabi for survey courses taught in diverse linguistic settings. The first of these was developed by a team of scholars in the United States for an American campus setting; the second also reflects English-language materials but emerges out of an entirely different national environment — South Africa. And the concluding syllabi are meant for the French, German, Russian, and Spanish reader respectively. The purpose of these syllabi is to identify the major readings available for classroom use in a range of languages, as well as to offset the intentional emphasis in this book on English-language readings. These syllabi also scant the so-called Early Modern or transitional era from the Middle Ages to the Modern on the grounds that this period requires a level of linguistic and textual preparation beyond the abilities of most undergraduates. Several essays in Part 1 address developments during this period, especially those by Miriam Bodian on "Early Modern Western and Central European Jewry" and David Fishman on "Hasidism and Its Opponents."

The Modern Jewish Experience, with its essays, bibliography, and syllabi, aims to guide the intelligent reader seeking orientation and direction through the maze of new research on modern Jewry. Though mainly intended as a resource for undergraduate instruction, this volume may be used profitably by educators of adults in synagogue and Jewish communal settings, as well as by individual students engaged in private study.

In planning this volume I benefited from the wisdom and support of numerous colleagues. Chancellor Ismar Schorsch of the Jewish Theological Seminary of America and Professor Moshe Davis of the International Center for the University Teaching of Jewish Civilization invited me to direct this project and subsequently offered their sage counsel. I am indebted to Professor Schorsch for his many years of enthusiastic encouragement and helpful advice, and to Professor Davis for welcoming me with great warmth into the academic circle of the International Center. He and members of his staff, particularly Haggai Lev, Priscilla Fishman, and Matelle Godfrey, have been most hospitable and helpful at every turn. At the Seminary a number of members of the administration helped move this project along, including the Provost, Professor Ivan Marcus; Vice Chancellor John Ruskay; Jean Highland, publications consultant; and Ann Appelbaum, counsel to the Seminary.

I was assisted in shaping the structure and content of this volume by two teams of scholars, one in the United States and one in Israel. The former consisted of Professors Miriam Bodian (University of Michigan); Jane Gerber (Graduate Center – CUNY); Marsha Rozenblit (University of Maryland); Michael Stanislawski (Columbia University); and three colleagues at the Jewish Theological Seminary of America, Professors David Fishman, Neil Gillman, and David Roskies. The first syllabus in Part 2 of the book is a tangible result of our deliberations. I also benefited from the collective wisdom of the Israeli team, with whom I consulted a half dozen times during the summers of 1989 and 1990. Members included Professors Haim Avni, Yisrael Bartal, Sergio DellaPergola, Paul Mendes-Flohr, and Gideon Shimoni, all of the Hebrew University. At meetings of the American team, constructive suggestions were offered by several guests, including Professors Harvey Goldberg and Gershon Shaked (both visiting from the Hebrew University).

In the production phase of this book, Niko Pfund, editor at New York University Press, helped speed the manuscript along and offered much valuable advice. Peter T. Daniels served superbly both as copy editor and as editor of an electronic manuscript. Timothy Hanssen assisted ably in a variety of technical tasks and also helped prepare the Annotated Bibliography. I could not have managed the task of coordinating and editing the work of scholars scattered widely between South Africa and the West Coast of the United States, in cities as diverse as Moscow and Toronto, Heidelberg and Bowling Green, without the cheerful collaboration of Peter and Timothy.

Finally, I wish to pay tribute to the professionalism and diligence of the two dozen colleagues who contributed so generously to this volume. I particularly appreciate their willingness to conform to my guidelines and to the severe constraints on length imposed upon them. Working in collaboration with scholars from diverse and far-flung habitations whose disciplinary and historical perspectives vary so greatly has reinforced my conviction that we need to rethink the conventional scope and emphases of teaching on the modern Jewish experience, a process of reconceptualization this volume seeks to foster.

Contributors

M. BODIAN is Assistant Professor of History at the University of Michigan, having previously taught at Yeshiva University. She is currently working on a book on the Portuguese and Spanish Jewish communities of Western Europe and has written several scholarly articles in this area.

RICHARD I. COHEN is Senior Lecturer in Modern Jewish History at the Hebrew University of Jerusalem. He is the author of *The Burden of Conscience: French-Jewish Leadership during the Holocaust* (1987) and editor of *Vision and Conflict in the Holy Land* (1985). He has also edited and contributed to Raymond-Raoul Lambert, *Carnet d'un Temoin, 1940–1943* (1985); *The French Revolution and Its Impact* (in Hebrew, 1991); and served as guest symposium editor of "Art and Its Uses: The Visual Image and Modern Jewish Society," *Studies in Contemporary Jewry*, 1990. He is currently at work on a book of essays on the interrelationship between Jewish art and Jewish social history in the Modern period.

SERGIO DELLAPERGOLA is Head of the Division of Jewish Demography and Statistics and Professor at the Institute of Contemporary Jewry, the Hebrew University of Jerusalem. He is the author of numerous books and articles on Jewish population trends in a wide range of Jewish communities and their significance for the continuity of those communities. His work has covered issues such as the changing demography of the Jewish family, Jewish international migrations, and the quantitative aspects of Jewish education worldwide.

DAVID E. FISHMAN is Assistant Professor of Jewish History at the Jewish Theological Seminary of America and Research Associate at YIVO Institute for Jewish Research. He is a specialist in East European Jewish history, with a particular interest in religious and ideological trends in Russian Jewry. He is the author of *The Early Russian Haskalah Bleter* and is currently writing a book on Russian Jewish Orthodoxy, 1897–1939. He is also the director of Project Judaica, a joint program in Jewish studies at the Russian State Humanities University.

JANE GERBER is Professor of Jewish History and Director of the Institute for Sephardic Studies at the Graduate Center of the City University of New York. She is the author of *Jewish Society in Fez* (1980) and *The Jews of Spain* (1992). From 1981 to 1983 she was president of the Association for Jewish Studies.

NEIL GILLMAN is Aaron Rabinowitz and Simon H. Rifkind Associate Professor and Chair of the Department of Jewish Philosophy at the Jewish Theological Seminary of America. He is the author of *Gabriel Marcel on Religious Knowledge* (1980), *Sacred Fragments: Recovering Theology for the Modern Jew* (1990), and *A Partisan Guide to Conservative Judaism* (1992). His current areas of research are in the phenomenology of religion and the relationship of liturgy and ritual in Judaism.

NANCY L. GREEN is Maître de conférences (Associate Professor) at the École des Hautes Études en Sciences Sociales in Paris, and co-organizer of the Jewish Studies program there. Her research interests include comparative migrations studies. She is the author of *The Pletzl of Paris: Jewish Immigrant Workers in the Belle Epoque* (1986) and is coauthor of *La révolution française et l'émancipation des Juifs de France* (1989). She is currently editing a collective volume entitled *Jewish Workers in the Diaspora*, as well as preparing a book on the comparative social and economic history of immigrants in the garment industries of Paris and New York.

URI KAUFMANN is Professor at the Hochschule für Jüdische Studien, in Heidelberg. His principle area of scholarly research is the social history of Jews in Central Europe in the eighteenth and nineteenth centuries. He is the author of *Jüdische und christliche Viehhandler in der Schweiz, 1780–1930* (1988) and is editor of *Bibliographien zur deutsch-jüdischen Geschichte* (1992). He is currently at work on a comparison of the Emancipation process in Alsace, Baden, and the north of Switzerland, 1800–1870.

SILVIA SCHENKOLEWSKI-KROLL is Lecturer in the Department of Information

Studies and Archive Librarianship at Bar Ilan University and at the School of Library and Archive Studies at the Hebrew University in Jerusalem. She is a founding member of the Asociacion de Investigadores del Judaismo Latinoamericano. Her research interests include the political organization and ideology of Argentinian Jewry, and archival science. She is at work on a book on the history of Zionism in Argentina.

MARK KUPOVETSKY is Ethnodemographer and Director of the Scientific Center for Judaic Studies and Jewish Culture, in Moscow. He is currently conducting a special course on Russian-and Soviet-Jewish history at the new Judaica program at the Russian State University of the Humanities, coorganized and sponsored by the Jewish Theological Seminary of America and YIVO. He has published studies and papers on demography and the modern history of Soviet Jews and ethnography of non-Ashkenazic Jews of the former Soviet Union. His articles have appeared in *Soviet Ethnography, Publications of the Geographic Society of the Soviet Academy*, and in the Soviet-Yiddish literary monthly *Sovetish heymland*.

ELI LEDERHENDLER is Lecturer in Contemporary Jewry at the Hebrew University's Institute of Contemporary Jewry. From 1986 to 1990 he taught East European Jewish history at Tel-Aviv University. He is the author of *The Road to Modern Jewish Politics* and other writings in East European and American Jewish history.

NEIL W. LEVIN is Assistant Professor of Jewish Music at the Jewish Theological Seminary of America, Editor-in-Chief of *Musica Judaica: Journal of the American Society for Jewish Music*, and Director of the National Center and Archives for Jewish Music, in New York. His research focuses on the sacred and secular music of modern European Jewry, and his books include *Zemirot Anthology, Songs of the American Jewish Experience*, and *Voices of Jewish Russia*. He is currently working on a comprehensive historical study of the liturgical music of German-speaking Jewry and is editing the critical edition of the complete works of the first modern cantor and synagogal composer, Salamon Sulzer.

SHULAMIT S. MAGNUS is Acting Assistant Professor of History, Department of History, Stanford University. Her areas of research include modern German Jewry, Jewish women's history, and German Jewish Emancipation. She is currently at work on *Jewish Emancipation in a German City: Cologne, 1798–1870* and *A Woman's Enlightenment: The Memoirs of Pauline Wengeroff*.

Victor A. Mirelman is Rabbi at West Suburban Temple Har Zion in River Forest, Illinois, and Adjunct Professor of Jewish History at Spertus College of Judaica in Chicago. His areas of research are Latin American and Sephardic Jewry. He is the author of *Jewish Buenos Aires, 1890–1930: In Search of an Identity.*

Alan L. Mittleman is Assistant Professor of Religion at Muhlenberg College, Allentown, Pennsylvania. Author of *Between Kant and Kabbalah: An Introduction to Isaac Breuer's Philosophy of Judaism*, his areas of scholarly interest include German Jewish Orthodoxy and Judaism and politics.

Allan L. Nadler is Director of Research at the YIVO Institute for Jewish Research and Dean of YIVO's graduate program, the Max Weinreich Center for Advanced Jewish Studies. Prior to holding this position, he was Assistant Professor of Jewish Studies at McGill University. He is the author of *A Religion of Limits: The Faith of the Mithnagdim* (1992).

David G. Roskies is Professor of Jewish Literature at the Jewish Theological Seminary of America. He is cofounder and editor of *Prooftexts: A Journal of Jewish Literary History*, which began publication in 1981. He is the author of two books on Jewish literary responses to catastrophe: *Against the Apocalypse* (1984), which received the Ralph Waldo Emerson Prize from Phi Beta Kappa, and *The Literature of Destruction* (1989). He was awarded a Guggenheim Fellowship in 1985 and began work on the modern Jewish return to folklore and fantasy. The products of this work are *The Dybbuk and Other Writings* by S. Ansky (1992), and *The Lost Art of Yiddish Storytelling*, slated for completion in 1993.

Marsha L. Rozenblit is Harvey Meyerhoff Associate Professor of Modern Jewish History at the University of Maryland, College Park. She is a social historian who specializes in the history of the Jews of Austria-Hungary and is the author of *The Jews of Vienna, 1867–1914: Assimilation and Identity.* She has also written several articles on Austrian Jewry generally, on the reform movement in Vienna, and on the Jews of Baltimore. She is currently working on a book studying the impact of World War I on Jews in Austria-Hungary.

Stuart Schoenfeld is Associate Professor of Sociology at Glendon College, York University, in Toronto. He is the current chair of the Research Network in Jewish Education. He has written extensively on many aspects of contemporary Jewish life in Canada and the United States. He has a long-standing interest in studying the experience of bar/bat mitzvah as an entré into issues of individual, familial, and communal Jewish identity.

MILTON SHAIN is Instructor of Medieval and Modern Jewish History at the University of Cape Town, South Africa. He is the author of *Jewry and Cape Society* (1983) and the forthcoming *From Pariah to Parvenu: The Foundations of Antisemitism in South Africa*. He is currently engaged in a comparative study of South African Jewry and Jews of the American South.

GIDEON SHIMONI is senior lecturer in the Department of Contemporary Jewry of the Hebrew University of Jerusalem and incumbent of the Shlomo Argov Chair in Israel–Diaspora Relations; he also serves as Director of the Continuing Workshop on Contemporary Jewish Civilization of the International Center for University Teaching of Jewish Civilization. He has written and edited various studies in English and Hebrew on the history of Zionism and on Jewish communities in the Western world. These include *Jews and Zionism: The South African Experience* (1980), *Contemporary Jewish Civilization: Selected Syllabi* (1985), *Zionism and Its Jewish Opponents* (in Hebrew; 1990), and *The Holocaust in University Teaching* (1991).

CHAIM I. WAXMAN is Professor of Sociology at Rutgers University. Among his many publications are *America's Jews in Transition* (1983) and *American Aliya: Portrait of an Innovative Migration Movement* (1989). He served as President of the Association for the Sociological Study of Jewry from 1979 to 1981, and is a member of the board of directors of the Association for Israel Studies and an Editorial Board member of *Studies in Zionism: A Journal of Israel Studies*. He is currently working on a study of American Jewish "baby boomers," based on the 1990 National Jewish Population Survey.

DAVID WEINBERG is Professor of History at Bowling Green State University, Bowling Green, Ohio. His research interests are the history of modern French Jewry and the development of secular Jewish identity in late ninteenth century Europe. Ho is the author of *A Community on Trial. The Jews of Paris in the 1930s* (1977) and is presently preparing a monograph comparing the ideas and activity of Haim Zhitlowski, Simon Dubnow, and Ahad Ha-Am.

JACK WERTHEIMER occupies the Joseph and Martha Mendelson Chair in American Jewish History at the Jewish Theological Seminary of America, where he also directs the Joseph and Miriam Ratner Center for the Study of

Conservative Judaism. He is the author of *Unwelcome Strangers: East European Jews in Imperial Germany* (1987) and is completing a book on the transformation of American Judaism in the second half of the twentieth century. He is also the editor of *The American Synagogue: A Sanctuary Transformed* (1987) and *The Uses of Tradition: Jewish Continuity in the Modern Era* (1992).

Part I

A GUIDE TO FIELDS OF STUDY

Area Studies

1. The Jews in Early Modern Central and Western Europe

M. Bodian

For the sake of convenience, I define Early Modern Europe as the period extending from the rise to dominance of the Atlantic states up to the eve of the Enlightenment, or, roughly, from the mid-sixteenth through the mid-eighteenth centuries. While this period is of crucial importance, it lacks the clearcut dynamics of post-Enlightenment Jewish history and suffers from an absence of overarching themes. I would suggest four class sessions.

The Resettlement of Jews in Western and Central Europe: Mercantilism, *Raison d'état*, and the Idea of Tolerance

The best overall discussion of this topic can be found in Jonathan Israel, *European Jewry in the Age of Mercantilism*.[1] This overview takes into account the variety of factors involved in Jewish resettlement patterns in Western Europe after the devastations of the Late Medieval and Reformation periods. A more narrowly demographic presentation of an important aspect of this development—the westward movement of East European Jews—is M. A. Shulvass, *From East to West: The Westward Migration of Jews from Eastern Europe during the Seventeenth and Eighteenth Centuries*.[2]

The standard and still useful discussion of changing attitudes toward the

1. New York: Oxford University Press, 1989: 5–69.
2. Detroit: Wayne State University Press, 1971.

Jews in this period is S. Ettinger, "The Beginnings of Change in the Attitude of European Society towards the Jews."[3] Eli Hecksher's *Mercantilism*[4] still provides a sound survey of emerging economic attitudes which generally proved favorable to Jewish resettlement.

Various studies exist describing how new attitudes and policies regarding Jews crystallized in particular states. Among these the following can be consulted. For France, see A. Hertzberg, *The French Enlightenment and the Jews*,[5] pp. 12–48; for England, David Katz, *Philo-Semitism and the Readmission of the Jews into England, 1603–1655*;[6] for Holland, H. I. Bloom, *The Economic Activities of the Jews of Amsterdam in the Seventeenth and Eighteenth Centuries*,[7] pp. 1–32. The best analysis of the interaction of forces in Prussia is Selma Stern, *Die Preussischen Staat und die Juden*, vol. 1, part 1, *Die Zeit des Grossen Kurfürsten und Friedrichs I.*[8] For Italy, see Benjamin Ravid, *Economics and Toleration in Seventeenth-Century Venice: The Background and Context of the* Discorso *of Simone Luzzatto.*[9]

The impact of changing European conditions and attitudes on Jewish society in the pre-Enlightenment period is discussed succinctly in Jacob Katz, *Exclusiveness and Tolerance*,[10] pp. 131-68.

The major scholars who have studied this episode are not in basic disagreement. The most difficult issue is one of balance: although new ideas and policies are emerging in this period, old ideas and interests persist. Different scholars weigh the impact of the forces of change differently. I recommend that the session devoted to the topic under discussion stress the more novel trend of the period, that is, the trend toward integration of Jews, without ignoring the considerable opposition to this trend.

Recommended reading for students: Israel (n. 1), pp. 5–69; excerpts from Menasseh ben Israel, "How Profitable the Nation of the Jews Are," and John Toland, "Reasons for Naturalizing the Jews in Great Britain and Ireland," in *The Jews in the Modern World*,[11] pp. 9–16.

This reading can provide the basis for a discussion focusing on the mutual reinforcement of—and inherent tension between—mercantilist economic

3. *Scripta Hierosolymitana* 7 (1961): 193–219.

4. 2 vols., trans. Mendel Shapiro (London: Allen & Unwin, 1935; repr. New York: Garland, 1983).

5. New York: Columbia University Press, 1968.

6. New York: Oxford University Press, 1982.

7. Williamsport, Pa.: Bayard, 1937.

8. Tübingen: Mohr, 1962.

9. Jerusalem: American Academy for Jewish Research, 1978.

10. New York: Behrman, 1961.

11. Ed. Paul Mendes-Flohr and Jehuda Reinharz (New York: Oxford University Press, 1980).

ideas, on the one hand, and philosophical notions of tolerance, on the other. The student should gain an understanding of how both sets of ideas clashed with still powerful particularistic interests, hierarchical social views, and emotional antisemitism associated with the Late Medieval period.

Intellectual and Religious Ferment among the Ex-*Conversos*

This is a difficult topic to teach, especially in a single session. The issues cannot be grasped without some knowledge of intellectual and spiritual trends in both Christian and Jewish society. Moreover, while the literature on this topic is extensive, it is often highly specialized, and there is as yet no adequate survey for the general reader.

One way to simplify the task would be to focus on three figures who represent, to a degree, different responses to a single cultural environment: Uriel da Costa, Baruch Spinoza, and Isaac Orobio de Castro. All three lived in the Portuguese and Spanish Jewish community of Amsterdam. Their lives and thinking are well documented, and their diverse paths reflect the complexity of belief among ex-*conversos* in seventeenth-century Europe.

On the particular cultural matrix of the ex-*conversos*, I would recommend Y. H. Yerushalmi's richly textured biography of Isaac Cardoso, *From Spanish Court to Italian Ghetto*.[12] A classic if somewhat dated history of the *conversos* is Cecil Roth, *A History of the Marranos*[13] (see especially pp. 168–270). A number of important scholarly studies have been published by I. S. Révah. Two of these seek to place Marranism and *converso* society in broad perspective: "Les Marranes"[14] and "L'hérésie marrane dans l'Europe catholique du 15e au 18e siècle."[15] See also related studies in the recent collection *Menasseh ben Israel and His World*.[16] For a bibliographical survey, see G. Nahon, "Les Marranes espagnols et portugais et les communautés juives issues du Marranisme dans l'historiographie récente (1960–1975)."[17]

On Uriel da Costa and the controversies related to his heterodox ideas, the basic work remains Carl Gebhardt, *Die Schriften des Uriel da Costa*,[18] which includes the relevant documents in their original language. Most important

12. New York: Columbia University Press, 1971.
13. Philadelphia: Jewish Publication Society, 1947.
14. *Revue des études juives* 118 (1959–60): 29–77.
15. In *Hérésies et sociétés dans l'Europe préindustrielle, 11e–18e siècles,* ed. J. Le Goff (Paris and The Hague: Mouton, 1968), pp. 327–37.
16. Ed. Y. Kaplan, H. Mechoulan, and R. Popkin (Leiden: Brill, 1989).
17. *Revue des études juives* 136 (1977): 297–367.
18. Amsterdam: Hertzberger, 1922.

among subsequent studies are those of I. S. Révah, particularly "La religion d'Uriel da Costa, Marrane de Porto."[19]

The literature on Spinoza and his thought is vast. I note here only the most important works which examine Spinoza in the historical and cultural context we are concerned with. Indispensable are the studies of I. S. Révah, *Spinoza et le Dr. Juan de Prado*;[20] "Aux origines de la rupture spinozienne";[21] and "Spinoza et les hérétiques de la communauté judéo-portugaise d'Amsterdam."[22] See also, recently, Yirmiyahu Yovel, *Spinoza and Other Heretics*, vol. 1.[23]

On Isaac Orobio de Castro there is now one important monograph, recently published in English translation: Yosef Kaplan, *From Christianity to Judaism, The Story of Orobio de Castro*.[24]

The scholarly controversies in this area are almost as abundant as the controversies among the ex-*conversos* themselves. It is clear that the ideas of many of these figures deviate from "normative" rabbinic thinking. But it is difficult to establish the salient influences. To what degree are *converso* perceptions conditioned by the *conversos'* unique psychocultural background? Is there nevertheless a parallel between these circumstances and certain aspects of the Jewish condition in the Modern period? To what degree are the *conversos'* perceptions conditioned by their intense involvement in, and familiarity with, philosophical and religious trends in non-Jewish society? These issues are still being debated, and will no doubt continue to be.

The discussion in the class session could be focused by comparing and contrasting the basic positions vis-à-vis rabbinic Judaism and communal authority adopted by Da Costa, Spinoza, and Orobio de Castro. How do the relations of each of these figures with the community reflect major issues concerning authority within *converso* society, and what do these issues augur for the future? Such a session will admittedly entail considerable work for an instructor unfamiliar with the material.

Suggested reading for students: Yosef Kaplan (n. 24), pp. 122–78; Uriel Da Costa, *A Specimen of Human Life*,[25] pp. 9–45.

19. *Revue de l'histoire des religions* 161 (1962): 45–76.
20. Paris and The Hague: Mouton, 1959.
21. *Revue des études juives* 123 (1964): 359–431.
22. *Revue de l'histoire des religions* 154 (1958): 173–218.
23. Princeton: Princeton University Press, 1989.
24. Trans. Raphael Loewe (New York: Oxford University Press, 1989).
25. New York: Bergman, 1967.

The Sabbatian Movement in Western and Central Europe

The Sabbatian movement originated and developed in the Ottoman Empire. Nevertheless, the movement's enormous impact on European Jewish society and its implications for early modern Jewish life seem to me to justify including a session devoted to the participation of European Jewry in the movement.

There is one work which stands alone in this field: Gershom Scholem's monumental *Sabbetai Sevi: The Mystical Messiah.*[26] A briefer survey of the movement can be found in G. Scholem, *Major Trends in Jewish Mysticism,*[27] pp. 287–324. Most of the secondary literature on the movement is highly specialized. The important contributions concerning the movement as it spread and evolved in Western and Central Europe are cited in Scholem (n. 26), pp. 461–602.

The major scholarly controversies concerning the Sabbatian movement have to do with (a) its underlying causes and (b) its repercussions. Scholem's thesis that the background to this far-flung movement was the spread of Lurianic Kabbalah has been challenged by Moshe Idel; see his *Kabbalah: New Perspectives,*[28] pp. 258f. As for its impact, the movement has been regarded by Scholem as an underlying stimulus for the emergence of both Hasidism and the Jewish Enlightenment. See, inter alia, Scholem (n. 27), pp. 304, 327–30; "Redemption through Sin," in his *The Messianic Idea in Judaism,*[29] pp. 137–41; and I. Tishby, "Between Sabbatianism and Hassidism: The Sabbatianism of the Kabbalist R. Yaakov Lifshitz of Mezhirech."[30] Scholem's thesis has been challenged by J. Katz, "On the Question of the Connection between Sabbatianism, the Enlightenment and the Reform."[31] For a detailed survey of other critiques of Scholem's thesis see the sources cited in Shmuel Werses, Haskalah and Sabbatianism: The Study of a Controversy (in Hebrew),[32] pp. 9–20, to which may be added Idel (n. 28), pp. 258f., 266.

Suggested reading for students: G. Scholem (n. 26), pp. 461–602; or the broader treatment in Scholem's article "Shabbetai Zevi."[33]

26. 2 vols., trans. R. J. Zwi Werblowsky (Princeton: Princeton University Press, 1973).

27. 3rd ed. (New York: Schocken, 1954).

28. New Haven: Yale University Press, 1988.

29. New York: Schocken, 1971.

30. In *Nethivei Emunah u-Minut* (Paths of Faith and Heresy) (Tel Aviv: Agudah ha-Sopherim be-Israel, 1964), pp. 204–26.

31. (In Hebrew), in *Studies in Jewish Religious and Intellectual History Presented to Alexander Altmann,* ed. S. Stein and R. Loewe (University, Ala.: 1979), pp. 83–100.

32. Haskalah ve-Shabta'ut: Toledotav shel maavak (Jerusalem: Mercaz Zalman Shazar, 1988).

33. *Encyclopaedia Judaica* (1971), vol. 14, cols. 1219–53.

The Court Jew

The classic and pioneering work in this field is Selma Stern, *The Court Jew*.[34] The scope of this work is narrow when compared to her masterly seven-volume work *Der Preussischen Staat und die Juden*.[35] It is, however, brief and in English. An adequate if dated summary can be found in F. L. Carsten, "The Court Jews, A Prelude to Emancipation."[36] The best concise discussion is Israel (n. 1), pp. 123–44. For a view from a Marxist perspective, see Raphael Mahler, *A History of Modern Jewry, 1780–1815*,[37] pp. 129–35.

For those who are interested in pursuing the subject more deeply, a knowledge of German is essential. Among the major works are H. Schnee, *Die Hoffinanz und der moderne Staat*,[38] vol. 1; H. Rachel and P. Wallich, *Berliner Grosskaufleuten und Kapitalisten*, vol. 2;[39] M. Grunwald, *Samuel Oppenheimer und sein Kreis: Ein Kapitel aus der Finanzgeschichte Oesterreichs*;[40] D. Kaufmann, *Samson Wertheimer, der Oberfaktor und Landesrabbiner (1658–1728) und seine Kinder*.[41]

Scholars of different backgrounds and persuasions agree that the court Jews played a role in carving out a place for the Jews in the modern state. See, for example, Schnee (n. 38), vol. 3, p. 215; Jacob Katz, *Out of the Ghetto*,[42] p. 30; and Jacob Toury, "Der Eintritt der Juden ins deutsche Bürgertum."[43] Further exploration is needed concerning the impact of court Jews' roles on their relation to the Jewish community and Jewish life. A somewhat modified view of the modernizing impact of these roles is presented in M. Bodian, "The Jewish Entrepreneurs in Berlin and the 'Civil Improvement of the Jews' in the 1780s and 1790s."[44]

Recommended reading for students: *The Memoirs of Glueckel of Hameln*,[45] pp. 10–22; Israel (n. 1), pp. 123–44. In a session on this topic, I would emphasize the dichotomy inherent in the court Jew's position: its medi-

34. Philadelphia: Jewish Publication Society, 1950.

35. Tübingen: Mohr, 1962–71.

36. *Leo Baeck Yearbook* 2 (1958): 140–56.

37. London:Vallentine and Mitchell, 1971.

38. Berlin: Duncker & Humblot, 1953.

39. Berlin: von Gaellius, 1938.

40. Vienna and Leipzig: Braunmüller, 1913.

41. Vienna: Beck, 1888.

42. New York: Schocken, 1978.

43. In *Das Judentum in der deutschen Umwelt 1800–1850*, ed. H. Liebeschutz and A. Paucker (Tübingen: Mohr), pp. 153–56.

44. (In Hebrew) *Zion* 49 (1984): 159–84.

45. Trans. Marvin Lowenthal (New York: Schocken, 1977).

eval character, on the one hand (the court Jew's personal dependence on the ruler; his responsibility for the Jewish community as a whole), and its modern character, on the other (integration of his roles into the structure of the modern state).

2. Polish Jewry to the Partitions

David E. Fishman

Whether the history and culture of the Jews in pre-Partition Poland (1500–1795) should be included in a course on the Modern Jewish Experience is itself an open question. The harbingers of change in the political and social status of the Jews and in Jewish culture and ideology appeared in Western and Central Europe in the seventeenth and eighteenth centuries and had little resonance at the time in the East. Historians have therefore tended to consider Old Polish Jewry under the rubric of "the Late Middle Ages" rather than that of "early modernity." Historical documents from Poland in this period can thus be found in Jacob R. Marcus, *The Jew in the Medieval World: A Source Book, 315–1791*,[1] pp. 179f., 205–11, 279–86, 343–48, 422–25, 443–66, and not in Paul Mendes-Flohr and Jehuda Reinharz, *The Jew in the Modern World: A Documentary History.*[2]

The basic features of this Jewry were quite "Medieval": its corporate legal status and system of communal self-government, its religious culture and linguistic insularity, the powerful influence of the Catholic church on Polish–Jewish relations, and so on. And yet, it would be inconceivable to omit this community—which in the mid-eighteenth century numbered seven hundred fifty thousand and constituted one third of world Jewry—from a course on Modern Jewish History. Textbooks such as H. M. Sachar, *The Course of Modern Jewish History*,[3] and Raphael Mahler, *History of Modern Jewry*,[4] deal

1. New York: Atheneum, 1974.
2. New York: Oxford, 1982.
3. Cleveland: World, 1958; repr. New York: Vintage, 1990.
4. London: Vallentine, Mitchell, 1971.

with this anomaly by discussing Poland in their introductory chapters on the Jews before the onset of modernity. Pre-Partition Poland thus serves as a useful foil or contrast to the incipient processes of Emancipation and Enlightenment occuring in Holland, England, France, and Germany.

A growing literature of sophisticated specialized studies has appeared in recent years, and it can be followed on the pages of *Polin: A Journal of Polish-Jewish Studies* (1986–), which includes a sizable book review section. Unfortunately, this body of scholarship has not yet been incorporated into an overview history of Polish Jewry, and the available works of sythesis are rather dated in their style, method, and contents. The single best survey remains Simon Dubnow, *History of the Jews in Russia and Poland*,[5] vol. 1, which strikes a good balance in sketching the political, socioeconomic, communal, and cultural dimensions of Polish Jewish history. For a fuller exposition of the legal, political, and socioeconomic themes going back to the Middle Ages, Bernard D. Weinryb, *The Jews of Poland: A Social and Economic History of the Jewish Community in Poland from 1100 to 1800*,[6] should be used. Weinryb's book is clearly written and richly annotated, but its virtual neglect of Jewish communal institutions and cultural/intellectual developments renders it somewhat skewed and fragmentary. A textured and sophisticated treatment of social and economic trends between 1500 and 1648 is found in Salo Baron, *Social and Religious History of the Jews*, vol. 16, *Poland–Lithuania 1500–1650*.[7] The volume, like much of Baron's work, is intended for readers with prior training in European history and is beyond the ken of most undergraduates.

One of the hallmarks of pre-Partition Polish Jewry was its social and cultural separateness from the surrounding milieu. Although recent studies have refined and moderated this image, the Jewish community was largely a world unto itself. Jacob Katz, *Tradition and Crisis: Jewish Society at the End of the Middle Ages*,[8] offers an analysis of the institutions, norms, and values of the Jewish communities in Central and Eastern Europe in the sixteenth to eighteenth centuries. It covers such key themes as the rabbinate, lay leadership, the powers of the *kahal*, the family, education, and social life. Katz's book can thus complement and compensate for some of the gaps in Weinryb's history. For a one-volume survey of Jewish intellectual history in Poland until the rise of Hasidism (in Halakhah, mysticism, religious thought, homiletics, and moralistic literature), Israel Zinberg, *History of Jewish Literature*, vol. 6, *Ger-*

5. Philadelphia: Jewish Publication Society, 1916; repr. New York: Ktav, 1973.
6. Philadelphia: Jewish Publication Society, 1973.
7. Philadelphia: Jewish Publication Society, 2nd ed., 1976.
8. New York: Schocken, 1971.

man–Polish Cultural Center,[9] remains solid and stimulating. Moshe Avigdor Shulvass, *Jewish Culture in Eastern Europe: The Classical Period,*[10] is a shorter (and unannotated) alternate.

The volumes by Katz and Zinberg treat the Jews of Poland, Germany, and the lands between as a single cultural unit, and this is the commonly held approach. Polish Jewry originated as a child of Medieval German Jewry and conceived of itself as heir to the Ashkenazic tradition. In the period under consideration, there were strong ties between the communities of Cracow, Lublin, Prague, and Franfort, with rabbis, merchants, books, and ideas moving back and forth between them. One basic feature of this Ashkenazic cultural realm was the Yiddish language spoken by its inhabitants, and the popular Yiddish literature read by women and unlearnèd men. Max Weinreich, *History of the Yiddish Language,*[11] is an interdisciplinary work of linguistics and cultural history which probes the development of Yiddish and the role of Yiddish in Ashkenazic Jewish life. (A brief, simplified presentation of Weinreich's work is available in the first part of Benjamin Harshav, *The Meaning of Yiddish.*[12]) The various genres of Old Yiddish literature are examined by Zinberg (n. 9), vol. 7.

So much for single-volume surveys. I now turn to a number of special topics. In recent years, the most lively scholarly activity has been in the area of Polish–Jewish relations. The near-total annihilation of Polish Jewry in the Holocaust and the enduring potency of antisemitism in postwar Poland have led historians to turn to the past in search of a deeper understanding of the entangled and painful relationship between Poles and Jews. The period of the sixteenth to mid-seventeenth centuries has been seen as a golden era in which Poland was, if not the proverbial *"paradisum Judaeorum,"* then at least a place of relative security and prosperity for Jews. The late seventeenth and the eighteenth centuries are considered a period of growing tensions between burghers and Jews and increased anti-Jewish agitation by the Church.

The logical point of departure for this topic is an examination of the charters granted by kings and magnates to Jewish communities dwelling in their territories. The classic charter of 1264 by Boleslow of Kalisz is available in Robert Chazan's compendium, *Church, State, and Jew in the Middle Ages.*[13] More relevant to our chronological period is Jacob Goldberg's comprehensive

9. (In Yiddish, 1929), trans. and ed. Bernard Martin (Cleveland: Press of Case Western Reserve University, 1976).

10. New York: Ktav, 1975.

11. (In Yiddish; New York: YIVO, 1973) abridged trans. S. Noble (Chicago: University of Chicago Press, 1980).

12. Berkeley: University of California Press, 1990.

13. New York: Behrman, 1980.

collection, *Jewish Privileges in the Polish Commonwealth.*[14] Although the texts of the *privilegia* are given in Latin, there are English prefaces and summaries for each item, as well as a fine introduction to the volume.

For a broader analysis of the position of the Jews in the mix of social, religious, and ethnic groups that constituted Poland, see Jacob Goldberg, "Poles and Jews in the 17th and 18th Centuries: Rejection or Acceptance,"[15] and Gershon Hundert, "An Advantage to Peculiarity? The Case of the Polish Commonwealth"[16] and "The Implications of Jewish Economic Activities for Christian–Jewish Relations in the Polish Commonwealth."[17] See also Murray J. Rosman, "A Minority Views the Majority: Jewish Attitudes toward the Polish-Lithuanian Commonwealth and Interaction with Poles,"[18] and Janusz Tazbir, "Images of the Jew in the Polish Commonwealth,"[19] in a journal volume which is devoted to mutual images and stereotypes among Poles and Jews.

The relations between Jews and the landed gentry, which grew in importance and complexity over the course of this period, have received close attention in two recent studies: Murray J. Rosman, *The Lords' Jews: Jews and Magnates in Old Poland,*[20] and Gershon D. Hundert, *The Jews in a Polish Private Town: The Case of Opatow in the Eighteenth Century.*[21]

A key event—and according to many historians a turning-point in the fortunes of Polish Jewry—is the Cossack uprising of 1648 led by Bogdan Chmielnicki, which included the massacre of scores of Jewish communities in the Ukraine and southern Poland. The classic Hebrew chronicle of the Chmielnicki massacres, Nathan Hanover's *Yeven metsulah*, is available in an English translation by Abraham Mesch as *Abyss of Despair.*[22] One can also consult the analysis of this and similar works in Bernard D. Weinryb, "Hebrew Chronicles on Bohdan Khel'nyts'kyi and the Cossack-Polish War."[23]

Polish Jewry developed a broad system of communal self-government on the local, regional, and national levels, culminating in the confederative body of Polish communities known as the Council of Four Lands (1580[?]–1764).

14. Jerusalem: Israel Academy of Sciences and Humanities, 1985.
15. *Jahrbücher für Geschichte Osteuropas* 22/2 (1974): 248–82.
16. *Association for Jewish Studies Review* 6 (1981): 21–38.
17. In *The Jews in Poland*, ed. Chimen Abramsky, Maciej Jachimczyl, and Antony Polonsky (Oxford: Blackwell, 1986), pp. 55–64, 226–31.
18. *Polin* 4 (1989): 31–41.
19. *Polin* 4 (1989): 18–30.
20. Cambridge: Harvard University Press, 1991.
21. Baltimore: The Johns Hopkins University Press, 1992.
22. New Brunswick, N.J.: Transaction, 1983.
23. *Harvard Ukrainian Studies* 1 (1977): 153–77.

A useful case study of a local *kahal* can be found in Israel Cohen, *History of the Jews in Vilna*,[24] pp. 114–81, and interesting materials from Cracow, the capital of Old Poland, are presented in Bernard D. Weinryb, "Studies in the Communal History of Polish Jewry."[25] For an example of the extensive powers and prerogatives exerted by regional bodies, see Isaiah Trunk, "The Council of the Province of White Russia."[26] A concise portrait of the Council of Four Lands is available in Hayyim Hillel Ben-Sasson, *Trial and Achievement: Currents in Jewish History*,[27] which also contains sketches of other topics relevant to Polish Jewry.

The prominent role played by religious learning in the life of pre-1648 Polish Jewry is eloquently portrayed in the final chapters of Hanover (n. 22). Several classic works of rabbinic literature were produced in this period. On the latter, see Isadore Twersky, "The Shulhan Arukh: Enduring Code of Jewish Law";[28] Lawrence Kaplan, "Rabbi Mordechai Jaffe and the Evolution of Jewish Culture in the 16th Century";[29] and Eugene Newman, *Life and Teachings of Isaiah Horowitz*.[30] The sermons of Rabbi Ephraim of Lunshtshitz, Polish Jewry's most famous preacher and social critic, are examined by Israel Bettan, *Studies in Jewish Preaching*,[31] pp. 273–316.

Several other topics in the history of Jewish religious life and thought in Poland merit consideration. Anti-Christian religious polemics are best exemplified by *Faith Strengthened*, a treatise by the Karaite scholar Isaac of Troki (ca. 1600).[32] Kabbalistic literature and the Jewish Messianic movements known as Sabbateanism and Frankism in Poland have been examined by Gershom Scholem in *Sabbetai Sevi: The Mystical Messiah*,[33] pp. 77–93, 591–602, 620–27; *Kabbalah*,[34] pp. 287–309, 429–31, 452–54; and in his classic essay "Redemption Through Sin."[35] The popular literature of Yiddish devo-

24. Philadelphia: Jewish Publication Society, 1943.

25. *Publication of the American Academy for Jewish Research* 12 (1942): 121–40; 15 (1945): 93–129.

26. *YIVO Annual for Jewish Social Science* 11 (1957): 188–210.

27. Jerusalem: Keter, 1974.

28. In his *Studies in Jewish Law and Philosophy* (New York: Ktav, 1982), pp. 130–47; also in *The Jewish Expression*, ed. J. Goldin (New Haven: Yale University Press, 1976), pp. 322–43.

29. In *Jewish Thought in the 16th Century*, ed. Bernard Cooperman (Cambridge: Harvard University Press, 1983), pp. 266–82.

30. London: Newman, 1972.

31. Cincinnati: Hebrew Union College, 1939.

32. Ed. and trans. Trude Weiss-Rosmarin (New York: Ktav, 1970).

33. Princeton: Princeton University Press, 1973.

34. New York: Quadrangle/New York Times Books, 1974.

35. In *The Messianic Idea in Judaism and Other Essays in Jewish Spirituality*, (New York: Schocken, 1971), pp. 78–141.

tional prayers for women called *tkhines* is illuminated by Chava Weissler, "The Traditional Piety of Ashkenazic Women."[36]

Social tensions and divisions within Polish Jewry seem to have heightened in the mid-eighteenth century, as the community experienced an economic, political, and moral crisis. These developments are examined by Ben Zion Dinur, "The Origins of Hasidism and Its Social and Messianic Foundations."[37] Another perspective on the trials and tribulations of the mid-eighteenth century is provided in *The Memoirs of Ber of Bolechow (1723–1805)*,[38] one of the few first-person narrative works we have from this era.

Important primary sources on the Jews in pre-Partition Poland can be found in several anthologies, including Walter Ackerman, *Out of Our People's Past*,[39] pp. 103–34; Franz Kobler, *A Treasury of Jewish Letters*,[40] vol. 2, pp. 368–77, 486–503; and Leo Schwarz, *Memoirs of My People*,[41] pp. 68–74, 144–48. One may also use imaginative fiction as a gateway into this period. I.B. Singer's novels *The Slave*[42] and *Satan in Goray*[43] are engaging, if not always accurate, in their evocation of Poland in the era of Chmielnicki and Sabbetai Sevi.

36. In *Jewish Spirituality*, vol. 2, ed. Arthur Green (New York: Crossroad, 1989), pp. 245–75.

37. In *Essential Papers on Hasidism: Origins to the Present*, ed. Gershon D. Hundert (New York: New York University Press, 1991), pp. 86–133.

38. Ed. and trans. Mark Wischnitzer (New York: Oxford University Press, 1922, repr. 1973).

39. New York: United Synagogue, 1977.

40. New York: Farrar, Straus and Young, 1952.

41. Philadelphia: Jewish Publication Society, 1943.

42. New York: Farrar, Straus, Cudahy, 1962.

43. New York: Farrar, Straus and Giroux, 1955.

3. The Jews in Imperial Russia

Eli Lederhendler

When Catherine II of Russia helped to complete the dismemberment of the Polish–Lithuanian Commonwealth in 1795, she also thereby determined the fate of the world's largest Jewish community. The addition of Polish lands to the Russian empire (which began in 1772 and continued until the Congress of Vienna in 1815) brought most of the Jews of Eastern Europe under czarist rule.

During the century and a half that separated the first partition of Poland from the October Revolution, "Russian" Jewry entered the Modern era, achieved formidable demographic strength (more than quadrupling in size from the beginning to the end of the nineteenth century), sent over two million of its men, women, and children out into the world to change the Jewish map forever, and gave to Jewish history such cultural treasures and outstanding sociopolitical movements as Hasidism, the Lithuanian yeshivas, modern Yiddish and Hebrew literature, Zionism, and the Jewish labor movement. It took the combined force of the two most murderous totalitarian regimes in history—Nazi Germany and Stalinist rule in Russia—to bring down this once-flourishing and vital Jewish society. Even today, in what must be considered the twilight of its existence, Russian Jewry engages our attention as few other diaspora communities do.

Small wonder, then, that its history exerts a powerful fascination on students and scholars and that (after some lean years, and despite the competition from other fields—American Jewish history, Zionism and Israel studies, Holocaust studies, etc.), more and more is being published on the subject. A new generation of historians, primarily in the United States and Israel, is engaged

3. The Jews in Imperial Russia 19

in the task of reexamining, reinterpreting, and rewriting the history of the Jews in Russia.

Perhaps it is inevitable that the emphasis today is on specialized studies. Since Simon Dubnow, *History of the Jews in Russia and Poland*,[1] almost no books have appeared that can be called general surveys of Russian Jewry in the Imperial period. The two works that come the closest are Salo Baron, *The Russian Jew under Tsar and Soviets*,[2] which treats both the Czarist and the Soviet periods, and Louis Greenberg, *The Jews in Russia: The Struggle for Emancipation*,[3] which—as the title implies—is not really a comprehensive social and cultural history.

There is, in fact, no up-to-date, good synthetic treatment that can be recommended wholeheartedly as a textbook. The next best thing is to use Baron (n. 2, chs. 2–10), or else the relevant sections in general histories (e.g., *A History of the Jewish People*,[4] chs. 46, 50, 57–59; Robert Seltzer, *Jewish People, Jewish Thought: The Jewish Experience in History*,[5] parts of chs. 11, 14, and 15; and also Howard M. Sachar, *The Course of Modern Jewish History*,[6] chs. 4, 9, 10, 12, and 15). Those wishing to focus primarily on the Soviet period, but interested in starting with a synopsis of the Imperial period, could turn to the first chapter of Benjamin Pinkus, *The Jews of the Soviet Union: The History of a National Minority*.[7] Finally, one can build class discussions around readings selected from *The Jew in the Modern World*[8] as well as Lucy Dawidowicz, *The Golden Tradition: Jewish Life and Thought in Eastern Europe*.[9] The latter also contains a useful introduction (89 pages) to intellectual trends in East European Jewry.

As I have intimated, however, the best of recent scholarship in the field is less concerned with summing up the history of Russian Jewry prior to 1917 than with expanding and deepening our understanding of cultural, social, economic, and intellectual processes within the larger story. It may be premature, at this stage, to embark on anything as ambitious as a new synthesis, given the amount of ground that still has to be covered.

1. 3 vols. (Philadelphia: Jewish Publication Society, 1916; repr. New York: Ktav, 1975).
2. New York: Macmillan, 1964; 2nd ed. 1976.
3. 2 vols. (New Haven: 1944, 1951; 2nd ed. 1976).
4. Ed. H.H. Ben-Sasson (Cambridge: Harvard University Press, 1976).
5. New York: Macmillan, 1980.
6. New York: Dell, 1958; repr. New York: Vintage, 1990.
7. Cambridge: Cambridge University Press, 1988.
8. Ed. Paul R. Mendes-Flohr and Jehuda Reinharz (New York: Oxford University Press, 1980).
9. New York and Chicago: Holt, Rinehart and Wilson, 1967; repr. Northvale, N.J.: Aronson, 1989.

In his recent autobiography, Jacob Katz relates that he once speculated about the dearth of Jewish historical literature written in the spirit of Jewish Orthodoxy: "If there is no Orthodox historiography, that is because there is no such thing as orthodoxy in history."[10]

In a way, the problem of Orthodoxy and its place in historiography forms one of the decisive axes (and dilemmas) of scholarship on Russian Jewry. This is because Orthodoxy as such is so much a part of Russian Jewish history, but it has proven problematic for scholars to deal with. This is an issue not just of methodology, but of the sociology of knowledge. Professional historians, themselves the products of Western academic traditions, are predisposed to find historical interest primarily in the forces of change and modernization that affected East European Jewry.

Even the earliest Russian Jewish historians, writing a century ago, were non- or anti-Orthodox in their personal orientation (as was the case among Jewish historians elsewhere in Europe), and that tended to affect their treatment of the traditionalist trends in Russian Jewry. In turn, that has colored our perceptions as well as the scholarly agenda of their successors.

Though it is fair to describe the Jews of the Russian empire as, in some respects, a modernizing society (see Eli Lederhendler, "Modernity without Emancipation or Assimilation? The Case of Russian Jewry"[11]), one nevertheless risks losing sight of basic historical facts if one fails to place modernizing trends in Russian Jewry in context and in relative perspective. (A lack of such perspective is precisely the problem readers may confront in reading Greenberg [n 3].) It is worth keeping always in mind, therefore, that the Jews who came under the czar's scepter in the late eighteenth century, and most of their descendants, were not Russian-speaking intellectuals, radical socialists, factory workers, or Hebrew poets; nor did most of them emigrate to America.

The transition from a traditional to a posttraditional society was a long, uneven process that was never smooth. Jacob Katz, *Tradition and Crisis: Jewish Society at the End of the Middle Ages*,[12] provides excellent background on the social significance of tradition for the Jews of Central and Eastern Europe until the mid-eighteenth century and on the crisis that Hasidism represented. The best portrayal of traditional Jewish communal life in Russia from the 1770s to the mid-nineteenth century is still Isaac Levitats, *The Jewish Community in Russia, 1772–1844*.[13]

10. *Bemo 'einay: Autobiografia shel historion* (With my own eyes: Autobiography of a historian) (Jerusalem: Keter, 1989), p. 73.

11. In *Assimilation and Community: The Jews in Nineteenth-Century Europe*, ed. Jonathan Frankel and Steven Zipperstein (Cambridge: Cambridge University Press, 1991), pp. 324–43.

12. New York: Free Press of Glencoe; Schocken, 1971.

13. New York: Columbia University Press, 1943.

By the same token, however, Russian Jewry was hardly so rooted in age-old communal, religious, and cultural patterns (shades of Tevye singing "Tradition, Tradition" in *Fiddler on the Roof*, © Sunbeam Music Corp., 1964) that it could remain immune to the social impact of urbanization, the coming of the railroad, the decline of the nobility, the opening of new territories and the founding of new cities, the closing of economic options in the countryside, the shrinking viability of the small crafts, or changing norms in marriage and childbirth.

The challenges of modernity were hardly avoidable. The responses they elicited varied widely: from a new, self-conscious, and remarkably durable Orthodoxy to equally new, acculturated strata in major Russian and Polish cities (see Shaul Stampfer, Three Lithuanian yeshivas in the nineteenth century [in Hebrew];[14] Immanuel Etkes, Rav Israel Salanter and the beginning of the Musar Movement [in Hebrew];[15] Michael Stanislawski, *Tsar Nicholas I and the Jews: The Transformation of Jewish Society in Russia, 1825–1855*;[16] Steven Zipperstein, *The Jews of Odessa: A Cultural History, 1794–1881*;[17] David E. Fishman, "Science, Enlightenment, and Rabbinic Culture in Byelorussian Jewry, 1772–1804";[18] Stephen D. Corrsin, *Warsaw before the First World War: Poles and Jews in the Third City of the Russian Empire, 1880–1914*[19]); from economic restratification to emigration (Simon Kuznets, "Immigration of Russian Jews to the United States: Background and Structure";[20] Arcadius Kahan, *Essays in Jewish Social and Economic History*[21]); from a politics of accommodation and integration to a politics of "autoemancipation" (Ezra Mendelsohn, *Class Struggle in the Pale: The Formative Years of the Jewish Workers Movement in Tsarist Russia*;[22] David Vital, *The Origins of Zionism*;[23] Alexander Orbach, *New Voices of Russian Jewry: A Study of the Russian Jewish Press of Odessa in the Era of the Great Reforms, 1860–1871*;[24] Jonathan Frankel, *Prophecy and Politics: Socialism, Nationalism, and the Russian Jews, 1862–1917*;[25] Stanislawski [n. 16]; Eli Lederhendler, *The*

14. "Shalosh yeshivot litaiot ba-mea ha-teshʻa ʻesreh," Ph.D. dissertation, Hebrew University, 1981.

15. *Rav Israel Salanter ve-reishita shel tenu'at ha-musar* (Jerusalem: ha-Otsar Seforim, 1982).

16. Philadelphia: Jewish Publication Society, 1983.

17. Stanford: Stanford University Press, 1985.

18. Ph.D. dissertation, Harvard University, 1985.

19. New York: Columbia University Press, 1989.

20. *Perspectives in American History* 9 (1975): 35–124.

21. Ed. Roger Weiss (Chicago: University of Chicago Press, 1986).

22. Cambridge: Cambridge University Press, 1970.

23. Oxford: Clarendon, 1975.

24. Leiden: Brill, 1980.

25. Cambridge: Cambridge University Press, 1981.

Road to Modern Jewish Politics: Political Tradition and Political Reconstruction in the Jewish Community of Tsarist Russia[26]).

Students of Russian Jewish history have, as it were, to keep all these balls in the air simultaneously in order to achieve a balanced picture. As if that were not enough, they should also have a grasp of Russian state policies vis-à-vis the Jews (see Greenberg [n. 3]; Levitats [n. 13]; Stanislawski [n. 16]; John Doyle Klier, *Russia Gathers Her Jews: The Origin of the "Jewish Question" in Russia, 1772–1825*;[27] Michael J. Ochs, "St. Petersburg and the Jews of Russian Poland, 1862–1905";[28] Hans Rogger, *Jewish Policies and Right-Wing Politics in Imperial Russia*[29]); and understand the development of the "Jewish Question" in the Russian setting, in the era of modern antisemitism (Heinz-Dietrich Löwe, *Antisemitismus und reaktionäre Utopie: Russischer Konservatismus im Kampf gegen dem Wandel von Staat und Gesellschaft, 1890–1917*;[30] Rogger [n. 29]).

In the absence of a book that might summarize the results of this new scholarship, a few points might be made here about recent trends: trends which should have classroom applicability as well.

First, there is a greater sensitivity today to the role of the traditionalist majority in Russian Jewish society. For some reason, more work has been done on this by Israeli scholars (Etkes and Stampfer, for example), but American scholars have readily chimed in (e.g., Stanislawski and Fishman). This has been a necessary historiographical corrective.

Second, the accusations of antisemitism once leveled almost indiscriminately against Russian policies and Russian officialdom—a staple of earlier works—have given way to more subtle, sophisticated, and nuanced analysis. Stanislawski's treatment of Count Uvarov stands out as one example of such revision, as does Klier's study on the period before 1825. The result is by no means a whitewash, but a more careful, more discerning approach.

Third, greater attention is being paid to local history and to the factors specific to certain cities or regions (Zipperstein [n. 17], Fishman [n. 18], Corrsin [n. 19]). This is an important development, because Russian Jewry was highly differentiated, culturally, economically, and even politically, as one traveled from north to south in the Pale of Settlement, or from the Russian provinces to the Polish provinces that lay to the west. The treatments of Odessa by Zipper-

26. New York: Oxford University Press, 1989.
27. DeKalb, Ill.: Northern Illinois University Press, 1986.
28. Ph.D. dissertation, Harvard University, 1986.
29. Berkeley and Los Angeles: University of California Press, 1986.
30. Hamburg: Hoffmann & Campe, 1978.

stein and of Warsaw by Corrsin show the impact on Jewish historiography of recent emphases in social history generally.

Finally, where once one dealt mainly with movements and with "the masses," some of the most talented younger scholars have recently turned to the vehicle of biography to illuminate aspects of cultural and intellectual history (Etkes [n. 15]; Michael Stanislawski, *For Whom Do I Toil? Judah Leib Gordon and the Crisis of Russian Jewry*;[31] Steven Zipperstein, *Ahad Ha'am: An Interpretive Study of His Life*[32]).

Altogether, this appears to be a process of revision, refinement, fine-tuning.

Our vision of the Jewish past in Eastern Europe is inevitably clouded by the Holocaust. This can lead to hagiography and nostalgia, in which the Jews of the shtetl take on mythic, rather than real-life, proportions. On the other hand, the failure of realism can just as easily take the form of seeing East European Jewry as a doomed society of perpetual victims. Both these tendencies (which are natural enough in the context of the popular imagination) are to be avoided in the classroom. In fact, both extremes—idealization of the shtetl and demonization of the non-Jewish environment—might be profitably discussed, once students have a modicum of factual knowledge.

The fact that Jews lived, for the most part, in urban settings by the end of the nineteenth century should be impressed on students, as should the fact that the majority of the Jewish population stayed on in Russia, where conditions for some were not as bad as for others. Indeed, there were some Jews who returned to Eastern Europe from the United States (although these were admittedly the exceptions; see Kuznets [n. 20] and Jonathan Sarna, "The Myth of No Return: Jewish Return Migration to Eastern Europe, 1881–1914"[33]).

Similarly, it can be argued with some justice that the reason why the pogroms of the 1880s came as such a shock was that they followed a long period of relative security. Demographic strength, cultural vitality, and economic muscle were as much a part of the Russian Jewish situation as were grinding poverty and official discrimination.

The urban experience of the Jews of the Pale placed them in the approximately ten percent of the Russian population that did not till the soil—a social position that carried distinct benefits. The Jews capitalized on that experience and on those advantages when they emigrated abroad or when, after the Revolution, they streamed to the major cities of the new Russia. Rapid socioeconomic mobility and a high investment in education were characteristic of both

31. New York: Oxford University Press, 1988.
32. Berkeley and Los Angeles: University of California Press/Weidenfeld, forthcoming.
33. *American Jewish History* 71/2 (1981): 256–68.

Soviet Jews and Russian Jews in America during the twenties, thirties, and forties of the twentieth century. The dynamism of the societies in which they lived surely made this great leap possible, but it is also true that Jews were particularly well placed to take full advantage of what each system had to offer, partly because of their history.

Therefore, Russian Jewish history should not be taught as a history of victims—though victimization is part of the story. Nor should tradition and modernity be depicted as two polar opposites that collided suddenly in nineteenth-century Russian Jewish society—though modernization was fraught with turmoil and social dislocation.

Rather, the degree of historical insight one gains is directly proportional to one's sensitivity to the subject's complexity. If that is a general truism, then this is one case in which it surely applies.

4. Soviet Jewry

Eli Lederhendler

Since the writing of this essay, the face of what was formerly the Soviet Union has changed drastically and this chapter of East European history has ended. It will take time before we can properly assess the consequences of the many changes, and it is not my intention to do so prematurely. Much of what I wrote in 1990 still applies. The situation of the Jews in the new republics or States of the Commonwealth is still in flux, the emigration continues, and no sweeping new assessments can be made at this time.

Surely teaching Soviet Jewry is one of the most difficult tasks facing the teacher of Jewish history today. Everything that has been written on the subject until now has lost a great deal of its contemporary relevance, and any prognoses made today are liable to be obsolete by next week. The years 1989–91 were a watershed in Soviet history unlike any other since Lenin, Trotsky, Stalin, and their cohorts made their revolution. The best source of information on Soviet Jewry today is the daily newspaper, and full use should be made of this resource. Even tracking developments over the course of a year or two can be a worthwhile project for students of the subject.

Naturally, one cannot fully appreciate the extent of the changes that took place in 1989–91 without first having a background knowledge of historical trends, and here is where the pre-Gorbachev literature is still very useful. Actually, a good case can now be made for revising the standard periodization which divided Russian Jewish history into two neat parts, pre- and post-Revolution. One way to do that might be to treat the entire period from the pogroms of 1881 to 1991 as a single episode, with critical events in 1881, 1917, 1940–45, and 1967.

Alternatively, one could view the period from the 1940s to the 1990s as a prolonged, final dénouement of the East European era in Jewish history, continuing after the trauma of the Holocaust with the "black years" of the late 1940s and early 1950s (to borrow a phrase from Yehoshua Gilboa[1]), the exodus of the remaining Jews from Poland in 1968, the mounting difficulties Jews faced in the 1970s in maintaining past levels of social mobility and professional integration, and finally, the Soviet Jewish emigration itself.

Either way, this would place historical studies of "Soviet Jewry" into a self-contained rather than open-ended framework. That would leave history to the historians, put current events squarely in the hands of the journalists, and reduce the temptation to speculate about the future. I fear, however, that it is still too soon to call the past truly past, and certain continuities will doubtless remain, even if we accept 1991 as a turning point (just as there are important continuities that transcend the divide created by 1917).

In any case, Gorbachev has made the use of the past tense de rigueur in teaching or writing about Soviet Jewry. Statements in the present tense that you may find in works devoted to the subject automatically require qualification, if not significant revision.

Sovietologists, having been taken by surprise by recent developments, are already engrossed in the business of deploying hindsight, the better to make sense of the *perestroika* phenomenon. Social and political trends of the 1970s and 1980s, from the ills of the sclerotic Communist party apparatus to the growth of nationality consciousness in the national republics and in Russia itself,[2] and from detente to Afghanistan on the foreign policy front, will be used to explain what occurred under Gorbachev.

Clearly the Jewish factor is not marginal to this story, and taking it into account ought to be part of any social-scientific assessment. As in other times and other places, the "Jewish question" has been something of a catalyst in the process of social and political change. In the Soviet case "the question" has been linked to major policy initiatives in such areas as arms limitation, multilateral agreements on European security and human rights, and economic cooperation with the West, to say nothing of nationalist ferment at home (*Soviet Jewry in the 1980s: The Politics of Anti-Semitism and Emigration and*

1. *The Black Years of Soviet Jewry, 1939–1953* (Boston: Little Brown, 1971).
2. There is a considerable literature on the Soviet nationalities question. See, e.g., Edward Allworth, *Soviet Nationality Problems* (New York: Columbia University Press, 1971); *Nationality Group Survival in Multi-Ethnic States: Shifting Support Patterns in the Soviet Baltic Region*, ed. Edward Allworth (New York: Praeger, 1977); *The Soviet West: Interplay between Nationality and Social Organization*, ed. Ralph S. Clem (New York: Praeger, 1975); Victor Kozlov, *The Peoples of the Soviet Union* (Bloomington: Indiana University Press, 1988).

the Dynamics of Resettlement;[3] Peter Reddaway, *Uncensored Russia: Protest and Dissent in the Soviet Union*;[4] A. Axelbank, *Soviet Dissent: Intellectuals, Jews, and Detente).*[5] If the demand for *glasnost'* and *perestroika* had something to do with the crisis of credibility suffered by the old Soviet system, surely the long-festering debate over Soviet Jewish rights played an important part in that crisis. It made a mockery of claims made by party officials in defense of their system, and in that context it can be placed alongside other nationality-related issues, Solzhenitsyn, the dissident movement, the Berlin Wall, and the chronic failures in the production of consumer goods and services.

Those who wish to read up on Soviet Jewry in the decade leading up to Gorbachev's revolution can consult Freedman (n. 3), which contains valuable essays on domestic Soviet politics, foreign policy, Jewish emigration, and the process of resettlement abroad. There are also a number of valuable documents and statistics in the Appendix. The book can be used easily by students.

Probably the best single overview of Soviet Jewish history as a whole, however, is Benjamin Pinkus, *The Jews of the Soviet Union: The History of a National Minority.*[6] Nora Levin, *The Jews in the Soviet Union since 1917: Paradox of Survival*[7] is a good second choice, but its length makes it unwieldy as a textbook in comparison with Pinkus. Pinkus takes the story from the Czarist period (in a short first chapter) until 1983. He subdivides the post-1917 period into three shorter periods: "the years of construction" (1917–39), "the years of destruction" (1939–53: World War II to the death of Stalin), and "the post-Stalin period." The chronological arrangement and the focus on the Soviet period per se make the book not only more up to date, but also easier to follow than the thematically arranged chapters in Salo Baron, *The Russian Jew under Tsar and Soviets.*[8] But for anyone who wishes to have more background on the pre-1917 period and the early Soviet years, Baron's book is still a valuable introduction. An older book that nevertheless provides detailed historical insight on the Soviet period up to 1950 is Solomon Schwarz, *The Jews in the Soviet Union.*[9]

A good companion volume for Pinkus's book, though it deals only with the years from 1948 to 1967, is the collection of documents which Pinkus himself

3. Ed. Robert O. Freedman (Durham: Duke University Press, 1989).
4. New York: American Heritage Press, 1972.
5. New York: Watts, 1975.
6. Cambridge: Cambridge University Press, 1988.
7. 2 vols. (New York: New York University Press, 1988).
8. New York: Macmillan, 1964; 2nd ed., 1976.
9. Syracuse, N.Y.: Syracuse University Press, 1951.

compiled, *The Soviet Government and the Jews, 1948–1967: A Documented Study.*[10] Several key documents from the Revolutionary period may be found in *The Jew in the Modern World.*[11]

A rather good collection of essays (again, somewhat dated) is *The Jews in Soviet Russia Since 1917.*[12] It is still useful, when read in conjunction with updated material. The essays by Ettinger, Abramsky, Korey, and Shmeruk are of particular value. A good socioeconomic and demographic study, with data from Soviet censuses up to 1980, is Mordecai Altshuler, *Soviet Jewry since the Second World War.*[13] This book contains an overwhelming wealth of tables but with judicious selection can be used profitably by students. A concise and accurate presentation of the development of Soviet Jewry up to the 1970s is Zev Katz, "The Jews in the Soviet Union."[14]

All these studies stress the duality of Soviet policies affecting Jews from the revolution to the 1980s: policies that allowed for considerable individual advancement and civil equality while at the same time subjecting Jews (both individually and as a group) to the same repressive conditions that were the lot of Soviet citizens generally. They also point out where and when the Jews constituted an exceptional case (whether to their benefit or otherwise) in Soviet society. These are important themes to pursue in class discussions.

Finally, visual and literary materials can add color to works of history or social analysis. Some fine examples are Zvi Gitelman's album of photographs, *A Century of Ambivalence: The Jews of Russia and the Soviet Union, 1881 to the Present*;[15] Isaac Babel's "Red Cavalry" stories (available in English editions of his collected stories);[16] works included in Irving Howe and Eliezer Greenberg's anthology, *Ashes out of Hope: Fiction by Soviet-Yiddish Writers*;[17] the novel *Gates of Bronze* by Haim Hazzaz;[18] or the Russian film *Commissar*, directed by Aleksandr Askoldov (made in 1967 but released only twenty years later).[19]

10. Cambridge: Cambridge University Press, 1984.

11. Ed. Paul R. Mendes-Flohr and Jehuda Reinharz (New York: Oxford University Press, 1980).

12. Ed. Lionel Kochan (London: Institute of Jewish Affairs, 3rd ed., 1978).

13. New York: Greenwood, 1987.

14. In *Handbook of Major Soviet Nationalities*, ed. Zev Katz et al. (New York: Free Press, 1975), pp. 355–89.

15. New York: Schocken, 1988.

16. Isaak Babel, *The Collected Stories*, ed. and trans. Walter Morison (Cleveland: World Publishing Co., 1960, 1970).

17. New York: Schocken, 1977.

18. Trans. S. Gershon Levi (Philadelphia: Jewish Publication Society, 1975).

19. Distributed by International Film Exchange, 201 W. 52nd St., New York.

Now we come to the area of special topics. By their nature they are of interest to the more specialized reader, but also to students writing papers on specific topics, and may be used, as well, to link class discussion of Soviet Jewry with aspects of European Jewish history discussed elsewhere in the curriculum. Thus, for example, there is a substantial literature on the Holocaust in the German-occupied areas of the USSR. The first mass killings by special squads were carried out on Soviet soil (Babi Yar at Kiev is only the most famous example); the largest and most active Jewish partisan groups were located in areas like Lithuania and Belorussia; and the Soviet Union provided refuge for many thousands of Jews (Schwarz [n. 9]; Raul Hilberg, *The Destruction of the European Jews*[20] and *Documents of Destruction: Germany and Jewry, 1933–1945*;[21] Dov Levin, *Fighting Back: Lithuanian Jewry's Armed Resistance to the Nazis, 1941–1945*[22] and "Lithuanian Jewish Refugees in the Soviet Union During World War II";[23] Reuben Ainsztein, *Jewish Resistance in Nazi-occupied Eastern Europe*;[24] Ilya Ehrenburg and V. Grossman, *The Black Book*;[25] and the novel by Anatolii Rybakov, *Heavy Sand*[26]). Moreover, memorialization of the Holocaust became a strong and early basis for the emergent Jewish national or dissident movement in the 1960s and early 1970s (Eli Lederhendler, "Resources of the Ethnically Disenfranchised"[27]).

Similarly, one can study antisemitism in the Soviet Union against the background of, or in comparison with, modern antisemitism in Europe. Here I would consult Schwarz (n. 9); William Korey, *The Soviet Cage: Anti-Semitism in Russia*;[28] and Pinkus (n. 10). A volume of essays on the subject, *Antisemitism in the Soviet Union: The Brezhnev Era*,[29] deals specifically with the Brezhnev era, and there is also a wealth of material on this topic in periodicals such as *Soviet Jewish Affairs*. See also *Soviet Publications on Judaism, Zionism, and the State of Israel, 1984–1988: An Annotated Bibliography*[30] and *Antisemitism: An Annotated Bibliography*, vol. 1.[31]

Of special relevance to Soviet Jewish history is the topic of Jewish partici-

20. Chicago: Quadrangle, 1961, 2nd ed., 1967; repr. New York: Holmes and Meier, 1985.
21. Chicago: Quadrangle, 1971.
22. New York: Holmes and Meier, 1985.
23. *Studies in Contemporary Jewry* 4 (1988): 185–209.
24. New York: Schocken, 1979.
25. New York: Holocaust Library, 1981.
26. London: Penguin, 1982.
27. In Allworth (n. 2), pp. 194–227.
28. New York: Viking, 1973.
29. Ed. Yehuda Bauer (forthcoming).
30. Ed. Boris Korsch (New York: Garland, 1990).
31. Ed. Susan S. Cohen (New York: Garland, 1987).

pation in the Revolutions of 1917 and, subsequently, in the Communist government. The best study is Zvi Gitelman, *Jewish Nationality and Soviet Politics: The Jewish Sections of the CPSU, 1917–1930*.[32] Also relevant here are Joseph Nedava, *Trotsky and the Jews*,[33] and Israel Getzler's biography of Iulii Martov, *Martov: A Political Biography of a Russian Social Democrat*,[34] as well as an essay by Leonard Schapiro, "The Role of the Jews in the Russian Revolutionary Movement."[35] Always thought-provoking (and, again, interesting from a wider, comparative perspective) is the consideration of Jewishness and social alienation as a factor in the modern radical temperament or in the critique of capitalist society generally, by Isaac Deutscher, *The Non-Jewish Jew and Other Essays*.[36] Jewish Communism is a fascinating subject in its own right and has not been thoroughly researched. A pro-Soviet book that contrasts the Jews' status in the USSR of the 1930s favorably with the Jewish predicament elsewhere in Europe is L. Dennen, *Where the Ghetto Ends: Jews in Soviet Russia*.[37]

On the Soviet Jewish exodus there is a growing literature, and some of the most interesting books are not necessarily the academic ones. Basic reading for anyone interested in the origins of the aliyah movement are Leonard Schroeter, *The Last Exodus*,[38] and Elie Wiesel, *The Jews of Silence: A Personal Report on Soviet Jewry*.[39] There are a number of very moving human documents, including Natan (Anatolii) Shcharansky, *Fear No Evil*;[40] Esther Markish, *The Long Return*;[41] and Mark Azbel, *Refusenik: Trapped in the Soviet Union*,[42] among a growing list. Of interest here is also the collection edited by David Prital, *In Search of Self: The Soviet Jewish Intelligentsia and the Exodus*.[43] Works dealing with the integration of Soviet Jewish emigrés into American and Israeli society include *The Soviet Jewish Emigre: Proceedings of the National Symposium on the Integration of Soviet Jews into the American Jewish Community, December 26–27, 1976*;[44] Studies of the Third

32. Princeton: Princeton University Press, 1972.
33. Philadelphia: Jewish Publication Society, 1972.
34. Cambridge: Cambridge University Press, 1967.
35. *The Slavonic and East European Review* 40 (1961): 148–67.
36. London: Oxford University Press; New York: Hill and Wang, 1968.
37. New York: King, 1934.
38. New York: Universe, 1974.
39. New York: Bibliophile, 3rd ed., 1987.
40. New York: Random House, 1988.
41. New York: Ballantine, 1978.
42. New York: Paragon, 1987.
43. Jerusalem: Mount Scopus Publications, 1982.
44. Ed. Jerome Gilison (Baltimore: Johns Hopkins University Press, 1977).

Wave: Recent Migration of Soviet Jews to the United States;[45] Zvi Gitelman, *Becoming Israelis: Political Resocialization of Soviet and American Immigrants* ;[46] and Freedman (n. 3).

The history of the Jews under the Soviet regime seemed to lurch from high drama to catastrophe to pathos and back again. Whether the cycle repeats itself or is finally playing itself out remains to be seen. Until that question is itself history, all we can do is compare the present to the past.

One thing is certain: change on an unprecedented scale is taking place today for Jews in the new Commonwealth. As indicators we need only mention two facts: the pace and volume of emigration, and the establishment of a national conference of Jewish organizations (the "Vaad"). For the historian, these events are so extraordinary as to invite use of the term "miraculous"— they seem to lie so much outside the trajectory of Soviet Jewish history.

No less extraordinary has been the establishment of an academic program in Judaica, a yeshiva, and an open university for Jewish Studies in Moscow (with instructors from Israel and America). Add to this the international scholarly conference on Russian Jewish history held in Moscow (December 1989) and you have an embarrassment of riches. "Can it last?" is the question we hardly dare to ask, but which many recent emigrés seem to be answering with their feet.

45. Ed. Dan Norman Jacobs and Ellen Frankel (Boulder: Westview, 1981).
46. New York: Praeger, 1962.

5. The Jews of Austria-Hungary

Marsha L. Rozenblit

The historiography on European Jewry has largely focused on the experiences of the Jews of Germany, and that experience has been taken as paradigmatic for all Jews in Western and Central Europe. Even though important books like Todd Endelman's *The Jews of Georgian England, 1714–1830: Tradition and Change in a Liberal Society*[1] argued against this trend and revealed how the German model of Jewish modernization—a model based on the development of an ideology of Emancipation—simply did not apply to liberal England, studies of German Jewry still dominate the field and form the basis of most courses on the Modern Jewish Experience. This domination is rather remarkable, given the fact that Germany as a unified state did not exist until 1870 and then only six hundred thousand Jews lived there. Of course, this domination can easily be explained in terms of the significance of much of the German-Jewish experience. The Haskalah and Jewish religious reform both began in Germany. Moreover, German Jews had to struggle hard for Emancipation and against antisemitism. The fact that the Holocaust began in Germany has also played a significant role in establishing the centrality of the German-Jewish experience.

The Jews of the Habsburg Monarchy—numbering two million and representing the entire spectrum of modern Jewish ideology and behavior—have generally been ignored in courses on the Modern Jewish Experience, tending as they do to focus on Germany and Eastern Europe. At best, such courses only mention the Edict of Toleration of Joseph II (1782), the first attempt by a European monarch to modernize the Jews and urge their integration into the

1. Philadelphia: Jewish Publication Society, 1979.

larger society, and the proliferation of antisemitism in the late nineteenth century which prompted Theodor Herzl, a Viennese Jewish journalist, to inaugurate the Zionist movement.

Habsburg Jewry, however, deserves to be studied in its own right. Such a study reveals the true complexity of modern Jewish identity and the importance of national context in determining that identity. Habsburg Jewry was infinitely more varied that Jewries elsewhere, largely because the Habsburg Monarchy itself was not a nation-state and because it experienced economic modernization more slowly than Western Europe. The Monarchy contained both modern, acculturated Jews and large masses of utterly traditional Jews. Moreover, the nature of the nationality struggle in Austria-Hungary, accompanied as it was by antisemitism, precipitated a larger measure of Jewish ethnic assertiveness in Austria than was true elsewhere in Western and Central Europe.

In many ways the Jews of Germany and of Austria-Hungary resembled each other. In both states Jews modernized, abandoning traditional Jewish occupations and behavior patterns and adopting German culture. In Germany, however, adopting German culture assumed loyalty to the German state and a sense of belonging to the German people, even if the racial antisemites ultimately denied Jews membership in the German *Volk* (people). In Austria, on the other hand, culture, state, and nation were not coextensive. The Habsburg Monarchy contained scores of nationalities, each struggling, by the end of the nineteenth century, for some measure of autonomy and self-determination. Hungarian nationalism had been assuaged by the compromise agreement of 1867 which created "Austria-Hungary" and gave Hungary independence in most areas except foreign policy, the army, and loyalty to the crown. The Poles too seemed satisfied with a large measure of autonomy in Galicia. But the Czechs, Slovaks, Ruthenes, Croats, and others demanded similar rights, and the Germans resented any infringements on their traditional domination of the Monarchy. In the ensuing conflict, no one—except the emperor, the army, the bureaucracy, and the Jews—had any idea what it meant to be "Austrian."

In this multinational empire, modernizing Jews in the nineteenth century had embraced German culture, but this embrace did not mean that they had become Germans. Jews adopted German culture because it was the dominant elite culture and because the German liberals had emancipated the Jews in 1867. In Hungary, modern Jews switched their allegiance to Magyar culture by midcentury; many modernizing Jews in Galicia adopted Polish culture; and some Bohemian Jews declared their loyalty to Czech culture. Nevertheless, in the Austrian half of the Monarchy, Jews retained their loyalty to German culture down to the dissolution of the Monarchy in 1918. Whether they lived in

German Vienna or among warring Germans and Czechs in Bohemia and Moravia, Jews proudly asserted that they were adherents of German culture.

Although they adhered to German culture, Austrian Jews of all religious and political stripes declared themselves "Austrian." Alone among the peoples of the Reich, Jews felt intense loyalty to the supranational Austrian state and especially to the person of the Emperor Franz Joseph. Jews—whether traditionally religious, liberal, or Zionist—perceived that only Austria and the Emperor protected them from the antisemitism which seriously infected almost all the national camps. Thus Jews who adopted German culture were not Germans, but Austrians. When their beloved "Austria" dissolved at the end of World War I, Austrian Jews faced a very serious identity crisis as they had to adjust their loyalties to the new German, Czech, or Polish nation-states which succeeded Austria.

This reality also encouraged greater Jewish ethnic consciousness. In Austria, adopting German culture did not require the Jews to belong to the German people. Loyalty to the supranational Austrian state, and love of German culture, did not preclude continued Jewish solidarity and ethnic loyalty. Both because of the nature of the state and the success of antisemitism, Jews were freer to admit their sense of belonging to the Jewish people here than in Germany or France. Thus ideological reform with its rejection of Jewish peoplehood and Zion never took root in Austria; thus liberal Jews who asserted their Germanness unselfconsciously spoke about Jewish peoplehood. The presence of large numbers of ultra-Orthodox Jews, who continued to espouse a traditional religio-national Jewish self-definition, only served to augment this ethnic self-consciousness.

Until recently, few historians have dealt with Austro-Hungarian Jewry. Traditional studies of these Jews, like Max Grunwald, *Vienna*,[2] Hans Tietze, *Die Juden Wiens*,[3] or Hugo Gold's histories of the Jews of Bohemia and Moravia, written in the 1920s and 1930s,[4] focused exclusively on the assimilation of the liberal elite and paid no attention to the context of the nationality struggle or to the ways modernity affected ordinary Jews. The bulk of scholarship in the decades after World War II focused either on the very interesting question of why so many Jews in Austria participated in culture, especially its avant garde, or on the issue of antisemitism and its causes.

Austria, especially Vienna, was justly famous for its role in crafting mod-

2. Philadelphia: Jewish Publication Society, 1936.

3. Leipzig: Tal, 1933.

4. *Die Juden und Judengemeinden Mährens in Vergangenheit und Gegenwart* (Brno: Jüdischer Buch und Kunst Verlag, 1929); *Die Juden und Judegemeinden Böhmens in Vergangenheit und Gegenwart* (Brno: Jüdischer Verlag, 1934).

ernist culture, and many of Vienna's most famous writers, musicians, and thinkers were men of Jewish origin. The enormous contributions to modernism of such Jews or former Jews as Gustav Mahler, Arnold Schoenberg, Sigmund Freud, Arthur Schnitzler, Karl Kraus, Otto Weininger, and others prompted their biographers and general historians of culture to explain such a phenomenon. Although Carl Schorske's evocative *Fin-de-Siècle Vienna: Politics and Culture*[5] paid no attention to the Jewish dimension of late nineteenth century Viennese culture, other historians like William Johnston, *The Austrian Mind: An Intellectual and Social History 1848–1938*;[6] William J. McGrath, *Dionysian Art and Populist Politics in Austria*;[7] Hans Kohn, *Karl Kraus, Arthur Schnitzler, Otto Weininger: Aus dem jüdischen Wien der Jahrhundertwende*;[8] and certainly the biographers of Freud, Kraus, Weininger, and others paid a lot of attention to the significance of the Jewish background of these cultural luminaries. For example, on Freud, see Marthe Robert, *From Oedipus to Moses: Freud's Jewish Identity*;[9] Dennis Klein, *Jewish Origins of the Psychoanalytic Movement*;[10] Peter Gay, *A Godless Jew: Freud, Atheisim, and the Making of Psychoanalysis*[11] and *Freud: A Life for Our Time*;[12] on Karl Kraus, see Wilma Iggers, *Karl Kraus, A Viennese Critic of the Twentieth Century*;[13] Harry Zohn, *Karl Kraus*;[14] or Edward Timms, *Karl Kraus, Apocalyptic Satirist: Culture and Catastrophe in Habsburg Vienna*.[15] Although some of the biographies do an excellent job of explaining how Jewish background influenced the creativity of certain individuals, none of the general studies does an adequate job of explaining why such a huge percentage of cultural figures in late Habsburg Vienna was Jewish. The most recent attempt, Steven Beller's *Vienna and the Jews, 1867–1938: A Cultural History*,[16] fails in its attempt to explain the phenomenon. Although Beller's notion that Jews were prominent in culture because they formed a large percentage of the educated bourgeoisie is an important point, he exaggerates the prominence of Jews in the educated bourgeoisie in order to make it. Moreover, Beller's argument that traditional

5. New York: Knopf, 1980.
6. Berkeley & Los Angeles: University of California Press, 1972.
7. New Haven: Yale University Press, 1974.
8. Tübingen: Mohr, 1962.
9. Garden City, N.Y.: Anchor Books, 1976.
10. New York: Praeger, 1985.
11. New Haven: Yale University Press, 1987.
12. New York: Norton, 1988.
13. The Hague: Nijhoff, 1967.
14. New York: Twayne, 1971.
15. New Haven: Yale University Press, 1986.
16. Cambridge: Cambridge University Press, 1989.

Jewish concern with ethical individualism led many Jews into modern culture misunderstands the nature of Jewish tradition.

The success of antisemitic political parties in Austria has also received a great deal of scholarly attention. Before the advent of Nazism, modern antisemitism achieved its greatest successes in Austria. Georg von Schöner-er's Pan-German Party, for example, while not particularly successful at the polls, nevertheless influenced many upper middle class Germans in Austria. Schönerer's party glorified the German *Volk* in racist terms, called for the dismemberment of the Habsburg Monarchy and the *Anschluss* of its German lands with the German Reich, and vilified the Jews. In Vienna, the Christian Social Party under Karl Lueger appealed to middle-class voters angry with liberalism and with economic modernization. On Austrian antisemitism generally, see Peter Pulzer, *The Rise of Political Anti-Semitism in Germany and Austria*,[17] and most recently Bruce Pauley, *From Prejudice to Persecution: A History of Austrian Anti-Semitism*.[18] On Schönerer, see Andrew Whiteside, *The Socialism of Fools: Georg von Schönerer and Austrian Pan-German-ism*.[19] On the incredible success of the Christian Social Party in Vienna, see John Boyer, *Political Radicalism in Late Imperial Vienna: Origins of the Christian Social Movement, 1848–1897*[20] and Richard Geehr, *Karl Lueger: Mayor of Fin-de-Siècle Vienna*.[21]

Only recently has a body of literature emerged which deals in a sophisticated, scholarly way with the unique dilemmas of Austro-Hungarian Jewry, attempting to analyze the nature of Jewish identity there. For Vienna, see Marsha Rozenblit, *The Jews of Vienna, 1867–1914: Assimilation and Identity*,[22] a quantified analysis of Jewish birth, marriage, tax, and school attendance records, which attempts to get beyond the cultural luminaries and the communal leaders in order to understand the social mechanisms of Jewish assimilation and the brakes that the Jews themselves placed on that process. Thus Rozenblit deals with migration patterns, occupational transformation, residential concentrations, intermarriage and conversion, and Jewish organizational networks. She argues that although Jews migrating to Vienna from the Austrian and Hungarian provinces did transform themselves in the capital, abandoning many traditional Jewish behavior patterns, they nevertheless continued to be an identifiable group on the urban scene and developed new ideologies

17. New York: Wiley, 1964; rev. ed., Cambridge: Harvard University Press, 1988.
18. Chapel Hill: University of North Carolina Press, 1992.
19. Berkeley and Los Angeles: University of California Press, 1975.
20. Chicago: University of Chicago Press, 1981.
21. Detroit: Wayne State University Press, 1990.
22. Albany: State University of New York Press, 1983.

to justify continued Jewish separateness. Although Robert S. Wistrich returned to an earlier historiographic focus on Jewish leaders, his *The Jews of Vienna in the Age of Franz Joseph*[23] presents a nuanced and sensitive explanation of Jewish identity in the Habsburg capital. His book reveals the extent to which antisemitism deepened the Jewish identity of the liberal establishment and its Zionist and religious critics, and of many cultural luminaries, whom he treats in great detail. An important collection of articles on this subject is *Jews, Antisemitism, and Culture in Vienna.*[24]

The Jews of Bohemia, as well, have been the focus of a great deal of historical research in the past decade. Traditionally loyal to German culture and Austria, Bohemian Jews were beset by a vehement struggle between Czechs and Germans in the late nineteenth century. Castigated as Germans by the Czechs, and hated as Jews by both Czechs and Germans, Bohemian Jewry had to decide if they were Germans, Czechs, or just simply Jews. In his study of Prague Germans, *The Politics of Ethnic Survival: Germans in Prague, 1861–1914,*[25] Gary Cohen argues that, at least in Prague, Jews persisted in a loyalty to German culture because the Germans there eschewed the antisemitic exclusiveness they adopted elsewhere. See also his article, "Jews in German Society: Prague, 1860–1914."[26] On the other hand, Hillel Kieval, *The Making of Czech Jewry: National Conflict and Jewish Society in Bohemia, 1870–1918,*[27] argues that in Bohemia many Jews began to adopt a Czech national identity in the late nineteenth century. Moreover, a small group of Zionists adopted a specifically Jewish national identity. See also his article, "The Modernization of Jewish Life in Prague."[28] The Jews of Moravia, who persisted in German loyalties or who adopted a Jewish national identity, have unfortunately not yet been studied by scholars.

Galician and Hungarian Jewries have also not come under the scholarly scrutiny that they so justly deserve. In Galicia—a province of Catholic Poles, Orthodox Ruthenians, and large numbers of densely concentrated Jews— many Jews continued to espouse a tradional Jewish self-definition, others became active Zionists, and many tried to modernize on the so-called Western model. In Hungary as well, large masses of ultra-Orthodox Jews and equally large numbers of modern, acculturated Jews lived together; both groups

23. London: Oxford University Press, 1989.

24. Ed. Ivar Oxaal, Michael Pollak, and Gerhard Botz (New York: Routledge and Kegan Paul, 1987).

25. Princeton: Princeton University Press, 1981.

26. *Central European History* 10 (1977): 28–54.

27. New York: Oxford University Press, 1988.

28. In *Toward Modernity: The European Jewish Model*, ed. Jacob Katz (New Brunswick, N.J.: Transaction, 1987).

espoused Magyar culture and political loyalty. Michael Silber, at the Hebrew University in Jerusalem, is currently working on Hungarian Jewry and his work should contribute to an understanding of this important group of Jews. Many Hungarian scholars are also hard at work on this subject.

These Jewries do come under scrutiny in general works on Jews in the Habsburg Monarchy. William O. McCagg, Jr., *A History of Habsburg Jews 1670–1918,*[29] for example, is an attempt at grand synthesis. Uniquely equipped with the necessary linguistic skills for this task, McCagg seeks to explain the nature of Jewish modernization within the context of Austro-Hungarian politics and society in the past three centuries. Although idiosyncratic, McCagg's book is always suggestive and interesting. Very helpful at overview is Ezra Mendelsohn's important book *The Jews of East Central Europe between the Wars.*[30] In German see Wolfdieter Bihl, "Die Juden,"[31] and Wolfgang Häusler, "Das österreichische Judentum zwischen Beharrung und Fortschritt."[32]

For the instructor wishing to give a lecture on Austro-Hungarian Jewry, I would recommend focusing on this issue of the nature of Jewish identity within the context of Austrian society and politics. For familiarity with the nationality conflict, the instructor should read Robert Kann, *The Multinational Empire: Nationalism and National Reform in the Habsburg Monarchy, 1848–1918,*[33] or Oscar Jászi, *The Dissolution of the Habsburg Monarchy.*[34] On the Jews, I would recommend Rozenblit (n. 22); Cohen (n. 26); Kieval (n. 27); Wistrich (n. 23), chs. 5 and 6, and "The Modernization of Viennese Jewry";[35] and McCagg (n. 29).

As for a student assignment, I would recommend Cohen's and Wistrich's articles (nn. 26, 35) or the introduction and chapter 4 of Rozenblit (n. 22).

29. Bloomington: Indiana University Press, 1989.

30. Bloomington: Indiana University Press, 1983.

31. In *Die Habsburger Monarchie, 1848–1918,* vol. 3, ed. Adam Wandruszka and Peter Urbanitsch (Vienna: Verlag der Österreichischen Akademie der Wissenschaften, 1980), pp. 880–948.

32. In *Die Habsburger Monarchie, 1848-1918,* vol. 4, ed. Adam Wandruszka and Peter Urbanitsch (Vienna: Verlag der Österreichischen Akademie der Wissenschaften, 1980), pp. 633–69.

33. New York: Columbia University Press, 1950.

34. Chicago: University of Chicago Press, 1929.

35. In Katz (n. 28).

6. The Jews of North Africa and the Middle East

Jane Gerber

The inclusion of the Sephardic experience in a curriculum on the Modern Jewish Experience is a desideratum today. Sephardim constitute sixty percent of the population of Israel, a majority of the Jewish population of France, and approximately one quarter of the Jewish people. Their experience, in many ways, is the experience of all the Jewish people in modern times. Moreover, the Sephardic chapter of the modern Jewish experience is open-ended — the story of change is ongoing. The Sephardic loyalty to their traditions in the face of secularism, nationalism, expulsion, and migration provides many fundamental perspectives on the tenacity as well as the transformation of the Jewish people in modern times.

Napoleon's invasion of Egypt in 1798 marked a turning point in the history of the Middle East and its Jewish communities. Formerly autonomous minorities soon came under the influence of European culture and rival political interests, resulting in new patterns of social relations both within and among the various communities. Modernization and Westernization affected all the peoples of the Muslim world to varying degrees: Sephardic Jews moved from the position of *dhimma*, protected and humiliated minority, to quasi-Westernized subject in a colonial empire, to eventual refugee, emigré, and new citizen in the nascent State of Israel and the major component of the Jewish community of France. The modern period is thus an era of radical transformations and their attendant destabilizing effects for deeply rooted, ancient Jewish communities.

On the eve of the Napoleonic invasion, Sephardic Jews lived in a vast area stretching from Morocco to India. Although less than one million in number, Sephardic communities exhibited great diversity and internal richness, ranging from urban concentrations of Ladino (or Judeo-Spanish)-speaking Jews in the Balkans and Turkey, Arabic-speaking urbanites in Syria, Iraq, and the imperial cities of North Africa, to thousands of farmers in Yemen, Aramaic-speaking villagers in the Kurdish hinterland, and widely dispersed Persian Jews in Iran and the Central Asian steppes (Bukhara, Azerbaijan, Uzbekistan). The variety of relationships with their Muslim neighbors was particularly striking, ranging from relative tolerance in Turkey and paternalistic protection by tribal chicftains in large areas of Morocco, Algeria, and Kurdistan to extreme degradation in Yemen and some parts of North Africa (where Jews were subject to discriminatory laws, debased occupations, seizing of orphans to be raised as Muslims, and the requirement that they clean the public latrines). Some of these communities were quite isolated from contact with the outside Jewish world, while others retained strong ties with Europe through familial connections with Europe's Sephardic populations or commercial relations with local representatives of European powers.

Constructing an inclusive curriculum on the modern Jewish experience does not require a discussion of all the Jewries of the Sephardic diaspora; beneath this mosaic of diversity there was a basic similarity of response to the major challenges of Westernization, modernization, and migration. The larger Sephardic communities in North Africa, Iraq, and Turkey all experienced direct contact with Europeans. Ultimately, even the most isolated community was not spared the destructive consequences of nationalism and expulsion or the more subtle effects of Westernization. Most of those who made policy for Sephardim over the past 150 years assumed reflexively that Westernization meant progress and was ipso facto desirable.

Use of the term "Sephardic" (from Hebrew *Sefarad*, "Spain," Obadiah 20) requires some explanation. Many of the communities under discussion actually bore little historic relationship to the Jews of Spain. While the largest Sephardic communities in modern times, those of North Africa, were deeply influenced culturally and demographically by the exiles of 1492, Kurdish, Yemenite, and Iraqi Jews had little contact with Spanish refugees in the sixteenth century. After the expulsion of the Jews from Spain in 1492, one of the main routes of exile of the emigrés was back into the world of Islam. The largest concentration of Sephardic exiles went to the Ottoman empire, where new centers of Jewish life such as Salonika, Istanbul, and Edirne began to flourish. A much smaller Sephardic migration left Portugal as secret Jews in the course of the sixteenth century, moving primarily to Holland, France, and Italy. Turkey and the Balkans were strongly Hispanic, while Yemen was barely touched by the migration of Iberian exiles. What united the mosaic of Jewries dotting the Mediterranean was a shared cultural tradition, albeit peppered by deep regional and local variants, based on common legal traditions derived from ancient and Medieval times and a basically similar historic evolution under Muslim rule. All these communities were deeply touched by the exhilaration and subsequent despair of the false messianic movement of Sabbetai Sevi in the seventeenth century and disfigured by the long decline and stagnation of the Muslim world in the seventeenth and eighteenth centuries. By the twentieth century the Jewish societies of the various Muslim regions faced common dilemmas posed by the twin challenges of colonialism and nationalism. To the extent that a curriculum on the modern Jewish experience is representative of the breadth and varieties of Jewish life in modern times, such a curriculum can comfortably treat the Sephardim from a thematic point of view; unity amid local diversity can be accommodated without dilution or distortion.

The scientific study of the Jews in Muslim lands in modern times is quite recent and still in its early stages. The nineteenth-century pioneers of European Jewish scholarship tended to ignore Sephardic Jewry, especially in the post-expulsion period, in part because the depressed condition of the community was not relevant to the concerns of a European generation seeking models of Emancipation. When at the end of the century scholarship did quicken as a result of the discovery of the Cairo Geniza (a treasure-trove of documents stored in a Cairo synagogue that reflect the world of the Jew in the Mediterranean for centuries — hundreds of thousands of fragments in Hebrew and Judeo-Arabic have been analyzed, shedding light on all aspects of the economic, familial, and communal life of Mediterranean Jewry), its fruits reflected the world of the Mediterranean Jew of Medieval times so richly documented in its fragments. In addition, Sephardic communities did not possess scholars trained in western sciences until very recently. Those learned people who commanded the requisite variety of Middle Eastern languages in which Jewish material was preserved were generally uninterested in the questions that define modern scholarship. Moreover, with the notable exception of the Ottoman archives, Muslim records were remarkably indifferent to the lot or even the presence of the Jews.

With the rise of the State of Israel, Sephardic Jewry has become the subject of systematic study by scholars at Israel's major universities. The Ben Zvi Institute in Jerusalem houses an extensive manuscript collection and publishes numerous monographic studies in *Sefunot* and *Pe'amim*. Smaller institutes of separate communities such as the Iraqis house individual collections with separate publications. Publishing programs by the national Misgav Yerushalayim and Bar Ilan University have added to the growing scientific literature in the Hebrew language. The significant manuscript holdings of the Sephardic collection at Yeshiva University constitute the material for the research arm of that institution's Sephardic Program. Yeshiva University is the first American institution of higher learning that has a funded program of Sephardic studies, but it has no systematic publishing program.

The most salient characteristic of the field of Sephardic Studies is its highly interdisciplinary character. Ethnolinguists (primarily in Israel) are delving into the various linguistic traditions of Sephardim, while a new generation of historians have succeeded the the older generation of pioneering scholars H. Z. Hirschberg and S. D. Goitein. The music of Sephardim is now receiving critical analysis, and the insights of folklorists are increasingly enriching scholars. Since one major impetus toward the study of Sephardim was their sudden immigration en masse to Israel, it is not surprising that anthropologists, quintessential cultural relativists, were the first to direct their attention toward Sephardim. So far, anthropology has dominated the field of Sephardic Studies, providing many of the innovative studies in Israel and the United States. Shlomo Deshen, Moshe Shokeid, Harvey Goldberg, Walter Zenner, Yoram Bilu, and Alex Weingrod are among the anthropologists whose work has illuminated such areas of inquiry as leadership and charisma, family and community, festivals like the *mimouna* and the Zaharani, and the more practical questions of immigrant acculturation. Anthropologists have tended, as one would expect, to be somewhat skeptical of the social engineering of Israeli statebuilders and quite sympathetic to the preservation and transformation of folk customs.

The area of concern of anthropologists is far removed from the work of scholars in language and literature. For the latter, Sephardic studies began as an outgrowth of a more general concern with what it meant to be Spanish, not what it meant to be Sephardic. For that generation, the work of Américo Castro and his disciples, which posited the importance of the Semitic element in Spanish culture, was positively revolutionary. Those who endeavor to explore Judeo-Spanish themes in the Balkans rarely interact with historians and anthropologists working on aspects of the culture of Jews from Muslim lands. Since Sephardic Studies is still in its early stages of development and not crisply defined, it is not surprising that translated source material, teaching aids such as maps and readers, and English renditions of some of the major works of scholarship remain a desideratum. There are as yet no bibliographical studies along the lines of *Index Islamicus* in English. Such works are especially necessary in the Sephardic field in light of its highly interdisciplinary character.

Change is a hallmark of the Modern period of Jewish history. Both Sephardim and Ashkenazim faced profound challenges to the traditional community and its assumptions. But the context of change was quite different for the two sectors. Change did not come to Sephardic Jews in the context of an emancipation debate, nor was the achievement of equality with the dominant Muslim majority ever a realistic goal. It was European Jews, concerned and chagrined by the abject condition of their co-religionists, who introduced change in the traditional Near Eastern Jewish community. With the establishment of the Alliance Israelite Universelle in 1860, a vast network of Western-style schools reached Jews in the remote corners of Islam. The native Western-educated teachers and their growing cadre of students challenged the older elites and traditional social structure. They generally lacked the degree of ideological fervor of the Ashkenazi reformers in Europe, scarcely touched the area of religious reform, and generally operated without the bitter divisiveness and rancor that characterized European Jewry as it confronted modernization. The role of the Alliance Israelite Universelle as a catalyst of change in North Africa has received scholarly attention in Michael Laskier, *The Alliance Israelite Universelle and the Jewish Communities of Morocco, 1862–1962*.[1] Aron Rodrigue in *De l'instruction à l'emancipation*[2] and *French Jews, Turkish Jews: The Alliance Irsaélite Universelle and the Politics of Jewish Schooling in Turkey, 1860–1925*[3] has traced the attitude of the Alliance toward the Middle Eastern Jews and the various stages of influence which the schools exerted on the local population in the Turkish Jewish community. His study is drawn from a close reading of Alliance archives and a larger perspective on questions of modernization. Both the Alliance Israelite Universelle and later the Jewish Agency served as the major instruments of change in the Sephardic world. Both assumed that progress required fundamental changes within the leadership and the rank and file of the Sephardic communities.

Given the absence of an Emancipation debate in Muslim lands and the continued acceptability of traditional religious institutions and their leaders, it is not surprising that the modern period was less radical in results and less corrosive in its impact on the traditional Sephardic Jewish family and community. Indeed, for many Sephardic Jews, the modernization process had only recently begun when the traditional community was destroyed by flight to Israel with its resultant dispersal and destruction of the old community, leaving an unanticipated void. The Sephardic family has received recent attention by Moshe Shokeid and Shlomo Deshen in articles in *The Jewish Family:*

1. Albany: State University of New York Press, 1983.
2. Paris: Calmann-Levy, 1989.
3. Bloomington: Indiana University Press, 1990.

Myths and Reality.[4] One fascinating study of the transformation of a North African saintly leader into a politico-religious personality in contemporary Israel and the broader question of the resuscitation of saint cults among Israeli Sephardim can be found in Alex Weingrod, *The Saint of Beersheba.*[5]

The Sephardic Jewish experience in modern times thus offers a variant mode in which to study the multifaceted question of change and tradition. Substantial changes did occur: family and lifestyle, the role of women and the education of children, economic and fertility patterns were all altered as a byproduct of Westernization rather than as a result of ideological debate and political utopianism. Among the many useful articles in the volume *Jewish Societies in the Middle East*[6] is an essay "Traditional Society and Modern Society" by Jacob Katz (pp. 35–47), which explores the meaning and mechanisms of change as they relate to Middle Eastern Jewish societies.

Sephardic Jewish history in modern times offers an additional fascinating variant to the Ashkenazi model. European Jews who set out to protect and modernize their Jewish brethren in Muslim lands began their involvement as protectors, most prominently with the Damascus Blood Libel of 1840. Gradually their ambitions expanded. They introduced new schools with a Western secular curriculum in the Muslim world, hoping thereby to "civilize," "productivize," and "uplift" their Jewish brethren languishing under the yoke of Islam. It was anticipated that a new Jew, adept at European languages and possessing new vocational skills, would be able to negotiate the transition from Mellah — the Jewish ghetto in Morocco, established in the fifteenth century — to modernity. This transition, however, did not lead to the integration of Jews in their native societies, since the presence of European colonialism was a disruptive force. The European presence was naturally attractive to the Jew because it spelled greater security and economic advancement; to the Muslim it was a humiliation and indeed a religious challenge. In which community would the Jew be integrated? The colonial one in which the *colon* was both a stranger to the native Muslim and frequently an antisemite as well, or the emergent nationalist society with its Islamic exclusivism? The dilemma of the Sephardic Jew caught in the middle of the cultural and political stresses of colonial domination lies at the heart of the autobiography of Albert Memmi, *Pillar of Salt.*[7]

The twentieth century witnessed a new political consciousness on the part of

4. Ed. Steven M. Cohen and Paula Hyman (New York: Holmes and Meier, 1986).
5. Albany: State University of New York Press, 1990.
6. Ed. Shlomo Deshen and Walter Zenner (Washington: University Press of America, 1982).
7. New York: Criterion, 1955.

the Jews in Muslim lands. In some measure this consciousness stemmed from the rise of Arab nationalism. In other instances, however, it was a result of the gradual penetration of Zionist ideology into the area. Calls for identification with France, petitions for British citizenship, and the dissonance and separatism of Balkan nationalism led to furtive attempts at establishing a Zionist presence among the Jewish youth. Zionism as an ideology, however, was European, "foreign" in language and assumptions to Middle Eastern Jews. Even the Zionist emissaries sent to North Africa barely spoke a word of French, the lingua franca of North African Jews by the early twentieth century. Moreover, as a political movement it was dangerous, suspect to the already overheated nationalist passions of Arabs in the Near East. Yet, the notion of return to Zion as a traditional expression of Sephardic Jewish activism remained alive through the centuries.

The modern European notion of national patriotism did not offer an option for Sephardim either, since no *patrie* existed. Wherever the Europeans became entrenched, be it British in Iraq and Egypt, French in North Africa and the Levant, or Italians in Libya, Sephardic Jews faced complex problems of identity unlike those in Europe. If their reaction was less traumatic, it was probably a result of the fact that their communities remained more coherent, their families more cohesive, and the possibility of integration less attainable. Until their last days in Muslim lands it was unclear what would be the entity in which a Jew would be allowed to integrate.

Sephardic history in the Ottoman heartland followed a different course from that of the Jews in the Arab Near East or North Africa. In the Ladino-speaking Sephardic communities of Turkey and the Balkans, the nineteenth century ushered in a new period. Nineteenth-century reforms, known as the *tanzimat* movement, restructured the relationship of all minorities to the Muslim majority. On the one hand, the Tanzimat recognized equality among the various Muslim, Christian, and Jewish minorities. Its reorganization efforts also extended to include reorganizations within the various religious groups (*millets*). Inadvertently, however, Ottoman reforms served to aggravate relations among the minorities, further polarizing the intercommunal relationships between Muslims and among Muslims, Christians, and Jews. Relations between Muslim sects and Christians turned violent, economic changes brought new antagonisms between Christians and Jews, and the European protection of the Ottoman Christian minorities enabled them to displace their Jewish competitors. Thus the combined forces of minority Christian nationalism, Jewish economic deterioration, and emergent pan-Turkish movements impoverished the Jews of Turkey. Turkish reforms had never really been intended by the Turks to ensure the wellbeing of the religious minorities but rather to stave off dismemberment and to win the goodwill of the powers. Indeed, the socioeconomic and nationalist forces set in motion in the Balkans eventually led the Jews to conclude that their only hope lay in emigration to the West. This realization was undoubtedly reinforced by the unprecedented and repeated instances of Blood Libels throughout the Ottoman East introduced by native Ottoman Christians (particularly Greeks) with the occasional connivance of European diplomatic representatives.

Culturally, the Jews of Turkey and the Balkans underwent a renaissance in the nineteenth century, expressed most vividly in an expansion of secular Ladino literature. This renaissance occurred, ironically, precisely at the moment that the Alliance Israelite Universelle was working to downgrade Judeo-Spanish in its schools. The Ladino flowering continued in diminished form in the Greek and Balkan states that split off from the Ottoman Empire in the twentieth century. David Bunis, *Sephardic Studies*,[8] presents an invaluable bibliography of Ladino history, literature, and language studies.

As the teacher of the modern Jewish experience moves from the nineteenth century discussion of Emancipation, modernization of community and economy, and the emergence of political antisemitism and nationalism, he or she will notice that the force of these Western movements was refracted in Muslim lands. Ideally, it would be desirable to integrate a discussion of antisemitism in Algeria while surveying modern antisemitism and the Dreyfus Affair in France. Similarly, the discussion of educational reform and the schools of the Alliance Israelite Universelle gains richness when viewed in the context of both the general European movement of Haskalah and the specifics of the debate of Jewish Emancipation in France. In such a fashion, the modern Jewish experience could be seen from the perspective of both branches of world Jewry. Moreover, the breakdown of Jewish life in Muslim lands could then be understood as part and parcel of the process of Ottoman decline and the evolution of modern Arab nationalism rather than primarily as a reflection of the emergent Arab–Israeli conflict. Such an integrative approach, moreover, mutes the differences between Ashkenazim and Sephardim frequently postulated by scholars in both communities.

As the curriculum moves beyond the nineteenth century with its transcendent questions of Jewish individual and group identity and the corresponding issues of nationalism and Jewish integration, the curriculum planner is faced with the question of how to interweave the disparate trends occurring in

8. New York: Garland, 1981.

Europe and the Near East. Post–World War I nationbuilding in Europe confronted the Jew with a host of problems — antisemitism, competing nationalisms, assimilating the refugees from the East, to name only a few. Sephardic Jews confronted dissimilar challenges in the interwar period. The collapse of the Ottoman Empire was superseded by the further entrenchment of the colonial regimes of France and England in North Africa and the Middle East. Jews witnessed an initial dramatic improvement in their condition in their respective countries as rapid urbanization and population expansion followed in the footsteps of the establishment of European control in the form of mandates and outright occupation. Jews played a particularly prominent role in the economic development of Iraq and Egypt, forming a vital part of the middle class in these countries. Culturally as well, they became increasingly identified with the occupying powers, especially in North Africa. Pressures increased on the Jews on all fronts — from European occupiers who wanted the Jews to disavow Zionism, from Arab nationalists radicalized by the continuing presence of the European powers. As the Arab–Jewish conflict in Palestine mounted, the Jews in Muslim countries were increasingly vulnerable to mob violence and suffered declining protection by the European occupiers. Arabs were entranced by anti-Western slogans and pro-fascist blandishments. The deterioration of the Jewish position in the interwar period was therefore global, sparked by different forces in Europe and Muslim lands. If some Sephardic Jews believed that the presence of the West spelled greater security, they were sadly mistaken. Ultimately, the Western presence introduced more lethal forms of antisemitism than any traditionally known in the Middle East, accelerating the breakdown of Muslim–Jewish coexistence. This complex process should be included in discussions of post-War developments regarding Palestine and the rise of fascism in Europe.

The Holocaust looms large in any consideration of Jewish fate in twentieth-century Europe. The tragic fate of Sephardic Jewry should be recalled in this portion of the curriculum. Jews throughout the Sephardic diaspora were affected, from outright deportation and annihilation in Salonika, Yugoslavia, and parts of Bulgaria to expropriations, forced labor, and even limited deportation in parts of North Africa. The Ladino civilization of the Balkans which had survived one-half millennium in exile was destroyed between 1939 and 1945. The abrogation of the Cremieux Decree stripped the Jews of Algeria of their French citizenship and struck a terrifying chord throughout the Maghreb. The unfettered pogrom known as the *Farhud* in Iraq in 1941 signaled the danger which fascism posed to Iraqi Jewry, shocking the community to the core. Jews in Egypt and Libya moved toward greater Zionist involvement as the presence of Palestinian Jewish units of the British Army shielded them from the tentacles of the Final Solution. One of the most comprehensive accounts of the Holocaust period in North Africa is Michel Abitbol, *The Jews of North Africa during the Second World War.*[9] Autobiographical accounts such as Rafael Uzan, *Days of Honey,*[10] or Naim Kattan, *Farewell Babylon,*[11] depict how the Holocaust and indigenous antisemitism shattered the security of integrated Jews in Iraq and North Africa. The impact of political change on the fate of the Jews of Egypt is carefully delineated by Güdrun Kramer in *The Jews of Modern Egypt, 1914–1952.*[12] Only a small minority of Jews engaged in the anticolonialist struggle in Muslim countries, while the majority fearfully watched the anticolonial conflict unfold, realizing that their safety hinged on a victory for the Allied forces.

Among the last units in a curriculum devoted to the modern Jewish experience is the epic story of the rise of the State of Israel in 1948 and the mass migration of the Sephardim. Within three years after the declaration of Israeli independence, most Sephardic communities had been evacuated from Muslim countries. Once again the themes of change and unresolved identity dominate the scientific literature of the period. Early studies like S. Eisenstadt, *The Absorption of Immigrants,*[13] were concerned with the dynamics and mechanics of immigrant absorption rather than with the unique cultures and crises of the immigrant communities. The research of S. Smooha, *Israel: Pluralism and Conflict;*[14] M. Shokeid, *The Dual Heritage: Immigrants from the Atlas Mountains in an Israeli Village;*[15] S. Deshen and Moshe Shokeid, *The Predicament of Homecoming;*[16] and Harvey Goldberg, *Cave Dwellers and Citrus Growers,*[17] have greatly enhanced our knowledge of how the Sephardim adapted to and were transformed by Israeli society. The vitality of particular customs of North African Jews such as the *mimuna* (festival of Moroccan Jews at the end of Passover), the *hillulot* (pilgrimages to and the veneration of graves of particular saintly rabbis) have been the subject of studies by Harvey Goldberg, "The Mimouna and the Minority Status of Moroccan Jews";[18] S. Deshen,

9. Detroit: Wayne State University Press, 1989.

10. Ed. I. Awret (New York: Schocken, 1984).

11. New York: Taplinger, 1980.

12. Seattle: University of Washington Press, 1989.

13. London: Routledge and Kegan Paul, 1954.

14. Berkeley and Los Angeles: University of California Press, 1978.

15. Manchester: Manchester University Press, 1971.

16. Ithaca: Cornell University Press, 1974.

17. Cambridge: Cambridge University Press, 1972.

18. *Ethnology* 17 (1978): 75–85.

"Tunisian Hilluloth";[19] Yoram Bilu, "Dreams and Wishes of the Saint";[20] and, most recently, Weingrod (n. 5). The unique community of Djerba has been the subject of anthropological analysis by L. Valensi and A. Udovich in *The Last Arab Jews*.[21]

Numerous specialized studies of individual communities have been published in Hebrew and English. Daniel Schroeter, *Merchants of Essaouira: Urban Society and Imperialism in Southwestern Morocco 1844–1886*;[22] H. Goldberg, *Jewish Life in Muslim Libya: Rivals and Relatives*;[23] and Norman Stillman, *The Language and Culture of the Jews of Sefrou, Morocco: an Ethnolinguistic Study*,[24] fill in important gaps in our knowledge. The instructor must bear in mind that the contemporary literature is frequently problem-oriented and weighted toward questions of immigrant absorption to the Israeli ethos. Younger Sephardic scholars in Israel are frequently engaged in an ongoing appraisal and critique of Israeli social policies connected with immigrant absorption, a critique which fortunately has not generally marred their scientific objectivity. A particularly provocative study of this genre is M. Inbar and C. Adler, *Ethnic Integration in Israel: A Comparative Case Study of Moroccan Brothers Who Settled in France and in Israel*.[25]

No study of the Sephardic Jews should ignore the fact that Sephardim still possess a rich lore and legacy and a keen sense of the importance of their past. While it would require special expertise to master the nuances of custom and law which differentiate Sephardim from Ashkenazim, a useful breakdown of Sephardic (i.e., Spanish), Moroccan, and Syrian Jewish customs has been compiled by H. Dobrinsky, *A Treasury of Sephardic Laws and Customs*.[26] Between the Dobrinsky study and Daniel Elazar's discussion of contemporary Sephardim, *The Other Jews*,[27] the instructor can equip herself with very basic outlines of Sephardic cultural and geographic diversity today.

Several useful maps with annotations can be found in E. Friesel, *Atlas of*

19. (In Hebrew) in *Dor ha-temurah* (The Generation of Transition), ed. M. Shokeid and S. Deshen (Jerusalem: Zvi Institute for Research on Jewish Communities in the Middle East, 1977), pp. 110–21.
20. In *Judaism Viewed from Within and Without*, ed. H. Goldberg (Albany: State University of New York Press, 1987), pp. 285–313
21. New York: Harwood Academic, 1984.
22. Cambridge: Cambridge University Press, 1988.
23. Chicago: University of Chicago Press, 1990.
24. Manchester: University of Manchester – *Journal of Semitic Studies*, 1988.
25. New Brunswick: Transaction, 1977.
26. New York: Yeshiva University Press, 1986.
27. New York: Basic Books, 1989.

Modern Jewish History,[28] providing visual evidence of the legal situation of Sephardim prior to their emigration, graphic illustrations of population breakdown in various countries, as well as Sephardic routes of migration in recent centuries.

Teaching the Sephardic dimension of the modern Jewish experience falls into several broad categories, each of which could form the core of a separate class discussion. (1) The Jews of Muslim lands in the nineteenth century and the impact of the West. (2) Internal changes affecting the Sephardim. (3) The crisis of identity: the Jews between the forces of colonialism and nationalism in the interwar period. (4) Zionism and anti-Jewishness and the tragedy of World War II. (5) Emigration and expulsion and the return to the land of Israel. (6) The contemporary Sephardic condition; retrieving a shattered past in Israel and the diaspora.

The basic texts for these core units on Sephardic Jews are readily available. The best single work for teaching purposes is Norman Stillman, *The Jews of Arab Lands*.[29] The first volume, covering the period until the 1870s, contains a brief introductory narrative on this period and a generous collection of primary documents. The second volume discusses developments from the end of the nineteenth century until the emigration movement to Israel. The texts in both volumes, culled from a variety of languages, illuminate a wide range of issues. Stillman does not deal with the inner life of Sephardic Jewry, but his two volumes facilitate the inclusion of the Sephardim in any modern Jewish history course. Stillman's volumes can be supplemented by Bernard Lewis, *The Jews of Islam*,[30] for a new discussion of the causes of Jewish decline in the Ottoman Empire.

Several films have been produced in Israel, France, and the United States depicting a variety of ethnographic aspects of the Sephardic tradition. Some include extracts of historical film footage on the emigration to Israel (for example, *The Last Chapter* and *Routes of Exile*), and others skillfully attempt to preserve a visual record of customs threatened by modernization. *The Jews of Jerba* by Alain Cohen, *The Mimouna* by Haim Shiran, and *The Jews of Turkey* by Laurence Saltzman fall into this category. The screen adaptation of Memmi's autobiography (n. 7) depicting his childhood in Tunisia supplements some of the more academic discussions of the anguish of identity conflict

---

28. New York: Oxford University Press, 1990.
29. 2 vols. (Philadelphia: Jewish Publication Society, 1983, 1990).
30. Princeton: Princeton University Press, 1986.

experienced in the 1940s and 1950s by North African Jews. Israeli commercial films such as *The House on Chelouche Street* by Moshe Mizrahi capture the chaotic period of the late 1940s with empathy and sensitivity. While the importance of the utilization of film for ethnographic purposes cannot be over-emphasized, caution should be employed so that Sephardic Jews do not become an exotic, folkloristic phenomenon in the mind of the student.

7. American Jewish History

Jack Wertheimer

In a survey of recent research on American Jewish history, the historian Jonathan Sarna noted the massive expansion of the field during the past decades. He measured this growth by the rising number of publications recorded in "Judaica Americana," a regular feature of the journal *American Jewish History*: whereas in 1965 a total of 175 publications were listed, by 1989, the figure had jumped to 515 publications. Other measures of expansion include the burgeoning of courses on American Jewish history at institutions of higher learning, the easy availability of scholarly books in the field, and the acceptance of articles on American Jewry by the most prestigious academic journals. The outpouring of new scholarly literature makes it impossible even for specialists in the field to keep track of all the new research. Fortunately, several excellent bibliographic guides are available: most highly recommended are a superb volume written by Jeffrey S. Gurock, *American Jewish History: A Bibliographic Guide*,[1] and Sarna's masterful survey of the most recent literature, "American Jewish History."[2] Further works on curriculum by Jonathan Sarna and others are being sponsored by the International Center for the University Teaching of Jewish Civilization, Jerusalem. The first of these has appeared as *Jews and the Founding of the Republic*.[3]

Rather than duplicate those assessments of the state of the field, the present essay is addressed solely to the question of how to incorporate material on the history of Jews in the United States into a survey course on the Modern Jewish

1. New York: Anti-Defamation League, 1983.
2. *Modern Judaism* 10 (1990): 343–65.
3. Ed. Jonathan D. Sarna and Benny Kraut (New York: Markus Wiener, 1985).

Experience. I identify six themes and illustrate how they offer rich possibilities for comparative discussions. My approach therefore emphasizes continuities and discontinuities between the American Jewish experience and that of other Jewries in regard to a half dozen historical issues.

The Emancipation Experience

The struggle of Jews to attain Emancipation is perhaps the central theme of courses on the Modern Jewish Experience. To trace varying models of Emancipation, courses routinely embark on a Cook's tour, generally beginning with revolutionary France, moving on to German-speaking Europe, continuing eastward to Russia, and concluding with Arab lands. The American experience often goes unmentioned, in part due to the Eurocentric bias of modern Jewish historiography, in part because of the relative absence of controversy in America. Why belabor an Emancipation debate that never was? It is precisely the relative absence of controversy that warrants comment in class discussions as a means of highlighting what happened when the "Jewish Question" did become a matter of public debate.

An analysis of Jewish Emancipation in the United States should begin with a survey of how the civil, religious, and political rights of Jews were treated in various colonies prior to the Revolutionary War. The session should emphasize the absence of an organized struggle for rights and the trial-and-error methods employed by individual Jews to expand their own opportunities. This may be compared to the efforts organized by Jewish elites in other lands to sway government officials and prove the worthiness of Jews for equality. As background reading, Abraham Vossen Goodman, *Jewish Rights in Colonial Times*,[4] remains helpful. On the acquisition of citizenship, see Jonathan D. Sarna, "The Impact of the American Revolution on American Jewry,"[5] and Stanley F. Chyet, "The Political Rights of the Jews in the United States, 1771–1840."[6] Emphasis may be placed on the passive role of Jews in this process and the ways in which granting them equality was imperative from the American perspective.

The discussion should then move to the requirements set forth in state constitutions of a religious test oath required prior to participation in the political process. There can be a discussion of differences between Federal and state prerogatives. The class should then examine the controversy between 1819

4. Philadelphia: Jewish Publication Society, 1947.
5. *Modern Judaism* 1 (September 1981): 149–60.
6. *American Jewish Archives* 10 (April 1958): 14–75.

and 1826 over the so-called Maryland Jew Bill as a case study. Comparisons can be made between the surfacing of antisemitism in Maryland and in European lands once the "Jewish Question" was raised for public debate. The Jew Bill controversy stands as an important exception to the general absence of political antisemitism in early America and illustrates what Jews were spared because they were included in general guarantees offered by the Federal Constitution. The attitudes expressed during the controversy about Catholics provides an opportunity to reflect on the hostility of Protestant denominations toward other Christian groups, thereby placing antisemitic utterances into a comparative framework. Many of the important documents from the Jew Bill debate are reprinted in Joseph L. Blau and Salo W. Baron, *The Jews in the United States, 1790–1840: A Documentary History,*[7] vol. 1, documents 22–37. For a good discussion of the social and economic context of the debate, see Edward Etches, "Maryland's 'Jew Bill.'"[8]

The Development of Reform Judaism

In the context of classes on the modernization of Judaism, it is useful to discuss the rise and development of Reform Judaism in nineteenth-century America. Any discussion of organized religious reforms must offer an explanation of why such activities succeeded in some countries and failed in others. The American case is extraordinary both because Reform achieved such a wide measure of popular success by the end of the century, as well as because the American environment was so different from the Central European region which initially spawned movements of religious modernization.

A discussion of American Reform begins with the controversy in Beth Elohim of Charleston. In 1824 some members of the Sephardic synagogue in Charleston petitioned the board for reforms in the synagogue service. When their demands were rejected, a group of disgruntled members organized a Reformed Society, which apparently sponsored worship services including instrumental music, English prayers, and male participants who did not cover their heads. By 1840, the reformers gained control of Beth Elohim and remade it as the first Reform Temple in the United States. There is considerable dispute over the factors causing this early effort at religious reform, let alone the relationship of Beth Elohim to other contemporaneous movements of religious reform. Some of the basic documents appear in Blau and Baron (n. 7), vol. 2, documents 209–11. For a recent discussion linking this effort to the

7. New York: Columbia University Press, 1963.
8. *American Jewish Historical Quarterly* 60 (March 1971): 258–80.

Maryland Jew Bill, see Robert Liberles, "Conflict over Reforms: The Case of Congregation Beth Elohim, Charleston, South Carolina."[9]

By the second half of the nineteenth century, and particularly in the post–Civil War era, Reform swept across American Jewry. Historians differ as to the sources of this movement: Was it an indigenous or an imported phenomenon? What role did rabbis play in its spread? And how important was its ideology in the success of Reform Judaism? For an analysis stressing the European origins of the movement and the centrality of ideology, see Michael A. Meyer, *Response to Modernity: A History of the Reform Movement in Judaism,*[10] chs. 6–8.This approach has been challenged by Leon Jick, *The Americanization of the Synagogue 1820–1870.*[11] Jick argues that Reform emerged in the United States when German-speaking Jews gradually Americanized and rose on the socioeconomic ladder: Reform was a response to indigenous needs of Jews who wished to accommodate to America, rather than an imported ideology. Thus, for Jick, the ideology came at a later stage to justify earlier changes, and rabbis were not very significant in spreading Reform. An attempt to mediate between the two positions regarding the origins of Reform and the role of ideology has been set forth by Naomi W. Cohen, *Encounter with Emancipation: The German Jews in the United States, 1830–1914.*[12] Meyer reprints the text of the Pittsburgh Platform defining Classical Reform, as well as subsequent formulations of Reform ideology (pp. 387–94).

Constructing a Jewish Community in America

The collapse of the traditional Jewish community and efforts to find a suitable replacement for the kehillah are central themes explored in courses on modern Jewry. The American case is especially rich in this regard because of the virtually complete absence of governmental intervention in the establishment and maintenance of Jewish communities. From the onset of their arrival in the United States, Jews were forced to devise new communal structures and rules of membership. A discussion of organizational experiments by American Jews will enrich students' understanding of the Jewish community in the modern era and particularly will highlight the tension between voluntarism and coercion.

Such a discussion can begin with the first congregations established by

9. In *The American Synagogue: A Sanctuary Transformed*, ed. Jack Wertheimer (New York: Cambridge University Press, 1987), pp. 274–96.

10. New York: Oxford University Press, 1988.

11. Hanover, N.H.: University Presses of New England, 1976.

12. Philadelphia: Jewish Publication Society, 1984.

Jews in North America. By reading the regulations of those synagogues, students will learn about the scope of synagogue activities in the colonial era, as well as the efforts of congregations to monopolize organized Jewish activities. Subsequent synagogue constitutions illustrate the growing impact of American democratic norms and the challenges to the authority of the early congregations. A useful document on the colonial synagogue is reproduced in "The Earliest Extant Minute Books of the Spanish Portuguese Congregation Shearith Israel in New York, 1728–1786."[13] On subsequent revisions of synagogue constitutions and acts of disobedience against synagogue leaders, see Blau and Baron (n. 7), vol. 2, documents 193–207.

Once the monopolistic synagogues collapsed, American Jewry struggled to redefine the role of the congregation. The evolving roles assumed by synagogues in the United States are analyzed in Abraham J. Karp, "Overview: The Synagogue in America: A Historical Typology."[14] Karp analyzes the functions assumed by synagogues in different eras to meet the changing needs of the American Jewish population. Other essays in Wertheimer (n. 10) offer case studies that can be used to explore the Americanization of the synagogue. Among the themes warranting attention in a comparative context are how synagogues revised their worship services, accommodated to the changing aspirations of women, coped with voluntarism, and educated youth. The relationship of the synagogue to the general and Jewish community is also a topic rich in comparative possibilities. With the displacement of the synagogue as the central address of the Jewish community, a variety of competing institutions vied for preeminence in the lives of Jews. Students can benefit from a lecture that identifies the origins and purpose of the numerous organizations in Jewish communal life. Such a discussion could seek to explain the relationship between defense activities (now known as "community relations" work) and the assertion of leadership in the Jewish community: agencies that defended Jews from antisemitic attacks arrogated to themselves the right to speak on behalf of American Jews on other issues as well.

Most important, the discussion needs to analyze efforts at achieving communal unity in the face of ever greater institutional fragmentation—and to assess the relative success of those efforts. How well did experiments to establish a kehillah fare in places such as New York City early in the twentieth century, and why did these experiments ultimately fail? To what extent did federations of Jewish philanthropy become the central address of local Jewish communities? And how potent are umbrella organizations such as the Council

13. In *The Jewish Experience in America*, ed. Abraham J. Karp (Waltham, Mass.: American Jewish Historical Society, 1969), vol. 1, pp. 240–65.

14. In Wertheimer (n. 9), pp. 1–34.

of Jewish Federations, the National Jewish Relations Advisory Council, and the Conference of Presidents of Major Jewish Organizations in our own time? Finally, the class can assess the means used by American Jews to achieve unity, as compared to the bonds that unite other Jewish communities. Many of these questions are discussed in the now somewhat dated, but still crucial, volume, by Daniel J. Elazar, *Community and Polity: The Organizational Dynamics of American Jewry.*[15] For a first-rate discussion of an early effort to achieve communal cohesion, see Arthur Goren, *New York Jews and the Quest for Community: The Kehilla Experiment, 1908–1922.*[16] On the civil religion that animates Jewish communal leaders, see Jonathan Woocher, *Sacred Survival: The Civil Religion of American Jews.*[17] For somewhat unsophisticated but helpful discussions of the activities of federation-sponsored agencies, see Harry L. Lurie, *A Heritage Affirmed: The Jewish Federation Movement in America,*[18] and Philip S. Bernstein, *To Dwell in Unity: The Jewish Federation Movement in the United States since 1960.*[19] Two helpful organizational histories that are attuned to the larger American Jewish scene are Naomi W. Cohen, *Not Free to Desist: A History of the American Jewish Committee, 1906–1966,*[20] and Deborah Dash Moore, *B'nai B'rith and the Challenge of Ethnic Leadership.*[21]

The Americanization of Immigrants

A course on the Modern Jewish Experience offers the possibility of comparing Jewish migrants before and after their passage to a new setting. Since American Jewry was built through successive waves of immigration, it provides a particularly worthwhile frame for comparison. Students will profit, for example, from a comparison of German Jews in Central Europe and the United States during the nineteenth century: How did these two German-speaking Jewish groups distribute themselves geographically and occupationally, acculturate, modernize their religion, and organize communal and cultural programs? A similar comparison of East European Jews in the Old and New Worlds would underscore the dislocations wrought by the migratory experience and the losses to Jewish religious and cultural life due to migra-

15. Philadelphia: Jewish Publication Society, 1975.
16. New York: Columbia University Press, 1970.
17. Bloomington: Indiana University Press, 1986.
18. Philadelphia: Jewish Publication Society, 1961.
19. Philadelphia: Jewish Publication Society, 1983.
20. Philadelphia: Jewish Publication Society, 1972.
21. Albany: State University of New York Press, 1981.

tion. There is equal value in comparing the experiences of Sephardim in the Levant with Syrian or Turkish Jews in Seattle. Such discussions would force students to clarify terms like "modernization," "acculturation," and "Americanization." On the German Jews of the nineteenth century, Cohen (n. 13) and Meyer (n. 11) are recommended. On East European immigrant Jews, see *People Walk on Their Heads: Moses Weinberger's Jews and Judaism in New York*,[22] and Irving Howe, *World of Our Fathers*.[23] The Americanization of German-Jewish refugees from Nazism is the subject of two wonderfully sophisticated works: Steven M. Lowenstein, *Frankfurt on the Hudson: The German-Jewish Community of Washington Heights, 1933–1983, Its Structure and Culture*,[24] and Benny Kraut, "Ethnic–Religious Ambiguities in an Immigrant Synagogue: The Case of New Hope Congregation."[25] There is still only a small literature on Sephardic Jews in the United States, but a discussion can be based on Marc Angel, "The American Experience of a Sephardic Synagogue"[26] and *La America: The Sephardic Experience in the United States*,[27] and Joseph M. Papo, *Sephardim in Twentieth Century America: In Search of Unity*.[28]

Antisemitism, American Style

The incorporation of material on Jew-hatred in America would enrich a discussion of modern antisemitism because it could help sharpen the distinction between the presence of antisemitic ideologies and the enactment of anti-Jewish policies. It is amply clear that every version of antisemitic propaganda prevalent in Europe was expressed publicly in the United States as well. And yet Jews fared differently in the United States than in European settings: political antisemitism has been negligible, as have been physical attacks on Jews in the United States. By discussing American antisemitism within the broader context of other antisemitic movements it is possible to explore the role of constitutional protections, pluralism, ideals of toleration, cultural heterogeneity, and other factors that may shield Jews from rabid attacks. Among the most useful readings on American antisemitism, the following are recommended:

22. Trans. and ed. Jonathan D. Sarna (New York: Holmes and Meier, 1981).
23. New York: Harcourt Brace Jovanovich, 1976.
24. Detroit: Wayne State University Press, 1989.
25. In Wertheimer (n. 9), pp. 231–73.
26. In Wertheimer (n. 9), pp. 153–69.
27. Philadelphia: Jewish Publication Society, 1982.
28. San Jose: Pele Yoetz Books, 1987.

Ben Halpern, "America is Different";[29] Lloyd P. Gartner, "The Two Continu-
ities of Antisemitism in the United States";[30] Jonathan D. Sarna, "American
Anti-Semitism";[31] Michael Dobkowski, *The Tarnished Dream: The Basis of
American Antisemitism*;[32] Leonard Dinnerstein, "The Historiography of
American Anti-Semitism";[33] and *Anti-Semitism in American History*.[34]

American Jewry Assumes International Leadership

Since the destruction of European Jewry during World War II, leadership of
world Jewry has fallen disproportionately onto the shoulders of American
Jewish leaders. This has occurred both because of the decimation of most
other large Jewish communities, aside from Israel, as well as because of the
international leadership assumed by the United States in the second half of the
"American century." As courses on the Modern Jewish Experience increasingly incorporate a unit on the postwar era (an imperative when we realize that
nearly half a century has elapsed since the end of World War II), a discussion
of the leadership activities of American Jewry is in order.

A point of entry for such a discussion which is dramatic and highly controversial concerns the behavior of the American government and the American
Jewish community during the years of the Holocaust. On the most basic level,
a discussion of this period must account for the efforts of various Jewish
groups to rescue and lobby on behalf of European Jews; then there is a need to
analyze the bitter debates over strategy that divided these groups; and finally,
there is a need to consider the limits to the power of Diaspora Jewries and the
debates over what Jewish leaders of one community may risk to aid Jews in
other communities. These topics are intertwined with questions concerning
the failures of the American government to protect and rescue the victims of
Nazism: Did Jewish leaders willfully blind themselves to the horrors of the
Holocaust rather than challenge the failures of their government? And did the
American Jewish "love afffair" with Franklin D. Roosevelt enable the Ameri-

29. In *The Jews: Social Patterns of an American Group*, ed. Marshall Sklare (New York: Free
Press, 1958), pp. 23–39.

30. In *Antisemitism through the Ages*, ed. Shmuel Almog (Oxford: Pergamon Press, 1988), pp.
311–20.

31. In *History and Hate: The Dimensions of Anti-Semitism*, ed. David Berger (Philadelphia:
Jewish Publication Society, 1986), pp. 115–28.

32. Westport, Conn.: Greenwood, 1979.

33. In *Uneasy at Home: Antisemitism and the American Jewish Experience*, ed. L. Dinnerstein
(New York: Columbia University Press,1987), pp. 256–67.

34. Ed. David A. Garber (Urbana: University of Illinois Press, 1986).

can president to avoid an active policy to aid and rescue European Jewry?

The role of the United States during the Holocaust is the subject of several major books. Most important are: David Wyman, *Paper Walls: American and the Refugee Crisis, 1938–1941;*[35] Henry Feingold, *The Politics of Rescue: The Roosevelt Administration and the Holocaust;*[36] David Wyman, *The Abandonment of the Jews: America and the Holocaust;*[37] Richard Breitman and Alan M. Kraut, *American Refugee Policy and European Jewry;*[38] and Deborah Lipstadt, *Beyond Belief: The American Press and the Coming of the Holocaust.*[39] All these books discuss the roles played by individual Jews in public life as they tried to shape American government policy. Wyman (n. 38) is the most important study in regard to the role of organized Jewish efforts to influence the government. Wyman is quite critical of many establishment Jewish organizations and sympathetic to the more radical groups. Other works that examine the leadership of Jewish organizations during this era are Haskel Lookstein, *Were We Our Brothers' Keepers? The Public Response of American Jews to the Holocaust,*[40] and Aaron Berman, *Nazism, the Jews, and American Zionism, 1933–1948.*[41] The challenges facing American government officials and Jewish leaders in the United States as well as their responses may be compared to those of responsible officials in other lands.

The postwar leadership of American Jewry addressed a range of other issues that were central to the international Jewish agenda—the fight to create a Jewish state, lobbying to protect the interests of Israel, the struggle to aid Soviet Jewry, and other campaigns on behalf of beleaguered Jews. Since many of these efforts were waged quite recently, there is still a shortage of historical works analyzing these activities. For an overall history of United States Jewry that emphasizes the postwar era and the mobilization of American Jewry on behalf of Jews abroad, see Howard M. Sachar, *A History of the Jews in America,*[42] especially chs. 16, 17, 20, 24, and 25. On the internal battles waged within the American Jewish community between Zionists, non-Zionists, and anti-Zionists during the thirties and forties, see Menahem Kaufman, *An Ambiguous Partnership: Non-Zionists and Zionists in America, 1939–1948,*[43] and Thomas A. Kolsky, *Jews against Zionism: The American Council for*

35. New York: Pantheon, 1985.
36. New Brunswick, N.J.: Rutgers University Press, 1970.
37. New York: Pantheon, 1984.
38. Bloomington: Indiana University Press, 1987.
39. New York: Free Press, 1986.
40. New York: Hartmore House, 1985.
41. Detroit: Wayne State University Press, 1990.
42. New York: Knopf, 1992.
43. Jerusalem: Magnes, 1991.

Judaism, 1942–1948.[44] Several works have begun to analyze Jewish lobbying within the administration and Congress on behalf of Jewish interests abroad. For a few examples of different types of studies, see Michael J. Cohen, *Truman and Israel*;[45] Melvin I. Urofsky, *We Are One: Amercian Jewry and Israel*;[46] William W. Orbach, *The American Movement to Aid Soviet Jews*;[47] and Marvin C. Feuerwerger, *Congress and Israel: Foreign Aid Decision-making in the House of Representatives, 1969–1976.*[48]

Three additional topics in the history of United States Jewry that are suitable for comparative treatment are ably discussed elsewhere in this volume. For suggested bibliography and teaching approaches on the history of women and children in the United States, see Shulamit Magnus's essay "Jewish Social History"; on the unique character of Zionism in America, see Gideon Shimoni's essay "Zionist Ideology"; and for a comparison of the experiences of Jewish immigrants from Eastern Europe in the United States with their counterparts in other countries, see my essay "The Mass Migration of East European Jews." Particularly in the North American setting, survey courses on the Modern Jewish Experience would benefit from periodic comparisons between developments in the United States and other lands.

44. Philadelphia: Temple University Press, 1990.
45. Berkeley: University of California Press, 1990.
46. Garden City, N.Y.: Anchor, 1978.
47. Amherst: University of Massachusetts Press, 1979.
48. Westport, Conn: Greenwood, 1979.

8. Jews in Commonwealth Countries

Gideon Shimoni

Introductory Remarks

There is no tradition of scholarship or even of university teaching marking off the English-speaking Jewish communities outside the United States as a special field. Apart from the Jews of Great Britain, whose emancipated status and involvement in salient events of worldwide significance for Jews usually draws some attention in a Modern Jewish History survey, these communities seldom are mentioned, let alone studied closely. There also exist no historical works predicated on any conception of these communities as a single unit.

Yet it is a fact that these communities have a great deal in common in terms of their historical experience. This is owing to the formative influence of the English language and British political culture on the development of those countries that initially were dependent colonies of the British Empire and in which European settlement had occurred on a large scale. They progressed in the early twentieth century to the status of self-governing Dominions of the Empire, and thence to that of independent countries in the British Commonwealth, a status legally formulated in the Statute of Westminster of 1931. Finally, in the mid-twentieth century they formed today's Commonwealth, a free association of sovereign nations (49 in number), sharing a common nominal allegiance to the British Crown. So profound was the British influence that it has continued to be felt even in South Africa well after that country seceded from the Commonwealth in 1961. Nor has the gigantic shadow of the United States effaced the imprint of the British political culture and system on Canada to this very day. According to the most authoritative recent demographic estimates,[1] in 1986 there were in the United Kingdom 326,000 Jews; in Canada 310,000; in South Africa 115,000; and in Australia 80,000. Taken together they comprise a Jewish population of 831,000 and constitute about 6.4% of the total Jewish population in the diaspora. Of course to these one may add some smaller Jewish communities such as those of Ireland, 2,000; New Zealand, 4,000; Zimbabwe, 1,200; India, 5,200; and Hong Kong, 1,000, totaling an additional 13,400. However, since these pockets of Jewish population are far too small to command any attention in the framework of modern Jewish history surveys, they shall not concern us here.

A Suggested Conceptual Framework for Teaching

The absence of literature delineating these communities in any sense as a field of inquiry necessitates the formulation of a conceptual framework by the university teacher who seeks to incorporate them meaningfully in a course on the modern historical experience of the Jews. Given the limited scale of the envisaged supplement—the working assumption here is that no more than three class sessions might be allowed—it is advisable to focus on only one major facet: the integration and status of the Jews in the majority society. Examination of other aspects, such as the organizational structure, religious patterns, Zionism, education, and economic stratification of each community must, of necessity, be waived. On the basis of the writer's own experience, the following is suggested.

The first desideratum is a summation of the salient factors shaping the special historical experience of the Jews in Britain in the period of advancing Jewish integration and Emancipation. This is most meaningful when compared and contrasted with the nineteenth-century experience of Continental Europe, by considering such factors as the social mobility of the Jews, the potency of liberal political ideas, and the character of nationalism. The interplay of such factors in the experience of Anglo-Jewry might be further illustrated by examining the reception of Jewish immigration from Eastern Europe at the turn of the century, particularly the controversy over the Aliens Act of 1905, as well as the British record in regard to the problem of Jewish refugees after the rise of Hitler. Also, the manifestations of antisemitism in British society between the two World Wars might be considered with particular emphasis on the limited capacity of such manifestations to undermine the status of the Jews in Britain.

1. *American Jewish Year Book* 89 (1989): 436–39.

Second, having clarified the above, the focus might move to a brief characterization of the major British Dominions overseas—Canada, South Africa, and Australia—as societal fragments of the home society itself. The principal point calling for attention in this respect is the fact that for the Jewish immigrant to these Dominions the advantages of emancipated status in the context of the British political culture were available from the outset.

Third, the discussion until this point will have placed emphasis on the common environmental heritage that influences these Jewish communities. The next phase of analysis should shift the emphasis to the environmental variables that distinguish the situation of each of these communities from each other as well as from the "home model"—Anglo-Jewry. From this perspective, the logical sequence might be: first Australia, since of all the Dominions its ethnic composition was the most purely British; followed by Canada and South Africa, which have in common a core society of dualistic ethnic composition, respectively French–British and Dutch–British. They also have in common an environment relatively conducive to multicultural pluralism resulting from the significant presence of other ethnic groups. In the case of South Africa, however, this pluralism is vastly complicated by the legally enforced system of racial discrimination known as apartheid.

Anglo-Jewry

The teacher who seeks guidance for reading on Anglo-Jewry in general should consult the discerning survey, Lloyd P. Gartner, "A Quarter Century of Anglo-Jewish Historiography."[2] A comprehensive bibliography of Anglo-Jewry is also available and can serve as an aid for specific student assignments where necessary: Ruth P. Lehmann, *Anglo-Jewish Bibliography 1937–1970*.[3]

Given the limited scope of the present proposal for mere supplementation to a course on the Modern Jewish Experience, the following brief selection of works is recommended. It is predicated on the conceptual outline suggested above.

A recently published concise survey that may serve as background text on Anglo-Jewry is Vivien D. Lipman, *A History of the Jews in Britain since 1858*.[4] Parts of this work may be selected as readings for the students.

Todd M. Endelman, *The Jews of Georgian England, 1714–1830: Tradition*

2. *Jewish Social Studies* 48/2 (Spring 1986): 105–26.
3. London: Jewish Historical Society of England, 1973.
4. Leicester: Leicester University Press, 1990.

and Change in a Liberal Society,[5] explores in depth the social development of Anglo-Jewry in the above period and is important if the proposed course extension is to place the social bases of Jewish emancipation in Britain within the comparative context of the Jewish experience in Continental Europe. A concise essay incorporating major conclusions from the above work is Todd M. Endelman, "The Englishness of Jewish Modernity in England."[6]* This essay focuses on issues particularly germane to our conceptual framework and might also be a prescribed reading for students. (Herein an asterisk marks references recommended for student readings.)

Of the many studies focusing on the Jewish Emancipation debate within Britain, the most recent overview is Abraham Gilam, *The Emancipation of the Jews in England, 1830–1860*.[7]* Further student readings might be drawn from sections of Gilam's work and/or by prescribing one of the following articles: M. Henriques, "The Jewish Emancipation Controversy in 19th Century Britain";[8]* Polly Pinsker, "English Opinion and Jewish Emancipation, 1830–1860";[9]* or Cecil Roth, "The Anglo-Jewish Community in the Context ˮ ˮ World Jewry."[10]* Another article which focuses on the issues d̲ᶜ attention is Howard Brotz, "The Position of the Jews in English Soc̲ᵢ However, this article must be used very critically as the analysis it pr̲ ̲ᴝ̲ᴣ, while stimulating for discussion, is a rather outdated and romanticized interpretation.

For the second phase of the suggested discussion of Anglo-Jewry, focusing on the immigration wave from Eastern Europe and its reception in Anglo-Jewry, the teacher is referred to Lloyd P. Gartner, *The Jewish Immigrant in England, 1870–1914*.[12] In recent years, Gartner's emphasis on the Jewish identity and solidarity of the immigrants has been disputed in studies emphasizing the immigrants' proletarian, rather than Jewish, solidarity. See, for example, Joseph Buckman, *Immigrants and the Class Struggle: The Jewish Immigrant in Leeds, 1880–1914*.[13] See also Gartner's review of this book.[14]

5. Philadelphia: Jewish Publication Society, 1979.

6. In *Toward Modernity: The European Jewish Model*, ed. Jacob Katz (New Brunswick: Transaction, 1987), pp. 225–46.

7. New York: Garland, 1982.

8. *Past and Present* 40 (July 1968): 126–46.

9. *Jewish Social Studies* 14/1 (January 1952): 51–94.

10. In *Jewish Life in Modern Britain*, ed. Julius Gould and Shaul Esh (London: Routledge and Kegan Paul, 1964), pp. 93–110.

11. *Jewish Journal of Sociology* 1/1 (1959): 95–113.

12. London: George Allen and Unwin, 1960; 2nd ed., 1973.

13. Manchester: Manchester University Press, 1983.

14. *Jewish Journal of Sociology* 26/1 (June 1984): 63–65.

On the problematics of the immigrant Jews' reception in British society, one may recommend Bernard Gainer, *The Alien Invasion: The Origins of the Aliens Act of 1905*;[15] also John A. Garrard, *The English and Immigration: A Comparative Study of the Jewish Influx 1880–1910*.[16] An innovative examination of the Jews in British society is provided in *The Making of Anglo-Jewry*,[17] especially the contribution of Tony Kushner, "The Impact of Anti-Semitism, 1918–1945" (pp. 191–208). This and other studies in the volume depart from the comparative perspective that has tended to treat the tragic case of Germany as the model against which to measure the impact of antisemitism. On the premise that British antisemitism should be evaluated within its own national context, the focus is shifted from crude fascist and conservative antisemitism (such as Oswald Mosley's British Union of Fascists) to the British liberal creed's own distinctive form of hostility to Jews, the "antisemitism of tolerance." It is argued that the failure of British liberalism to tolerate diversity, and its manifesting of subtle modes of antisemitism, not only had an inhibiting and warping effect on Jewish behavior and self-esteem in Britain but also had a political spin-off in certain governmental policies toward Jews. An appreciative but critical comment on this revisionist perspective may be found in the perceptive survey by Todd M. Endelman, "English Jewish History,"[18] especially pp. 98–101.

British governmental attitudes and policies toward reception of Jews are treated in Louis London, "Jewish Refugees, Anglo-Jewry, and British Government Policy, 1939–1940."[19] Also useful is Bernard Wasserstein, "The British Government and the German Immigration 1933–1945,"[20] which sums up the conclusions drawn in Wasserstein's major work, *Britain and the Jews of Europe 1939–1945*,[21] as well as in A.J. Sherman, *Island Refuge: Britain and the Refugees from the Third Reich 1933–1939*.[22] See also Bernard Wasserstein, "Patterns of Jewish Leadership in Great Britain during the Nazi Era."[23]

From the perspective of teaching on the Jewish communities in the countries associated with the British Commonwealth, a word of caution is in place

15. London: Heinemann, 1972.
16. London: Oxford University Press, 1971.
17. Ed. David Cesarani (Oxford: Blackwell, 1990).
18. *Modern Judaism* 11 (1991): 99–109.
19. In Cesarani (n. 17), pp. 163–90.
20. In *Exile in Great Britain*, ed. Gerhard Hirschfeld (London: Berg; Atlantic Highlands, N.J.: Humanities Press, 1984), pp. 63–82.
21. Oxford: Clarendon, 1979.
22. London: Elek, 1973.
23. In *Jewish Leadership during the Nazi Era: Patterns of Behavior in the Free World*, ed. Randolph L. Braham (New York: Columbia University Press, 1985), pp. 29–43.

in regard to some of the works recommended above: since they focus heavily on the negative responses to Jewish immigrants and to the Jewish presence in Britain, they must be counterbalanced with an explanatory framework that accounts for the fact that, in the final analysis, Jews enjoyed great personal and communal security and freedom in Britain, especially when viewed in the comparative perspective of Continental Europe. This requires consideration of such factors as the strength of the liberal tradition in Britain, the relative facility with which the aristocracy accommodated middle class wealth including that of Jews, the relative maturity of the British political culture (note especially the British understanding of the rule of law), and the relatively satisfied and moderate character of nationalist sentiment in Britain, resulting, perhaps, from the deflection of nationalist aggressiveness and racism onto the imperial arena. Also of note is the stable parliamentary form of government in which two broad-spectrum parties tended to occupy the central stage of politics. Such parties were less conducive to the adoption of antisemitic policies than were the splintered parties that characterized the unstable political systems of Europe.

The New Societies of Australia, Canada, and South Africa in Comparative Perspective

The Founding of New Societies[24] offers a comparative historical perspective on the societies of Australia, Canada, and South Africa (as well as the United States and Latin America). They are treated as "fragments" of the mother societies in Europe, British as well as French and Dutch in the cases of Canada and South Africa respectively. The relevant chapters are Richard N. Rosecrance, "The Radical Culture of Australia" (pp. 275–318); Kenneth D. McRae, "The Structure of Canadian History" (pp. 219–74); and Leonard M. Thompson, "The South African Dilemma" (pp. 178–218). Although these expositions are bound to a particular theory accounting for the development of new societies which is disputable, they do provide illuminating and stimulating background material for our subject.

Consonant with Hartz's approach, the emergence of the Jewish communities in Australia and South Africa is discussed in Daniel J. Elazar with Peter Medding, *Jewish Communities in Frontier Societies: Argentina, Australia, and South Africa*[25] (esp. pp. 137–222, 225–335).

24. Ed. Louis Hartz (New York: Harcourt, Brace and World, 1964).
25. New York: Holmes and Meier, 1983.

An impressionistic but well-informed depiction of the contemporary character of the Jewish communities in Britain, Australia, and South Africa may be found in Howard M. Sachar, *Diaspora: An Inquiry into the Contemporary Jewish World*.[26] For the university teacher who has never had the opportunity of visiting these communities, an impression of the Jewish atmosphere that characterizes them may be gained from Sachar's descriptions. See ch. 6, "The Jews of Complacence: Great Britain" (pp. 140–68), and ch. 7, "The Progeny of Empire: Australia and South Africa" (pp. 169–97). (Sachar's volume does not include Canada and the United States.) In addition, a useful reference work providing up-to-date information on salient developments in all communities is the annual *American Jewish Yearbook*.

Another comparative perspective of value to the teacher, although one that focuses on structural and organizational aspects of the various Jewish communities, is Daniel J. Elazar, *People and Polity: The Organizational Dynamics of World Jewry*,[27] ch. 11, "Jewries of the British Commonwealth" (pp. 234–61).

Australian Jewry

From the vantage point adopted here, the most serviceable survey of the Australian Jewish community is Peter Medding, "Australia."[28]* This chapter might also serve as a prescribed reading for students. It draws in brief upon Medding's more detailed earlier works, such as *Jews in Australian Society*,[29] especially "Introduction: Ethnic Minorities in Australian Society" (pp. 1–13). His treatment of the subject highlights the distinctive aspects of that community against the background of Australia's markedly British heritage. A more recent work that may be consulted for a complete overview of Australian Jewry's development until the present time is Hilary L. Rubinstein, *Chosen: The Jews in Australia*.[30]

For the teacher who places particular emphasis on the period of Nazism's rise and the Holocaust, a work which parallels Wasserstein (n. 21) is Michael Blakeney, *Australia and the Jewish Refugees 1933–1948*.[31] See also Suzanne D. Rutland, "Australian Responses to Jewish Refugee Migration before and after World War II."[32]

26. New York: Harper and Row, 1985.
27. Detroit: Wayne State University Press, 1989.
28. In Elazar and Medding (n. 25), pp. 225–335.
29. Ed. Peter Y. Medding (Melbourne: Macmillan, 1973).
30. Sydney: Allen and Unwin, 1987.
31. Sydney: Croom Helm Australia, 1985.
32. *The Australian Journal of Politics and History* 31/1 (1985): 29–48.

Canadian Jewry

The incorporation of Canadian Jewry within the context of a course on the modern Jewish experience requires that attention be given to at least four interacting factors. These are: the influence of the British heritage; the French sector of Canadian society (estimated at 28.7% of the total population in 1986) and its direct impact upon the Jews of Quebec as well as indirect influence on the cultural and political dualism of Canadian society; the significantly large presence of other ethnic groups in Canada (estimated at 26.7% in 1986) and the consequent encouragement of multiculturalism that characterizes contemporary Canada; and, finally, the impact of Canadian Jewry's gigantic neighbor community in the United States.

The teacher may be referred to *The Canadian Jewish Mosaic*,[33] especially W. Shaffir and M. Weinfeld, "Canada and the Jews: an Introduction" (pp. 7–20);* Harold M. Waller and M. Weinfeld, "The Jews of Quebec and 'Le Fait Francais'" (pp. 415–41);* Stuart Schoenfeld, "Canadian Judaism Today" (pp. 129–50); and H. M. Waller, "Power in the Jewish Community" (pp. 151–70).

Another useful volume for the university teacher is *The Jews of North America*.[34] From the vantage point adopted here, two chapters of this work are recommended: Harold Troper, "Jews and Canadian Immigration Policy, 1900–1950" (pp. 44–56), and Irving Abella, "Anti-Semitism in Canada in the Interwar Years" (pp. 235–46). For the origins of the Jewish community and the early phases of the Jews' position within Canada's dualistic society, the teacher should consult Michael Brown, *Jew or Juif? Jews, French Canadians, and Anglo-Canadians, 1759–1914*.[35]

For the teacher who places particular emphasis on the period of Nazism's rise and the Holocaust, a work paralleling Wasserstein (n. 21) is Irving Abella and Harold Troper, *None Is Too Many: Canada and the Jews of Europe 1933–1948*.[36]

Since the status of Quebec in the Canadian confederation is still much at issue, the teacher who wishes to incorporate up-to-date reference to the situation may have to resort to current newspapers and periodicals.

33. Ed. Morton Weinfeld, William Shaffir, and Irwin Cotler (Toronto: Wiley, 1981).
34. Ed. Moses Rischin (Detroit: Wayne State University Press, 1987).
35. Philadelphia: Jewish Publication Society, 1987.
36. Toronto: Lester and Orpen Dennys, 1982.

South African Jewry

The case of South African Jewry attracts obvious attention to the unique situation of a Jewish community enjoying the privileges of a caste-like minority that dominates a majority by means of a system based on racial discrimination. However, prior consideration ought to be given to the similarity with Canada. Much like the British–French dualism of Canada, the British–Afrikaner dualism of South Africa has had a compound effect on the Jews. Not only did the Jews experience, at certain historical stages, particular hostility emanating from the frustrated French/Afrikaner sector, but their ethnic self-awareness was stimulated by the cultural and political division between those of British stock and those of French/Afrikaner stock. However, the multicultural values of the Canadian polity, in which members of all ethnic groups enjoyed equal civic rights, may be contrasted with the enforced segmentation of South African society on the basis of apartheid. In South Africa the Jews enjoyed equal rights in the privileged intrawhite dualism that dominated the polity and enforced a broader intercolor pluralism. But at the present time this entire system is in process of disintegration, with important consequences also for the Jewish community.

The university teacher may acquire an understanding of the complex context in which South African Jewry has developed from Gideon Shimoni, *Jews and Zionism: The South African Experience, 1910–1967*.[37] The emphasis placed in this work on the markedly Zionist character of South African Jewry reflects a major effect of the societal context referred to above. The Jewish religious identity of Jews was greatly reinforced by an overlapping ethnic identity expressed as Zionism. A more updated, concise survey is Gideon Shimoni, "South African Jews and the Apartheid Crisis."[38]* This might be assigned for student reading. This is further updated by Milton Shain and Sally Frankenthal, "South African Jewry, Apartheid, and Political Change."[39] Since the remarkable transformation of South Africa is taking place at the time of writing, further updating will have to depend on current newspaper and periodical articles.

South African Jewry: A Contemporary Survey[40] is a useful survey of various dimensions of South African Jewish life, such as communal structure, religious expression, education, and economic activities. However, as I have

---

37. Cape Town: Oxford University Press, 1980.
38. *American Jewish Yearbook* 88 (1988): 3–58.
39. *Patterns of Prejudice* 25/1 (1991): 62–74.
40. Ed. Marcus Arkin (Cape Town: Oxford University Press, 1984).

already remarked, the limited time available will not permit more than the most cursory attention to these aspects. For the teacher who places particular emphasis on the period of Nazism's rise and the Holocaust, there is no full-scale study relating to South Africa. However, Shimoni (n. 37) contains some relevant material: ch. 4, "The Emergence of the Jewish Question"; ch. 5, "The Response to the Jewish Question."

Use of Historical Documents in Teaching

The teacher who is able to incorporate analysis of historical documents might select a few items from *Michael*, published by Tel Aviv University, which provides well-annotated manuscript documents or unknown or unusual printed matter on the history of the Jews in various lands. One volume contains documents relating to the Jewries of Britain and Canada in the nineteenth and twentieth centuries.[41]

41. Vol. 10, ed. Robert A. Rockaway and Shlomo Simonsohn (Tel Aviv: The Diaspora Research Institute, Tel Aviv University, 1986).

9. Israeli Society and Culture

Chaim I. Waxman

To understand Israeli society and culture it is important to be aware that although Israel is in many respects a modern society, it has a number of characteristics which make it unique; and, as the dean of Israeli sociologists, Shmuel N. Eisenstadt, argues,[1] to more fully comprehend the nature of its society and culture, its dynamism must be analyzed within the context of both its similarities to and differences from other modern societies.

Eisenstadt points to four distinctive characteristics as paramount. First, Israel developed as a pioneering and ideological society, in contrast to most others except, perhaps, the early Puritan settlement of the United States. In addition, Israel's development took place within an environment teeming with hostility and which, therefore, made the security issue a central one in the process of nation-building. The ideological character of Israeli society derives from its being founded on Zionism, a movement for the reconstruction of national Jewish life. Within this context, Eisenstadt provides an overview of Jewish history, from the early Biblical period, as the background within which Zionism developed as a movement containing elements of both rebellion and continuity. Finally, Israel is distinguished by the fact that, although it is a small society similar in certain respects to other small modern societies, its Zionist ideology aims to make it the center of the cultural activity of the Jewish people around the world. It is within this context that the intricate and often ambivalent relationship between Israel and Jewish communities in the Diaspora is more adequately understood.

1. *The Tranformation of Israeli Society: An Essay in Interpretation* (Boulder, Colo.: Westview, 1986).

Exactly what has been happening in Israeli society and culture since 1967, and especially the implications of those developments on the future, are subject to very deep debate among social scientists as well as among the Israeli public at large. Eisenstadt and indeed most prominent Israeli social scientists, such as his colleagues at the Hebrew University Dan Horowitz and Moshe Lissak, are rather pessimistic. The latter, for example, argue that although the Labor Zionist center which formed the political, economic, and cultural elite leadership of Israel in the initial decades of Israeli statehood envisioned it as a "utopia," there is now "trouble in utopia."[2] The "trouble"—the nation-state's inability to cope with the excessive demands placed upon it and the "contradictions that cannot be or, at least, have not as yet been 'resolved'" (p. 257)— largely began, according to the authors, with the Six Day War of June 1967. The contradictions, or "cleavages," are numerous, but the five broadest are identified as the Jewish–Arab, religious–secular, ethnocultural (Ashkenazi–Sephardi), social class, and ideological ones. Within each of these are a host of subissues and subcleavages which, Horowitz and Lissak argue, threaten the social cohesion and ultimately the democratic character of Israel.

Nor is the air of pessimism about Israel's internal sociopolitical development limited to Israeli social scientists. It pervades the work of a number of American scholars as well, such as that of the American political scientist Myron J. Aronoff,[3] for many of the same reasons. Both the pessimists and such optimists as Daniel J. Elazar[4] agree that Labor Zionism is waning and that the defeat of the Labor alignment in 1977 was a manifestation of very deep social and cultural changes within Israeli society.

However, where Eisenstadt and Horowitz and Lissak are dismayed by these developments and fear that Israel is being overtaken by populism and particularism which may stifle its social, cultural, and moral creativity—in part probably because they are personally much closer to the ideology of Labor Zionism—Elazar continues to view Israel as a beacon and a model of Jewish dynamism. He is much more sanguine about the consequences of the increasing Sephardi power, largely because he rejects the prevailing view that civil politics was an exclusively Ashkenazi characteristic. He is also much more sanguine about the interrelated issues of religious–secular strife and the ideological cleavages, perhaps because of his own background as both an American and a traditionalist.

2. *Trouble in Utopia: The Overburdened Polity of Israel* (Albany: State University of New York Press, 1989).
3. *Israeli Visions and Divisions: Cultural Change and Political Conflict* (New Brunswick, N.J.: Transaction, 1989).
4. *Israel: Building a New Society* (Bloomington: Indiana University Press, 1986).

The impact of the interplay between the boundaries and frontiers of Israel as both state and society is examined in a broad range of essays edited by the Israeli sociologist Baruch Kimmerling.[5] The fact that even among the contributors to that volume there is a range of conceptions of Israel underscores one very complex aspect of the social scientific analysis of Israeli society and culture—that is, delineating a range of focus without distorting the picture by artificially removing it from the wider spheres which impinge upon it.

A good collection of current essays on the major domestic and foreign policy issues in Israeli politics is *Israeli Politics in the 1990s*.[6] Written from a variety of perspectives, these essays evaluate, among others, the historical, religious, demographic, and economic components of the contemporary political reality in Israel, without which the complexity of current events concerning Israel cannot be understood.

A discussion of Israeli society and culture within the context of the modern Jewish experience would, certainly, cover a broad range of issues. For background and perspective, Walter Laqueur, *A History of Zionism*,[7] and Howard M. Sachar, *A History of Israel*,[8] are basic. Both provide comprehensive and penetrating analyses of the varieties of conceptions of Zionism and the dynamic relationship between those conceptions and the shape of Israeli society and culture.

Israel is a country of immigration and, as a result, it experiences complex patterns in the relations among the variety of Jewish ethnic groups there. Sammy Smooha, *Israel: Pluralism and Conflict*,[9] and Alex Weingrod, *Israel: Group Relations in a New Society*,[10] are two good macrosocial studies of the nature of ethnic relations in Israel, with Smooha being much more critical as compared to Weingrod's more functionalist perspective. *Migration, Ethnicity, and Community*[11] is a representative collection of very fine social scientific analyses of a variety of aspects of immigration and ethnicity. Among studies of specific ethnic groups in Israel are Shlomo Deshen and Moshe Shokeid, *The Predicament of Homecoming: Cultural and Social Life of North African Immigrants in Israel*;[12] Chaim I. Waxman, *American Aliya: Portrait of An*

5. *The Israeli State and Society: Boundaries and Frontiers* (Albany: State University of New York Press, 1989).

6. Ed. Bernard Reich and Gershon R. Kieval (Westport, Conn.: Greenwood, 1991).

7. London: Weidenfeld and Nicholson, 1972; repr. New York: Schocken, 1989.

8. New York: Knopf, 1981.

9. Berkeley and Los Angeles: University of California Press, 1978.

10. New York: Praeger, 1965.

11. *Studies of Israeli Society*, ed. Ernest Krausz, vol. 1 (New Brunswick, N.J.: Transaction, 1980).

12. Ithaca, N.Y.: Cornell University Press, 1974.

Innovative Migration Movement;[13] and Walter F. Weiker, *The Unseen Israelis: The Jews from Turkey in Israel.*[14]

The kibbutz is a phenomenon which has been a source of fascination to both social scientists and laymen alike, and the literature on the subject far exceeds it real place in Israeli society. Among the classic studies are Melford E. Spiro's two books, *Kibbutz: Venture in Utopia*[15] and *Children of the Kibbutz,*[16] as well as Bruno Bettelheim, *Children of the Dream.*[17] Of somewhat more recent vintage, and with a more specific focus, is Lionel Tiger and Joseph Shepher, *Women in the Kibbutz.*[18] For an even more specific aspect of the kibbutz phenomenon, see *Religious Kibbutz Movement.*[19] For penetrating personal reflections on kibbutz life, see Yosef Criden and Saadia Gelb, *The Kibbutz Experience: The Dialogue at Kfar Blum.*[20] The best collection of social scientific articles dealing with a broad range of issues relating to the kibbutz is *The Sociology of the Kibbutz.*[21] For a good study of the unique variety of Judaism which has emerged within the secular kibbutz movement, see Shalom Lilker, *Kibbutz Judaism: A New Tradition in the Making.*[22] With all of these, however, it should be remembered that the reality of the kibbutz has changed dramatically in the last decade—for example, in almost all kibbutzim young children now live with their parents and in many the economic base has shifted from agriculture to manufacturing—and there are no accounts yet available of the kibbutz under those changes.

The works of Israel's major writers of fiction are readily available in English, especially those of such figures as Amos Oz, A. B. Yehoshua, and David Grossman. Their works in particular can serve as the basis for an in-depth discussion of the Jewishness of Israeli-Jewish writers, because each of them emphasizes a somewhat different aspect of Jewishness; yet Jewishness is basic to each of them. For a good selection of Israeli poetry, see *Israeli Poetry: A Contemporary Anthology.*[23] For a study of mass communications

13. Detroit: Wayne State University Press, 1989.

14. Lanham, Md: University Presses of America, 1988.

15. Cambridge: Harvard University Press, 1956; repr. New York: Schocken, 1971.

16. New York: Schocken, 1958; repr. Cambridge: Harvard University Press, 1975.

17 New York: Avon, 1969

18. New York: Harcourt Brace Jovanovich, 1975.

19. Ed. A. Fishman (Jerusalem: Religious Section of Youth and he-Halutz Dept. of the Zionist Organization, 1957).

20. New York: Herzl, 1974.

21. Krausz (n. 11), vol. 2 (New Brunswick, N.J.: Transaction, 1983).

22. New York: Cornwall, 1982.

23. Ed. and trans. Warren Bargad and Stanley F. Chyet (Bloomington: Indiana University Press, 1986).

and leisure time in Israel, see Elihu Katz and Michael Gurewitch, *The Secularization of Leisure: Culture and Communication in Israel.*[24]

Although this literature guide applies in the context of a course on the Modern Jewish Experience and thus emphasizes Jewish life in Israel, it must be emphasized that all of Israel—its entire population, as well as its society and culture—is affected by the Arab minorities there. The student of Israeli society might therefore want to consult Ian Lustick, *Arabs in the Jewish State,*[25] which is written by an American with a critical perspective. A noteworthy account of the Palestinian Arab perspective, written by an Israeli Arab who is a news editor for the Israeli broadcasting system, is Rafik Halabi, *The West Bank Story.*[26] Especially since the onset of the Intifada, the situation is very different from that described by Halabi.

An impressive in-depth sociological analysis of a number of the social cleavages discussed by Horowitz and Lissak (n. 2) is found in a recent book by Eliezer Ben-Raphael and Stephen Sharot, *Ethnicity, Religion, and Class in Israeli Society.*[27] As its title indicates, this work spans the dimensions of ethnicity, religion, and social stratification and systematically examines each individually as well as the interplay between the various dimensions.

Since, as suggested earlier, politics plays such a central role in Israeli society and culture, it is inevitable that some time will be spent on the subject, even if the course is not given by a social scientist. In addition to the broad sociopolitical analyses mentioned previously, the following might be consulted for specific aspects of Israeli political life: Asher Arian, *Politics in Israel: The Second Generation;*[28] *Israel's Odd Couple: The 1984 Knesset Elections and the National Unity Government;*[29] *Studies in Contemporary Jewry,* vol. 5, *Israel: State and Society, 1948–1988;*[30] Peter Y. Medding, *The Founding of Israeli Democracy, 1948–1967;*[31] and Gregory S. Mahler, *Israel: Government and Politics in a Maturing State.*[32]

When all is said and done, probably the greatest risk for anyone speculating about the future is that the speculations invariably assume that other things will continue as they have been. That is the implicit assumption of all scien-

24. Cambridge: Harvard University Press, 1976.
25. Austin: University of Texas Press, 1980.
26. New York: Harcourt Brace Jovanovich, 1981.
27. Cambridge: Cambridge University Press, 1991.
28. Chatham, N.J.: Chatham House, rev. ed. 1989.
29. Ed. Daniel J. Elazar and Shmuel Sandler (Detroit: Wayne Sate University Press, 1990).
30. Ed. Peter Y. Medding (New York: Oxford University Press, 1989).
31. New York: Oxford University Press, 1990.
32. San Diego: Harcourt Brace Jovanovich, 1990).

tific predictions—*ceteris paribus* ("other things being equal"). But as anyone in the social sciences who has risked predicting knows, all other things rarely are equal. The implicit predictions of Horowitz and Lissak, for example are a case in point. Three major developments which they could not have anticipated will almost definitely have major immediate impact on the "trouble" in the Israeli polity: the massive immigration of Soviet Jews, the Persian Gulf war, and the airlift of some sixteen thousand Ethiopian Jews to Israel. As of this writing, it is much too early to know what the consequences of any of those will be. At the same time, it is also abundantly clear that they will have major impact on Israeli society for a long time to come. Since Israeli society is a major component of the modern Jewish experience, those developments will unquestionably have ramifications well beyond the geographical location of the State of Israel.

That, in fact, brings us to the matter of the location of the study of Israeli society within a course on the modern Jewish experience. There are various ways in which the subject of Israeli society can be approached within a course on the Modern Jewish Experience. One way, and perhaps the most straightforward, is to view it as the culmination, or at least the most revolutionary aspect, of that experience, and thus to discuss it as the last part of the course. Within that context, Jewish sovereignty might be viewed as that to which many Jews have aspired for centuries, and to look at how Jews have actually fared in their own sovereign state. To what extent have the dreams of Zionism and sovereignty been realized? Which goals are taking longer than anticipated to be realized, and why? What are some of the uniquely new problems which sovereignty has created? How has the existence Israel impacted upon Jewish communities in the Diaspora? A number of these questions were addressed either explicitly or implicitly in many of the essays in *World Jewry and the State of Israel.*[33] Today, however, the situation is very different from what it was even fifteen years ago, because of major political and social upheavals in the countries of most Diaspora communities, as well as within Israel itself.

Another way of dealing with Israel is to indicate, at the very beginning of the course, the uniqueness of Jewish sovereignty from the perspective of at least the past two thousand years of Jewish history, and to then compare and contrast every subject discussed in the course in terms of its development in the Diaspora and its development in Israel. For example, in a discussion of the subject of Jewish identity, the differences between traditional and modern society and the nature of Jewish identity in both would be discussed, followed by a discussion of differences between modern Jewish identity in Diaspora

33. Ed. Moshe Davis (New York: Arno, 1977).

communities, where Jews are social minorities, and Jewish identity in Israel, where Jews are the dominant group. Within this context, there could be a fruitful discussion of the question raised in Charles S. Liebman and Steven M. Cohen, *Two Worlds of Judaism*,[34] as to whether at least two separate and distinct types of Judaism are developing, one Israeli and one American, with the former becoming increasingly particularistic and the latter becoming increasingly universalistic.

Perhaps as a counterbalance to the image of Judaism in Israel conveyed by Liebman and Cohen, it would be advisable to integrate a very good collection of essays reflecting the diversity and rich variety of religious expression in Israel, *Tradition, Innovation, Conflict: Jewishness and Judaism in Contemporary Israel*.[35] This volume is unique in its colorful portrayal of a range of communal dimensions which manifest the significance of the religious factor, as well as its informed discussions of religious dissent and alternatives including analyses of Reform and Conservative Judaism in Israel, the newly religious, and religious defectors.

Another example of the contrast between Jewish development in the Diaspora and in Israel would be in a discussion of the organic Jewish community, the kehillah, in the modern Jewish experience. Comparisons and contrasts could be drawn between the organic community in the Diaspora, where Jews may or may not have a measure of political autonomy as Jews but they do not have political sovereignty, and Jewry in Israel, where in many respects the state has replaced, or at least deposed, the kehillah. The point is that with every subject within the context of the modern Jewish experience, comparisons and contrasts will be made throughout between the Diaspora and Israel.

A third example would be in a discussion of the causes and consequences of antisemitism in the modern world. Here again, there are many significant differences between Diaspora communities of various kinds and Israel. An important issue to discuss and explore in this context is the role of antisemitism in Israeli nationalism, both on the political as well as on the social-psychological level. One of the benefits of the significant role which Israel plays in American Jewish identification is the availability of reading material on Israel. In addition to the works cited previously, many useful brief articles— which students are more likely to actually read—are available in Jewish periodical literature, ranging from the weekly International Edition of the *Jerusalem Post*, almost any communal Anglo-Jewish weekly, and the somewhat

34. New Haven: Yale University Press, 1990.

35. Ed. Zvi Sobel and Benjamin Beit-Hallahmi (Albany: State University of New York Press, 1991).

more in-depth *Jerusalem Report*, to such magazines as *Midstream* and *Commentary*, as well as the denominational—Orthodox, Conservative, Reconstructionist, Reform—publications, and up to the more scholarly journals, such as *Judaism*, *Modern Judaism*, and *AJS Review*, the journal of the Association of Jewish Studies. There is sufficient material available to allow the instructor to assign relatively brief articles as backgrounders for class lectures and discussions, as well as more lengthy, sophisticated, and scholarly material for class reports and papers. Also, given the prominent place of Israel in current affairs, the class lectures and discussions will very often have a very timely quality to them. It is important, however, to stress those features of the issues which transcend the specific timeliness of the events.

10. Latin American Jewry

Victor A. Mirelman

The scientific study of the Jewish communities of Latin America is a relatively new endeavor that has produced few works in English, and this dearth of literature hampers teaching about Latin American Jewry in English-speaking settings. Happily, a slow correction is under way with the publication of some studies in English. This is due in no small measure to the proliferation of Latin American Studies on American campuses on the one hand, and a keener awareness of Jews in Latin America by scholars of Jewish studies, who as of late have emphasized the Modern and Contemporary periods in Jewish history, on the other.

Although the scholarly universe is not too vast, some controversial issues have divided researchers, including the following questions: (1) Was the Jewish Colonization Association assimilationist, and was it unfair economically to the colonists in Argentina (Avni)? (2) What was the extent of antisemitism in Argentina during the early decades of the twentieth century (Mirelman, Elkin, Senkman)? (3) What role did Jews play in the white slave traffic (Mirelman)? (4) How do we assess the relationship between Argentina's military junta and the leadership of the Jewish community (Timerman and his opponents)? I will highlight these controversies as I briefly survey the history of Latin American Jewry.

A Jewish presence in Latin America has been claimed since the first trips by the conquistadors. It has been also noted that there were some Jews, or *conversos*, even in Columbus's first voyage in 1492.

Once the Spanish and Portuguese dominions in the New World were established, the prohibition of Judaism was extended from the metropole to the American possessions as well. Thus, from the point of view of Jewish history, the central issues during the Colonial period concerned the question of Judaizing. In addition to New Christians or *conversos*, there were some Jews living in areas of Brazil, though not openly. For a short while (1630–1654), when the Dutch conquered northeast Brazil, a substantial number of Sephardim moved from the Netherlands to the area around Recife, where the first Jewish synagogues in the New World were founded. Jews left Recife when the Portuguese reconquered the area.

Early writings on Jews during the Colonial period by Jewish scholars in the United States had the purpose of legitimatizing the Jewish presence in the continent. Many articles first published in the *American Jewish Historical Quarterly* were gathered in the set edited by Martin A. Cohen, *The Jewish Experience in Latin America*.[1] Alongside Cohen's study, *The Martyr: Luis de Carvajal: The Story of a Secret Jew and the Mexican Inquisition in the Sixteenth Century*,[2] other scholars in the United States such as Arnold Wiznitzer, "Crypto-Jews in Mexico during the Sixteenth Century" and "Crypto-Jews in Mexico during the Seventeenth Century,"[3] and Seymour Leibman, *The Jews in New Spain: Faith, Fame, and the Inquisition*,[4] have contributed to the subject. Scholars in Latin America have also added to our knowledge of crypto-Jews in Latin America with the works of Boleslao Lewin, *Mártires y conquistadores judíos en Latinoamérica*;[5] Anita Novinsky, *Cristãos novos na Bahia*[6] and "Jewish Roots of Brazil";[7] Günter Böhm, "El bachiller Francisco Maldonado de Silva, 1592–1639";[8] Iṭic Croitoru Rotbaum, *De Sefarad al Neosefaradismo: Contribución a la historia de Colombia*;[9] and Rachel Mizrahi Bromberg, *A Inquisição no Brasil: Um capitão-mor judaizante*.[10] The various authorities are especially divided as to the "Jewishness" of those accused of Judaizing by the Inquisition, a question that splits scholars of *conversos* in Spain and Portugal as well. There is also debate over how to interpret accusations of Judaizing: Did such charges imply that the accused was a Jew, as

1. 2 vols. (Waltham, Mass.: American Jewish Historical Society, 1971).
2. Philadelphia: Jewish Publication Society, 1973.
3. In Cohen (n. 1), vol. 1, pp. 88–132 and 133–77, respectively.
4. Coral Gables, Fla.: University of Miami Press, 1970.
5. Buenos Aires: Editorial Candelabro, 1968, 1976.
6. São Paolo: Editôra Perspectiva, 1972.
7. In *The Jewish Presence in Latin America*, ed. Judith L. Elkin and Gilbert Merkx (Boston: Allen and Unwin, 1987), pp. 33–44.
8. *Judaica Iberoamericana* 4–5 (1983–84): 3–168.
9. Bogotá: Editorial Kelly, 1967.
10. São Paulo: Centro de Estudos Judaicos, 1984.

some claim; were they merely a reflection of some observance that smacked of Judaism; or were they simply denunciations based on personal or economic rivalries or vendettas? In regard to the Inquisition, historians have generally adhered to interpretations along the lines of two legends: the Black Legend, which asserts that the Spaniards dealt most cruelly with dissenters such as Jews and Protestants; and the White Legend, which states that the Inquisitors were no more cruel than other contemporaries. Jewish historians have been criticized for clinging to the Black Legend (see Stanley M. Hordes, "Historiographical Problems in the Study of the Inquisition and the Mexican Crypto-Jews in the Seventeenth Century"[11]).

The short-lived Jewish community in northeast Brazil was studied in depth by Arnold Wiznitzer, *Jews in Colonial Brazil*[12] and "The Exodus from Brazil and the Arrival in New Amsterdam of the Jewish Pilgrim Fathers, 1654";[13] Isaac and Suzanne Emmanuel have contributed a *History of the Jews in the Netherlands Antilles*,[14] while Frances P. Karner wrote on *The Sephardics of Curaçao: A Study of Sociocultural Patterns in Flux.*[15]

Independence was achieved throughout the continent during the first quarter of the nineteenth century. The new countries inherited the Iberian culture of Spain and Portugal and a strong adherence to Catholicism. However, there were strong regional differences that made for distinctive patterns of immigration, education, secularization, industrialization, and eventually also pluralism. It is therefore extremely important to study each Jewish community in the context of the nation in which it was situated. In some instances it is also desirable to consider regions within a country—for example, different areas of Brazil. An approach comparing Jewish life in different Latin American countries can be highly illuminating.

Although major immigration to Latin America began after 1889, Jewish individuals and families arrived earlier. Some originated in Morocco and settled in northern Brazil, Venezuela, and the Amazon area. Later they moved to the larger cities in Brazil and Argentina and to their hinterlands. A second group of Jews, mainly from Curaçao, established a presence in Coro, Venezuela, where they resided, in small numbers, for most of the nineteenth century. Jews from Central Europe—France, Germany, and especially Alsace-Lorraine—as well as England and Italy, formed small communities in major cities such as Buenos Aires, Rio de Janeiro, Lima, Valparaiso, and Mexico City.

11. *American Jewish Archives* 34/2 (November 1982): 138–52.
12. New York: Columbia University Press, 1960.
13. In Cohen (n. 1), vol. 2, pp. 313–30.
14. 2 vols. (Cincinnati: American Jewish Archives, 1970).
15. Assen: Van Gorcum, 1969.

There is a growing number of studies of these early Jewish migrants to the Latin American mainland. The following are the best contributions. On Argentina: Victor A. Mirelman, "A Note on Jewish Settlement in Argentina, 1881–1892"[16] and "Jewish Life in Buenos Aires before the East European Immigration (1860–1890)";[17] H. Avni, *Argentina and the Jews: A History of Jewish Immigration,*[18] and Bernard D. Ansel, "The Beginnings of the Modern Jewish Community in Argentina, 1852–1891."[19] On Chile and Peru: Günter Böhm, *Judíos en el Perú durante el siglo XIX*[20] and "Judíos en Chile durante el siglo XIX."[21] On Coro: Isidoro Aizenberg, *La comunidad judía de Coro 1824–1900: Una historia,*[22] and Isaac S. Emmanuel, *The Jews of Coro, Venezuela.*[23] On Mexico: Corinne Azen Krause, "The Jews of Mexico: A History with Special Emphasis on the Period from 1857 to 1930."[24] And on Brazil: Egon and Frieda Wolff, *Os Judeus no Brasil Imperial.*[25] In addition, Mark Wischnitzer, "Historical Background of Settlement of Jewish Refugees in Santo Domingo,"[26] has written on the attempt by the Dominican Republic to settle Jews in the 1880s.

The first mass migration of Jews to the South American continent started in 1889 with the arrival in Buenos Aires of a ship with over 800 Jews from Russia. In time, this migration was facilitated by the founding of the Jewish Colonization Association (JCA) by Baron Maurice de Hirsch in 1892. The JCA promoted a unique program to return Jewish colonists to the land, especially in Argentina, but also in southern Brazil. Parallel to this, a large concentration of Jews grew in Buenos Aires, and minor centers started in the hinterland of Argentina and in the major capitals of South America. The areas of settlement depended on a variety of factors but were especially determined by local conditions in each individual Latin American country. A comparative survey of Jewish immigrant experiences in different countries can illuminate the nature and consequences of this mass migration to Latin America.

Brief local histories, memoirs, and personal vignettes dealing with the

16. *Jewish Social Studies* 33 (January 1971): 3–12.
17. *American Jewish Historical Quarterly* 67 (1978): 195–207.
18. Trans. Gila Brand (Tuscaloosa: University of Alabama Press, 1991).
19. Ph.D. dissertation, University of Kansas, 1969.
20. Santiago: Universidad de Chile, 1985.
21. In *Comunidades judías de Latinoamérica 1971–1972* (Buenos Aires: , 1972).
22. Caracas: Biblioteca de Autores y Temas Falconianos, 1983.
23. Monograph of the American Jewish Archives 8 (Cincinnati: Hebrew Union College – Jewish Institute of Religion, American Jewish Archives, 1973).
24. Ph.D. dissertation, University of Pittsburgh, 1970.
25. São Paolo: Centro de Estudos Judaicos, 1975.
26. *Jewish Social Studies* 4 (1942): 50–58.

diverse communities have been printed, especially since World War II. Some monographs of worth have also been written. The *Argentiner IWO Shriftn* has published articles on the JCA colonies as well as on other issues in the history of Argentine Jewry. In addition, early commissioned reports on Jewish life in Latin America provide fundamental data. Interestingly, these reports were sponsored by major Jewish organizations, first in Europe and later in the United States. Particularly noteworthy are: Rabbi Samuel Halphon, "Enquête sur la population israélite en Argentine," sponsored by the Alliance Israélite Universelle and JCA in 1909;[27] Harry Sandberg, "The Jews of Latin America," commissioned by the American Jewish Committee;[28] J. X. Cohen, *Jewish Life in South America*, by the American Jewish Congress;[29] and Jacob Shatzky, *Comunidades judias en Latinoamérica*,[30] again by the AJC. In addition, an Experts Conference on Latin America and the Future of Its Jewish Communities was convened in London in 1972, and its *Proceedings* were published in 1973.[31] Various studies were also published by the Latin American office of the American Jewish Committee[32] and in publications of the Jewish Agency[33] during the 1960s and early 1970s.

Around this time, more intensive scholarly inquiry about Latin American Jewry began. Students in both American and Israeli universities wrote doctoral dissertations on subjects dealing directly with Latin American Jewry. Some of the latter have now appeared as books, which constitute the first serious research on these communities. Local community leaders and scholars also began examining their own communities' history.

Argentine Jewry, by far the largest community in the continent, has been the subject of the greatest number of scholarly endeavors. Haim Avni of the Hebrew University published three works on this Jewry, all in Hebrew as well as Spanish. Avni's first study, *Argentina, "ha-Aretz ha-Yeuda,"*[34] is a thoroughly researched examination of the JCA project in Argentina from its inception until the death of Baron Hirsch in 1896. The second book (Avni, n. 18) concentrates on Jewish migrations to Argentina from 1810 to 1950. And his

27. In *Rapport de l'Administration Centrale au Conseil d'Administration pour l'Année 1909* (Paris: JCA, 1910), pp. 251–308.
28. *American Jewish Year Book* 19 (1917–18): 35–105.
29. New York: Bloch, 1941.
30. Buenos Aires: American Jewish Committee, 1952.
31. *Proceedings of the Experts Conference on Latin America and the Future of Its Jewish Communities* (London: Institute of Jewish Affairs, 1973).
32. Three volumes of *Comunidades Judías de Latinoamérica* for the years 1968, 1970, and 1971–72 (Buenos Aires).
33. The journal *Dispersion and Unity* and its Hebrew edition *Bi-tefutsot ha-gola*.
34. (Argentina, "The Promised Land") (Jerusalem: Magnes, 1973).

latest work, Emancipation and Jewish Education: A Century of Argentinian Jewry's Experience, 1884–1984 (in Hebrew),[35] deals with Jewish education in Argentina during the past century. Avni presents the reader with solid scholarship that reflects the Argentine reality and the particular Jewish postures.

In 1982 Eugene F. Sofer published *From Pale to Pampa: A Social History of the Jews of Buenos Aires,*[36] a concise study of Jewish mobility during the early decades of this century. His subject is limited to the Ashkenazi Jews affiliated with the Hevrah Kedushah Ashkenazi, later to become the kehillah of that sector of Jews in Buenos Aires. A more recent work by Victor A. Mirelman, *Jewish Buenos Aires 1890–1930: In Search of an Identity,*[37] offers a detailed study of the greatest concentration of Jews in Latin America from its beginnings to 1930, with particular attention given both to the Ashkenazim and the various Sephardic groups. It also includes a description of the internal fight against Jews involved in prostitution and white slavery, as well as other controversies such as the struggle between Zionists and Communists, antisemitism, and mixed marriages.

Some noteworthy recent publications in Spanish include two useful books on Argentinian Jewry by the historian Boleslao Lewin, *Cómo fue la inmigración judía a la Argentina*[38] and *La colectividad judía en la Argentina.*[39] Though not with an academic apparatus nor fully analytical, they contain abundant information. Also in Spanish, Leonardo Senkman authored a thoughtful essay, *La identidad judía en la literatura argentina,*[40] regarding Jewish identity in Argentina as reflected in the literature produced by Jews there.

Studies of the other Latin American Jewish communities have been published in their respective countries. Thus Henrique Rattner has produced a valuable sociological study of São Paulo Jewry, *Tradição e Mundança: A comunidade judaica no Brasil.*[41] This was followed by Nachman Falbel's work on Brazilian Jewry, *Estudos sobre a Comunidade Judaica no Brasil.*[42] The small community of Costa Rica is the subject of a study by Jacobo Schifter Sikora, *El judío en Costa Rica,*[43] and that of Paraguay was described

35. *Emantsipatsi'ah ve-khinukh yehudi: Me'ah shenot nisyonah shel yahadut Argentinah* (Jerusalem: Mercaz Zalman Shazar le Historiyah Yehudit, 1985).

36. New York: Holmes and Meier, 1982.

37. Detroit: Wayne State University Press, 1990.

38. Buenos Aires: Plus Ultra, 1971.

39. Buenos Aires: Alzamor Editores, 1974.

40. Buenos Aires: Editorial Pardes, 1983.

41. São Paolo: Editora Atica, 1977.

42. São Paolo: Federação Israelita do Estado de São Paolo, 1984.

43. San José: Editorial Universitad Estatal a Distancia, 1979.

by Alfredo M. Seiferheld, *Los judíos en el Paraguay.*[44] Leon Trahtemberg Siderer wrote an account of Jewish immigration to Peru, *La inmigración judía al Perú, 1848–1948*,[45] and Moshe Nes-El a historical chronicle of the Sephardic community in Chile, *Historia de la comunidad israelita sefaradí de Chile.*[46]

For a general overview of Jewish life in the continent, *Jews of the Latin American Republics*[47] by Judith Laikin Elkin is the best available text. The author describes the major developments from colonial times to our days and summarizes the various positions regarding issues of scholarly debate. Her article "Latin American Jewry Today"[48] dwells on the contemporary situation. The demography of Latin American Jewry has long been a partial guessing game, but the recently published studies of Sergio DellaPergola, "Demographic Trends of Latin American Jewry,"[49] and U. O. Schmelz and S. Della-Pergola, "The Demography of Latin American Jewry,"[50] have given us a much better perspective.

In recent years, Latin American Jewry has received greatest attention due to the controversy engendered by different interpretations and rationalizations of the military juntas, especially in Argentina during the so-called Dirty War (1976–1983) and Chile under Pinochet (1973–1990). Jacobo Timerman, *Prisoner Without a Name, Cell Without a Number*,[51] kindled heated debate within the Jewish community in Argentina and abroad regarding antisemitism on the one hand, and the Jewish response to the dictatorship on the other. The literature is vast, though research is still an ongoing process.

To complete the picture of a Jewish role in Latin America, one must account for the Israel dimension. The relationship between Israel and Latin American countries began in the early days of UNSCOP and the United Nations vote to partition Palestine and continued with the establishment of ties between the State of Israel and the various nations on the continent. These ties have at times been the source of international controversy and have prompted the publication of various politically tendentious works, such as Edy Kaufman, Yoram Shapira, and Joel Barromi, *Israel–Latin American Relations*,[52]

44. Asuncion: Estudios Paraguayos, 1981.
45. Lima: Asociacion Judia de Beneficencia y Culto de 1870, 1987.
46. Santiago: Ed. Nascimento, 1984.
47. Chapel Hill: University of North Carolina Press, 1980.
48. *American Jewish Year Book* 85 (1985): 3–49.
49. In Elkin and Merkx (n. 7), pp. 85–133.
50. *American Jewish Year Book* 85 (1985): 51–102.
51. New York: Knopf, 1981.
52. New Brunswick, N.J.: Transaction, 1979.

and Bishara Bahbah, *Israel and Latin America: The Military Connection.*[53] Most recently, an anthology in Spanish was edited in Israel, *Los latinoamericanos en Israel: Antología de una aliá,*[54] documenting Latin American aliyah to Israel and its contributions to the State.

As noted at the outset, scholarly work on Latin American Jewry has lagged, but it has been gaining momentum in recent years. Especially critical to this development has been the founding of the Latin American Jewish Studies Association (LAJSA), as well as internal developments in Latin America that have affected Jewish life. LAJSA has organized several scholarly conferences in the United States, Israel, and Argentina, and some of the papers have been published in book form. Elkin and Merkx (n. 7) contains scholarly articles on a variety of historical, sociological, and cultural issues that will prove worthwhile in a discussion of Latin American Jewry. It includes works by some of the scholars already cited in this essay (Avni, Elkin, Mirelman, Novinsky, Rattner, Senkman, and others). In addition, the November 1982 issue of *American Jewish Archives* is entirely devoted to articles on Latin American Jewry. From time to time, other scholarly journals such as *Jewish Social Studies* and *American Jewish History* publish articles devoted to this field of history. All these developments suggest that the field of Latin American Jewry will continue to grow as a topic of scholarly endeavor.

Teaching about Latin American Jewry

For the teacher of the Modern period in Jewish history who wants to devote three classes to Latin America, I would suggest the following themes. (1) The question of massive waves of migration during the late nineteenth and early twentieth centuries should be part of the general overview; likewise the question of refugees during the Nazi period. On migration: Elkin (n. 47), chs. 3 and 4; Mirelman (n. 37), chs. 1 and 2; and Avni (n. 18). On refugees: Arthur Morse, *While Six Million Died,*[55] chs. 11 and 19; Henry Feingold, *The Politics of Rescue: The Roosevelt Administration and the Holocaust,*[56] pp. 22–44, 99–102; Haim Avni, "Latin America and the Jewish Refugees: Two Encounters, 1935 and 1938."[57] (2) For an overview of the continent and the formation of the largest community: Elkin (n. 47); Mirelman (n. 37); Moshe Davis, "Cen-

---

53. New York: St. Martin's in association with Institute for Palestine Studies, 1986.
54. Ed. Florinda Goldberg and Iosef Rozen (Buenos Aires: Contexto, 1988).
55. New York: Random House, 1967.
56. New Brunswick, N.J.: Rutgers University Press, 1970.
57. In Elkin and Merkx (n. 7), pp. 45–68.

tres of Jewry in the Western Hemisphere: A Comparative Approach."[58] (3) On contemporary conditions: Haim Avni, "Latin America";[59] Robert M. Levine, "Adaptive Strategies of Jews in Latin America."[60] (4) On contemporary antisemitism and Jewish leadership: Timerman (n. 51); Benno Weiser Varon, "The Canonization of Jacobo Timerman";[61] Mark Falcoff, "The Timerman Case."[62] Themes (3) and (4) could be combined in one class.

58. *Jewish Journal of Sociology* 5/1 (June 1963): 4–26.

59. In *World Politics and the Jewish Condition*, ed. Louis Henkin (New York: Quadrangle, 1972), pp. 238–74.

60. In Elkin and Merkx (n. 7), pp. 71–84.

61. *Midstream* 27/7 (August–September 1981): 36–44.

62. *Commentary* 72/1 (July 1981): 15–23.

Social and Political Issues

11. The Traditional Jewish Community
M. Bodian

The community as a flexible framework for Jewish life in the Medieval period was first studied by Louis Finkelstein, *Jewish Self-Government in the Middle Ages*.[1] Finkelstein's work is largely confined to the study of major internal ordinances adopted in Medieval European communities. The basis for Jewish communal life in the context of Christian society was studied by James Parkes, *The Jew in the Medieval Community*.[2] A far more encompassing view of the community as the basic organizing structure in Jewish life was developed by Salo Baron in his pioneering work, *The Jewish Community: Its History and Structure to the American Revolution*.[3] The scope of this work and the wealth of material examined make the work useful to this day. The third volume contains a 110-page bibliography rich in primary sources. The most rigorous analysis of traditional Jewish communal life has been carried out by Jacob Katz in his *Tradition and Crisis: Jewish Society at the End of the Middle Ages*,[4] a work which has had a lasting impact. For a briefer discussion of Jewish communal life, see H. H. Ben-Sasson, "The 'Northern' European Jewish Community and Its Ideals."[5]

As to the origins of Jewish communal structure, Yitzhak Baer's article "The Foundations and Beginnings of a Jewish Community Structure in the

1. New York: Jewish Theological Seminary of America, 1924.
2. London: Soncino, 1938; repr. New York: Hermon, 1976.
3. 3 vols. (Philadelphia: Jewish Publication Society, 1942).
4. New York: Free Press of Glencoe, 1961.
5. In *Jewish Society through the Ages,* ed. H.H. Ben-Sasson & Shmuel Ettinger (London: Vallentine, Mitchell, 1971).

Middle Ages"[6] challenges Baron's conviction that the Jewish community had its origins in diaspora life and argues that its early origins were in Eretz Israel. Irving Agus has argued that the Jewish community in fact contributed to shaping institutional life in Christian Europe, not vice versa, in his introduction to *Urban Civilization in Pre-Crusade Europe*.[7] This thesis has been criticized in a review by Robert Lopez.[8]

In recent years, scholars have begun to take an increased interest in Jewish life in Moslem lands, where traditional communal life had its own variations. Bibliography on this topic can be found in Jane Gerber's essay in this volume, "The Jews of North Africa and the Middle East." While earlier scholars have tended to emphasize the overall issues of legal status and communal structure, drawing a sharp distinction between the Jewish and the non-Jewish spheres, contemporary scholars have examined communal life with a deeper interest in the interaction between the community and the majority society in economic, social, and cultural life.

Specialized studies of the various aspects of communal life abound; however, many of them are not in English and have not been translated. I organize the discussion of bibliography according to three topics around which a course unit might be built: (1) The Jewish community within the structure of Medieval society; (2) The autonomous community and its institutions; and (3) The maintainance of traditional patterns: family life, social welfare, local custom, and education. I consider only the European Jewish community.

The Jewish Community within the Structure of Medieval Society

A session devoted to this topic should give the student a conception of the corporate and hierarchical structure of Medieval society in general, and the particular place of the Jewish community within this society. While emphasis would probably be placed on the late medieval period, discussion should be focused on those forces which produced the conditions for Jewish life throughout the Middle Ages. The most thorough discussion of this topic can be found in Salo Baron, *A Social and Religious History of the Jews*,[9] especially 4: 3–88; 9: 3–54, 135–92; 11: 3–121. See also his "'Plenitude of Apos-

---

6. (In Hebrew) *Zion* 15 (1950): 1–41; trans. Joseph Dan, *Binah*, vol. 1 (New York: Praeger, 1989).

7. 2 vols. (New York: Yeshiva University Press, 1965).

8. *Speculum* 42 (1967): 340–43.

9. 18 vols., 2nd ed. (New York: Columbia University Press, 1952–83).

tolic Powers' and Medieval 'Jewish Serfdom'";[10] Abraham Neuman, *The Jews in Spain,*[11] 1: 3–33; and Guido Kisch, *The Jews in Medieval Germany: A Study of Their Legal and Social Status.*[12] The bibliography on this topic is vast; Baron can be consulted for specific areas. Some familiarity with works dealing with broad problems in European Medieval history would also be helpful. Among the classics are Marc Bloch, *Feudal Society;*[13] R.W. Southern, *Making of the Middle Ages;*[14] and G. Tellenbach, *Church, State, and Christian Society.*[15]

Suggested reading for students: Baron (n. 3), 1: 208–82.

The Autonomous Community and Its Institutions

A session on this topic should help the student grasp the essential independence and vitality of Jewish communal existence, despite the legal restrictions imposed from without. It should also allow the student to consider the collective benefit attained at the cost, from a contemporary point of view, of individual freedom. The outstanding works in this area are Baron (n. 3) and Katz (n. 4). There are, in addition, many more specialized works. On the internal legal foundations, for example, see Menahem Elon, "The Nature of Communal Ordinances in Jewish Law."[16] On the rabbinate, see Jacob Katz, "Towards a Rabbinate at the Close of the Middle Ages."[17] On the organization of welfare, see Jacob Marcus, *Communal Sick-Care in the German Ghetto.*[18]

Suggested reading for students: Jacob Katz, *Out of the Ghetto,*[19] 9–27, and (n. 4), 79–209.

10. Trans. in Baron, *Ancient and Medieval Jewish History* (New Brunswick, N.J.: Rutgers University Press, 1972), pp. 284-307.

11. 2 vols. (Philadelphia: Jewish Publication Society, 1948).

12. Chicago: University of Chicago Press, 1949.

13. London: Routledge and Kegan Paul, 1962.

14. New Haven: Yale University Press, 1953.

15. Oxford: Blackwell, 1958.

16. (In Hebrew) in *Mehqarei mishpat le-zekher Avraham Rosenthal* (Legal Studies in Memory of Avraham Rosenthal), ed. Guido Uberto Tedeschi (Jerusalem: Hebrew University, 1964).

17. (In Hebrew) in *Benjamin de Vries Memorial Volume*, ed. A. Melamed (Jerusalem: Tel-Aviv University, Reshut ha-Mehqar, 1968), pp. 281–94.

18. Cincinnati: Hebrew Union College Press, 1978.

19. New York: Schocken, 1978.

The Maintenance of Traditional Patterns: Family Life, Social Welfare, Local Custom, and Education

Because of the great diversity of communal life in different regions, a session on this topic can perhaps best be approached by using a first-hand account describing a particular community. Unfortunately, there have been relatively few efforts to reconstruct the fabric of everyday life in the community. Worthy of note are Israel Abrahams, *Jewish Life in the Middle Ages*,[20] and Hermann Pollack, *Jewish Folkways in Germanic Lands (1648–1806): Studies in Aspects of Daily Life*.[21] On family life, consult Katz (n. 4), chs. 14–15, and "Family, Kinship and Marriage in the Sixteenth to Eighteenth Centuries."[22] Jewish scholars have begun to take an interest in the realm of popular culture and piety; see, for example, E. S. Horowitz, "Jewish Confraternal Piety in the Veneto in the Sixteenth and Seventeenth Centuries."[23]

Suggested readings for students: excerpts from *The Memoirs of Glueckel of Hameln*[24] and from Leon Modena, *Life of Judah*.[25] The latter has the advantage of extensive scholarly notes.

For students, the crucial issues and points which should be addressed in this unit are (a) the relation of the Jewish community to medieval social organization in general; (b) the variety of communal patterns among different Jewries as a result of differing adaptive demands; and (c) the uniting factor, virtually world-wide on the eve of the Modern period, of acceptance of halakhic norms as defined by the *Shulhan Arukh*.

20. Philadelphia: Jewish Publication Society, 1896; repr. London: E. Goldston, 1932.
21. Cambridge: MIT Press, 1971.
22. *Journal of Jewish Studies* 1 (1959): 4–22.
23. In *Gli ebrei e Venezia secoli XIV–XVIII*, ed. G. Cozzi (Milan: Edizioni Comunità, 1987), pp. 301–14.
24. Trans. Marvin Lowenthal (New York: Schocken, 1977).
25. Trans. and ed. Mark Cohen (Princeton: Princeton University Press, 1988).

12. Jewish Emancipation

David Weinberg

Two hundred years have passed since the first proclamation of Jewish civil equality in Europe, yet the issue of Emancipation continues to absorb and fascinate Jewish scholars. The reasons are not hard to find. The granting of legal rights to Jews not only brought about significant changes in their economic and social status but also had a profound impact on the internal administrative structure and ideology of the Jewish community. The repercussions of the entrance of the Jew into the modern world continue to reverberate among contemporary Jews. Indeed, the variety of forms of Jewish identity in the two contemporary centers of Jewry, the United States and Israel — from ultra-Orthodoxy to militant secularism — can be viewed in large part as responses to the ongoing challenges of Emancipation.

Given the centrality of Emancipation in modern Jewish consciousness, it is not surprising that the question of the granting or denial of civil rights continues to be the major theme of the teaching of modern Jewish history. In attempting to incorporate the varied histories of Jewish communities in the Modern era into a comprehensive and comprehensible whole, scholars and educators have tended to frame the development of the five major areas of modern Jewish settlement in terms of clearly defined yet intersecting challenges of and responses to Emancipation: legal equality and assimilationism in Western Europe; persecution and "auto-emancipation" in Eastern Europe; the dilemma of unemancipated Arab Jewish communities who, under the influence of European imperialism, were caught between East and West; and the contrasting fates of American and Israeli Jews, heirs to emancipated Jewry, seeking to forge a distinctive identity in a pluralistic society and under conditions of political sovereignty, respectively.

The foundations for the standard view of Emancipation can be found at the very beginnings of modern Jewish historiography in the writings of the nineteenth-century German scholar, Heinrich Graetz. Graetz and his followers emphasized the formal nature of Emancipation, focusing on the writings and declarations of non-Jewish and Jewish "notables" who supported civil equality. At the same time, they stressed the problematic nature of the Jewish response, viewing the integration of Jewry into the larger society in terms of the conflict between the political concerns of the dominant society and the "spirituality" of a powerless Jewish community in its midst. In this sense, Emancipation came to be seen as a challenge as much as an opportunity, opening the doors for Jews to integrate into society but creating immense psychological and ideological problems for both individual Jews and the community as a whole.

In the early twentieth century, such views were incorporated with little critical examination in the popular Jewish histories by Solomon Grayzel and Alexander Marx and Max Margolies. In the period after World War II, the topic of Emancipation underwent new scrutiny as contemporary Jews sought to define the relationship between Israel and the Diaspora in what many defined as a "post-Emancipation" era. Of particular significance was the work of Zionist-oriented historians such as Uriel Tal,[1] Shmuel Ettinger,[2] and Haim Hillel Ben-Sasson,[3] who, writing after the Holocaust, emphasized the role that the integration of Jews into European society played in weakening the community and leading to the onslaught of modern antisemitism. Today, Emancipation continues to be a dominant theme of texts and readers such as *The Jew in the Modern World*[4] that have been published to cater to the growing interest of American students in undergraduate and adult education courses in the modern Jewish experience.

Whether because of ideological preference, the lack of a suitable alternative model, or simple inertia, it is unlikely that Emancipation will soon be dethroned as the central topic of the study and teaching of modern Jewish history. Thanks to the work of two historians, Salo Baron and Jacob Katz, however, in recent years there has been a significant transformation in the understanding of its nature and impact in Jewish history. As early as 1928 in an article entitled "Ghetto and Emancipation" published in *The Menorah*

1. E.g., *Christians and Jews in Germany: Religion, Politics, and Ideology in the Second Reich, 1870–1914* (Ithaca: Cornell University Press, 1975).
2. E.g., "The Modern Period," in *A History of the Jewish People*, ed. H. H. Ben-Sasson (Cambridge: Harvard University Press, 1976), pp. 727–1096.
3. E.g., *Jewish Society through the Ages* (New York: Schocken, 1972).
4. Ed. Paul Mendes-Flohr and Jehuda Reinharz (New York: Oxford University Press, 1980).

Journal,[5] Baron had argued for the need for a more critical examination of the alleged gains made by Jews after the French Revoution and for a more sophisticated understanding of the status of Jews during the Middle Ages. In a more expansive essay entitled "Newer Approaches to Jewish Emancipation,"[6] the dean of Jewish historians in the United States argued that the situation in pre-Emancipation Europe was not as bleak as generally portrayed. At the same time, he called for a more nuanced view of Emancipation that would place the granting of civil equality to Jews within the general context of European modernization. Finally, Baron strongly urged Jewish historians to examine not only legal developments in the process of Emancipation but also social and cultural changes within both the Jewish community and the larger society that both preceded and resulted from the granting of legal rights to Jews.

In books such as *Exclusiveness and Tolerance*,[7] *Tradition and Crisis*,[8] and *Out of the Ghetto*,[9] the Israeli scholar Jacob Katz introduced English-speaking readers to the complexities of the transformation of the European Jewish community from tradition to modernity. As noted earlier, previously Emancipation had been commonly understood as the legal granting of civil rights to Jews and was generally associated with a series of specific laws and proclamations that originated in the French Revolution and culminated with the triumph of Bolshevism in Russia. In arguing that notions of toleration and equality for Jews preceded formal Emancipation, Katz stressed the importance of the changing social, economic, and intellectual interactions between Jews and Christians in the late Middle Ages and Early Modern era. The result was that supporters of Emancipation in the late eighteenth century, both Christian and Jewish, saw citizenship as conveying social and economic as well as political equality. The misunderstandings between the dominant society and the Jewish community concerning the exact nature of Emancipation, however, meant that social acceptance often lagged behind while economic integration generally preceded the granting of civil rights. In short, Katz argued, Emancipation had to be understood as an ongoing process rather than a sudden transformation which was initiated by a political and intellectual elite but was realized only in the unconscious daily interchange between Jew and Christian in European society as a whole.

In the 1970s and 1980s, young scholars have drawn upon Baron's and

5. Repr. in *The Menorah Treasury*, ed. Leo W. Schwarz (Philadelphia: Jewish Publication Society, 1964), pp. 50–63.

6. *Diogenes* 29 (Spring, 1960): 56–86.

7. New York: Behrman, 1962.

8. New York: Schocken, 1971.

9. Cambridge: Harvard University Press, 1973.

Katz's works to examine the genesis of Emancipation and the Jewish response in specific European countries in the late eighteenth and the nineteenth centuries. In arguing that Emancipation was a developing process that differed from country to country, works such as Todd Endelman, *The Jews of Georgian England, 1714–1830,*[10] and Marsha Rozenblit, *The Jews of Vienna,*[11] have demonstrated that the Jew's entrance into modern society was neither progressive nor unilinear. In the case of Western and Central Europe, for example, historians now tend to divide the struggle for Jewish rights roughly into three distinct periods — an initial stage marked by legal emancipation at the beginning of the century, a period of reaction paralleling the accession of Restoration monarchs to power, and a revival of support for full Jewish participation in society after the Revolutions of 1848. At the same time, attitudes toward Jewish Emancipation are now understood to have varied horizontally according to country and vertically according to socioeconomic group. Thus, for example, while British concerns generally were mild because of the relatively small number of Jews in England and the comparatively advanced stage of economic development, the German states were forced to confront the impact of the integration of a sizable Jewish population in a society that was slow to industrialize and in which economic opportunities were restricted. Responses to Jews were also shaped by the close association between Jewish Emancipation and modernization in general. Thus it was far more likely that elements of the middle and upper-middle classes who benefited from economic, social, and political liberalism would support Jewish equality rather than members of the petite bourgeoisie and working class who were adversely affected by or were unable to take advantage of increased economic opportunity, social mobility, and democratization.

Other scholars have called for an appropriate understanding of the entrance of Jewry into the larger society within the framework of European modernization in general. In *The Transformation of the Jews,*[12] Calvin Goldscheider and Alan Zuckerman argued that the integration of European Jewry must be viewed within the general context of the rise of industrial capitalism and democracy in nineteenth-century Europe. Without minimizing the ambivalent nature of Christian Europe's attitudes toward Jews (though at times ignoring the distinctiveness of Jewish communal life and values), the two authors help to corroborate Baron's and Katz's claim that Jewish Emancipation was part of a larger process of the destruction of the Old Regime characterized by the

10. Philadelphia: Jewish Publication Society, 1979.
11. Albany: State University of New York Press, 1983.
12. Chicago: University of Chicago Press, 1984.

breakdown of corporate feudal structures and the creation of a new polity and economic structure based on allegiance to the State and individual self-betterment.

One of the major contributions of the recent studies of emancipated Jewish communities in nineteenth-century Europe has been a recognition that the Jewish response to modernity cannot be defined simply by the polarities of total acceptance and total rejection. As Michael Marrus has demonstrated in a masterful essay on European Jewry before the Holocaust, "European Jewry and the Politics of Assimilation: Assessment and Reassessment,"[13] if it is true that most Jews eagerly partook of the new opportunities afforded by the bestowal of civil equality, they were not unaware of the risks. In contrast to the generally negative Zionist-oriented view of the Jewish response to the granting of civil equality, Rozenblit and others have clearly demonstrated that though the impact of Emancipation was often deleterious to traditional belief and practice, integration into the larger society also created new opportunities for Jewish expression and identification.

Borrowing from the techniques of European social history and quantification, Jewish historians have also begun to examine the impact of Emancipation on all sectors of the Jewish population. Despite the importance of the writings of young Jewish intellectuals who either eagerly embraced assimilation or anguished over the cost of integration into society, for most Jews the entrance into modern society was gradual and occasioned little soul-searching. As Endelman (n. 7) notes in his analysis of British Jewry in the eighteenth and early nineteenth centuries, for example, Jewish integration developed its own "rhythm" which was not necessarily dependent on formal political equality. In the daily interchange between Christian and Jew, patterns of thought and behavior formed unconsciously with little concern for logical and ideological consistency especially among the less articulate members of the Jewish community. More often than not, Jewish and general attitudes and values were compartmentalized, existing side by side with little interaction and thus with little contradiction. As Steven Zipperstein has shown in *The Jews of Odessa: A Cultural History, 1794–1881*,[14] the unconscious absorption of "alien" ideas and behavioral patterns could even occur in Russia, where formal equality was lacking and where the acceptance of modernity flew in the face of both general and Jewish social and cultural norms.

Jewish historians have also discovered that the exact nature of the Jewish response depended on the nature of both general and Jewish political, social,

13. *Journal of Modern History* 49/1 (1977): 89–109.
14. Stanford: Stanford University Press, 1985.

and economic conditions in the particular country. As Michael Meyer has demonstrated in *The Origins of the Modern Jew*[15] and *Response to Modernity*,[16] the highly conscious and reasoned reactions of religious reformers and political activists which form the basis of most popular studies of Emancipation and its effects generally were limited to countries such as Germany where formal equality had to be won in the face of an often hostile population and political leadership. In other countries, such as England and to a lesser extent France, where political and economic modernization advanced more quickly and traditional Christian belief and observance were weaker, Jewish apologetics were less in evidence. So too, middle-class elements within the Jewish community were far more likely to defend the Jews' entrance into society than either the already successfully integrated *haut bourgeois* heirs to the Court Jews or the preindustrial working poor.

In arguing for a reassessment of the nature and role of Emancipation, thoughtful scholars do not wish to deny its central importance in the study and teaching of modern Jewish history. Arising and developing concomitantly with modern Jewish historiography, the Jew's confrontation with the implications of his full participation in the modern world is inextricably linked with his understanding of the recent past. As long as that confrontation continues to be marked by a creative tension between Jewish and general commitments, the implications of Emancipation seem certain to affect not only contemporary Jews' appreciation of their history but their education of future generations as well.

Readings

Teachers interested in introducing students to the complex nature of Emancipation (and countering commonly held assumptions about Jewish assimilation) would do well to assign selections from Jacob Katz's books, especially *Out of the Ghetto* (n. 6). In examining the circumstances leading to the granting of civil rights, Katz demonstrates that supporters of Emancipation were not always motivated by altruism. In turn, he argues forcefully that integration into the larger society did not necessarily lead to the destruction of Jewish collective identity and solidarity. Baron (n. 3) may be also be used to highlight the complex nature of the Emancipation process, though it presumes a general knowledge of modern Jewish historiography. Selections in Mendes-Flohr and Reinharz (n. 1) provide valuable primary documentation on both the formal

15. Detroit: Wayne State University Press, 1967.
16. New York: Oxford University Press, 1988.

acts of Emancipation and the response of the Jewish community in the nineteenth century.

Meyer (n. 12) personalizes the early Jewish response to Emancipation by examining the reactions of individual German Jewish intellectuals who were instrumental in the development of religious reform and modern Jewish thought in general. Teachers may wish to balance their views by asking students to read the comments from nineteenth-century Orthodox rabbis contained in the Mendes-Flohr and Reinharz reader who feared that the granting of legal equality would lead to the disappearance of religious tradition and the destruction of the Jewish community. Marrus (n. 10) is an excellent summary of the contemporary debate over the "costs" of Emancipation viewed in light of the reactions of European Jewry to antisemitism before the Holocaust. In emphasizing the complex nature of the issue, the article serves as an important corrective for students (and others) who are quick to point an accusatory finger at "assimilated" Jewry in the prewar era for their alleged failure to respond effectively and soon enough to the threat of Nazism.

13. Secular Jewish Culture

David Weinberg

The study of secularism and secularization in the West has made enormous strides over the past few decades. In breaking down the simplistic association of secularism with atheism and social progress typical of nineteenth-century thought, cultural historians and sociologists of religion have helped to broaden the scope and sophistication of the field. Scholars now recognize that there can be no uniform definition of the ideology of secularism and the process of secularization since they differ from community to community according to the nature of the particular society's religion and religious institutions. Similarly, they have grown to realize that religious belief and practice are not inextricably linked. As students of the psychology and phenomenology of religion have pointed out, religious practice serves a multitude of nontheological purposes that remain unaffected by the decline in faith. Scholars have also discovered that there are significant differences between anticlerical and antireligious attitudes and that attacks on religious leaders may signal not a rejection of religion but a reaffirmation of what are perceived as its basic truths. In a more general sense, students of secularization have recognized that the decline of traditional beliefs and practices is part of the larger process of modernization itself. The secularization of a society thus is increasingly understood as including decidedly nonreligious developments such as the growing emphasis upon pragmatism, the rationalization of social, economic, and political institutions, and the emergence of mass culture.

Until recently, these discoveries were lost on Jewish historians. While modern historiography abounded in provocative analyses of the phenomenon of secularization and secular thought in almost all societies, most scholars of

Jewish history seemed strangely oblivious to its relevance to their research. Respected historians such as Salo Baron, Raphael Mahler, Jacob Katz, and Milton Himmelfarb, for example, use the terms "secularism" and "secularization" interchangeably with unbelief, integration, and assimilation, with little attempt at definition or analysis. Too often, the secularization of Jewry is associated with the conscious attitudes of the most articulate elements of the Jewish community with little regard for the impact of modern ideas and institutions on the general Jewish population. With the notable exception of Calvin Goldscheider and Alan Zuckerman, *The Transformation of the Jews*,[1] which attempts to place the secularization of European and American Jewry within the general context of Western modernization, Jewish historians have generally limited their discussion of secularization to the decline of traditional Judaism. As a result, there is a commonly held assumption among Jews (and among non-Jews who read the numerous popular Jewish histories that have recently been published) that the transformation of Jewish thought and behavior from traditional to modern can be explained simply as a sudden and dramatic shift from a religious to a nonreligious identity.

Similar problems are evident in classic studies of the so-called "secular Jew." Especially disappointing have been the various studies of the modern Jewish intellectual, who is generally viewed as the harbinger of secular ideas. The most penetrating analyses, such as Isaac Deutscher's "non-Jewish" Jew,[2] John Murray Cuddihy's "uncivil Jew,"[3] and Hannah Arendt's "Jew as pariah"[4] generally describe individuals whose ties with Jewish culture and community were minimal and whose marginality often led them to be alienated from both the larger society and fellow Jews. The result, as the cases of Karl Marx, Rosa Luxemburg, and Leon Trotsky clearly demonstrate, was a bold and incisive critique of evils of modern society in which the Jewish plight was glaringly absent, even deliberately ignored.

In the past two decades, there have been signs of a growing understanding among Jewish historians of the need to apply the findings of general studies of secularization to their own research. A few studies of the impact of social and economic integration on premodern Jewish attitudes and behavior in specific West and East European communities have appeared, including Todd Endelman, *The Jews of Georgian England, 1714-1830*,[5] and Steven Zipperstein,

1. Chicago: University of Chicago Press, 1984.

2. *The Non-Jewish Jew and Other Essays* (London: Oxford University Press, 1968).

3. *The Ordeal of Civility: Freud, Marx, Levi-Strauss, and the Jewish Struggle for Modernity* (New York: Basic Books, 1970).

4. *The Jew as Pariah: Jewish Identity and Politics in the Modern Age* (New York: Grove, 1978).

5. Philadelphia: Jewish Publication Society, 1979.

The Jews of Odessa: A Cultural History, 1794–1881.[6] They are noteworthy both for their attempt to incorporate religious and nonreligious components of secularization in their discussion and for their emphasis on the gradual and often unconscious way in which traditional Jewish attitudes and behavior were altered by the impact of modern society. Along with other European Jewish social historians, these young scholars have corroborated the findings of general historians and sociologists that modernization led not necessarily to the rejection of religion, but rather to its relegation to one of many concerns of daily life.

Other recent works have helped to clarify our understanding of the impact of modern ideas upon traditional Jewish leadership and belief. Israeli historians such as Immanuel Etkes in his study, R. Yisrael Salanter and the Origins of the Musar Movement,[7] have provided a fascinating insight into the manner in which radical attacks on Orthodoxy in Central and Eastern Europe in the nineteenth century forced rabbis in Russia and Poland to adopt some of the political and ideological strategies of their freethinking opponents. More generally, scholars such as Jacob Katz in works such as *Tradition and Crisis: Jewish Society at the End of the Middle Ages*,[8] though not directly focusing on the process of secularization itself, have sought to investigate the historical precedents within the premodern Jewish community in the seventeenth and eighteenth centuries that provided the framework for both religious reform and the rejection of religion by nineteenth-century Jewish intellectuals.

By far the most developed aspect of the study of secularism within the Jewish community has been the investigation of the various self-professed "secular" movements in modern Jewish history. Borrowing ideas and behavioral patterns from the larger society, yet convinced that the modernization of Jewry must come from within the community, these movements sought not only to distance themselves from traditional religious belief and practice but also to develop a new basis for individual and collective survival and growth. In particular, historians have fruitfully examined the ideology of Bundism or Jewish socialism that flourished from the turn of the century until the Bolshevik Revolution and again in Poland during the interwar period. In works such as Moshe Mishkinsky, The Beginning of Opposition to Jewish Activities in Russia: Basic Directions;[9] Ezra Mendelsohn, *Class Struggles in the Pale*;[10] Henry

6. Stanford: Stanford University Press, 1985.
7. *R. Yisrael Salanter ve-reshitah shel tenuat ha-Musar* (Jerusalem: Hebrew University, 1982).
8. New York: Free Press of Glencoe, 1961.
9. *Reshit tenu'at ha-poalim ha-yehudit be-Rusyah: megamot yesod* (Tel Aviv: University of Tel Aviv, 1981).
10. Cambridge: Cambridge University Press, 1970.

Tobias, *The Jewish Bund in Russia from its Origins to 1905*;[11] and Nora Levin, *While Messiah Tarried: Jewish Socialist Movements, 1871–1917*,[12] scholars have described how Bundism not only preached the virtues of social and economic equality but also envisioned a new Jewish culture grounded in the Yiddish language which would replace the religious obscurantism of Jewish orthodoxy with so-called "progressive" values and ideals. Studies such as Emmanuel Goldsmith, *Architects of Yiddishism at the Beginning of the Twentieth Century*,[13] and Joshua Fishman, *Never Say Die: A Thousand Years of Yiddish in Jewish Life and Letters*,[14] have examined the general movement of Yiddishism that arose in late-nineteenth-century Russia and Poland and sought to create an authentic folk culture resting on the daily experiences of the Jewish laboring masses rather than on the sacred Hebrew texts of traditional Judaism.

There was a similar "secular" strain in the Zionist movement, especially among those who saw the settlement in Palestine as the beginning of the development of a new Jewish social and economic system. Here, the various biographies of socialist Zionists such as Anita Shapira's study of Berl Katznelson, *Berl: The Biography of a Socialist Zionist: Berl Katznelson, 1887–1944*,[15] and Marie Syrkin's study of her father, *Nachman Syrkin, Socialist Zionist: The Biographical Memoir*,[16] have given us an important insight into the ideology of secular Zionist thinkers, many of whom were more tied to Jewish religious symbolism and ideology than they were willing to admit publicly. Historians are also beginning to discover that the roots of the current controversy between religionists and secularists in Israel are to be found in the history of the *yishuv* or pre-State Jewish community. A few studies by Israeli scholars, including Ehud Luz, *Parallels Meet: Religion and Zionism in the Early Zionist Movement*,[17] have examined the changing attitudes of the Labour-dominated *yishuv* toward religion and religious parties in the pre-State period that led to the establishment of the so-called "status quo" on religious questions and that explain the power and influence of religious leaders and parties in modern-day Israel.

A number of Jewish historians, many of them children of immigrants themselves, have also begun to investigate the heritage of East European Jewish

11. Stanford: Stanford University Press, 1972.
12. New York: Schocken, 1977.
13. Rutherford, N.J.: Fairleigh Dickinson University Press, 1976.
14. The Hague: Mouton, 1981.
15. Cambridge: Cambridge University Press, 1985.
16. New York: Herzl, 1961.
17. Philadelphia: Jewish Publication Society, 1988.

secular movements in the new Jewish settlements of the United States and Israel. Irving Howe, *World of Our Fathers*,[18] for example, traces the plight of newly arrived immigrants to America at the turn of the century and examines the slow demise of the secular Yiddish culture that they brought with them as it fell victim to the inexorable pull of assimilation. Within the American Jewish community itself, interest in East European secular Jewish culture was spurred momentarily in the 1960s and 1970s by the general search for ethnic "roots." In particular, aging immigrant militants sincerely believed that native-born Jewish radical youth would find their way back to Jewish life through their exposure to the ideas of Yiddishists and Jewish socialists. Beyond the publication of a number of anthologies of East European "secular" writings and a revival of interest in the Yiddish language, however, little came of their effort.

There have been some attempts to develop a distinctive American form of secular Jewish culture, most notably the Society for Ethical Culture at the end of the nineteenth century. As Benny Kraut notes in *From Reform Judaism to Ethical Culture: The Religious Evolution of Felix Adler*,[19] however, though the Ethical Culture movement did make an attempt to develop a nonsectarian and secular alternative to both traditional Christianity and Judaism, its base remained largely German-Jewish and its ideals reflected the values of prophetic Judaism. A recent example of Jewish secularism in the United States is the Movement for Humanistic Judaism led by Rabbi Sherwin Wine of Birmingham, Michigan. Wine's journal, *The Secular Jew*, and his various books outline the movement's views and examine the heritage of secular Jewish thought.

There is much discussion among Jews about the religious–secular debate in modern-day Israel, yet little has been written about it of a scholarly nature. An important start has been made by Charles Liebman, an American-born Israeli sociologist. In two books co-authored with Eliezer Don-Yehiya, *Civil Religion in Israel*[20] and *Religion and Politics in Israel*,[21] Liebman has examined the creation of what he calls an Israeli "civil religion," namely the legitimization and sanctification of society through the use of religious symbols and rituals borrowed from traditional Judaism. The authors argue that through ceremonies such as *Yom ha-Shoah ve-ha-Gevurah* (The Day of Remembrance of the Holocaust and Acts of Valor) and the creation of national myths such as Masada, where a group of Jews chose mass suicide rather than capture and subse-

18. New York: Harcourt Brace Jovanovich, 1976.
19. Cincinnati: Hebrew Union College Press, 1979.
20. Berkeley and Los Angeles: University of California Press, 1983.
21. Bloomington: Indiana University Press, 1984.

quent enslavement by Rome after the destruction of the Second Temple in 70 C.E., a largely secular Israeli society and leadership has imbued its political culture with transcendent significance in order to assure collective loyalty.

"Secularization" and "secularism" have become buzzwords in contemporary sociological and historical writing and research. For Jewish scholars, on the other hand, the concepts are still relatively new and there is still great uncertainty over how and when the terms should be used. Most scholars are in agreement, however, that the findings of generalists need to be more consistently applied to the study of the impact of modernization on Jewish history.

For the lay Jew, on the other hand, the concepts of secularization and secularism seem abstract and irrelevant. Despite a certain continuing popular fascination with Yiddish and Jewish socialism, secular Jewish culture is largely a thing of the past, destroyed by the ravages of the Holocaust and the inexorable power of assimilation. Even the efforts of Israeli secularists to develop a distinctive ideology have not had great success. In part their difficulties reflect the weaknesses inherent in secular Zionist ideology in general — its failure to find justification for Jewish survival in the past and its inability to develop appropriate methods of transmission of belief and loyalty to future generations of Jews. In part the problems of Israeli secularists can be explained by the daily struggle for survival in the Jewish State which leaves little time for philosophical speculation. Nevertheless, as long as Jews continue to maintain a separate identity that is grounded in a distinctive history yet is alive to contemporary developments, both the process of secularization and the challenges that avowed Jewish secularists attempted to meet almost a century ago — the impact of modern ideas and institutions on traditional attitudes and behavior — will continue to have relevance to Jewish life.

Readings

In order for students to understand specific manifestations of secular Jewish culture, it is important that they first become familiar with the history of the Jews' entrance into modern society. Goldscheider and Zuckerman (n. 1) is an especially valuable introduction to the subject because of its attempt to place the modernization of Jewish life within the general context of European political, social, and economic development over the past two centuries. Teachers should be aware, however, that in its effort to emphasize external rather than internal factors affecting the Jewish community, the work tends to minimize the distinctiveness of Jewish thought and behavior. Another useful survey of modernization in Jewish life is Robert Seltzer, *Jewish People, Jewish*

Thought,[22] particularly the chapters devoted to the decline of religion and the development of Jewish ethnicity among both European and American Jewry in the Modern era.

Works dealing with specific communities, such as Endelman (n. 5) and Zipperstein (n. 6), may also be helpful, especially since they stress how the decline of traditional belief and practice in Europe was often unconscious and occasioned few outward concerns. Teachers may wish to "personalize" the crisis of modernization and secularization as well as to counter romanticized images of East European Jewry before the Holocaust by having students read Isaac Bashevis Singer's novels, especially *The Family Moskat*.[23] Singer's works can be read profitably along with more historical works, such as Ezra Mendelsohn's excellent and concise chapter on interwar Poland in *The Jews of East Central Europe between the World Wars*.[24]

Despite its polemical tone and awkward title, Saul Goodman's anthology *The Faith of Secular Jews*[25] remains one of the few sources available in English of the writings of East European Jewish Yiddishists and socialists of the late nineteenth and early twentieth centuries. There is a growing number of books on Bundism, the most readable for undergraduates (though not necessarily the most historically accurate) being Levin (n. 12). An excellent selection of writings by socialist and utopian Zionists is contained in Arthur Hertzberg's anthology *The Zionist Idea*.[26] Students might also profit by reading Lucy Dawidowicz's overview of East European secular Jewish thought in *The Golden Tradition*.[27]

A very readable survey that examines the fate of secular Jewish movements and thought in America is Howe (n. 18). It should not be used as a definitive work on the immigrant Jewish experience, however, since it ignores almost completely the culture of religious Jewish immigrants. There is little written about secularism and secularization in Israel that can be easily adapted to an undergraduate curriculum. The more sophisticated student might benefit from reading Liebman and Don-Yehiya (nn. 20, 21), which deal with the attempt by Israeli politicians to use Jewish religious tradition to bolster the secular Jewish State. A balanced study of the controversy between religionists and secularists in Israel today remains to be written, however.

22. New York: Macmillan, 1980.
23. New York: Knopf, 1988.
24. Bloomington: Indiana University Press, 1983.
25. New York: Ktav, 1976.
26. New York: Doubleday, 1970.
27. New York: Holt, Rinehart and Winston, 1967; repr. Northvale, N.J.: Aronson, 1989.

14. Modern Jewish Social History

Shulamit S. Magnus

Origins and Recent Directions

Social history is the study of society in history. A relatively recent approach, social history developed as historians of Europe and the United States redefined the criteria of what was historically significant and worthy of study. Rather than examining "great events" or extraordinary personalities, social historians shifted the focus to the average, ordinary, but more typical masses of people and their behavior, who merited study because they were the vast majority of humanity throughout history. Migration, marriage patterns, fertility, occupational stratification and mobility, dress, manners, and mores replaced wars, diplomacy, kings, and philosophers as objects of study.

Jewish social history emerged under the influence of this trend. Since the creation of *Wissenschaft des Judentums* ("science of Judaism") in nineteenth-century Germany, most Jewish historical writing focused on religious and intellectual concerns, in part because it adopted then-reigning biases about what was important historically; in part because this focus suited programmatic needs of the German Jewish community in the age of Emancipation. At a time when Jews struggled to gain respectability for themselves and their culture, Jewish scholars felt the need to present Judaism in its best light, as "high culture." Jewish historians minimized or overlooked the experience of the masses of Jews, downplaying or even condemning movements such as mass messianism or Hasidism. This bias is associated particularly with the name of one of the early giants of Jewish historical writing, Heinrich Graetz (1817–1891), who typified all of Jewish history as that of "scholarship and suffering."

This filtering of the Jewish experience distorted historical reality, presenting the experience of elites—rabbis and scholars—as expressive of the Jewish experience as a whole. Yet the vast majority even of male Jews were not members of these elites, and at least half the population, women, were excluded by definition. In order truly to understand "the Jewish experience," social historians broadened their lenses to study Jewish society in all its complexity. Since most Jews were "inarticulate"—did not leave written records of their lives and thoughts—the social historical study of the Jews requires new approaches to traditional literary sources, as well as quantitative analysis of statistical sources.

While giving some background to the emergence of Jewish social history, this essay does not pretend to review the field comprehensively, but it presents basic questions social historians raise, recommends some writing (mostly in English) which I have found useful in teaching, and suggests how this material can be used.

Background

Simon Dubnow (1860–1941) was the first scholar to take a social-historical approach to the study of modern Jewry, correcting a reigning Germanocentric, as well as intellectualist, bias in Jewish historiography. Dubnow studied mass messianism (the Sabbetai Zevi movement and Frankism) and Hasidism in Eastern Europe, reconstructed communal history of the seventeenth and eighteenth centuries from Lithuanian kehillah records, and championed a campaign to have lay workers collect folk material from the Russian Jewish masses for a major project on popular culture. His major works, *History of the Jews in Russia and Poland*[1] and *Weltgeschichte des jüdischen Volkes*,[2] are still indispensable. Two other pioneers in the field of Jewish social history are Salo Wittmayer Baron (1895–1989) and Jacob Katz (b. 1904). Baron, a prolific scholar with an encyclopedic grasp of Jewish history, was particularly interested in the Jewish community as a social unit and in its structures, organization, and function. His *The Jewish Community*[3] ranges over several periods and regions of Jewish history, studying membership, education, social welfare, and criminality. Baron also pioneered in the study of Jewish demography, using Jewish and non-Jewish sources, literary and communal records, and census and tax lists to estimate Jewish population size, fertility, and mortality

---

1. 3 vols. (Philadelphia: Jewish Publication Society, 1916–20; repr. New York: Ktav, 1975).
2. 10 vols. (Berlin: Jüdischer Verlag, 1925–30).
3. 3 vols. (Philadelphia: Jewish Publication Society, 1942).

rates. A good introduction to Jewish demography from the biblical era on is Baron's "Population."[4] Baron presents an overview of major issues in modern Jewish social history in "The Challenge of Material Civilization"[5] and documents the interconnectedness of material and religious and cultural life throughout his monumental *A Social and Religious History of the Jews.*[6]

Jacob Katz has done extensive research on Jewish–gentile relations, a central theme in the history of the Jews in every era but especially in modernity, when traditional barriers to interaction fell and the rules of Jewish–gentile relations were rewritten. A master of responsa literature, Katz seeks the social reality which underlay rabbinic pronouncements, showing how these pronouncements were signposts of changing relations between Jews and non-Jews. Thus, he shows a positive revaluation of Christianity at the end of the Middle Ages and beginning of modernity reflected in liberal rulings on Jews dealing in Christian-produced wine and ritual objects (*Exclusiveness and Tolerance: Studies in Jewish–Gentile Relations in Medieval and Modern Times*[7]). Particularly interested in identifying what sparks attitudinal and behavioral shifts by Jews toward non-Jews, Katz wrote a classic study of the traditional Ashkenazi Jewish community and the disintegration of its foundations, structure, and institutions in modernity (*Tradition and Crisis*[8]). Katz made a signal contribution to conceptualizing the change between Medieval and modern conditions in his depiction of the emergence of "neutral" (later amended to "semi-neutral") ground between Jews and non-Jews, which was a *novum* in their relations. His *Out of the Ghetto: The Social Background of Jewish Emancipation, 1770–1870*[9] is a study of Jewish society in transition to modernity and the struggle to devise social institutions and ideologies of identity and affiliation appropriate to changed circumstances. Katz's work is indispensable in any course on Jewish modernity.

In the last twenty years, there has been an outpouring of writing on modern Jewish social history: studies of particular communities, as well as research on migrational and occupational trends, family, fertility, and communal patterns which characterize Jews in modernity. Some of the major works in English are: Todd M. Endelman, *The Jews of Georgian England, 1714–1830: Tradition and Change in a Liberal Society*;[10] Paula Hyman, *From Dreyfus to Vichy:*

4. *Encyclopaedia Judaica* 13 (1971): cols. 2–6.

5. In *Great Ages and Ideas of the Jewish People*, ed. Leo W. Schwarz (New York: Random House, 1956), pp. 391–419.

6. 18 vols. (New York: Columbia University Press, 1952–83).

7. New York: Behrman, 1961.

8. New York: Free Press of Glencoe, 1971.

9. Cambridge: Harvard University Press, 1973.

10. Philadelphia: Jewish Publication Society, 1979.

The Remaking of French Jewry, 1906–1939[11] and, more recently, *The Emancipation of the Jews of Alsace*;[12] Marsha L. Rozenblit, *The Jews of Vienna, 1867–1914: Assimilation and Identity*;[13] Vicki Caron, *Between France and Germany: The Jews of Alsace-Lorraine, 1871–1918*;[14] Ezra Mendelsohn, *The Jews of East Central Europe between the World Wars*;[15] *Modern Jewish Fertility*;[16] *The Jewish Family: Myths and Reality*;[17] and *The Jewish Family: Metaphor and Memory.*[18]

Scholars have also begun to devote sustained attention to the experience of Jewish women in modernity, a major new area of research about Jewish society and a logical extension of social history's attention to non-elites. Until very recently, almost nothing has been known about how the basic events of Jewish modernity—the emergence from the ghetto, the breakdown of traditional society, the Jewish rise into the middle class, Jewish acculturation and assimilation—affected or were experienced by women. Nor is much known about women's religious responses in this age of religious upheaval and new ideologies. Yet research is showing that what has been depicted as the Jewish experience of modernity was, in reality, male experience (itself highly influenced by education and class), and that women fared and behaved differently from men. Gender, in short, is being recognized as a crucial variable in the modern Jewish experience.

Marion A. Kaplan has pioneered in this study. Her articles and, more recently, her book *The Making of the Jewish Middle Class*[19] have shown how women's work in nineteenth- and early twentieth century Germany contributed to the spectacular Jewish rise from poverty to middle class standing, even as women were increasingly shut out of gainful employment; how women became prime carriers of the new bourgeois credo which Jews hoped would gain them respectablity; how women as a whole, contrary to the spectacular but highly unrepresentative image of a few salon Jewish women at the turn of the nineteenth century, tended to retain traditional behavior and to be slower to assimilate than Jewish men. (Deborah Hertz, *Jewish High Society in Old Regime Berlin*,[20] a social history of salon society, shows just how exceptional

11. New York: Columbia University Press, 1979.
12. New Haven: Yale University Press, 1991.
13. Albany: State University of New York Press, 1983.
14. Stanford: Stanford University Press, 1988.
15. Bloomington: Indiana University Press, 1983.
16. Ed. Paul Ritterband (Leiden: Brill, 1981).
17. Ed. Steven M. Cohen and Paula E. Hyman (New York: Holmes and Meier, 1986).
18. Ed. David Kraemer (New York: Oxford University Press, 1989).
19. New York: Oxford University Press, 1991.
20. New Haven: Yale University Press, 1988.

it was.) See Kaplan, "Tradition and Transition—The Acculturation, Assimilation, and Integration of Jews in Imperial Germany—A Gender Analysis,"[21] "Priestess and Hausfrau: Women and Jewish Tradition in the German-Jewish Family,"[22] and "Tradition and Transition: Jewish Women in Imperial Germany."[23] Kaplan's work both uncovers an important chapter in the history of Jewish women and shows how women's history will revise our view of Jewish modernity as a whole.

Themes and Sources

All modern Jewish historians study when and why modernity began for Jews. While the intellectual or religious historian sees Spinoza and Mendelssohn as seminal figures, with Mendelssohn often called "the first modern Jew," the social historian seeks to establish how the masses of Jews behaved in the seventeenth, eighteenth, and nineteenth centuries, and whether this behavior signified any fundamental change from traditionalism.

Rabbinic case law (responsa) and moralistic literature are prime sources for this investigation, culled not for what was held to be normative, but for evidence of changing social reality such as Jewish fraternization and eating of forbidden foods with non-Jews—in short, transgressing the laws and behavioral norms of traditional society. If appreciable numbers of such cases appear, and if this marked a departure from the type of cases previously reported in responsa literature, social historians might conclude that a popular shift occurred in a prime area demarcating modernity: the quality of social relations between Jews and non-Jews. Jacob Katz adds two crucial qualifications for such infractions to be considered true indicators of modernity: evidence that the perpetrators were unrepentant and that rabbinic authorities were powerless to enforce controls.

Katz argues that while behavioral violations did occur in eighteenth-century Central Europe, the sources do not report a lack of remorse. This became common only in the nineteenth century, and even then, as other scholars have shown, with great regional and class variations. Most Jews remained traditional well into the nineteenth century, and even Jews in congregations headed by Reform rabbis debated reforms we would consider moderate—most having to do with decorum, rather than profound doctrinal or behavioral change (See

21. *Leo Baeck Institute Yearbook* 27 (1982): 3–35.
22. In Cohen and Hyman (n. 17), pp. 62–81.
23. In *Jewish Women in Historical Perspective*, ed. Judith R. Baskin (Detroit: Wayne State University Press, 1991), pp. 202–21.

Katz [n. 9], pp. 34–36; Steven M. Lowenstein, "The Pace of Modernisation of German Jewry in the Nineteenth Century"[24] and "The 1840s and the Creation of the German Jewish Reform Movement";[25] and Michael Meyer, *Response to Modernity.*[26]) Jewish modernity, then, cannot be dated from Spinoza or Mendelssohn. A much more complex picture of the pace, progress, and nuances of change in Jewish society emerges from study of larger, more representative samples of Jews.

Because earlier Jewish historiography focused on extraordinary individuals, it highlighted change and emphasized assimilation. Social historical research, by contrast, has yielded insight into the persistence of tradition in modern Jewish society and has tended to highlight continuity more than rupture. Three works cited above illustrate the dynamics of continuity in important Jewish communities.

Rozenblit (n. 13) studied Jews in *fin-de-siècle* Vienna. Judging by the many Viennese Jewish luminaries who either were highly assimilated or converted—Sigmund Freud, Arthur Schnitzler, Gustav Mahler, Arnold Schoenberg—historians have viewed Vienna as the very cauldron of Jewish assimilation. Modern French Jewry, too, has often been characterized as the essence of an assimilated community. Yet Caron (n. 14) and Hyman (n. 12), who studied the Jews of Alsace-Lorraine, the heartland of French Jewry, conclude that Jewish assimilation was not as extreme as is often portrayed and that potent forms of Jewish affiliation and identification persisted or were created. Hyman argues persuasively that the focus on the French Jewish urban elite has produced an exaggerated view of the pace and prevalence of French Jewish assimilation, while study of the numerically preponderant, largely rural and small-town Jews of Alsace demonstrates the persistence of tradition in ninetenth-century France. This is an important addition to Hyman's own earlier work (n. 11), which showed traditionalism to be an expression of East European Jewish immigrants in the twentieth century.

Rozenblit, Caron, and Hyman analyzed large quantities of social data—on occupation, income, education, residential, and marriage patterns—and found that, for all the changes which Jewish society underwent, peculiarly Jewish patterns of behavior persisted. Jews moved up the occupational scale yet concentrated in certain sectors that came to be seen, and experienced, as "Jewish." Jews tended to live in certain neighborhoods, so although their children attended secular schools, they did so in the company of other Jews. Since Jews

24. *Leo Baeck Institute Yearbook* 21 (1976): 41–56.
25. In *Revolution and Evolution: 1848 in German Jewish History*, ed. Werner E. Mosse et al. (Tübingen: Mohr, 1981), pp. 255–97.
26. New York: Oxford University Press, 1988.

tended to socialize with other Jews, endogamy remained high. Despite the creation of a modernized, "official" Judaism in France, traditional forms of worship persisted alongside it. Assimilation made inroads in Vienna, yet ideologies rejecting assimilation—Orthodoxy, Zionism—either persisted or arose. Some of these behaviors were conscious; some lacked an ideology. Some were the result of antisemitism; some merely expressed the desire of a minority group to seek comfort within its own circle. In any case, Jewish accomodation to modernity was not as linear as the history of Jewish elites had suggested. These findings, combined with Kaplan's on women, seriously challenge the older view (particularly pronounced in Zionist historiography) of a headlong Jewish plunge into assimilation once legal Emancipation occurred.

When measuring the transition to modernity, social historians look at important behavioral indicators: language, dress, names, education, marriage patterns (endogamy or exogamy). The more a group distinguishes itself in these areas, the less it is said to be acculturated; the more Jews approach non-Jewish norms, the more they are said to have acculturated. Acculturation can be quite compatible with continued, if "modern," Jewish identity; "assimilation," on the other hand, is used to connote loss of all group identity, its most extreme expressions being outmarriage (since non-Jewish partners rarely converted) and conversion.

In studying where Jews were on the continuum between these poles, social historians pay close attention to two crucial, related variables: date and region. To take an example from Germany, often depicted as the paradigmatic modern Jewish community: Jews in Berlin may have acculturated to a high degree as early as the turn of the nineteenth century, as attested by their modern attire in portraits and their writings, but was their behavior typical? Did the majority of German Jews share their experience?

The evidence from communal records—kehillah minute books, synagogue ordinances, responsa literature—does not sustain such a conclusion. When, then, and why, did modernity make popular inroads? The results of this research change our view of German Jewish modernity as a whole, since for much of the nineteenth century, large numbers of German (like French) Jewry lived in villages and towns where the pace and nature of change was much slower than in cities. (See Lowenstein [n. 24]; Monika Richarz, "Emancipation and Continuity—German Jews in the Rural Economy".[27])

The continuity of Jewish identity and its reworking in new guises is one of the most important themes of Jewish modernity. How did Jews respond to the

27. In Mosse et al. (n. 25), pp. 95–115.

fall of a clearly demarcated sphere of being in non-Jewish society—to Emancipation, in short? How did Jews define themselves after affiliation became voluntary, and the content of Jewish identity was no longer subject to effective definition by rabbinical or communal authorities?

Religious and intellectual historians look at the ideologies of movements: of Reform, in particular. Social historians ask how representative the Reform movement was, even for German Jews. One scholar, Steven M. Lowenstein, has done illuminating research which shows that in the 1840s, a decade of great organizational activity in the Reform movement, relatively few German rabbis considered themselves Reform, and that most of these served small communities. Moreover, in contrast to the conspicuous rhetoric of Reform leaders like Geiger, not to mention the more radical Samuel Holdheim, actual reforms introduced in most of these rabbis' communities were relatively moderate: sermons in German, confirmation ceremonies, choirs ("The 1840s and the Creation of the German Jewish Reform Movement"[28]). "Reform," then, signified something quite different to congregants than to movement ideologues, and there was quite a different social reality in the Reform movement at midcentury than organizational activity or ideological pronouncements would lead us to believe.

The causes of modern outlook or behavior are different for philosophers and average Jews, and this too will dictate differences in approach between scholars of elites and social historians.

Todd Endelman's book on English Jewry (n. 10) illustrates the importance of social structures in determining attitudes and behavior. Endelman shows that, unlike the Jewish experience on the Continent, traditionalism broke down early and thoroughly for most English Jews—not because of the inroads of modern ideologies but because of the lack of traditional communal controls in a country with no preexisting kehillah. The absence of internal restraints in a liberal, tolerant, secularizing environment meant that there was little impediment to Jewish cultural integration. Equally important, Endelman investigates the class basis of Jewish acculturation and assimilation and shows that cultural change was not restricted to the middle and upper Jewish classes who are the focus of most historical investigations. Instead, he shows, Jews adopted the mores of their respective class counterparts in English society as they acculturated: wealthy Jews aping the manners of wealthy Anglicans; poor Jews adopting "many of the patterns of urban life of the social class to which they belonged ... [including] criminal activity, sexual promiscuity, street violence and prize-fighting" (pp. 166f. Little wonder earlier Jewish historians,

---

28. In Mosse et al. (n. 25), pp. 264–68.

concerned with the image of Jewish probity, avoided studying or publicizing this type of material!)

Social historians study occupational and economic change which occurred as a result of modern conditions. With Emancipation, some or all (depending on the country) occupational, residential, and educational restrictions against Jews were lifted. How did Jews respond? This is an important question, since much of the argument for emancipating the Jews turned on the assertion that Jews had concentrated in trade and finance because of external constraints rather than innate proclivity, and that their occupational profile would "normalize" once discrimination ceased. Jews would enter crafts and agriculture; more, they were expected to diversify occupationally, in the minds of some, as the "price" of Emancipation. What were Emancipation's actual occupational effects, social historians ask?

Arthur Prinz, Jacob Toury, and Monika Richarz have written on this subject for Germany; Phyllis Cohen Albert and Paula Hyman for France (Prinz, *Juden in Deutschen Wirtschaftsleben, 1850–1914;*[29] Toury, *Soziale und politische Geschichte der Juden in Deutschland, 1847–1871;*[30] Richarz, *Jüdisches Leben in Deutschland,*[31] "Jewish Social Mobility in Germany During the Time of Emancipation (1790–1871),"[32] and [n. 27]; Albert, *The Modernization of French Jewry;*[33] Hyman [nn. 11–12].)

All find that while considerable occupational and economic change took place in the nineteenth century as a result of lessened discrimination and an expanding industrial economy, Jews continued to predominate in commerce. Both custom (Jewish familiarity with the money economy) and general economic trends (the take-off of capitalism) determined this outcome. Thus, while petty trade—peddling, secondhand, rag dealing—declined dramatically, Jews moved into retail trade—establishing shops and later, department stores. Jews remained in the same sector of the economy as before Emancipation, there experiencing upward occupational mobility. This brought a higher standard of living and, in both countries, a phenomenal ascent into the middle class by a group which had been predominantly poor on the eve of Emancipation.

Social historians also found that Jews availed themselves of secular educational opportunities to a degree out of all proportion to their numbers in the population. Since education is a prime avenue to increased earnings and social

29. Tübingen: Mohr, 1984.
30. Düsseldorf: Droste, 1977.
31. Stuttgart: Deutsche Verlags-Anstalt, 1976.
32. *Leo Baeck Institute Yearbook* 20 (1975): 69–77.
33. Hanover, N.H.: University Presses of New England, 1977.

118 Shulamit S. Magnus

status, the statistics are eloquent nonliterary testimony to Jewish expectations of modernity. Education, of course, is also a prime fashioner of identity. With increased Jewish use of secular institutions and the decline of Jewish schools, documented by decreasing enrollments and school closings, Jewish acculturation proceeded apace (Monika Richarz, *Der Eintritt der Juden in die Akademischen Berufe*;[34] more briefly but in English, see [n. 32]).

Since both educational and occupational opportunities are superior and more abundant in cities than in towns or villages, Jews in the age of Emancipation urbanized at a rate far exceeding that of non-Jews. (For France, see Albert [n. 33], pp. 3–25. For Germany, see Lowenstein [n. 24] and "The Rural Community and the Urbanization of German Jewry,"[35] and Alice Goldstein, "Urbanization in Baden, Germany: Focus on the Jews."[36]) Social change occurs at an accelerated pace in cities, so Jewish urbanization went hand in hand with loss of traditional Jewish behaviors and adoption of those of the non-Jewish culture. The manners and mores of the new urban Jewish middle class increasingly approximated those of the non-Jewish bourgeoisie.

While the new research has shown that traditionalism persisted longer and was more widespread among Jews than the older historigraphy recognized, it has also demonstrated that Jews, in comparison to the non-Jewish society, participated to an exaggerated degree in trends which characterize modernity. This includes limitation of family size, something which occured among the urbanized middle classes of Europe as a whole over the course of the nineteenth century, but more so, and sooner, among Jews. (See Paula Hyman, "Jewish Fertility in Nineteenth Century France,"[37] and Steven M. Lowenstein, "Voluntary and Involuntary Limitation of Fertility in Nineteenth Century Bavarian Jewry."[38])

In sum: while the social profile of Jews in Western and Central Europe and England changed radically in response to modern economic developments and reforms in Jewish legal status, Jews remained recognizably Jewish as a social as well as a religious entity. The new research has shown that, for all the assimilatory pressures of modernity, social forces, as much as or more than religious movements or ideologies, also conspired to keep Jews Jewish.

Class conflict is a major chapter in modern Jewish social history. While not a novel phenomenon, modern conditions vastly exacerbated such tensions: the positing of "useful" Jews worthy of Emancipation also created a category of

34. Tübingen: Mohr, 1974.
35. *Central European History* 13/3 (1980): 218–35.
36. *Social Science History* 7/1 (1984): 43–66.
37. In Ritterband (n. 16), pp. 78–93.
38. In Ritterband (n. 16), pp. 94–111.

"useless," degenerate Jews, whom privileged Jews sought either to reform or to avoid, lest their own precarious status be jeopardized. A glaring instance of such behavior occurred in Revolutionary France, where Sephardi Jews, granted Emancipation before the Ashkenazim, argued that they were a separate nation. Endelman (n. 10) beautifully illustrates the emergence and implications of modern Jewish class distinctiveness. Class conflict is a central theme in Michael Stanislawski, *Tsar Nicholas I and the Jews*.[39] Though not a social history, the book, as the subtitle states, illustrates "the transformation of Jewish society in Russia" from 1825 to 1855. Stanislawski integrates cultural and communal history, a rarity; he also illustrates the social tensions exacerbated by government and Haskalah policies aimed at "modernizing" the Jews. Finally, he includes a chapter on changes in the economic structure of Jewish society in this period. Ezra Mendelsohn, *Class Struggle in the Pale*,[40] is most useful in studying the peculiar occupational stratification which antisemitism and economic decline produced in the Jews of the Pale of Settlement.

The fast pace and radical nature of change in nineteenth-century Jewish society created sharp intergenerational and spousal conflict. There were far-reaching consequences for family life, too, in the Musar movement's creation of a class of young Torah scholars, separated for years from their wives and families. A number of articles by Immanuel Etkes, David Biale, and Gershon Hundert treat marriage and the family in modern East European Jewish society, among elites—rabbinic scholars, *maskilim*—and the population at large. (Etkes, "Family and the Study of Torah among Lithuanian Talmudist Circles in the Nineteenth Century"[41] and "Marriage and Torah Study Among the *Lomdim* in Lithuania in the Nineteenth Century";[42] Biale, "Childhood, Marriage, and the Family in the Eastern European Enlightenment"[43] and "Eros and Enlightenment: Love Against Marriage in the East European Jewish Enlightenment";[44] Hundert, "Approaches to the History of the Jewish Family in Early Modern Poland-Lithuania"[45] and "Jewish Children and Childhood in Early Modern East Central Europe."[46])

Jewish modernity emerged quite differently in Eastern than in Western and Central Europe. Stanislawski (n. 39) is the best overall treatment for the nine-

39. Philadelphia: Jewish Publication Society, 1983.
40. Cambridge: Cambridge University Press, 1970.
41. (In Hebrew) *Zion* 51/1 (1986): 87–106.
42. In Kraemer (n. 18), pp. 15–78.
43. In Cohen and Hyman (n. 17), pp. 45–61.
44. *Polin* 1 (1986): 49–67.
45. In Cohen and Hyman (n. 17), pp. 17–28.
46. In Kraemer (n. 18), pp. 81–94.

teenth century. For the twentieth, see Mendelsohn (n. 15). While not a social history, this book is a model study of Jewish communities in seven countries in the interwar period, a time of great social and economic change, as well as cultural efflorescence. Mendelsohn crafts the profiles of these communities superbly, integrating analysis of Jewish politics, economics, and demographics. The book is engagingly written, has illustrative and accessible tables, and clearly shows how and why modernity emerged, and assumed a different visage, in different settings.

Beginning in 1881, mass Jewish migration from east to west is a major theme in Jewish social history, in which the clash of native and immigrant Jewries is an important chapter. Hyman (n. 11) explores the class and occupational differences of immigrant and French Jews, their sharply diverging notions of Jewish identity, and the impact of immigrant culture on the native community. Jack Wertheimer treats the clash of immigrant and native cultures and the social, religious, and occupational differences of the two communities in Germany between 1871 and 1914, in *Unwelcome Strangers: East European Jews in Imperial Germany.*[47] For the same period in England, see Todd Endelman, "Native and Foreign Jews in London, 1870–1914."[48]

Using This Material

A course on modern Jewish history can easily integrate a unit on the social impact of modernity on Jews. Such a unit can even help define the parameters and goals of study of elites. A survey course on Jewish Modernity should certainly cover both intellectual and social history. When I teach the latter type of course, I stress that I am not advocating the study of elites or of society in opposition, but as different and complementary approaches to the study of Jewish modernity. Thus, I couple readings on Mendelssohn, the German Haskalah, and Reform philosophy with social-historical studies of the Reform movement; we study the thought of the Neo-Orthodox maverick, Samson Raphael Hirsch, with Robert Liberles' analysis of the communal context of Hirsch's rise, *Religious Conflict in Social Context.*[49]

I have found the beginning chapters of Calvin Goldscheider and Alan S. Zuckerman, *The Transformation of the Jews,*[50] a useful, succinct introduction

47. New York: Oxford University Press, 1987.
48. In *The Legacy of Jewish Immigration: 1881 and Its Impact*, ed. David Berger (New York: Columbia University Press, 1983), pp. 109–30.
49. Westport, Conn.: Greenwood, 1985.
50. Chicago: University of Chicago Press, 1984.

to the main trends of modern Jewish social history. Useful, too, is S. Ettinger, "The Modern Period,"[51] a lengthy survey which gives particular emphasis to social, economic, and demographic trends in modern European Jewry, east and west. One might then use any of the specialized monographs mentioned above to study trends in greater detail, either in a particular community or in comparative perspective.

I integrate Kaplan's material on women (nn. 19, 21–23) to highlight gender as a category of analysis and to make students aware that what we normally study as "Jewish history" is, in fact, the study of Jewish men—and a minority of them, at that. (On this theme, see Paula Hyman, "Gender and Jewish History,"[52] and Shulamit Magnus, "'Out of the Ghetto': Integrating the Study of Jewish Women Into the Study of 'the Jews.'"[53])

To this end, I also use Kaplan's book on the German Jewish feminist movement, *The Jewish Feminist Movement in Germany*.[54] Here, Kaplan shows how the women of the Jüdischer Frauenbund adopted many of German society's bourgeois values about women—evidence of women's acculturation. I also use this book to discuss conflicted attitudes among German Jewish men, who harbored prejudice and practiced discrimination against Jewish women at a time when Jewish Emancipation was far from complete and (male-dominated) Jewish institutions were battling anti-Jewish discrimination in German society. While antiwoman prejudice existed in Jewish society independent of attitudes absorbed from German culture, the behavior Kaplan illustrates shows the influence of reigning bourgeois values on Jewish men (see especially p. 157). I treat this material as German Jewry's internal battle for Emancipation to emphasize that women, too, were German Jews, and to highlight the gender basis for this unrecognized, yet glaring, conflict between external and internal communal policy.

I treat East European Jewry after the Jews of England, France, Germany, and Austria, because modernity set in later in the East, and because both the czarist government and the Jewish community were very conscious of the French and German models of change, whether they viewed Emancipation and modernization as blessing or calamity. If students have studied Western Jewish communities, there can be very fruitful and exciting discussions of the commonalities and particularities of Jewish modernity in different settings. If the course allows only a few sessions on Eastern Europe, I use Mendelsohn's

51. In *A History of the Jewish People*, ed. H. H. Ben-Sasson (Cambridge: Harvard University Press, 1976), pp. 727–1096.
52. *Tikkun* 3 (January–February 1988): 35–38.
53. *Judaism* 39/1 (Winter 1990): 28–36.
54. Westport, Conn.: Greenwood, 1979.

chapters on Poland and Hungary, because the contrasts between these communities were so sharp.

Since the methodologies of social history are likely to be more foreign to students than those of intellectual and religious history, it is worth devoting some time to this, either as a special session or as part of the discussion of generally assigned readings. I photocopy and circulate particularly illustrative tables and charts from the readings, almost invariably finding that students have glossed over them. We then read these "primary sources" in class, with me asking leading questions. To see the emergence of Jewish occupational trends, I ask what percentage of the Jewish community practiced trade or the professions, in which decades. To highlight gender differences in Jewish occupational stratification, I use Kaplan's tables and ask students to compare what occupations women and men practiced. I use Mendelsohn's (n. 15) and Rozenblit's (n. 13) data on Jewish population concentration to illustrate their analyses of Jewish ethnicity in Eastern Europe and Vienna, respectively; the statistics in Albert (n. 33) and Hyman (n. 12) to illustrate Jewish migration and urbanization. While students initially may take statistical sources to be dry, when they realize what messages are "encoded" in the numbers and that these tell a story, there is a sense of excitement and discovery and often, I find, a sense of immediacy to historical reality not attained in the study of traditional literary sources. This is particularly true when I use Lowenstein's simple yet revelatory charts of the reforms actually introduced in Reform temples in the 1840s ([n. 28], pp.286–97).

The study of Jewish social history has so significantly enriched our understanding of the modern Jewish experience that its findings belong on any syllabus on Jewish Modernity. The nonspecialist has a wealth of fine studies from which to choose.

15. The Mass Migration of East European Jews

Jack Wertheimer

Evyatar Friesel highlights the significance of migration for the modern Jewish experience by beginning his magnificent *Atlas of Modern Jewish History*[1] with a series of maps (pp. 10–19) depicting the remarkable shifts in Jewish population centers from the seventeenth century to the present. A perusal of these maps makes it abundantly clear that Jews have repeatedly reconcentrated themselves demographically in the modern era: whereas the locus of Jewish settlement was primarily in Poland, the Ottoman Empire, and North Africa at the end of the seventeenth century, key centers soon arose in Central and Western Europe, and in our own time the greatest concentrations are found in North America, the land of Israel, and the former Soviet Union. These maps alert us to the dramatic odysseys of modern Jews—movements of vast populations within empires, from one country to the next, and eventually across continents.

Jewish migration may be understood as a response to crises—both physical and economic. After encountering czarist pogroms, Nazi death camps, Arab riots, and Communist prison states, Jews rebuilt their lives and communities in new centers. Others migrated primarily to improve their economic lot: they moved to places that offered greater opportunities—whether those places were in nearby urban settings or across the ocean. Jewish migration in the modern era therefore may be understood as a story of tenacious physical and economic reconstruction in the face of hardship, as a saga demonstrating the resiliency of Jewish people during the migration process and their ability to establish homes, businesses, and self-help institutions in new settings.

1. New York: Oxford University Press, 1990.

It is also the story of Jewish cultural transfer—and what was gained and lost as Jewish immigrants made their way in new environments. For much of the cultural baggage the migrants carried with them from their former homes was transformed in their new ones: whether they moved from Minsk to London, Lemberg to New York, Kovno to Capetown, or from Tunis to Tel Aviv, Jewish migrants had to adapt to the host culture as well as the culture and society of native Jews in those settings. The encounter was often bruising—for both the newcomers and the oldtimers. It provoked antisemites and fueled Jewish self-hatred. But the collision of Jewish cultures also ignited remarkable Jewish creativity.

This essay addresses only the question of international migration. It is important to bear in mind, however, that in the modern era Jews have also migrated internally within countries and particularly to urban centers. For a broad overview of such migrations, see Calvin Goldscheider and Alan S. Zuckerman, *The Transformation of the Jews*,[2] chs. 6, 7, 10, and 12. For a fine case study of internal migration and urbanization within the Austro-Hungarian empire, see Marsha L. Rozenblit, *The Jews of Vienna, 1867–1914: Assimilation and Identity.*[3]

Not surprisingly, international Jewish migrations have attracted much scholarly attention in recent decades and are the subject of exciting new research. One merely needs to compare some of the standard older works written at midcentury with recent studies to appreciate the richness of new offerings. Earlier works focused mainly on the causes for emigration, the dimensions of population movement, relief programs for the travelers, and the occupational and social characteristics of the immigrants. (The most important earlier works are: Jacob Lestchinsky, "Jewish Migrations, 1840–1946";[4] Liebman Hersch, "Jewish Migrations During the Last 100 Years";[5] and Mark Wischnitzer, *To Dwell in Safety: The Story of Jewish Migrations since 1800.*[6]) More recent scholarship is grounded in the new social history and poses entirely different questions: Was the experience of immigrant women different from that of their male counterparts? How did poor immigrant Jews adapt to sudden abundance? What was the impact of immigrants on both the agenda and the cultural life of native Jewish communities? And how did the children

2. Chicago: University of Chicago Press, 1984.

3. Albany: State University of New York Press, 1983.

4. In *The Jews: Their History, Culture, and Religion*, ed. Louis Finkelstein (Philadelphia: Jewish Publication Society, 3rd ed., 1960), pp. 1536–96.

5. In *The Jewish People, Past and Present* (New York: Jewish Encyclopedic Handbooks, 1955) vol. 1, pp. 407–30.

6. Philadelphia: Jewish Publication Society, 1948.

of immigrants construct their identities? Particularly in the North American setting, where immigrant history receives special attention, the new research on Jewish migrations deserves consideration in courses on the Modern Jewish Experience. This essay examines the literature on Jewish mass migration from Eastern Europe, the migration that has attracted greatest attention in recent scholarship and that was most critical in transforming the map of international Jewish life.

Literature and Themes

The beginnings of Jewish emigration from Eastern Europe are directly traceable to the Chmielnicki uprising of 1648–49 and the subsequent invasions of Poland. Prior to the seventeenth century, during the High and Later Middle Ages, Jewish migration in Europe had moved in an eastward direction: when West European countries successively ordered their Jews expelled, the refugees made their way first to Central Europe and later to Poland. Similarly, during the last major expulsions, when Jews were driven from the Iberian Peninsula, they traveled through North Africa to Italy and finally the Ottoman Empire. The flow of movement changed, however, after 1648 due to the destruction of Jewish communities in southern Poland and the weakening of the Polish monarchy. Gradually, Polish Jews made their way westward, first to German-speaking states and later to Western Europe and even the New World. Among the works describing this movement are: Moses A. Shulvass, *From East to West: The Westward Migration of Jews from Eastern Europe during the Seventeenth and Eighteenth Centuries*,[7] and Jonathan Israel, *European Jewry in the Age of Mercantilism, 1550–1750*.[8] By the eighteenth century there was also a small but significant movement of Polish and German Jews into the Netherlands, England, and North American colonies. Details about their numbers and impact can be gleaned from histories of those Jewries, such as Todd Endelman, *The Jews of Georgian England 1714–1830*,[9] pp. 170–73.

The movement from east to west remained quite small until well into the nineteenth century, when a mass flight of East European Jews began in earnest. Starting as a trickle in response to cholera epidemics and famines sweeping the western parts of Russia in the later 1860s, and slowly gaining momentum in the 1870s, the migration from Russia burst into a flood in the wake of the assassination of Czar Alexander II in 1881. In each succeeding

7. Detroit: Wayne State University Press, 1971.
8. Oxford: Oxford University Press, 1985.
9. Philadelphia: Jewish Publication Society, 1979.

decade, ever larger numbers departed, so that by the early years of the twentieth century, over one hundred thousand emigrated annually. By the last years of the nineteenth century, Jews from the Austro-Hungarian empire and Rumania joined this mass westward flight, a movement that ended only in the interwar era when travel restrictions imposed by the Bolshevik government and immigration restrictions in many Western lands effectively blocked the mass migration.

One of the pioneering works of Jewish immigrant history was Lloyd P. Gartner's study of the English experience. His book *The Jewish Immigrant in England*[10] has served as a model of research on immigrant society and especially workers and Yiddish culture. More recent examinations of labor movements appear in Joseph Buckman, *Immigrants and the Class Struggle: The Jewish Immigrant in Leeds, 1880–1914*,[11] and the essays by Bill Williams, Anne J. Kershen, and Rickie Burman in *The Making of Modern Anglo-Jewry*.[12] On the second generation, see Rosalyn Livshin, "The Acculturation of the Children of Immigrant Jews in Manchester, 1890–1930."[13] For an insightful historiographical survey of recent literature on East European Jews and other immigrants in England, see David Feldman, "There Was an Englishman, an Irishman, and a Jew ... : Immigrants and Minorities in Britain."[14] Two important volumes appeared in the early 1970s devoted to the responses of the British government and press: Bernard Gainer, *The Alien Invasion: The Origins of the Aliens Act of 1905*,[15] and John A. Garrard, *The English and Immigration, 1880–1910*.[16]

Whereas the vast majority of East European Jews in England arrived prior to the Aliens Act of 1905, the settlement of such Jews in France began in earnest early in the twentieth century and reached a peak only after World War I. Two important English-language studies examining this immigrant population are: Nancy L. Green, *The Pletzl of Paris: Jewish Immigrant Workers in the Belle Epoque*,[17] a careful analysis of working class Jews in Paris, conceived primarily as a study of labor history; and Paula E. Hyman, *From Dreyfus to Vichy: The Remaking of French Jewry, 1906–1939*,[18] which surveys the pre–

10. Detroit: Wayne State Univeristy Press, 1960.
11. Manchester: Manchester University Press, 1983.
12. Ed. David Ceserani (Oxford: Blackwell, 1990).
13. In Ceserani (n. 12), pp. 79–96.
14. *Historical Journal* 26 (March 1983): 183–96.
15. New York: Crane, Rusak, 1972.
16. London: Oxford University Press for Institute of Race Relations, 1971.
17. New York: Holmes and Meier, 1986.
18. New York: Columbia University Press, 1979.

and post–World War I period from the perspective of Jewish history and therefore examines both the society and movements created by the immigrants, as well as relations between those immigrants and native Jewry. On the responses of immigrant and native Jews during the growing crisis of the thirties, see David H. Weinberg, *A Community on Trial: The Jews of Paris in the 1930s.*[19]

The conflict-ridden experience of East European Jews in Germany has attracted considerable attention in recent years. Steven E. Aschheim, *Brothers and Strangers: The East European Jew in German and German Jewish Consciousness, 1800–1923,*[20] focuses on the varying stereotypes of Eastern Jews in the minds of German Jews and gentiles. Aschheim analyzes responses to East European Jews in order to probe the nature of Jewish identity and antisemitism in modern Germany. Jack Wertheimer, *Unwelcome Strangers: East European Jews in Imperial Germany,*[21] offers a social history of the immigrant experience prior to World War I. The book examines the complex policies of German governments toward Jews from the East, characterizes the demographic, occupational, and social features of immigrant Jews, and analyzes the responses of organized German Jewry to the newcomers. Trude Maurer accounts for the period after the outbreak of World War I in *Ostjuden in Deutschland 1918–1933.*[22] The English reader is able to sample some of Maurer's wonderfully detailed research by reading her essay "The East European Jew in the Weimar Press: Stereotype and Attempted Rebuttal."[23] Ludger Heid, another German historian writing on the interwar era, focuses on working class East European Jews in the Ruhr industrial zone. For an overview of work in progress, see his essay, "East European Jewish Workers in the Ruhr, 1915–1922."[24]

The largest number of East European Jews migrated to the New World and principally to the United States. The sheer quantity of research on East European Jews in the United States is enormous, and therefore only a sampling is cited here. For an excellent survey of the most important recent research, see Jonathan D. Sarna, "American Jewish History,"[25] especially pp. 35–53 and notes. This essay is particularly useful in identifying journal literature of distinction. For a general account of immigration and especially the changing

19. Chicago: University of Chicago Press, 1974.
20. Madison: University of Wisconsin Press, 1982.
21. New York: Oxford University Press, 1987.
22. Hamburg: Hans Christian Verlag, 1986.
23. *Studies in Contemporary Jewry* 1 (1984) 176–98.
24. *Leo Baeck Institute Yearbook* 30 (1985): 141–68.
25. *Modern Judaism* 10 (1990): 343–65.

technology facilitating travel, see Philip Taylor, *The Distant Magnet: European Emigration to the U.S.A.*[26] On the political struggle to enact restrictionist legislation, see John Higham, *Strangers in the Land: Patterns of American Nativism 1860–1925.*[27]

The two classic accounts of immigrant life in New York City, the most important concentration of East European Jews in the United States, are Moses Rischin, *The Promised City: New York's Jews, 1870–1914,*[28] and Irving Howe, *World of Our Fathers: The Journey of the East European Jews to America and the Life They Found and Made.*[29] Both volumes emphasize secular Yiddish culture and downplay the role of religion, Zionism, and traditional culture. Rischin's heroes are the workers who created the Jewish labor movement, and Howe is most interested in the Yiddish cultural scene. To correct for the male-oriented biases and highlight the unique experiences of women, we now can read Paula E. Hyman, "Gender and the Immigrant Jewish Experience in the United States";[30] Susan A. Glenn, *Daughters of the Shtetl: Life and Labor in the Immigrant Generation;*[31] and Sidney Stahl Weinberg, *The World of Our Mothers: The Lives of Jewish Immigrant Women.*[32] For material on East European Jews who settled elsewhere in the United States, we can rely on most Jewish communal histories. Among those that are especially sophisticated in their examination of the immigrant population and its relationship to the broader gentile and Jewish societies, see William Toll, *The Making of an Ethnic Middle Class: Portland Jewry over Four Generations,*[33] and Stephen Hertzberg, *Strangers in the Gate City: The Jews of Atlanta, 1845–1915.*[34] Ewa Morawska breaks new ground with her sophisticated analysis of immigrants in a small community in her essay "A Replica of the 'Old Country' Relationship in the Ethnic Niche: East European Jews and Gentiles in Small-Town Western Pennsylvania, 1880s–1930s."[35] On the struggle to unify the Downtown immigrants and the Uptown native Jews within a broader communal agency, see Arthur Goren, *New York Jews in Quest of Community:*

26. New York: Harper and Row, 1971.

27. New Brunswick, N.J.: Rutgers University Press, 1954.

28. Cambridge: Harvard University Press, 1962.

29. New York: Harcourt, Brace Jovanovich, 1976.

30. In *Jewish Women in Historical Perspective*, ed. Judith R. Baskin (Detroit: Wayne State University Press, 1991), pp. 222–42.

31. Ithaca, N.Y.: Cornell University Press, 1990.

32. Chapel Hill: University of North Carolina Press, 1988.

33. Albany: State University of New York Press, 1982.

34. Philadelphia: Jewish Publication Society, 1978.

35. *American Jewish History* 77 (September 1987): 27–86.

The Kehilla Experiment.[36] There are numerous documentary collections, such as Irving Howe and Kenneth Libo, *How We Lived: A Documentary History of Immigrant Jews in America, 1880–1930.*[37] On the pursuits and identity of the second generation—children of immigrant Jews—see Deborah D. Moore, *At Home in America: Second Generation Jews in New York,*[38] and on the religious adaptations of second generation Jews, see Marshall Sklare, *Conservative Judaism: An American Religious Movement.*[39] A creative exploration of how poor East European Jews reacted to the riches of America is found in Andrew R. Heinze, *Adapting to Abundance: Jewish Immigrants, Mass Consumption, and the Search for an American Identity.*[40]

Thus far the scholarship on Jewish immigrants in Canada is not very extensive. For a popular overview, see Irving Abella, *A Coat of Many Colours: Two Centuries of Jewish Life in Canada,*[41] which also offers a bibliography for further reading. Several fine essays appear in *The Jews of North America,*[42] a work that is especially noteworthy because it reflects a growing interest in placing immigration to the United States and Canada—as well as other themes—into comparative perspectives (see the essays by Gideon Shimoni and Victor Mirelman in this volume for references to work on Jewish immigrants in British Commonwealth lands and Latin America, respectively).

The same cannot be said about scholarship on the immigration of East European Jews to Palestine, a subject almost uniformly treated in isolation as an aspect of Zionist history rather than of international Jewish migration. It is assumed that the ideological commitments of *'Olim* (immigrants to the land of Israel), as well as the unique circumstances of life in Palestine, militate against any comparisons of aliyah with other migrations. Yet patterns of education, religious traditionalism, occupational structure, and urbanization in the *yishuv* (the Jewish settlement in Palestine) bear comparing with patterns of other Jewish emigrants from Eastern Europe, even if only to highlight their uniqueness.

Although there is a huge literature in Hebrew on what is often perceived as the heroic age of immigration, the second aliyah, far less is available in English. For a general overview, see Walter Laqueur, *A History of Zionism,*[43]

36. New York: Columbia University Press, 1970.
37. New York: Richard Marek, 1979.
38. New York: Columbia University Press, 1981.
39. Glencoe, Ill.: Free Press, 1953.
40. New York: Columbia University Press, 1990.
41. Toronto: Lester and Orpen Dennys, 1990.
42. Ed. Moses Rischin (Detroit: Wayne State University Press, 1987).
43. New York: Schocken, 1976.

part 2, and Howard M. Sachar, *A History of Israel from the Rise of Zionism to Our Time*,[44] chs. 2, 4–7. A classic study of immigrant absorption is S. N. Eisenstadt, *The Absorption of Immigrants: A Comparative Study Based Mainly on the Jewish Community in Palestine and the State of Israel*.[45] One of the most notable biographies that brings this era to life is *Berl: The Biography of a Socialist Zionist*,[46] by Anita Shapira. There is a rich literature mainly in Hebrew on subthemes, ranging from social experiments such as the kibbutz to the creation of the Jewish infrastructure in Palestine; and there are works on the cultural creativity of the first Hebrew immigrants to the despair, suicide, and reemigration of others. Still, it is noteworthy that we have few anthropological studies of East European immigrant populations that settled in Palestine to match the rich work on their non-Ashkenazi counterparts.

In concluding this survey of literature, it is noteworthy that the greatest strides in scholarship have been made in our understanding of Jewish immigrants from Eastern Europe as they made their way in specific lands. Few works, however, venture a comparative perspective, even in analyzing a specific theme. (A notable exception is Edward Bristow's useful overview of the international struggle against Jewish white slavery, *Prostitution and Prejudice: The Jewish Fight against White Slavery, 1870–1939*.[47]) As the literature on immigrants in particular lands has grown more extensive, there is a need for comparative and synthetic analyses that will examine the mass migration from an international perspective. We will need to consider comparative issues ranging from labor history to the history of restrictionism, from studies of governmental responses to analyses of how different Jewries responded to the arrival of immigrant Jews. Finally, there is a need to compare the immigration experiences and adaptations of East European Jews who settled in Palestine with those who settled in Western lands: specifically, were the former so different by virtue of their ideological commitments that any comparisons are misleading; or conversely, are the first waves of aliyot more readily understood in the context of other migrations by East European Jews?

Since the era of great migration from Eastern Europe, world Jewry has witnessed three successive eras of mass migration. (1) During the thirties and forties, victims of Nazi persecution fled to havens of rescue, while others were denied the opportunity to migrate and consequently perished. Their experiences are discussed in other essays in this volume—principally, Marsha

44. New York: Knopf, 1976.
45. Glencoe, Ill: Free Press, 1955.
46. Cambridge: Cambridge University Press, 1984.
47. London: Oxford University Press, 1982.

Rozenblit, "The Holocaust"; Chaim Waxman, "Israeli Society and Culture"; and Stuart Schoenfeld, "American and Canadian Jewish Sociology." (2) During the same era and into the fifties, aliyah to Palestine and later Israel became a significant factor due to persecutions in Europe and Arab lands. References to these migrations may be found in essays herein: Jane Gerber, "Jews in Muslim Lands"; Sergio DellaPergola, "Jewish Demography"; and the aforementioned essays of Schoenfeld and Waxman. (3) Since the 1960s, international migration has continued with the largest numbers of Jewish emigrants departing from the former Soviet Union for Israel and Western lands, another significant population has emigrated from Israel to Europe and the United States, and smaller populations have fled Iran, Rhodesia, South Africa, and Latin American dictatorships. (See the essay herein of DellaPergola.) The collapse of Communism has set in motion yet another wave of emigration, principally of Jews fleeing from rising levels of antisemitism, political instability, and economic chaos. Although numerically the emigration from the Soviet Union is most significant, we should not overlook the stirring exodus of Jews from Ethiopia to Israel. As emigration from the former Soviet Union grows, it will continue an eastward movement that began ever so tentatively over three hundred fifty years ago, surged between 1880 and 1920, and was suspended for several decades by totalitarian regimes that have now fallen. After a hiatus of several decades, the mass migration of East European Jews has resumed.

Suggested Themes for Class Discussions

The mass migration of East European Jews provides rich opportunities for comparative discussions in courses. Three themes are particularly worthwhile: (1) a comparison of Jewish immigrants' lives in several Western lands, (2) a discussion of how immigrations affected native Jewish communites, and (3) an exploration of the role of Jewish immigration in the transfer of Jewish culture and the creation of new cultural forms.

The first of these three class sessions could draw on the tables in *The Jew in the Modern World: A Documentary History*,[48] which provide information on the scale of migration, occupations of Jews, and so on. Friesel (n. 1) offers additional tables and graphics to illustrate shifts in geographic concentration. The class discussion can then compare the dimensions of immigration to various lands and the possible role of population size in determining how immigrant Jews fared; a comparison of occupations will illuminate general patterns

48. Ed. Paul Mendes-Flohr and Jehuda Reinharz (New York: Oxford University Press, 1980).

of adaptation and economic choices; and there can be discussion of worker movements and immigrant mutual aid societies. Useful documents on the latter themes are found in Mendes-Flohr and Reinharz (n. 48), part 9, documents 12–20; chapters may be assigned from studies of Eastern Jews in France (Hyman [n. 18]), Germany (Wertheimer [n. 21]), England (Ceserani [n. 12]), and Argentina (Victor Mirelman, *Jewish Buenos Aires 1890–1930: In Search of Identity*[49]).

A second class can analyze the relationship between immigrants and their new environments. A comparative discussion of how various governments and societies responded to the immigrants will provide a useful perspective for an understanding of antisemitism. It can also illuminate the extent to which societies viewed themselves as a haven of refuge for victims. (Chapters from books on different countries could be assigned—e.g., Garrard [n. 16], Higham [n. 27], Wertheimer [n. 21].) Courses conducted in the United States may compare the American treatment of foreigners in theory and practice, as well as how Americans and other nations viewed immigration. The rest of the class session can examine how native Jews responded to the newcomers. Several documents in Mendes-Flohr and Reinharz (n. 48) illuminate the American setting (part 10, documents 21, 24–29). The works cited in the paragraph above contain ample chapters on the interactions of natives and immigrants.

A third class session could explore questions of cultural transfer and transformation. Specifically, how did Yiddish culture fare in new settings? What cultural and ideological baggage did East European Jews bring with them to new environments? And how were new cultural and religious syntheses negotiated when immigrant and native Jewish cultures collided? To highlight the transfer of culture, chapters may be assigned from Howe (n. 29), as well as the works of Gartner (n. 10) and Green (n. 17). Memoir literature is especially rich on the role of immigrant Jews in the spread of Zionism among native Jewish youth: the middle chapters of Gershom Scholem, *From Berlin to Jerusalem*,[50] may be assigned. On the clash of cultures, chapters may be assigned from books by Aschheim (n. 20) and Hyman (n. 18). Finally, there are several extraordinary novels that depict the upheaval in family life and traditional patterns wrought by the mass migration; see especially Henry Roth, *Call It Sleep*;[51] Anzia Yezierska, *Bread Givers*;[52] and Ephraim Lisitzky, *In the Grip of Cross-Currents*.[53]

49. Detroit: Wayne State University Press, 1990.
50. New York: Schocken, 1980.
51. 1934; New York: Avon, 1962.
52. Garden City, N.Y.: Doubleday, Page, 1925; repr. New York: Persea, 1975.
53. Trans. Moshe Kohn and Jacob Sloan (New York: Bloch, 1959).

16. Modern Antisemitism and Jewish Responses

Marsha L. Rozenblit

The shock of the Holocaust, the sheer fact that the Nazi regime had annihilated between five and six million European Jews in a systematic, bureaucratic, and utterly rational manner, precipitated an immediate inquiry into its root causes. Obviously, antisemitism—hatred of the Jews—had fueled Nazi success. The Nazis themselves had always espoused viscious anti-Jewish animosity, and their antisemitic ravings had found a ready ear in the large segment of the German population that had voted for them in the early 1930s. Even if the Germans who voted for the Nazis did not share all of Hitler's anti-Jewish views, clearly Nazi antisemitism did not repel them either. More importantly, the fact that the Nazis were so successful in deporting the Jews from most European countries to the death camps, often with the active cooperation of local populations, revealed that anti-Jewish animosity was widespread in European society. Nazi antisemitism may have been unique in its desire to murder the Jews, but a general willingness to believe antisemitic myths clearly helped the Nazis realize their goal.

The realization that the Holocaust could not just be blamed on a few crazy Nazis but that European civilization itself bore significant responsibility for Nazi genocide prompted a great deal of soul-searching in the immediate aftermath of World War II. Philosophers and social critics like Jean-Paul Sartre in France and Hannah Arendt in the United States attempted to come to grips with the phenomenon of antisemitism. In his powerful 1948 essay *Antisemite and Jew*,[1] Sartre explained antisemitism as a psychological phenomenon which permits the unsuccessful individual to blame an outsider for his own inadequacies. While castigating European society for using Jews as a scapegoat, Sartre argued that the solution was total Jewish assimilation and the disappearance of the Jews as a distinct group. On the other hand, Hannah Arendt's magnum opus *The Origins of Totalitarianism*[2] essentially blamed the Jews for antisemitism. She argued that the Jewish alliance with the nation-state and in particular with liberalism in the nineteenth century had been a misguided strategy which left the Jews defenseless against the illiberal forces which had come to dominate European society.

In response to the Holocaust and to the arguments of Sartre and Arendt, scholars for the past four decades have tried to explain the causes of European antisemitism. Since the main impetus to these studies has been the attempt to understand the Holocaust, these scholars have generally not focused on traditional Christian anti-Jewish polemic and the persistence of that polemic in a secular age. The Nazis, after all, represented an anti-Christian, pagan trend in European society, and they did not draw on religious arguments against the Jews. Instead, scholars have devoted their attention to "modern" antisemitism, that is, to the eruption of antisemitic movements in Western and Central Europe beginning in the late 1870s. These movements, coming in the wake of Emancipation and the extension to the Jews of full civil rights and equality in the countries in which they lived, represented a backlash against modernity and viewed the Jews as the embodiment of that hated modernity. Whether in France, Germany, Austria, or Hungary, antisemites blamed the Jews for all the ills of modern society: for the dislocations caused by capitalism, industrialization, and urbanization, and for the problems generated by liberalism and parliamentary democracy. Antisemites yearned for a premodern utopia, a place which existed, of course, only in their imaginations. In Germany, Austria, and Hungary antisemites even organized political parties which garnered significant numbers of voters, chiefly but not exclusively among the lower middle class of artisans and shopkeepers. These parties demanded that Jews be eliminated from public life and be reduced to second-class citizens. Their belligerent demagoguery on the streets and in parliaments accustomed people to antisemitic invective and helped make antisemitism "respectable." In Vienna, where political antisemitism achieved its greatest successes, the antisemitic Christian Social Party won a majority of seats on the city council and dominated urban political life after the 1890s.

1. Trans. George J. Becker (New York: Schocken, 1948).
2. New York: Harcourt, Brace, 1951.

Besides channeling resentment of modernity against the Jews, modern antisemitism also developed two new arguments. In the first place, many antisemites argued that the Jews were conspiring to destroy Western civilization. Through control of politics, culture, the press, and the economy, Jews sought to dominate and then destroy European society. Such works as *The Protocols of the Elders of Zion* or *La France juive* by Eduard Drumont characterized the Jews as rapacious capitalists and liberals, and as revolutionary Communists destroying all that was noble in human society. Even more ominously, other antisemites developed full-blown racial theories which not only viewed the Jews as an inferior race, but which held that this "Semitic" race was the avowed enemy of the "Aryan" race which it sought to destroy. Racial antisemites heralded an approaching apocalytpic struggle between the forces of light and goodness, the Aryans, and the forces of darkness and evil, the Semites, and they feared that the Aryans would lose this struggle to the all-powerful Semites who would then utterly destroy the world. All antisemites, however, agreed that the Jews were not really members of European society but were strangers, foreigners, and outsiders par excellence.

Since the conspiratorial and racial theories of nineteenth-century antisemitism, as well as widespread desire to blame the Jews for all the problems of society, had so obviously influenced Hitler and the Nazis in their world view, historians have tried to explain why such antisemitism flourished in the late nineteenth century. Because of the pan-European nature of this antisemitism, historians have wisely not limited themselves to understanding only German and Austrian antisemitism. Some historians have sought a socioeconomic explanation, others a political explanation, still others a psychopolitical or pschyosocial explanation, and others an explanation which combines all the above factors.

The earliest explanations of "modern" antisemitism to appear in the literature relied on a socioeconomic understanding of the appeal of that antisemitism. Paul Massing, *Rehearsal for Destruction: A Study of Political Anti-Semitism in Imperial Germany*,[3] for example, argued that the proliferation of antisemitic political parties in Germany at the end of the nineteenth century was due to the enormous resentment of the lower middle class, the *Mittelstand*, to capitalism, industrialization, and modernity. Artisans and shopkeepers feared that such new economic institutions as factories and department stores would force them out of business and hence out of the ranks of the middle class and into the ranks of the proletariat. They expressed their status anxiety in antisemitic invective, blaming the Jews for the competition caused by

3. New York: Harper, 1949.

136   *Marsha L. Rozenblit*

capitalism. Jews, disproportionately represented in the ranks of entrepreneurs and traditionally associated in European consciousness with money, provided a ready target. For a more recent study of artisanal economic antisemitism, see Shulamit Volkov, *The Rise of Popular Antimodernism in Germany: The Urban Master Artisans, 1873–1896.*[4] This socioeconomic interpretation is present even in the works which present other arguments about the rise and success of antisemitism.

While the socioeconomic argument is important, it does not explain why many upper middle class Europeans also subscribed to antisemitic myths. Thus, many historians argue that modern antisemitism can only be understood in political terms, that is, within the context of the rejection of liberalism by certain sectors of society in the late nineteenth century. The chief exponent of this view is Peter Pulzer, *The Rise of Political Anti-Semitism in Germany and Austria.*[5] Middle class Europeans who resented parliamentary democracy and such liberal values as free trade, equality before the law, anticlericalism, and freedom both blamed the Jews for the problems of liberalism and sought to destroy the liberal system itself. The Jews, who supported liberalism and relied on it for their newly won rights, provided a convenient target for the forces which opposed liberalism. Many local studies of antisemitism, such as Robert Brynes, *Antisemitism in Modern France*;[6] Stephen Wilson, *Ideology and Experience: Antisemitism in France at the Time of the Dreyfus Affair*;[7] Richard A. Levy, *The Downfall of the Anti-Semitic Political Parties in Imperial Germany*;[8] Reinhard Rürup, *Emanzipation und Antisemitismus: Studien zur 'Judenfrage' in der bürgerlichen Gesellschaft*;[9] and John Boyer, *Political Radicalism in Late Imperial Vienna: Origins of the Christian Social Movement, 1848–1897*,[10] essentially view antisemitism as a tool of illiberal forces in late nineteenth century Europe.

Still another approach to antisemitism views the movement in psychopolitical terms. George Mosse, for example in *The Crisis of German Ideology*[11] and also in *Toward the Final Solution: A History of European Racism*,[12] argued that many Germans, unhappy with the form that German unity had

4. Princeton: Princeton University Press, 1978.
5. New York: Wiley, 1964; rev. ed., Cambridge: Harvard University Press, 1988.
6. New Brunswick, N.J.: Rutgers University Press, 1950.
7. Rutherford, N.J.: Fairleigh Dickinson University Press, 1982.
8. New Haven: Yale University Press, 1975.
9. Göttingen: Vandenhoek & Ruprecht, 1975.
10. Chicago: University of Chicago Press, 1981.
11. New York: Grosset and Dunlap, 1964; rev. ed., New York: Schocken, 1981.
12. New York: Fertig, 1979.

taken in 1870, sought a more meaningful sense of community in a glorification of the German *Volk* (people). This *völkisch* ideology developed into a full-fledged racism which not only lauded such so-called Germanic virtues as rootedness, creativity, industriousness, honesty, and spirituality, but also denigrated the Jews as the antithesis of the German/Aryan race. Rejecting modernity as bourgeois and boring, young university students in particular sought fulfillment as part of the German *Volk* and they attacked the Jews, whom they depicted as dry, dessicated, hyperrational wanderers, as their eternal enemies. Important studies of this form of racism include such works as Fritz Stern, *The Politics of Cultural Despair*;[13] Uriel Tal, *Christians and Jews in Germany: Religion, Politics, and Ideology in the Second Reich*;[14] Geoffrey G. Field, *Evangelist of Race: The Germanic Vision of Houston Stewart Chamberlain*;[15] and Konrad Jarausch, *Students, Society, and Politics in Imperial Germany: The Rise of Academic Illiberalism*.[16] Psychological dissatisfaction with politics and a yearning for Germanic glory also explains support for the Austrian Pan-German antisemitic movement of Georg von Schönerer. On this movement see Andrew Whiteside, *The Socialism of Fools: Georg Ritter von Schönerer and Austrian Pan-Germanism*.[17] An important early study which also viewed antisemitism in psychological terms is Eva Reichmann, *Hostages of Civilization: The Social Sources of National Socialist Anti-Semitism*.[18]

Recently some historians have recognized the importance of the persistence of Christian hostility toward the Jews for the antisemitic movements of the late nineteenth century. Jacob Katz, *From Prejudice to Destruction: Anti-Semitism, 1700–1933*,[19] argues quite convincingly that traditional religious attitudes toward the Jews fueled much of modern antisemitism, even if the new antisemites stripped their arguments of their original religious language. This argument, of course, is not new. Already in 1943 Joshua Trachtenberg, *The Devil and the Jews*,[20] had revealed the continuties between Medieval and modern antisemitic images of the Jew as nonhuman outsider. Moreover, in her important 1956 study *Er ist wie Du: Aus der Frühgeschichte des Antisemitismus in Deutschland (1815–1850)*,[21] Eleonore Sterling had argued that early

13. New York: Doubleday, 1961.
14. Ithaca: Cornell University Press, 1975.
15. New York: Columbia University Press, 1981.
16. Princeton: Princeton University Press, 1982.
17. Berkeley and Los Angeles: University of California Press, 1975.
18. London: Gollancz, 1949.
19. Cambridge: Harvard University Press, 1980.
20. New Haven: Yale University Press, 1943.
21. Munich: Kaiser, 1956.

nineteenth century malcontents used Medieval myths about the Jews in their critique of modern society. In addition, all scholars recognize that traditional Christian views influenced the attitudes of East Europeans toward the Jews in the nineteenth and twentieth centuries.

The Jewish response to antisemitism has also been the subject of a great deal of historical inquiry in years since World War II. Most European Jews remained essentially passive in the face of antisemitic movements in France, Germany, and Austria. Regarding antisemitism as some sort of anachronistic holdover from premodern times or else a foreign import, many Jewish leaders felt that treating it with the silence of disdain was their best policy. They coupled their refusal to engage in public defense of Jewish interests with assertions of loyalty to and identity with their respective countries. They also preferred to rely on gentiles to speak out against antisemitism, fearing that they would only exacerbate antisemitism if they spoke out in their own defense. Nevertheless, in Germany and Austria Jews did form defense organizations which launched public campaigns against antisemitism and battled the antisemites in the courts.

Much of the original scholarship, following both the Zionist ideology of the late nineteenth century and the charges of Hannah Arendt, presented Jewish behavior in an essentially negative light. Although the policy of reliance on republican institutions and gentile public opinion actually worked in France, Michael Marrus criticized this policy in *The Politics of Assimilation: French Jewry at the Time of the Dreyfus Affair.*[22] Similarly, Yehuda Reinharz, *Fatherland or Promised Land: The Dilemma of the German Jew, 1893–1914,*[23] criticized German Jews for their undying love of *Deutschtum* (Germanness) in the face of antisemitic attack, and he viewed the German-Jewish defense organization solely in terms of their attempts to foster German consciousness among German Jews.

On the other hand, other scholars have regarded the German and Austrian defense organizations quite positively, not just as an activist response to antisemitism, but also internally as an important vehicle of post-Emancipation Jewish identity. Leading the way in this direction was Ismar Schorsch, *Jewish Reactions to German Anti-Semitism, 1870–1914,*[24] which argued that the German-Jewish defense organization—the Centralverein deutscher Staatsbürger jüdischen Glaubens (Central Organization of German Citizens of the Jewish Faith)—served an important function in bolstering Jewish pride and Jewish

22. New York: Oxford University Press, 1971.
23. Ann Arbor: University of Michigan Press, 1975.
24. New York: Columbia University Press, 1972.

culture in Imperial Germany. Similarly, Marsha Rozenblit, *The Jews of Vienna, 1867–1914: Assimilation and Identity*,[25] and Robert Wistrich, *The Jews of Vienna in the Age of Franz Joseph*,[26] see the parallel Austrian Jewish organization, the Austrian Israelite Union, as performing the same function in augmenting Jewish pride and a sense of separate Jewish identity in the face of antisemitic attack in Austria. Thus antisemitism served to propel Jews into a more public assertion of Jewishness than the ideology of Emancipation had dictated earlier in the nineteenth century.

The Zionist movement was yet another Jewish response to antisemitism in Western and Central Europe. For the historiography of Zionism see the essay by Gideon Shimoni in this volume.

To prepare a unit on antisemitism and the Jewish response for a course on the Modern Jewish Experience, the instructor would do well to read several of the major works on antisemitism cited above. In particular, I would recommend Pulzer (n. 5), Katz (n. 19), Mosse (n. 11), Wilson (n. 7), and Boyer (n. 10). On the Jewish response I would recommend Schorsch (n. 24) and Wistrich (n. 26), pp. 190–202, or Rozenblit (n. 25), pp. 154–61.

The best assignments for students would include Pulzer (n. 5; now in paperback) or Mosse (n. 11) and selections from several antisemitic texts of the late nineteenth century. In the sourcebook prepared by Paul Mendes-Flohr and Yehuda Reinharz, *The Jew in the Modern World*,[27] there are many selections from antisemitic writers of the period. Students should read and discuss the selections from Heinrich Treitschke, Adolf Stöcker, *The Protocols of the Elders of Zion*, and several others. The best pedagogic policy would be to present the major arguments of the antisemites and then try to deal with the causes for the eruption of this movement at the end of the nineteenth century.

25. Albany: State University of New York Press, 1983.
26. Oxford: Oxford University Press, 1989.
27. New York: Oxford University Press, 1980.

17. The Holocaust

Marsha L. Rozenblit

The Holocaust, the annihilation of European Jewry by the Nazis during World War II, is a central event both in Jewish and in German, indeed all European, history. Because of its centrality and power, it presents many difficult challenges to the instructor in a course on the Modern Jewish Experience. Although the events of the Holocaust call into question the very nature of Jewish–gentile relations in the Modern period, the Holocaust was not inevitable or predetermined. Thus any presentation of the Holocaust must place it within the specific social and political context in which it occurred. Students must understand both the nature of European Jewish life and why Nazi ideology flourished in order to come to grips with the behavior of the perpetrators, the victims, and the witnesses of the Holocaust. The Holocaust was no abstract example of racial hatred run rampant, but rather a specific event which occurred in a specific time and place.

Any study of the Holocaust must focus on certain key issues. In the first place, why did the Nazis want to kill the Jews? Prior to the Nazis, although antisemitism had developed an elaborate ideology which depicted the Jews as the enemies of the human race, no antisemites had ever even considered, let alone attempted, a systematic policy of annihilation. Nineteenth-century antisemites had blamed the Jews for all the ills of modern society: for the problems caused by modernization, industrialization, capitalism, urbanization, parliamentary democracy, and liberalism. Racial antisemites viewed the Jews as the racial enemy of the "Aryans," the forces of darkness and sterility who were seeking to destroy the forces of light, creativity, and goodness, and they spoke of an apocalyptic struggle between the Aryans and the Semites. Many antisemites argued that the Jews were conspiring to destroy Western civilization. Their solution to the "Jewish Problem," however, was simply to reduce the visibility and civil rights of the Jews. Hitler and the Nazis did not invent any new antisemitic arguments; they fervently believed all the racial and conspiratorial arguments made by antisemites before them. Yet they took these arguments to their logical conclusions and murdered all the Jews of Europe in order to find a "Final Solution to the Jewish Problem."

Why and when the Nazis decided to murder the Jews is a very controversial subject in scholarship on the Holocaust. One group of historians, the "intentionalists," argues that mass murder was always what Hitler and the Nazis indended to do, but they waited to implement their policy until conditions were ripe, that is, during World War II itself. The major exponents of this "intentionalist" school include Lucy Dawidowicz, *The War Against the Jews, 1933–1945;*[1] Gerald Fleming, *Hitler and the Final Solution;*[2] and Eberhard Jäckel, *Hitler's Weltanschauung: A Blueprint for Power.*[3] Other historians, the "functionalists," argue that while Hitler and the Nazis always hated the Jews and wanted to persecute them, they only decided to murder the Jews when they realized that their earlier policies—restricting Jewish rights, forcing Jews out of the German economy (Aryanization), forced emigration from Germany, and mass evacuation of the Jews of Europe to the island of Madagascar—did not "solve" the Jewish problem for them. Karl Schleunes, *The Twisted Road to Auschwitz,*[4] for example, clearly demonstrates that in the 1930s the Nazis possessed no master plan of annihilation but rather moved from policy to policy according to the needs of the moment and the struggle for power within the Nazi hierarchy. The functionalist argument about the Final Solution itself has been ably presented by Martin Broszat, "Hitler and the Genesis of the Final Solution";[5] Hans Mommsen, "The Realization of the Unthinkable: 'The Final Solution of the Jewish Question in the Third Reich'";[6] and Christopher Browning, *Fateful Months: Essays on the Emergence of the Final Solution.*[7] Recent biographies of Nazi leaders, like Richard Breitman's study of Heinrich Himmler, *The Architect of Genocide: Himmler and the Final Solution,*[8] shed important light on this dilemma.

The evidence, of course, is terribly problematic. In *Mein Kampf,*[9] Hitler

1. New York: Holt, Rinehart and Winston, 1975.
2. Berkeley and Los Angeles: University of California Press, 1984.
3. Middletown, Conn.: Wesleyan University Press, 1972.
4. Urbana: University of Illinois Press, 1970.
5. *Yad Vashem Studies* 13 (1979): 73–125.
6. In *The Politics of Genocide: Jews and Soviet Prisoners of War in Nazi Germany*, ed. Gerhard Hirschfeld (London: Allen & Unwin,1986), pp. 93–144.
7. New York: Holmes and Meier, 1985.
8. New York: Knopf, 1991.
9. Trans. Ralph Manheim (Boston: Houghton Mifflin, 1953).

had spoken in vague and general terms about eliminating the Jews, but readers did not necessarily take him to mean that he wanted to kill the Jews. Moreover, in the 1930s Nazi policy toward the Jews did not indicate any murderous intent. In those years the Nazis merely stripped Jews of their rights and possessions and urged them to leave Germany. Even when World War II began, the Nazis did not immediately begin a policy of annihilation but rather only concentrated the Jews in ghettos, and only in Poland. On the other hand, in 1941 the Nazis did decide to murder the Jews of Europe, and such a policy obviously did not simply appear out of nowhere. In all likelihood, a middle position between the intentionalists and the functionalists is closest to the truth. That is, Hitler and his closest associates wanted to eliminate the Jews utterly, but they only realized that this meant that they had to develop a master plan to murder the Jews when they encountered the reality of millions of East European Jews during Germany's conquest of Europe during World War II. In any case, the Holocaust derived from Hitler's own paranoid world view.

How Hitler and the Nazis succeeded in imposing that world view on millions of Germans is the second question which any study of the Holocaust must address. The answer to this question is not particularly controversial. Most historians agree that the dilemmas of Germany in the 1920s and 1930s— humiliating defeat in World War I, resentment of the Treaty of Versailles which rendered Germany's army nearly impotent and stripped Germany of some of her territory, a huge burden of wartime reparations to England and France, enormous economic problems caused by the inflation of the 1920s and especially by the world depression of the 1930s, and the weaknesses of the Weimar government—led many people to vote for the Nazis in the hope that this young, energetic party would solve Germany's problems and restore her glory. Good books on the Nazis and on their electorate include Michael Kater, *The Nazi Party: A Social Profile of Members and Leaders, 1919–1945*,[10] and Thomas Childers, *The Nazi Voter: The Social Foundations of Fascism in Germany, 1919–1933*.[11] Once in power, of course, the Nazis created a totalitarian dictatorship and used terror to enforce their will.

Still a third question raised by the Holocaust is simply how the Nazis managed to kill the Jews of Europe. The best and most important study of how the Nazis implemented mass murder is still Raul Hilberg, *The Destruction of the European Jews*,[12] now in a revised edition. Indeed, Hilberg, a political scientist, effectively launched Holocaust historiography. In clearly written, meticu-

10. Cambridge: Harvard University Press, 1983.
11. Chapel Hill: University of North Carolina Press, 1983.
12. Chicago: Quadrangle, 1961; rev. ed., 3 vols., New York: Holmes and Meier, 1985.

lous detail, Hilberg analyzed how the Nazi bureaucracy planned and executed the Holocaust in general and in every country of Nazi-occupied Europe. In so doing, he revealed the extent to which the regular German bureaucrats in the Railroad, Finance, and Foreign Ministries—not to mention the Army— assisted Nazi ideologues in the Holocaust. Hilberg, incidentally, could be grouped with the "functionalists" mentioned above. That is, he sees the Nazis only turning to the Holocaust after abandoning other anti-Jewish policies.

Despite a huge outpouring of scholarship on the Holocaust since 1961, Hilberg's book has not been superseded as a general treatment of the destruction process. In the thirty years since his magnum opus was published, many books have appeared which have provided much greater detail on the process of destruction in different countries, but in general they do not contradict his evaluation of that process. These regional studies, however, do raise yet another very important question about the Holocaust: Why were the Nazis more successful in killing the Jews in some places than in other places? The Nazis succeeded in murdering nearly all the Jews of Poland, Germany, Czechoslovakia, and some of western Russia; most of the Jews in Hungary, Holland, and Greece; half the Jews in Norway, Rumania, and Yugoslavia; only a quarter of the Jews in France and Italy; and almost none of the Jews in Denmark. In *Accounting for Genocide: National Responses and Jewish Victimization during the Holocaust,*[13] sociologist Helen Fein tried to develop a formula which explained this phenomenon. Fein argued that Nazi success depended on the complex interplay of local antisemitism, degree of Nazi control over a given area, timing of the destruction process in relationship to the end of World War II, nature of anti-Nazi resistance, and degree of Jewish concentration. While these factors are obviously crucial, the formula is frankly too complicated. Actual local studies, which place Nazi policy firmly within the context of local conditions, are far more satisfying in their attemps to explain Nazi success or lack thereof.

Randolph Braham, *The Politics of Genocide: The Holocaust in Hungary*[14] shows how the antisemitic, right-wing governments of Hungary, an ally of Nazi Germany, implemented their own anti-Jewish policy but resisted Hitler's requests to deport the Jews until the Nazis simply occupied Hungary in 1944 and accomplished the job themselves. The Nazis only killed three-quarters of Hungarian Jewry because the war ended before they could finish. On the other hand, in Poland, which the Nazis controlled from 1939, and where they began to implement the Final Solution in 1942, no obstacles existed and they killed

13. New York: Free Press, 1979.
14. 2 vols. (New York: Columbia University Press, 1981).

all the Jews within a year. Yitzchak Arad, *Treblinka, Sobibor, Belzec: The Operation Reinhard Death Camps*,[15] reveals in excruciating detail how the Nazis easily deported all the Jews of Poland to the gas chambers. Michael Marrus and Robert Paxton, *Vichy France and the Jews*,[16] shows how the Vichy French government not only cooperated with the Nazis, but even anticipated Nazi requests and implemented its own extremely harsh anti-Jewish policy. Other important regional studies include Meir Michaelis, *Mussolini and the Jews: German–Italian Relations and the Jewish Question in Italy, 1922–1945*;[17] Leni Yahil, *The Rescue of Danish Jewry*;[18] and Jacob Presser, *Ashes in the Wind: The Destruction of the Dutch Jews.*[19]

Of course, the nature of Jewish response to the onslaught against them has been extremely controversial ever since the end of World War II and must be one of the major issues in academic discussion of the Holocaust. Raul Hilberg himself criticized the Jews both for their passivity in the face of the Nazis and for their cooperation in their own destruction. In particular, he charged the Jewish Councils, established by the Nazis to act as intermediary bodies between themselves and the Jews, with participating in the Holocaust by providing the Nazis with the lists of people for deportation and assisting in the round-ups of the Jews. Hannah Arendt, an important social critic, went even further than Hilberg in *Eichmann in Jerusalem*[20] and charged that without the cooperation of the Jewish Councils the Nazis would have murdered far fewer Jews.

In response to Hilberg's and Arendt's criticism of Jewish behavior during the Holocaust, many scholars attempted to understand the true nature of Jewish response to the Nazi assault. Most influential at helping us understand Jewish behavior has been Isaiah Trunk, *Judenrat: The Jewish Councils in Eastern Europe under Nazi Occupation*,[21] a detailed study of the Jewish Councils in the ghettos in Poland. Trunk tried to place the Jewish Councils within the context in which the Nazis placed them, a context in which members of the Councils had no alternative but to cooperate. Moreover, he amply demonstrates that members of the Jewish Councils worked very hard to save Jewish lives, trying to bargain with and bribe Nazi officials, and developing novel strategies for survival that included establishing factories and enmeshing the ghettos in the German war economy. Unfortunately, *Judenrat* strategy

15. Bloomington: Indiana University Press, 1987.
16. New York: Basic Books, 1981.
17. New York: Oxford University Press, 1978.
18. Philadelphia: Jewish Publication Society, 1969.
19. London: Souvenir, 1968.
20. New York: Viking, 1963.
21. New York: Macmillan, 1972.

mistakenly assumed that the Nazis were rational and would not want to kill those who provided them with cheap labor. Believing Nazi promises, *Judenrat* leaders also hoped that by sacrificing some Jewish lives they would be able to save most of the Jews of the ghettos. Trunk repeatedly reminds his readers that it is hard to use normal moral criteria when dealing with an utterly immoral enemy.

The literature on Jewish resistance to the Nazis is also a response to the charges about Jewish passivity. In addition to Reuben Ainsztein, *Jewish Resistance in Nazi-occupied Eastern Europe*,[22] many local studies deal with the issue at length. About two-thirds of Arad (n. 15) deals with resistance activities in Treblinka and Sobibor. Similarly, Yisrael Gutman, *The Jews of Warsaw, 1939–1943: Ghetto, Underground, Revolt*,[23] mostly covers the famous Warsaw Ghetto Uprising in April 1943. Many memoirs also deal with the subject.

Resistance, of course, was not typical, despite the pride many feel about acts of resistance. Most Jews merely tried to stay alive as best they could. The best scholarly treatment of such attempts, restricted only to the concentration camps, is Terrence Des Pres, *The Survivor: An Anatomy of Life in the Death Camps*.[24] But the large memoir literature, and the extant diaries of Holocaust victims, amply reveal a very strong will to survive and the resourceful ways people managed to do so. Such memoirs as Elie Wiesel, *Night*;[25] Primo Levi, *Survival in Auschwitz*;[26] Alexander Donat, *The Holocaust Kingdom*;[27] Nehama Tec, *Dry Tears*;[28] Samuel Willenberg, *Surviving Treblinka*;[29] Rudolf Vrba, *I Cannot Forgive*;[30] Isabella Leitner, *Fragments of Isabella*;[31] Aranka Siegel, *Upon the Head of a Goat*;[32] or diaries like Emanuel Ringelblum, *Notes from the Warsaw Ghetto*;[33] Chaim Kaplan, *Scroll of Agony*;[34] Abraham Lewin, *A Cup of Tears*;[35] or the *Warsaw Diary of Adam Czerniakow*[36] reveal

22. New York: Barnes and Noble, 1975.
23. Bloomington: Indiana University Press, 1982.
24. New York: Oxford University Press, 1976.
25. New York: Hill and Wang, 1960.
26. New York: Collier, 1961.
27. New York: Holocaust Library, 1978.
28. New York: Oxford University Press, 1984.
29. Oxford: Blackwell, 1989.
30. London: Sidgwick, Jackson, Gibbs and Phillips, 1964.
31. New York: Dell, 1978.
32. New York: Farrar, Straus and Giroux, 1981.
33. New York: Shocken, 1974.
34. New York: Macmillan, 1965.
35. Oxford: Blackwell, 1988.
36. New York: Stein and Day, 1979.

the excruciating dilemmas faced by Jews and how they attempted to live and survive.

The last set of questions concerns the behavior of the "witnesses" to the Holocaust, chiefly America, Great Britain, and the Vatican, in the face of Nazi anti-Jewish policy. In the 1930s, when the Nazis began to persecute the Jews of Germany, why were most countries of the world unwilling to admit large numbers of German Jewish refugees? During the war and the Final Solution, why were the Allies and the Vatican relatively indifferent to the fate of the Jews and uninterested in attempting to rescue the Jews of Europe? The answers to these questions must be sought, of course, in the political context of the 1930s and 1940s. Important books seeking to explain American policy include Henry Feingold, *The Politics of Rescue: The Roosevelt Administration and the Holocaust, 1938–1945;*[37] David Wyman, *Paper Walls: America and the Refugee Crisis 1938–1941*[38] and *The Abandonment of the Jews: America and the Holocaust, 1941–1945;*[39] and Richard Breitman and Alan Kraut, *American Refugee Policy and European Jewry, 1933–1945.*[40] On British policy, see Bernard Wasserstein, *Britain and the Jews of Europe, 1939–1945,*[41] and A. J. Sherman, *Island Refuge: Britain and the Refugees from the Third Reich, 1933–1939.*[42] John Morley, *Vatican Diplomacy and the Jews during the Holocaust, 1939–1943,*[43] tries to explain the unwillingness of the Catholic Church to take a stand against Nazi policy.

The instructor who wants to include the Holocaust in a curriculum on the Modern Jewish Experience thus has a lot of reading to do. For a general overview of the Nazi and the Jewish side of the Holocaust, Dawidowicz (n. 1) is the most important book to read, despite its troublesome implication that the Holocaust was inevitable. The instructor should also certainly read Hilberg (n. 12), Schleunes (n. 4), Fein (n. 13), Trunk (n. 21), Des Pres (n. 24), Wyman (n. 39), and several memoirs, in particular Donat (n. 27), Levi (n. 26), and Ringelblum (n. 33).

Given the fact that the Holocaust will probably be treated in two or three lectures, I would recommend assigning the students only one book, preferably one of the memoirs. Donat (n. 27) is a perfect choice since it covers a variety of experiences: in the Warsaw Ghetto, in the Resistance, and in the concentra-

37. New Brunswick, N.J.: Rutgers University Press, 1970.
38. Amherst: University of Massachusetts Press, 1968.
39. New York: Pantheon, 1984.
40. Bloomington: Indiana University Press, 1987.
41. New York: Oxford University Press, 1979.
42. Berkeley and Los Angeles: University of California Press, 1973.
43. New York: Ktav, 1980.

tion camps. It is also extremely well written and moving, providing very deep insights into how Jews experienced the Holocaust. If the instructor prefers a textbook-type assignment, the best textbooks on the subject of the Holocaust are Leni Yahil, *The Holocaust: The Fate of European Jewry*,[44] and Yehuda Bauer, *A History of the Holocaust*.[45] Dawidowicz (n. 1) could also work for better students. Frankly, reading a memoir will leave a more lasting impression.

44. New York: Oxford University Press, 1990.
45. New York: Watts, 1980.

Religious and Ideological Movements

18. Hasidism and Its Opponents

David E. Fishman

A recent survey of scholarship on Hasidism suggested that no field in Jewish studies has undergone such thorough revision and transformation during the last decade as this one. Old conventional wisdoms have been undermined, and a whole new set of questions has been raised. Meanwhile, the author of another critical review of the historiography contends that nearly all the work done on Hasidism to date is impressionistic and methodologically flawed and suggests that the field should start from scratch all over again. (Morris M. Faierstein, "Hasidism: the Last Decade in Research";[1] Zeev Gries, "Hasidism: The Present State of Research and Some Desirable Priorities."[2]) When scholars talk about a field in such terms, it is a sure sign of ferment and growth. And indeed, measured by any criteria (the number of specialists, articles, and monographs; the proliferation of undergraduate courses and compendia of Hasidic sources), the study of Hasidism has come into its own.

This movement of mysticism and religious revivalism, centering around the charismatic leadership of the *tzadik* or *rebbe*, emerged in the Ukraine in the middle of the eighteenth century. Students of Jewish history and religion have focused their attention primarily on Hasidism's early history, in the period of its founder, Rabbi Israel Baal Shem Tov (1700–1760), and in the period of its expansion and classical literary creativity (ca. 1760–1815). A number of sociologists and anthropologists have studied contemporary Hasidic communities in North America and Israel. But scholarly research on the intermediate phases of the movement's history, between 1815 and the 1960s, is only in its infancy.

1. *Modern Judaism* 11/1 (1991): 111–24.
2. *Numen* 34/1 (1987): 97–108, 34/2: 179–213.

For the English reader, the best entree into the history of Hasidism, its religious ideas and practices, and the body of modern scholarship in this area is *Essential Papers on Hasidism: Origins to Present.*[3] *Essential Papers* includes lengthy selections from Shimon Dubnow's classical history of the movement (translated from the Hebrew), a sample of Gershom Scholem's scholarship on Hasidic mysticism, and studies by the historians Benzion Dinur, Shmuel Ettinger, and Raphael Mahler on the position of the Hasidic movement in Jewish society in the eighteenth and nineteenth centuries. The volume also features recent work by Ada Rapoport-Albert and Murray J. Rosman, which exemplify the methodological care and revisionist tendency of the "new scholarship." (Current research in this field is richly represented in a volume of *Polin: A Journal of Polish-Jewish Studies* entitled "Hasidism Reconsidered."[4])

In the absence of a book-length history of Hasidism in English, readers seeking an overview of major personalities, trends, and events should consult Israel Zinberg, *History of Jewish Literature*, vol. 9[5] (strongly influenced by Dubnow in its approach), and Harry Rabinowicz, *Hasidism: The Movement and Its Masters*[6] (unsophisticated in method, but comprehensive in scope). For many Hasidic figures of the eighteenth and nineteenth centuries, the only available resource in English is Martin Buber's two-volume collection of legends, *Tales of The Hasidim.*[7] The latter, however, should be used with extreme caution, since Buber's *Tales* are actually a recasting and reinterpretation of the Hasidic source materials.

The central figure in the movement's history, Rabbi Israel Baal Shem Tov (also known as "The Baal Shem Tov," and abbreviated as "the Besht") is shrouded in mystery. The Baal Shem Tov left no writings of his own, and the primary source of information on his life is a hagiographic work composed more than half a century after his demise—*In Praise of the Ba'al Shem Tov.*[8] The "quest for the historical Baal Shem Tov" has thus been a major preoccupation of Hasidic scholarship. (For a critical review of this effort, see Murray J. Rosman's article by that name in *Tradition and Crisis Revisited.*[9]) Dubnow's presentation (n. 3) remains a good point of departure, but the Besht's

3. Ed. Gershon D. Hundert (New York: New York University Press, 1991).
4. Ed. Ada Rapoport-Albert (forthcoming).
5. Cincinnati: Hebrew Union College Press; New York: Ktav, 1976.
6. Northvale, N.J.: Aronson, 1988.
7. New York: Schocken, 1975.
8. Ed. and trans. Dan Ben-Amos and Jerome Mintz (Bloomington: Indiana University Press, 1970).
9. Harvard Judaica Monographs (Cambridge: Harvard University Press, forthcoming).

role as mentor and teacher, and his mystical teachings per se, have been further elucidated by Joseph Weiss in several articles collected in his *Studies in East European Jewish Mysticism*[10] and by Emanuel Etkes, "Hasidism as a Movement: The First Stage."[11] Rosman's recent discovery of references to the Baal Shem Tov in Polish archival documents has shed new light on the latter's position in the Jewish community of Miedzyboz, "Miedzyboz and Rabbi Israel Baal Shem Tov."[12]

Since it is a movement centered around charismatic leaders and personalities, it is natural that much of the scholarly literature on Hasidism is in the form of critical biographical studies. For the undergraduate student, these may provide the most accessible introductions to the subject. Some of the best works of this genre are Abraham Joshua Heschel, *The Circle of the Baal Shem Tov*[13] (on three of the Besht's contemporaries); Samuel H. Dresner, *The Zaddik: The Doctrine of the Zaddik According to the Writings of Rabbi Yaakov Yosef of Polnoy*[14] (on a key figure in the generation after the Baal Shem Tov); and Arthur Green's magisterial *Tormented Master: A Life of Rabbi Nahman of Bratslav*,[15] a fascinating psychoreligious study of one of Hasidism's more vexing personalities.

The scholarly study of Hasidic mysticism and religion begins with the work of Gershom Scholem. His essay "Hasidism: The Latest Phase"[16] places Hasidism in the context of the history of kabbalah, by viewing the kabbalah of Isaac Luria (sixteenth century), Sabbatianism, and Hasidism as three stages in an unfolding development. Specific themes discussed in that essay are developed more fully in Scholem's articles "The Neutralization of the Messianic Element in Hasidism," "Devekut, Or Communion With God," and his polemical piece concerning "Martin Buber's Interpretation of Hasidism."[17] Scholem's contribution to Hasidic scholarship revolves around these three themes of Messianism, Devekut, and Tikkun ("the repairing of Divine sparks").

Scholem's disciples have delved into the varieties of Hasidic mystical theory and practice. For a sampling of their work, see Weiss (n. 10); Rivka Schatz

10. Ed. David Goldstein (New York: Oxford University Press, 1985).

11. In *Hasidism: Continuity or Innovation?*, ed. Bezalel Safran, Harvard Judaica Texts and Monographs (Cambridge: Harvard University Press, 1988), pp. 1–26.

12. In Hundert (n. 3), pp. 209–25.

13. Chicago: University of Chicago Press, 1985.

14. New York: Schocken, 1974.

15. New York: Schocken, 1981.

16. In *Major Trends in Jewish Mysticism* (Jerusalem: Schocken, 1941), pp. 325–50.

17. All in *The Messianic Idea in Judaism and Other Essays in Jewish Spirituality* (New York: Schocken, 1971).

Uffenheimer, "Contemplative Prayer in Hasidism";[18] Rachel Elior, "Habad: The Contemplative Ascent to God";[19] and Louis Jacobs, *Hasidic Prayer.*[20] Jacobs's book (a segment of which is included in Hundert [n. 3]) is the most accessible study for undergraduates and others without prior background. Naftali Loewenthal, *Communicating the Infinite: The Emergence of the Habad School,*[21] is the latest major work in the area of classical Hasidic thought.

The institution of the *tzadik* or *rebbe* is one of the hallmarks of Hasidism. The role of the *tzadik* as intermediary between heaven and earth, as expressed in Hasidic theory and practice, has been examined by Dresner (n. 14); Arthur Green, "Typologies of Leadership and the Hasidic Zaddiq";[22] and Aaron Wertheim, "The Hasid, the Zaddik, and Their Mutual Obligations."[23] There is also a more specialized study by Rachel Elior, "Between Yesh and Ayin: The doctine of the Zaddik in the Works of Jacob Isaac, the Seer of Lublin."[24]

The older historiography (Dubnow, Zinberg, S.A. Horodecki, and others) contended that Hasidism was a democratic and "populist" religious movement which elevated the religious dignity of "simple Jews," including that of women, and rejected the elitism of traditional rabbinic Judaism. This notion has been challenged in recent studies, including Ada Rapoport-Albert, "God and Zaddik as the Two Focal Points of Hasidic Worship,"[25] and with reference to the position of women, "On Women in Hasidism: S.A. Horodecky and the Maid of Ludmir Tradition."[26]

The Hasidic tale is a special topic which deserves to be singled out. Hasidism produced an abundant hagiographical literature, much of which is available in one form or another in English—*In Praise of the Ba' al Shem Tov* (n. 8); Buber (n. 7); Eli Wiesel, *Souls on Fire: Portraits and Legends of Hasidic Masters;*[27] and others. Telling tales in praise of the *tzadikim* became a sacred, indeeed ritualized, activity in Hasidism. The most extraordinary work of Hasidic storytelling is the collection of tales related by Rabbi Nahman of Bratslav (d. 1812), which are marked by their artistic sophistication and mys-

---

18. In *Studies in Mysticism and Religion Presented to Gershom G. Scholem* (Jerusalem: Hebrew University, 1968), pp. 209–26.

19. In *Jewish Spirituality*, ed. Arthur Green (New York: Crossroad, 1987), vol. 2, pp. 157–205.

20. Philadelphia: Jewish Publication Society; New York: Schocken, 1972.

21. Chicago: University of Chicago Press, 1990.

22. In Green (n. 19), vol. 2, pp. 127–56.

23. In Hundert (n. 3), pp. 372–400.

24. In *Jewish History: Essays in Honor of Chimen Abramsky*, ed. A. Rapoport-Albert and S. J. Zipperstein (London: Halban, 1988), pp. 393–455.

25. In Hundert (n. 3), pp. 299–329.

26. In Rapoport-Albert and Zipperstein (n. 24), pp. 495–525.

27. New York: Bibliophile, 1986.

tical profundity. *Nahman of Bratslav: The Tales*[28] provides a complete English translation with an excellent introduction and commentaries by Arnold J. Band, and a preface by Joseph Dan.

Selections from Hasidic homiletical literature are available in English translation in a variety of shapes and sizes. Joseph Dan, *The Teachings of Hasidism*,[29] consists of brief excerpts from the classics of Hasidic literature (until 1815) which are arranged in sections on God–Man–Israel, the Zaddik, and religious life. Louis Jacobs, *Hasidic Thought*,[30] offers the complete texts of select Hasidic homilies, ranging across the entire span of the movement's history. Louis Newman, *Hasidic Anthology*,[31] is a compendium of Hasidic aphorisms, short tales, and homilies about everything under the sun, drawn from a variety of primary, secondary, and tertiary sources. For the more serious student, there are several full-length treatises in English translation. Arthur Green's edition of the collected homilies of Menahem Nahum of Chernobyl, *Upright Practices: The Light of the Eyes*,[32] is an excellent specimen of the homiletical genre of Hasidic writing, with all its rhetorical creativity and religious depth. *Liqqute amarim (tanya)*[33] by Shneur Zalman of Liady, the founder of the Lubavitch Hasidic dynasty, is a more systematic work of Hasidic theology and ethics.

A fascinating subject, especially in light of today's interdenominational clashes in Judaism, is the virulent opposition to Hasidism which arose in Lithuania in the late eighteenth century and the campaign to eradicate the movement led by Rabbi Elijah of Vilna ("the Vilna Gaon," 1725–1796). For an outline of the main events in the conflict between Hasidim and Mitnaggedim ("opponents"), one should consult the overview in Bernard D. Weinryb, *The Jews of Poland*,[34] pp. 282–303. Mordechai Wilensky reviews the major allegations and criticisms against Hasidism which recur in the bans, letters, and controversialist literature of the period in "Hasidic–Mitnaggedic Polemics in the Jewish Communities of Eastern Europe."[35] Primary sources from this conflict are available in Walter Ackerman, *Out of Our People's Past*,[36] pp. 211–18.

The opposition to Hasidism was fueled by vested political interests con-

28. New York: Paulist Press, 1978.
29. New York: Behrman, 1983.
30. New York: Schocken, 1976.
31. New York: Schocken, 1963.
32. New York: Paulist Press, 1982.
33. Trans. Nissan Mindel, 2 parts (Brooklyn: Kehot, 1962–65).
34. Philadelphia: Jewish Publication Society, 1973.
35. In Hundert (n. 3), pp. 244–74.
36. New York: United Synagogue, 1977.

cerned about the weakening of the traditional loci of power and authority in the Jewish community. But there were also real differences between the religious outlooks of the two camps. Jacob Katz accentuates Hasidism's reordering of the traditional scale of values in the relevant chapters of *Tradition and Crisis*,[37] with religious enthusiasm and innerness taking priority over talmudic study and punctilious Halakhic observance. A comparison between the Baal Shem Tov and the Vilna Gaon reveals striking contrasts in these areas (as well as a few surprising similarities). For a portrait of the Gaon as an ascetic, recluse, and talmudist, see Louis Ginzberg's essay in *Students, Scholars, and Saints*.[38] Norman Lamm probes the religious thought of the Gaon's leading disciple, Rabbi Chaim of Volozhin, in *Torah Lishmah: Torah for Torah's Sake in the Works of Rabbi Hayyim of Volozhin and His Contemporaries*.[39] The lines of philosophical disagreement between the two religious trends are drawn sharply in Allan L. Nadler, *A Religion of Limits: The Theology of Mithnagdism*.[40]

There are few works of scholarly merit on Hasidism in the nineteenth and early twentieth centuries. Two noteworthy exceptions are Morris Faierstein, *All Is in the Hands of Heaven: The Teachings of Rabbi Mordechai Joseph Leiner of Izbica*,[41] and Nehemia Polen, "Divine Weeping: Rabbi Kalonymus Shapiro's Theology of Catastrophe in the Warsaw Ghetto."[42] Representative samples of later Hasidic thought can be found in Jacobs (n. 30). On Hasidism's virulent rejection of Zionism as a rebellion against God and the Messiah, see Ehud Luz, *Parallels Meet: Religion and Nationalism in the Early Zionist Movement*,[43] pp. 208–26, and Allan L. Nadler, "Piety and Politics: The Case of the Satmar Rebbe."[44]

The ability of contemporary Hasidic communities to resist the forces of modernity has attracted the attention of sociologists and anthropologists. The latter have studied Hasidic life in America utilizing interviews, fieldwork, and questionnaire surveys. Some of the more noteworthy studies are Jerome S. Mintz, *Legends of the Hasidim: An Introduction to Hasidic Culture and Oral Tradition in the New World*;[45] Solomon Poll, *The Hassidic Community of Wil-*

37. New York: Free Press of Glencoe, 1961.
38. (Lanham, Md.: University Press of America, 1985), pp. 125–44.
39. New York: Yeshiva University Press, 1989.
40. New York: Yeshiva University Press, 1993.
41. New York: Yeshiva University Press, 1989.
42. *Modern Judaism* 7/3 (1987): 253–69.
43. Philadelphia: Jewish Publication Society, 1988.
44. *Judaism* 31/2 (Spring 1982): 135–52.
45. Chicago: University of Chicago Press, 1968.

liamsburg;[46] and W. Shaffir, *Life in A Religious Community: The Lubavitcher Chassidim in Montreal.*[47] On Hasidim in contemporary Israeli society, see Menahem Friedman, "Haredim Confront the Modern City."[48]

In an introductory course on Modern Jewish History, it is probably most important to convey that Hasidism is not synonymous with traditional "orthodox" Judaism but is rather an innovative mystical movement which transformed Jewish religious and communal life in Eastern Europe. Many courses introduce Hasidism after discussing the Haskalah in Germany, in order to emphasize the divergent paths taken by West and East European Jewries in the eighteenth century. While the one came under the increasing influence of Englightenment and secularity, the other was engulfed by mysticism and religious revival. This sequence also lays the groundwork for explaining to students why the Haskalah was slow in making significant inroads into Poland and Russia. From this perspective, focusing on the movement's classical period rather than on its more recent stages seems totally appropriate.

There are, however, frameworks in which a broader treatment of Hasidism is possible. Courses on Judaism in Modern Times can include a unit on the history of Hasidism in the nineteenth and twentieth centuries, including its confrontation with modernity and transplantation to America and Israel. Courses on Contemporary Judaism are an appropriate context for studying Hasidic life from a sociological and anthropological perspective and can incorporate the conduct of original fieldwork. Indeed, any survey of contemporary Jewry should not neglect the Hasidic community, which remains a cultural and political force in the Jewish world today.

46. New York: Free Press of Glencoe, 1962.
47. Toronto: Holt, Rinehart, Winston of Canada, 1974.
48. *Studies in Contemporary Jewry* 2 (1986): 74–96.

19. Religious Movements in Nineteenth- and Twentieth-Century Eastern Europe

Allan L. Nadler

The critical study of the traditional religious movements of East European Jewry during the Modern period remains—with the notable exception of the remarkable recent efflorescence of scholarship on Hasidism—an exceedingly neglected field. This is particularly true of the English-language scholarship on nineteenth- and twentieth-century Orthodox Judaism, which is so scarce that it is difficult even to consider it as constituting an established realm of academic research. The paucity of works in this area, particularly when contrasted with the highly developed and impressive recent scholarship on Hasidism, is, however, at least somewhat understandable. Unlike Hasidism, which represents a strikingly original school of the Jewish mystical tradition and a very well defined social movement in modern Jewish history, the perceived hallmark of most other branches of traditional East European Rabbinic Judaism of the past two centuries, or Orthodoxy, has been that of a reactionary resistance to original theology and to religious or social change of any kind. Even those movements within East European Orthodoxy which possessed some degree of originality were largely reactions to the disintegration, in the last two centuries, of the traditional social order of Russian and Polish Jewry and the subsequent rise of major Jewish heterodoxies, such as Hasidism, the Haskalah, and Zionism. The dominant impulse of Orthodoxy—some might even say its very essence—is caution, conservatism, and resistance to change. All this renders the subject less than perfectly fascinating to doctoral candidates and scholars seeking out new and original areas of research.

Aside from some good work produced in Hebrew by a few Israeli scholars, the preponderance of material, in both Hebrew and English, on traditional East European Judaism takes the form of uncritical hagiographies of its leading religious leaders, usually written by their rabbinic heirs or their Orthodox disciples and admirers. Nevertheless, there is a sufficient core of critical monographs to render the world of traditional East European Judaism accessible to students of the modern Jewish experience.

The three principal developments within East European Orthodox Judaism in the last two centuries—Mitnaggedism (the Rabbinic movement of opposition to Hasidism and the Lithuanian yeshivas which it engendered), the Musar movement, and Religious Zionism and ultra-Orthodox anti-Zionism—were essentially reactions to the three respective major movements of change within East European Jewry—Hasidism, the Russian Haskalah, and the rise of secular Jewish nationalism. The study of each of these three trends within traditional Judaism can very profitably constitute a distinct and important section of any course on modern Judaism or Jewish history.

Mitnaggedism and the Lithuanian Yeshiva

The Rabbinic opponents of Hasidism—the Mitnaggedim—have not managed to attract the attention of many critical Western scholars. While there is a considerable Hebrew literature on the father of this movement of Lithuanian Orthodox Judaism, the Gaon of Vilna, R. Elijah b. Solomon, there exists only a single, long-outdated English biographical essay by Louis Ginzberg in his collection *Students, Scholars, and Saints.*[1]

The Gaon's most famous and important disciple, R. Hayyim of Volozhin, who founded the first great Lithuanian yeshiva, has fared only slightly better. Aside from a few brief biographical sketches on R. Hayyim, the best of which is the article by Walter Wurzberger in *Guardians of Our Heritage,*[2] there is a valuable study of his most important religious doctrine by Norman Lamm, *Torah Lishmah: Torah For Torah's Sake in the Works of Rabbi Hayyim of Volozhin and His Contemporaries.*[3] This fine volume is especially important in that it examines the central doctrine of Mitnaggedic Judaism which underlies the ideology of the yeshiva movement which became the institutional framework for its furtherance—that is, the belief that the study of Torah is

1. Philadelphia: Jewish Publication Society, 1928.
2. Ed. Leo Jung (New York: Macmillan, 1958), pp. 187–206.
3. New York: Yeshiva University Press, 1988.

Judaism's supreme spiritual value and the Jews' most important religious vocation. Also worthy of note is Lamm's article on the second generation of Mitnaggedism, "The Phase of Dialogue and Reconciliation."[4] The thought of another famous disciple of the Gaon of Vilna, the populist preacher Jacob Kranz of Dubno (popularly known as the Dubner Maggid), is treated in Herman A. Glatt, *He Spoke in Parables: The Life and Works of the Dubno Maggid*.[5]

The theology of mitnaggedic Judaism is an almost entirely neglected field. With the exception of Allan L. Nadler, *A Religion of Limits: The Theology of Mithnagdism*,[6] which examines the major beliefs of the Mitnaggedim in contrast to Hasidic theology, the positive religious thought of the early Rabbinic opponents of Hasidism has been completely ignored by scholars. A case study of the religious thought of the Mitnaggedim as reflected in the writings of a direct descendant of the Vilna Gaon is Nadler's essay, "Meir ben Elijah's Milhamoth Adonai: A Late Anti-Hasidic Polemic."[7]

Mordechai Wilensky, the editor of the most important collection of primary texts of the rabbinic opposition to Hasidism, *Hasidim u-mitnaggedim*,[8] wrote an article abstracting the basic substance of the massive early Mitnaggedic polemical literature, "Hasidic–Mitnaggedic Polemics in the Jewish Communities of Eastern Europe: The Hostile Phase."[9] Samuel Dresner, "Hasidism and its Opponents,"[10] displays a decidedly pro-Hasidic bias in its presentation of some of the theological issues which originally divided Mitnaggedim from Hasidim.

The yeshiva founded by R. Hayyim in the Belorussian town of Volozhin eventually gave rise to a significant network of talmudic academies which served as the most important bulwark against the dramatic inroads which Hasidism had been making across Eastern Europe during the course of the nineteenth century. A definitive history of the yeshivas has, unfortunately, yet to been written. Several articles are, however, worthy of note. The best for undergraduate reading are Abraham Menes' two overviews, "Yeshivas in Rus-

4. In *Tolerance and Movements of Religious Dissent in Eastern Europe*, ed. Bela K. Kiraly (New York: Columbia University Press, 1975), pp. 115–32.

5. New York: Jewish Theological Seminary, 1957.

6. New York: Yeshiva University Press, 1993.

7. *The Journal of Jewish Thought and Philosophy* 1 (1992): 247–80.

8. 2 vols. (Jerusalem: Hebrew University Press, 1970).

9. In Kiraly (n. 4), pp. 89–114.

10. In *Great Schisms in Jewish History*, ed. R. Jospe and S. Wagner (Denver: University of Denver, Center for Judaic Studies, 1981), pp. 119–75.

sia"[11] and "Patterns of Jewish Scholarship in Eastern Europe."[12] Gedalya Alon, "The Lithuanian Yeshivas,"[13] presents a somewhat rarefied, nostalgic portrait of the pre-war yeshiva world. Haim Hillel Ben-Sasson, "Lithuania: the Structure and Trend of its Culture,"[14] also contains valuable material about the Lithuanian yeshivas and the Musar movement.

Although they do not, strictly speaking, belong to the field of historical scholarship, Chaim Grade's Yiddish novels about religious life in Lithuania provide a most faithful and vivid depiction of a vanished religious culture. This is particularly true of his two-volume opus, *The Yeshiva*,[15] which provides the invaluable insight of an unusually perceptive and scholarly novelist into the world and psyche of the students and scholars of the Lithuanian yeshivas of which he himself was a rather notorious product. Finally, sociologist William Helmreich enrolled himself in an American "Lithuanian-style" yeshiva as part of an in-depth social and religious examination of the contemporary yeshiva. The resulting book, *The World of the Yeshiva*,[16] is a superb and insightful study of the American institutional successors to the yeshiva of Volozhin.

There have been numerous studies of assorted twentieth-century Mitnaggedic figures. The two volumes edited by Leo Jung, *Guardians of Our Heritage* (n. 2) and *Men of the Spirit*,[17] contain an assortment of factual, if reverent and uncritical, biographical sketches of some important later Mitnaggedic sages, such as R. Isaac Elhanan Spektor and Naftali Zevi Berlin.

The Lithuanian yeshivas were headed by some of the greatest religious leaders and scholars of non-Hasidic Orthodoxy. Almost all the literature available on these important figures has to date been written by their disciples from the yeshiva world and issued by partisan, Orthodox publishers. These books, mostly released as part of the ambitious ArtScroll Series,[18] include major monographs on such seminal rabbinic figures as Rabbi Elhonon Wasserman of Baranovitch, Abraham Isaiah Karelitz (popularly known as the Hazon Ish),

11. In *Russian Jewry*, ed. J. Frumkin, G. Aronson, and A. Goldenweisser (New York: Yoseloff, 1966), pp. 382–407.

12. In *The Jews: Their History, Culture, and Religion*, ed. L. Finkelstein (New York: Harper, 1949), vol. 1, pp. 376–426.

13. In *The Jewish Expression*, ed. Judah Goldin (New Haven: Yale University Press, 1976), pp. 452–68.

14. *Encyclopedia Judaica* 1973 Supplement, pp. 120–34.

15. Trans. Curt Leviant (Indianapolis: Bobbs-Merrill, 1976).

16. New York: Free Press, 1982.

17. New York: Macmillan, 1963.

18. Brooklyn: Mesorah Publications.

and Israel Meir Kagan of Radin (popularly known as the Hafetz Hayyim). While the biographies are rather worshipful and completely uncritical, they do provide some basic biographical and bibliographical information and contain some accurate and helpful references to the relevant primary texts. Due to their deeply religious adoration for their subjects, however, these works should be consulted, if at all, with critical caution.

Two important and original contemporary scions of the Lithuanian yeshiva world who spent most of their lives in America, Rabbi Joseph Baer Soloveitchik and Rabbi Isaac Hutner—and who are somewhat representative of two of the most important schools of the Lithuanian Yeshiva and Musar movements, Brisk and Kelm respectively—have received much critical attention recently.

While the extensive scholarship on R. Soloveitchik's original existentialist/ Orthodox religious philosophy properly belongs to the field of modern Jewish thought, his philosophy of Halakhah has been examined by Lawrence Kaplan, "Rabbi Joseph B. Soloveitchik's Philosophy of Halakha."[19] David Singer and Moshe Sokol, "Joseph Soloveitchik: Lonely Man of Faith,"[20] have argued the degree to which Soloveitchik's philosophy is in fact rooted in traditional Mitnaggedic Judaism. Soloveitchik's most influential and important work on the significance of Halakhic study and observance, *Ish ha-halakhah*, which has been characterized by Eugene Borowitz as "a Mitnaggedic phenomenology of awesome proportions," has been translated by Lawrence Kaplan.[21] Two fine general introductions to Soloveitchik's thinking are Lawrence Kaplan, "The Religious Philosophy of R. Joseph B. Soloveitchik,"[22] and Aaron Lichtenstein, "R. Joseph Baer Soloveitchik."[23]

R. Isaac Hutner, a considerably more conservative Mitnaggedic contemporary of Soloveitchik, has been treated recently in a number of essays, most of which have appeared in the Modern Orthodox journal *Tradition*. Most notable among these are the following essays: Hillel Goldberg, "R. Isaac Hutner: A Synoptic Interpretive Biography";[24] Lawrence Kaplan, "R. Isaac Hutner's Daat Torah Perspective on the Holocaust: A Critical Analysis";[25] and the translations by Steven Schwarzschild, "Two Lectures of Rabbi Isaac Hutner."[26]

19. *The Jewish Law Annual* 7 (1985): 139–97.

20. *Modern Judaism* 2/3 (1982): 227–72.

21. *Halakhic Man* (Philadelphia: Jewish Publication Society, 1983).

22. *Tradition* 14/2 (1973): 43–64.

23. In *Great Jewish Thinkers of the Twentieth Century*, ed. Simon Noveck (Washington, D.C.: B'nai B'rith Books, 1963), pp. 281–97.

24. *Tradition* 22/4 (1986): 18–46.

25. *Tradition* 18/3 (1980): 235–48.

26. *Tradition* 14/4 (1976): 90–109.

The ideology of Mitnaggedism, which centered around the spiritual dominance in Jewish life of *talmud torah*, or rabbinic scholarship, gave rise to a traditional society in which the very act of learning became the most hallowed religious experience, and among whose adherents scholarship was the sole criterion for spiritual prestige. A fascinating sociological study of the central role of *lernen*, or yeshiva-style learning, in contemporary American Orthodox society is Samuel C. Heilman, *The People of the Book*.[27]

The Musar Movement

The most distinctive school to emerge out of the world of the Lithuanian yeshivas was the Musar movement. Founded by Rabbi Israel Salanter, the intensely introspective Musar ideology, advocating the struggle for personal moral excellence, has been perceived by many scholars as a response to the emphasis on the ethical improvement and the aesthetic correction of East European Jewry in the ideology of the early Russian Haskalah.

Salanter's life and thought have been the subject of several book-length studies, of which the pioneering monograph by Menahem G. Glenn, *Israel Salanter: Religious Ethical Thinker*,[28] though somewhat lacking in critical depth, remains the most informative and accessible. Glenn's book also contains an English translation of the most important early manifesto of Musar ideology, Salanter's *Iggeret ha-musar* (Epistle on Ethics), which is an ideal primary text for class study. Hillel Goldberg's intellectual biography of Salanter, *Rabbi Israel Salanter: Text, Structure, and Idea*,[29] is a very detailed study of the chronological and intellectual development of R. Israel Salanter's religious thinking which might prove a bit too ponderous and esoteric for the average undergraduate. It is, however, supplemented by a most valuable "Essay on Bibliography" which provides a mine of references for further reading and research. A very early, but nonetheless helpful, portrait of Salanter is the biographical sketch by Ginzberg (n. 1), pp. 145–94. By far the best essay-length introduction to Salanter's ethics and the ideology of the early Musar movement is the English abstract of Immanuel Etkes's Hebrew book on Salanter, "Rabbi Israel Salanter and His Psychology of Musar."[30]

In the generations following Salanter's death, the Musar movement flourished and was divided into several distinct ethical and pietistic schools. However, in contrast to the abundance of good scholarly material on its founder,

27. Chicago: University of Chicago Press, 1983.
28. New York: Dropsie College, 1953.
29. New York: Ktav, 1982.
30. In *Jewish Spirituality from the Sixteenth Century Revival to the Present*, ed. Arthur Green (New York: Crossroad, 1989), pp. 206–44.

significantly less has been written in English about the subsequent masters of
the Musar movement and the various heads of the Musar yeshivas. There is a
long, uncritical, but helpful article by Rabbi J. J. Weinberg, "Lithuanian
Musar."[31] Jung (n. 2) also includes a study by Eliezer Ebner of a major disciple of Salanter, R. Simcha Zissel Broide.[32]

Two books by Lester Samuel Eckman provide the essential information on
the subsequent history of the movement and the key doctrines of its most
important rabbis: *The History of the Musar Movement*[33] is a simple, uncritical
chronological survey of the development of the movement and its important
masters and academies; *The Teachings of the Fathers of the Musar Movement*[34] is an almost entirely nonanalytical, somewhat paraphrastic introduction to the basic doctrines of the major figures of the Musar movement after
Salanter, from his students, R. Simha Zissel Broide and R. Isaac Blaser,
through to the famous mid twentieth century Sage, Israel Meir Kagan of
Radin (the Hafetz Hayyim). Despite the superficiality and absence of critical
scholarly analysis in Eckman's books, they remain somewhat objective and
are the only studies available in English which contain essential biographical
and intellectual information on the later Musar movement. Although, with the
exception of Salanter's *Iggeret ha-musar*, none of the early texts of the movement are available to English readers, the first part of one of the most important twentieth-century Musar works, ideal for class analysis, *Mikhtav me-
Eliyahu* by R. Elijah Dessler, has been translated.[35]

Religious Zionism and Ultra-Orthodox Anti-Zionism

The emergence of modern Jewish nationalism in Russia proved to be the
greatest and most divisive challenge to traditional Judaism in Eastern Europe,
which had long maintained a passive messianic posture regarding the vulnerable predicament of the Jews in exile. The rejection of the traditionally acquies-
cent rabbinic political posture of submission to the *Galut* implicit in early
Zionism, and more particularly the explicit renunciation of religious faith and
Halakhic practice by early twentieth-century Zionist theoreticians such as
A.D. Gordon and Micha Joseph Berdichevsky, provoked the anger of the vast
majority of the rabbis of Eastern Europe. By the first decades of this century,
anti-Zionism had already become a standard aspect of Orthodox ideology in

31. In Jung (n. 17), pp. 215–83.
32. Pp. 317–36.
33. New York: Shevgold, 1973.
34. New York: Shevgold, 1990.
35. *Strive For Truth*, trans. Aryeh Carmel (New York: Feldheim, 1978).

most parts of Eastern and Central Europe. Nevertheless, a small but distinguished group of rabbis was taken with the Zionist idea and gave rise to an important Orthodox wing within the Zionist movement, which ultimately became the Mizrachi Zionist Organization.

The best general introduction to the rather complicated history of the confrontation between traditional Judaism and modern Jewish nationalism in Russia during the formative years of the Zionist movement is the excellent study by Ehud Luz, *Parallels Meet: Religion and Nationalism in the Early Zionist Movement.*[36] Luz deals extensively with the wide variety of religious responses to Zionism from the perspectives of both the social and intellectual historian. There are important separate chapters on the development of ultra-Orthodox anti-Zionist theology and the emergence of religious Zionism and the Mizrachi movement. Luz, "Spiritual and Anti-Spiritual Trends in Zionism,"[37] provides a thematic exploration of some of the major issues resulting from the confrontation between Jewish nationalism and tradition.

The most famous rabbinic precursors of Modern Jewish nationalism were Zevi Hirsch Kalischer and Samuel Mohilever. Important selections from their writings, with brief introductions, are included in the first section of Arthur Hertzberg, *The Zionist Idea.*[38] Sam N. Lehmen-Wilzig's article on Zevi Hirsch Kalischer, "Proto-Zionism and its Proto-Herzl,"[39] provides a valuable introduction to his thought. There are also good articles on R. Kalischer by Jacob Katz[40] and on R. Mohilever by Eliyahu Moshe Genechovsky.[41]

The two most important pioneers of religious Zionism were R. Abraham Isaac Kook, the first Chief Rabbi of Jewish Palestine, and R. Isaac Jacob Reines, the founding father of the Mizrachi movement. Rabbi Kook's remarkably original mystical/messianic appreciation of the significance of modern Jewish nationalism has been studied by dozens of Israeli scholars, most of whose work is available only in Hebrew. There are, however, a number of decent English biographies as well as some fine translations from Rabbi Kook's vast literary corpus.

Of the two biographies of Rabbi Kook written by Jacob Bernard Agus, the better one is *High Priest of Re-Birth: The Life, Times, and Thought of Abraham Isaac Kook.*[42] Aside from the biography of this religious maverick, Agus includes a rudimentary introduction to aspects of R. Kook's religious philoso-

36. Philadelphia: Jewish Publication Society, 1988.
37. In Green (n. 30), pp. 371–401.
38. New York: Atheneum, 1973.
39. *Tradition* 16/1 (1976): 56–76.
40. In Jung (n. 2), pp. 207–28.
41. In Jung (n. 17), pp. 415–36.
42. New York: Bloch, 1972.

phy. Two other works on Rabbi Kook, neither of which is as good as Agus's, are the intellectual portrait by Leonard Gewirtz, *Jewish Spirituality: Hope and Redemption*,[43] and the brief, uncritical biography by Dov Peretz Elkins, *Shepherd of Jerusalem*.[44]

Rabbi Kook's writings have been edited and carefully translated into English, with helpful introductory essays, in two volumes by Ben Zion Bokser: *The Essential Writings of Abraham Isaac Kook*[45] and *The Lights of Penitence*.[46] Another translation of Kook's *Orot ha-teshuvah* (Lights of Penitence) is Alter Benzion Metzger, *Rabbi Kook's Philosophy of Repentance*.[47] An interesting sampling of R. Kook's correspondence which provides much insight into the sociopolitical and religious background of his activities as modern Palestine's first Chief Rabbi is the annotated translation by Tzvi Feldman, *Rav A. Y. Kook: Selected Letters*.[48]

The only good English biography of Rabbi Reines, which surveys both his career and his religious doctrines, is Joseph Wanefsky, *Rabbi Issac Jacob Reines: His Life and Thought*.[49] Two partisan histories of the political movement which Reines founded, both entitled *History of the Mizrachi Movement*, were written by J. L. Maimon[50] and S. Rosenblatt.[51]

Far less material is available on the history and theology of Orthodox anti-Zionism. The history and ideology of the non-Zionist Agudath Israel party, founded in Poland largely in opposition to the rise of religious Zionism, is the subject of an excellent dissertation by Gershon Bacon, "Agudath Israel in Poland 1916–1939: An Orthodox Jewish Response to the Challenge of Modernity."[52] A far less critical history of the Agudah, with a strong emphasis on the biographies of its leading rabbinic figures, is Joseph Friedenson, "A Concise History of Agudath Israel."[53] A good analysis of some of the political operations of the Agudath Israel is Ezra Mendelsohn, "The Politics of Agudas Yisrael in Inter-War Poland."[54]

Heaven at Bay: The Jewish Kulturkampf in the Holy Land, by Emil Mar-

43. New York: Ktav, 1986.
44. New York: Shevgold, 1975.
45. New York: Amity House, 1988.
46. New York: Paulist Press, 1978.
47. New York: Yeshiva University Press, 1968.
48. Maaleh Adumim, Israel: Maaliot Publications of Yeshivot Birkat Moshe, 1986.
49. New York: Philosophical Library, 1970.
50. New York: Mizrachi Hatzair of America, 1938.
51. New York: Mizrachi Organization of America, 1951.
52. Ph.D. dissertation, Columbia University, 1979.
53. In *Yaakov Rosenheim Memorial Anthology* (New York: Orthodox Library, 1968), pp. 1–64.
54. *Soviet Jewish Affairs* 2 (1972): 47–60.

morstein,[55] is the most sophisticated contemporary discussion of the extreme Orthodox anti-Zionist position. I. Domb, *The Transformation: The Case of Neturei Karta*,[56] also presents an intelligently formulated and rather learned argument in favor of the vehemently anti-Zionist ideology of that fringe group based in Jerusalem. A brief survey of the various contemporary Orthodox positions regarding Zionism, which contains copious notes comprising many very helpful references to the relevant textual and secondary material, is Immanuel Jakobovits, "Religious Responses to Jewish Statehood."[57]

The sole significant surviving voice of ultra-Orthodox anti-Zionism in the post-Holocaust period was the prolific Hasidic Grand Rabbi of Satmar, R. Joel Teitelbaum. Norman Lamm, "The Ideology of the Neturei Karta According to the Satmarer Version,"[58] paraphrases some of the most important aspects of Teitelbaum's writings. Allan L. Nadler, "Piety and Politics: The Case of the Satmar Rebbe,"[59] provides a more analytical study of Teitelbaum's extremist ideology.

The contemporary Satmar community has been examined in two books by sociologists: Solomon Poll, *The Hasidic Community of Williamsburg*;[60] and George Kranzler, *Williamsburg: A Jewish Community in Transition.*[61]

In the context of a survey course on Modern Jewish History, I would recommend that at least one separate lecture be devoted to Mitnaggedism, preferably at the very end of the section on Hasidism. An ideal required reading for this lecture would be Wilensky (n. 9). Depending on whether the course includes American Jewish history, one or two lectures on the Musar and contemporary yeshiva movements should follow the section on Hasidism. The single best required reading on the Musar movement is Glenn (n. 28), including the translation of *Iggeret ha-musar*; on the Lithuanian yeshivas I suggest Menes (nn. 11 and 12).

Finally, any discussion of the history of Zionism should include at least several classes on religious Zionism and Orthodox anti-Zionism. The selections from the writings of Alkali and Kalischer found in Hertzberg (n. 38) and selected chapters in Luz (n. 36) should provide adequate primary and secondary readings for this purpose.

It is clear from the gaps and shortcomings in the available material that the

55. New York: Oxford University Press, 1969.
56. London: Hamadfis, 1958.
57. *Tradition* 20/3 (1982): 188–204.
58. *Tradition* 19/3 (1971): 38–53.
59. *Judaism* 31/2 (1982): 135–52.
60. New York: Shocken, 1969.
61. New York: Feldheim, 1961.

academic study of East European Orthodox Judaism is still in its infancy. The real proof of the degree to which this remains an underexplored area of research is the fact that virtually none of the existing scholarship has been subjected to any critical revision. Nonetheless, as the above hopefully makes clear, there is more than sufficient material available in English to satisfy the needs of an undergraduate-level syllabus.

20. Modern Jewish Religious Movements

Alan Mittelman

The literature on modern Jewish religious movements, which—for the purposes of this essay—refers to Reform, Conservative, Orthodox, and Reconstructionist Judaism, is vast. Considerable historical, sociological, and philosophical/theological scholarship on the movements exists, as does an ongoing production of primary source materials found in such institutional self-expressions as sermon collections, rabbinic professional journals, institutional documents, and so on. I am (thankfully) spared the daunting task of bringing conceptual and bibliographic order to such a field, as my focus is modest and practical. My concern is pedagogic. I concentrate on how the field of modern Jewish religious movements can best be integrated into a curriculum on the Modern Jewish Experience. To do this, I explore some of the issues raised in the relevant scholarship and consider the best texts and approaches for the classroom.

There are, roughly, three scholarly approaches to these movements. Historians, sociologists and anthropologists, and philosophers are all working in the area. The following survey is intended to note some of the main titles which could be chosen depending upon which approach to the modern Jewish experience the professor wishes to take in the course. Some of the books are intended for the instructor's own preparation, others may be given to the student. The selection of materials presented here is representative, not exhaustive. My suggestions are just that. One must work with the materials on one's own to find out what best suits one's purposes and one's students.

Origins of Inquiry into Modern Jewish Religious Movements

Before we turn to the most contemporary studies, it is worth knowing how this field of inquiry originated. Scholarly attention to the rise of modern religious movements among the Jews is coeval with the development of modern Jewish studies as such. Founders of the *Wissenschaft des Judentums*, such as Abraham Geiger (1810–1874) or Leopold Zunz (1794–1886), even when not directly concerned with modern issues, wrote studies of antiquity influenced by their reformist agenda for the present. Geiger, for example, emphasized the theme of tradition and transformation. He sought to validate the nascent Reform movement as well as his own activism in it in a dynamic portrayal of ancient Judaism. Religious modernism and Jewish studies are thus joined at the hip.

In a more systematic manner, Heinrich Graetz (1817–1891), whose monumental *History of the Jews*[1] established modern Jewish historiography, treated the phenomena of Reform, Neo-Orthodoxy, and positive-historical Judaism, the precursor of Conservative Judaism, in the concluding chapters of his great work. Graetz depicts the formation of the movements as responses to the novel conditions of modern society, thus setting the basic interpretive pattern: religious change is an adaptation to modernity. Graetz focuses on leading personalities (*Gelehrtengeschichte*) rather than social or economic forces as the moving forces behind the movements and often polemicizes against them with remarkable vehemence. Both Geiger and Graetz were committed to partisan points of view. Contemporary historical scholarship, while no less committed to one or another Jewish point of view than Geiger or Graetz, does, however, strive for a fairness and dispassion which they did not achieve. As a generalization, then, we can maintain that attention to the religious movements is firmly embedded in the modern tradition of Jewish studies.

Historical Scholarship

Until recently, the principal genre of Jewish studies has been historiography. Twentieth-century scholars have produced numerous histories of the various movements or of phases or leading personalities within them. The earlier historical works often reflect an institutional or partisan stance, while more recent writing, even when it comes from within the movements, is more self-critical.

Reform Jews were the first to produce a systematic history of their move-

1. Philadelphia: Jewish Publication Society, 1941.

ment. The reason for this may be found in the fact that Orthodoxy resists categorization—for theological, historical, and sociological reasons—as a movement, and Conservatism, while amenable to the movement designation, has a controversial terminus a quo. Reform, on the other hand, has clearly delineated origins in the liturgical reforms of early nineteenth century Germany and acquires institutional articulation and self-consciousness earlier than the other constellations.

Thus David Philipson's 1931 work *The Reform Movement in Judaism*[2] probably counts as the first full-blown English-language history of a modern Jewish religious movement. Philipson, while seeing Reform as a uniquely appropriate response to modernity, embeds the reformist impulse in the whole sweep of healthy historical Judaism. A Conservative parallel may be found in Moshe Davis, *The Emergence of Conservative Judaism*,[3] which explored the transformation of the nineteenth-century historical school into the twentieth-century Conservative movement. Aaron Rothkopf, *Bernard Revel: Builder of American Orthodoxy*,[4] provides an account of the consolidation of Orthodoxy as a self-conscious movement in the United States through a biographical study of the founder of Yeshiva University. Of these works, Davis's and Rothkopf's merit continued study, while Philipson's has been superseded.

Contemporary Jewish historians are still producing comprehensive studies of the movements. Among contemporary works must be mentioned Michael A. Meyer, *Response to Modernity: A History of the Reform Movement in Judaism*,[5] and Mordechai Breuer, *Jüdische Orthodoxie im deutschen Reich 1871–1918*.[6] Meyer's work has become the standard history of Reform and will undoubtedly remain so for years to come. In this state-of-the-art intellectual history, Meyer pays close attention to the contemporary philosophical and cultural influences which played upon the architects of the movement. Unlike Philipson, Meyer offers a critical, honest assessment of Reform's contemporary dilemmas. Meyer sees Reform as an internally divided movement, characterized by genuine pluralism and hence by discontinuity with its past. The simple liberal faith and boundless optimism of Philipson's era has given way to a tone of tempered, wary hope. (One has only to compare Philipson with Meyer to see how far religion in America has veered from self-confident liberalism to resurgent traditionalism.) While too lengthy a treatment for the student (unless a full semester course is offered), Meyer's work is essential reading for the college teacher.

2. New York: Macmillan, rev. ed. 1931; repr. New York: Ktav, 1967.
3. Philadelphia: Jewish Publication Society, 1963.
4. Philadelphia: Jewish Publication Society, 1972.
5. New York: Oxford University Press, 1988.
6. Frankfurt am Main: Athenaeum, 1986.

Mordechai Breuer's volume—which is currently being translated into English—represents a different historiographic orientation from Meyer's. Rather than an intellectual history, Breuer has written a social history of German Orthodoxy. While not exactly the history of a movement, Breuer's work captures a way of life through thick description of its social institutions, practices, values, and cultural context. Unlike the other historical works considered, Breuer does not share the largely unstated presupposition that modernity is not only a challenge, but a blessing. He studies Orthodox figures from the same milieu as Franz Rosenzweig and Martin Buber, who had a keen sense of the limits and failures of the modern. When Breuer's work finally appears in English, the last chapter (on the quest of modern Orthodoxy to reach a post-Enlightenment synthesis) would impress students with the radical, creative character of German Orthodoxy in its last phase. The contrast between German Orthodoxy, which never abandoned sophisticated philosophical dialogue with contemporary culture, and American Orthodoxy, which has a tendency to succumb to cultural triumphalism, would be worth exploring.

Richard Libowitz, *Mordechai M. Kaplan And The Development of Reconstructionism*,[7] is one of the few full-length scholarly appraisals of Reconstructionism available. Like other works by Reconstructionists, it is a kind of scholarly hagiography which portrays Reconstructionism as a vanguard movement. It is as revealing of the mind of the Reconstructionist movement as it is of its proper subject matter.

There are a number of histories which treat the movements comparatively. For the classroom, Marc Lee Raphael, *Profiles in American Judaism*,[8] is probably the best. Despite the title, Raphael deals with both the European intellectual and social origins and the Americanization of the movements. Raphael also treats the contemporary problems and prospects of the movements. Students find it readable, and the scholarship is sound. Similar works include David Rudavsky, *Contemporary Jewish Religious Movements*,[9] which contextualizes the movements in a longer framework of European Jewish history than does Raphael (and includes a treatment of Hasidism), and Gilbert Rosenthal, *Four Paths to One God*.[10] Neither of these is as sound as Raphael's work, however. Nathan Glazer's classic, *American Judaism*,[11] is the most theoretically sophisticated of all these works. Strongly social-historical and sociological in orientation, he describes transdenominational American

7. New York: Edwin Mellen, 1983.
8. San Francisco: Harper and Row, 1984.
9. New York: Behrman House, 1979.
10. New York: Bloch, 1973.
11. Chicago: University of Chicago Press, 1974.

Judaism as a kind of civil religion. Such an approach influenced later studies such as Jonathan Woocher, *Sacred Survival: The Civil Religion of American Jews.*[12] *American Judaism* seems to have been written with the college classroom in mind.

An alternative to book-length studies of the movements is to use Robert Seltzer, *Jewish People, Jewish Thought,*[13] and Paul Mendes-Flohr and Jehuda Reinharz, *The Jew in the Modern World,*[14] coordinately to provide both a historical narrative and documentary materials. Both these texts lend themselves to a general course in Modern Jewish History, and there is sufficient material in them for a subunit on the movements.

For further reading in the German background of the movements, H. M. Graupe, *The Rise of Modern Judaism*;[15] David Sorkin, *The Transformation of German Jewry*[16] (particularly the last chapter); Noah Rosenbloom, *Tradition in an Age of Reform*;[17] Hans Bach, *The German Jew*;[18] Robert Liberles, *Religious Conflict in Social Context: The Resurgence of Orthodox Judaism in Frankfurt am Main, 1838–1877*;[19] and David Ellenson, *Rabbi Esriel Hildesheimer and the Creation of a Modern Jewish Orthodoxy,*[20] are all recommended for the instructor.

None of these studies treat the condition of the American movements in the last several years. That task is admirably accomplished by Jack Wertheimer, "Recent Trends in American Judaism."[21] Wertheimer surveys the past two decades of structural, environmental, and ideological change in American Jewish religious life as a whole and in the denominations. Although his study ends in 1989, the trends he depicts still prevail.

Sociological and Anthropological Scholarship

As historiography has come to be increasingly social in orientation through the pioneering work of Salo Baron and Jacob Katz, sociology per se has also taken a secure place in the field of Jewish studies. The first full-length treat-

---

12. Bloomington: Indiana University Press, 1986.
13. New York: Macmillan, 1980.
14. New York: Oxford University Press, 1980.
15. Trans. John Robinson (Huntington, N.Y.: Robert E. Krieger, 1978).
16. New York: Oxford University Press, 1987.
17. Philadelphia: Jewish Publication Society, 1976.
18. New York: Oxford University Press, 1984.
19. Westwood, Conn.: Greenwood, 1985.
20. Tuscaloosa: University of Alabama Press, 1990.
21. *American Jewish Year Book* 89 (1989): 63–162.

ment of a modern Jewish religious movement by a sociologist was Marshall Sklare, *Conservative Judaism: An American Religious Movement.*[22] First published in 1955, Sklare's work (like Glazer [n. 11], which first appeared in 1957) broke with the intellectual-historical method of describing the Weltanschauung of a movement. Sklare also rejected the unstated methodological presupposition that the movements are heroic, basically philosophical attempts to adapt to modernity. Sklare sees Conservative Judaism as an "ethnic church" defined more by its function of providing group cohesion for Americanized suburban Jews than for its abstract intellectual commitments. The final chapter, written for the 1985 edition, raises serious doubts about the Conservative movement's long-term viability in the face of cultural trends, such as the resurgence of traditional religion, which affect the American religious mainstream in general.

Sklare's book has long been considered a classic of American Jewish sociology, as has Charles Liebman, "Orthodoxy in American Jewish Life."[23] As early as the mid-1960s, Liebman noted the new vitality in Orthodoxy and tried to get at the social and cultural factors which nourished its persistence, indeed its flourishing. Liebman also dealt with Reconstructionism similarly, in "Reconstructionism and American Jewish Life."[24] Using the concepts of "folk religion" and "elite religion," he portrayed Reconstructionism as an intellectual formulation of American Jewish folk religion.

American Orthodoxy continues to attract sociological study. M. Herbert Danzger, *Returning to Tradition: The Contemporary Revival of Orthodox Judaism,*[25] is an up-to-date work in the Weberian interpretive tradition epitomized by Liebman. Danzger studies the mutual interaction of Weltanschauung and material factors as he analyzes the institutional growth and adaptation of Orthodoxy to American modernity. Other studies of Orthodoxy by sociological insiders include Samuel Heilman, *The People of the Book,*[26] and his less technical, autobiographical narrative, *The Gate Behind the Wall.*[27] The first work deals with the ritual of *lernen* (advanced talmudic study for its own sake). Heilman becomes a participant-observer in a *bes midrash* and analyzes the symbolic dimension of the interaction of the members of the group with their texts and with each other. The second book deals with Heilman's personal transformation from participant-observer to participant. Both works

22. Lanham, Md.: University Press of America, 1985.
23. *American Jewish Year Book* 66 (1965): 21–99.
24. *American Jewish Year Book* 71 (1970): 31–39.
25. New Haven: Yale University Press, 1989.
26. Chicago: University of Chicago Press, 1983.
27. New York: Penguin, 1984.

offer a thought-provoking passage into the inner world of authentic traditionalism. They represent the application of interpretive anthropology, once reserved for the culture of Bali and Java, to the culture of the yeshiva. The latter book is accessible to all students, the former only to advanced undergraduates.

Ethnographic studies such as Menachem Friedman's analysis of Haredim, "Life Tradition and Book Tradition in the Development of Ultra-Orthodox Judaism,"[28] or Steven Lowenstein, "Separatist Orthodoxy's Attitudes toward Community—The Breuer Community in Germany and America,"[29] also provide a penetrating insight into the traditional world. They offer persuasive analyses of how the most traditional elements in the Jewish world are also shaped by the encounter with modernity. By reading such essays, students will understand just how pervasive modernity is. While the Haredim are in no sense a "modern Jewish movement," the peculiar ways in which they are touched by the same cultural forces which produced the other religious movements can become clear. "Ultra-Orthodoxy" appears less as a fossil than as a participant in the dialogue with modernity.

A recent work by Charles Liebman, coauthored with Steven Cohen, *Two Worlds of Judaism: The Israeli and American Experiences*,[30] depicts the salient characteristics of American Judaism as a whole in contrast to those of Israeli Judaism. Liebman and Cohen characterize each society's "construction" of Judaism in terms of categories such as particularism/universalism, liberal individualism/communitarianism, and personalism/legalism, among others. They show how the very different cultures of Israel and America have shaped rather different fundamental understandings of what Judaism is and of how Judaism is lived. Relying on both survey data and the interpretation of popular Jewish culture, their portrayal of American Judaism is persuasive. I am less certain of the persuasiveness of their picture of Israeli Judaism.

Philosophical/Theological Scholarship

One of the important changes that has occured in Jewish studies, in my view, is the emergence of constructive Jewish philosophy. Jewish scholars are "doing" Jewish philosophy (or theology, if you will) rather than working on

28. In *Judaism Viewed from Within and Without*, ed. Harvey Goldberg (Albany: State University of New York Press, 1987), pp. 235–55.

29. In *Persistence and Flexibility*, ed. Walter P. Zenner (Albany: State University of New York Press, 1988), pp. 208–22.

30. New Haven: Yale University Press, 1990.

historical studies of ancient, Medieval, or modern German-Jewish thought. The emergence of Jewish thought in America carries an ambiguous import for the study of modern Jewish religious movements, indeed, for the movements themselves. Many of the thinkers at work today are not tied to any particular movement. Emil Fackenheim, to use the example of a senior figure, does not speak for the Reform movement, even though he has roots in it. The action in contemporary Jewish thought may well be occuring outside the identifiable institutional structures of the religious movements, signaling a loss of creativity for the movements themselves.

To appreciate what this means, one might turn to Arthur A. Cohen and Paul R. Mendes-Flohr, *Contemporary Jewish Religious Thought*.[31] The editors commissioned dozens of original philosophical essays on classical religious topics. The handful of essays which express the institutional self-definition of the religious movements lack the depth and excitement of the nondenominational essays. They state an ideological case rather than argue a philosophical point. Having said that, however, the four essays on the movements nonetheless provide handy summaries of current institutional thinking in a philosophical mode. Students find them easy to grasp, and the material will provoke discussion. Pairing the essays from this book with a historical overview of the movements and some documentary materials would create a workable course unit.

Perhaps the most important institutional self-expression in recent years is the Conservative movement's *Emet ve-emunah*,[32] a statement of principles of Conservative Judaism. After decades of resisting a single philosophical statement of Conservative beliefs, the movement finally worked out a consensual position. What is significant here is not only what the text says, but also what the event represents. Doctrinal articulation was perceived by the movement as a necessary survival strategy. The long-term inadequacy of an "ethnic church," which Sklare had predicted, had become apparent. The document lends itself to classroom discussion as it is only 57 pages long. Close attention to its nuances (for example, even while stating what Conservative Jews ought to affirm, it insists on excluding no one: it is not a catechism) reveals much of the contemporary intellectual and moral condition of Conservative Judaism.

While a statement such as *Emet ve-emunah* is a real departure for Conservative Judaism, American Reform Judaism has long issued pithy statements of its principles. The Pittsburgh Platform (1885), the Columbus Platform (1937), and, most recently, the 1976 San Francisco Platform ("A Centenary Perspec-

31. New York: Scribners, 1987.
32. New York: Jewish Theological Seminary of America, 1988.

tive") reveal the dramatic changes which Reform has undergone. The three platforms chart a course from unbridled liberal optimism to chastened realism, from universalist self-definition to a dialectical affirmation of Jewish particularism, and from anti-ritualism to a new embrace of traditional ritual. These texts may be found in the Appendix of Meyer (n. 5).

Rebecca Alpert and Jacob Staub, *Exploring Judaism: A Reconstructionist Approach*,[33] is the most current book-length philosophical presentation of Reconstructionism. It represents the work of third-generation Reconstructionists and reveals the on-going transformation of Kaplan's thought necessary to keep the movement viable.

A good anthology of contemporary views of leading thinkers in each tradition is available in *Understanding American Judaism: Toward the Description of a Modern Religion*, vol. 2.[34] The sixteen essays in this volume suffice to give the student an informed understanding of the intellectual character of each movement and an opportunity to weigh the quality of thinking against nondenominational projects.

Another approach one might take to explore the contemporary position of the movements is to look at how representatives of each group work on normative ethical issues. Menachem M. Kellner, *Contemporary Jewish Ethics*,[35] has three essays on abortion from Orthodox, Conservative, and Reform points of view. The contrast between the movements in terms of approach to and reliance on Halakhah, the understanding of individual conscience, the role of religion in public life, and so on is striking. A similar trio of pieces can be found in *B'nai B'rith National Jewish Monthly*.[36] The moral philosophical approach offers students an additional connection with issues that they may find personally relevant.

Finally, we note what might be called a thematic approach. Arnold Eisen, *The Chosen People In America*,[37] traces the trajectory of one concept, chosenness, through the manifold of successive American Jewish generations and denominations. Eisen establishes that general social and cultural factors, rather than movement-specific philosophical ones (with the exception of Reconstructionism), determined the form of the belief in chosenness. Eisen also points to the rise of independent, constructive Jewish thought and the decline in importance of institutional self expression. Another account of the development of constructive Jewish thought is Robert Goldy, *The Emergence*

33. New York: Reconstructionist Press, 1985.
34. Ed. Jacob Neusner (New York: Ktav, 1975).
35. New York: Sanhedrin, 1978.
36. August–September 1989.
37. Bloomington: Indiana University Press, 1983.

of Jewish Theology in America.[38] Goldy shows how the import of existential-ism from Europe both challenged and revitalized Jewish theology in Reform, Conservative, and Orthodox circles.

Woocher (n. 12), while not directly focused on the movements, describes an underlying form of religiosity which competes with the movement's elite theological formulations. Using the concept of "civil religion" popularized by Robert Bellah, Woocher investigates the religious reality of American Jewish life in a manner far more convincing than that obtained by studying the ideo-logical self-descriptions of the movements alone.

Pedagogic Approaches

It is perhaps presumptuous to tell another instructor how to teach about a sub-ject matter with which he or she also has some familiarity. At this point, I sim-ply want to share what has worked in my own teaching at my own institution.

I am convinced that, as valuable as the sociological, anthropological, and philosophical approaches are, history must provide the basic context for our exploration of modern Judaism. Accordingly, students should learn the partic-ular histories of these movements, both in Europe and the United States. As indicated above, Raphael (n. 8) is the best single history text.

Of course, one brings all sorts of presuppositions to one's interpretation and teaching of history. Methodologically, I am inclined to treat religion in America as a unique phenomenon rather than the essential continuation of a trajectory started in Europe. Historians of American religion such as Martin Marty have found that peculiar cultural values, such as voluntarism and exper-imentalism, come to characterize the religions brought here by Europeans and change them in fundamental ways. Religions long accustomed to state support (Anglicanism, for example) had to make crucial adjustments in order to sur-vive in America's disestablishmentarian society. Movements that were mar-ginal and deviant in Europe, such as the Baptist churches, have become mainstream here because they could take advantage of what William Lee Miller called the "deregulated religion market." If there is such a thing as "American religion," then one ought to look for elements within the American Jewish religious movements which reflect common trends and values. Pitts-burgh-Platform Reform may very well be closer phenomenologically to con-temporary liberal Protestantism than to other forms of Judaism.

This raises another methodological point. What sort of model do we use,

---

38. Bloomington: Indiana University Press, 1990.

either deliberately or in our presuppositions, to image the relationship of the movements to one another? Do we believe, for example, that they represent a spectrum of expressions (from left to right along a line) of one underlying reality? Perhaps we imagine a tree with a central stock and branches that fili- ate from it? We have an epistemological need to locate some constant such as the Jewish people and to see these formations as symbolic structures vis-à-vis a determinative ontology. Model-making such as this is an act of the imagina- tion. We ought to recognize that, although it is necessary (as Wittgenstein said, in order for the door to turn, the hinges must stand fast), it is also arbitrary. We could make other models. Indeed, we do. Few of us would use the model which assumes that "the new is forbidden by the Torah," that is, that the movements represent perverse rebellion and deviance from revealed norms. Yet it is clear that we could if we wished. Thus one goal of teaching about these movements, in my view, is to make the student critical of the epistemo- logical conventions that underlie our interpretations. I try to make my students self-conscious about their own constructions of denominational Judaism and increase their capacity to appreciate quite different ways of considering the matter. I am not advocating a kind of "reader response" view of Jewish reli- gious movements; I am simply calling for an awareness of the perspectival determinants of historiography.

Given a self-critical historical grasp of the rise of the movements in Europe and their transplantation and transformation here, one must then stress the open-ended, unfinished nature of the present. Orthodoxy, while experiencing new vitality and self-confidence, is also moving to the right. "Modern" Ortho- doxy, an Orthodoxy of synthesis and acculturation, has become discredited. Those elements of Orthodoxy most contemptuous of modernity today have the most prestige and authority. Reform Judaism is torn between the centripe- tal pressures of its commitment to individual autonomy and conscience, and the centrifugal forces of institutionalism. Coupled with this inherent dilemma is the relativization of liberalism and humanism, on which it has relied, in our now "postmodern" age. Conservative Judaism struggles to define itself as a Halakhic movement against a late twentieth century laity that is functionally post-Halakhic and no longer nourished by dropouts from Orthodoxy. Recon- structionism is both beholden to the thought of Mordecai Kaplan and embar- rassed by it.

Conclusion

The decade of the 1980s witnessed a realignment in American religion. The main-line churches virtually receded from public view as the evangelical and

Catholic churches rose to cultural leadership. Correlatively in the Jewish world, Orthodoxy continued its spectacular phoenix-like ascent while Conservatism and Reform, though hardly infirm, reconciled themselves to the dawn of a postliberal era. A civil Judaism of Soviet Jewry– and Israel-centered activism, denominated by Daniel Elazar and Jonathan Woocher "neo-Sadduceanism," daily overwhelmed the ideological commitments of the movements in the minds and hearts of many committed Jews. Finally, the proliferation of nonrabbinic Jewish scholars secured a rich Jewish creativity outside the movements and their seminaries. What all this means for the movements is, of course, unclear. What it portends for the study of the movements and how we teach about them is only a little less unclear.

While it is necessary to trace the historical rise and institutional articulation of the movements, it seems to me more interesting and relevant to subject them to the kind of sociological, anthropological, and thematic study sketched above. Such work clarifies the foundational interaction of American Jews with American culture and with America's distinctive religious experience. It also lays bare some of the general features of the religious experience (such as the relationship between worldview and ritual, for example), wherever it is found. Future scholarship will probably see continued growth in social-science and thematic approaches, although historical studies of figures and institutions will undoubtedly continue as well.

21. Modern Jewish Politics

Eli Lederhendler

There is a certain irony in the fact that Jewish political studies may justly be considered a new field—at one of the few conferences devoted specifically to the topic (held at the YIVO Institute in New York in the fall of 1989), one of the keynote speakers contended that the field of Jewish politics is still virgin territory. Given the Jews' proverbial contentiousness and their track record of survival and national self-regeneration against considerable odds, one might assume that Jews would be considered political animals par excellence. Why this has not been so in the past, and why Jewish political studies are still in their first generation, becomes clear when we consider the following facts.

First, political studies in general evolved from the study of the state. It is only in recent decades that political science has undergone a "social" transformation (similar to that which has affected the writing of history). That is, political analysis has come to include—in addition to the state and its international relations—a host of other players (interest groups, lobbies, elites and other social classes, ethnic groups, mobilized diasporas, etc.), structures (parties, bureaucracies, organizations, legislatures, churches, local government, tribes, even the family), and problems ("ethnopolitics," nationalism, colonialism, revolution, leadership, political "mobilization" or participation, labor relations, "modernization," "development," "civil religion," ideology, political myths, political culture and political socialization, public opinion and voter behavior, "core" vs. "periphery").

Thus, while a stateless group such as diaspora Jews would not have been treated as a political phenomenon in the traditional sense, the new scholarly agenda clearly takes in many areas in which the Jews are a relevant quantity. They appear either as a case study or subset within larger sociopolitical contexts (e.g., studies of domestic ethnic influence on American foreign policy or ethnic voting patterns—see Steven L. Spiegel, *The Other Arab–Israeli Conflict: Making America's Middle East Policy, From Truman to Reagan;*[1] Steven M. Cohen, *American Modernity and Jewish Identity;*[2] *The Politics of Ethnicity*[3]); or else as the subject of political-historical studies in their own right, affording comparative insights for the field generally (e.g., studies of Jewish socialist movements—Jonathan Frankel, *Prophecy and Politics: Socialism, Nationalism, and the Russian Jews, 1862–1917;*[4] Ezra Mendelsohn, *Class Struggle in the Pale: The Formative Years of the Jewish Workers' Movement in Tsarist Russia;*[5] Yoav Peled, *Class and Ethnicity in the Pale: The Political Economy of Jewish Workers' Nationalism in Late Imperial Russia*[6]).

Second, Jewish historical studies, having evolved from the *Wissenschaft des Judentums* tradition of literary, intellectual, and cultural history, rarely included political themes (except for such limited areas as the Jews' legal status, in relation to the struggle for Emancipation, or celebrated cases of Jewish diplomacy). The greatest diaspora Jewish historians (Graetz, Dubnow, and Baron) considered the Jewish people to be an international "spiritual" nation that had transcended political nationhood, and they therefore did not deal with the politics of the Jewish community as a legitimate area of study in its own right.

Third (and this point is connected to the first two), because politics is chiefly concerned with power and its uses, the prevailing assumption that the Jews were historically powerless (a view influenced by the Holocaust) necessarily implied that they stood somehow "outside" politics—even "outside history" (Yehuda Bauer, *The Jewish Emergence from Powerlessness;*[7] Gershom Scholem, *The Messianic Idea in Judaism and Other Essays*[8])—and lacked political acumen, "instincts," or "wisdom." This point of view generated what can only be described as a masterly, if controversial, interpretation of the role of Jews in European political development, based on their anomalous and, in the final analysis, insignificant position (Hannah Arendt, *The Origins of Totalitarianism*[9]).

1. Chicago: University of Chicago Press, 1985.

2. New York: Tavistock, 1983.

3. Ed. Stephen Thernstrom (Dimensions of Ethnicity series; Cambridge: Harvard University Press, 1982).

4. New York: Cambridge University Press, 1981.

5. Cambridge: Cambridge University Press, 1970.

6. New York: St. Martin's, 1989.

7. Toronto: University of Toronto Press, 1978.

8. New York: Schocken, 1971.

9. New York: Meridian, 1951.

A critique of this approach has been in the works for some time and has taken the form of challenges to the absolute categories used to set up the power–powerless polarity (Ismar Schorsch, "On the History of the Political Judgment of the Jew";[10] David Biale, *Power and Powerlessness in Jewish History*;[11] Eli Lederhendler, *The Road to Modern Jewish Politics: Political Tradition and Political Reconstruction in the Jewish Community of Tsarist Russia*[12]), yielding a more nuanced interpretation. One can also see the germ of this perspective in Zionist and Israeli historiography, which has unabashedly sought out the national, political, and class factors in the Jewish past, with a view toward explaining the Jewish national renaissance. This approach is typical of the lifework of such scholars as Haim Hillel Ben-Sasson, Ben-Zion Dinur, Israel Halperin, and Raphael Mahler, among others.

As the Jewish historical field came increasingly to be dominated by social rather than intellectual–cultural inquiry, and as the fact of Jewish statehood began to impinge on modern scholarship, a process of "repoliticization" has taken place. That is, politics was brought back into Jewish historiography and sociology, on the one hand, and Jews as a political phenomenon were reintroduced into political studies generally (Daniel J. Elazar, *Community and Polity: The Organizational Dynamics of American Jewry*;[13] *Kinship and Consent: The Jewish Political Tradition and its Contemporary Uses*;[14] Daniel J. Elazar and Stuart Cohen, *The Jewish Polity: Jewish Political Organization from Bibical Times to the Present*[15]).

In short, Jewish political studies have gone from a desert to a growth industry, permeated by the need to account for or come to terms with the Holocaust, Soviet nationality policy, and the impact of Israel. For the purposes of opening the discussion, having students read Biale (n. 11) and Peter Y. Medding, "Patterns of Political Organization and Leadership in Contemporary Jewish Communities"[16] or "Toward a General Theory of Jewish Political Interests and Behavior in the Modern World"[17] is a good idea.

There are several possible approaches to teaching the subject of modern Jewish politics, and I will briefly outline some of the options. The first might be called the 'historical–geographical" approach, in which the focus is on dis-

10. Leo Baeck Memorial Lecture 20 (New York: Leo Baeck Institute, 1977).
11. New York: Schocken, 1986.
12. New York: Oxford University Press, 1989.
13. Philadelphia: Jewish Publication Society, 1976.
14. Ed. Daniel J. Elazar (Ramat Gan: Turtledove, 1981).
15. Bloomington: Indiana University Press, 1985.
16. In Elazar (n. 14), pp. 259–88.
17. In Elazar (n. 14), pp. 313–43.

tinctive arenas of Jewish political activity; a second, the "political theory" approach, is concerned with structural and theoretical problems; a third, the "special problems" approach, addresses integrated topics.

Organizing three teaching units around the historical–geographical principle is fairly straightforward: one might deal successively with Eastern Europe, the United States, and Zionism/Israel (or, alternatively, Central and Western Europe). In each case, the point to get across would be the interplay between domestic politics in the particular social and political setting, on the one hand, and common features of modern Jewish politics that transcend national boundaries, on the other.

The East European arena produced a vibrant Jewish political life complete with parties, elections, parliamentary representation, international congresses and treaties, even government ministries devoted to Jewish affairs. The background to this phenomenal development lies in the nineteenth-century movement for social and cultural renewal known as the Haskalah (Lederhendler [n. 12]). The growth of ideological movements and parties from the 1860s to the Russian Revolution forms the first stage in the proliferation of organized Jewish political frameworks (Mendelsohn [n. 5], Biale [n. 11], Frankel [n. 4] and "The Crisis of 1881–82 as a Turning Point in Modern Jewish History"[18]). A key to understanding these phenomena is the twin process of secularization and the growth of nationalism in Eastern Europe between 1848 and 1914, and students ought to be able to discuss the consequences of both for Jewish society.

Thereafter, the scene is split between Soviet Russia, on the one hand (Zvi Gitelman, *Jewish Nationality and Soviet Politics*;[19] Benjamin Pinkus, *The Jews of the Soviet Union: The History of a National Minority*[20]), and interwar East Central Europe, on the other (Ezra Mendelsohn, *Zionism in Poland: The Formative Years, 1915–1926*,[21] *The Jews of East Central Europe between the World Wars*,[22] and "Reflections on East European Jewish Politics in the Twentieth Century";[23] he is at work on a major comparative study of interwar Jewish politics). Documents on key developments in the Soviet Union between 1948 and 1967 are presented in Benjamin Pinkus, *The Soviet Government and*

18. In *The Legacy of Migration: 1881 and Its Impact*, ed. David Berger (New York: Brooklyn College Press, 1983), pp. 9–22.

19. Princeton: Princeton University Press, 1972.

20. New York: Cambridge University Press, 1988.

21. New Haven: Yale University Press, 1981.

22. Bloomington: Indiana University Press, 1983.

23. *YIVO Annual of Jewish Social Science* 20 (1991): 23–37; this volume also contains other papers from the 1989 YIVO conference on Jewish politics.

the Jews, 1948–1967: A Documented Study.[24] For a more detailed discussion of Soviet Jewish history, see my essay on that topic in this volume.

For the study of American Jewish politics, several chapters in Henry Feingold, *Zion in America: The Jewish Experience from Colonial Times to the Present,*[25] provide a valuable introduction (chs. 6, 11, 14–16). On more specific and contemporary issues, there are studies of the way the Jewish community is organized and how it functions (Elazar [n. 13]; Chaim Waxman, "Challenges to Consensus in the Contemporary American Jewish Community";[26] Kenneth D. Roseman, "Power in a Midwestern Jewish Community"[27]); studies that focus on major debates and leaders (Ben Halpern, *Clash of Heroes: Brandeis, Weizmann, and American Zionism*[28]); and examinations of postwar developments and trends, especially in connection with Jewish liberalism and with activism on Israel's behalf (Charles S. Liebman, *The Ambivalent American Jew: Politics, Religion, and Family in American Jewish Life*[29] and "Changing Conceptions of Political Life and their Implications for American Judaism";[30] Cohen [n. 2]; Jonathan Woocher, *Sacred Survival: The Civil Religion of American Jews;*[31] Peter Y. Medding, "Segmented Ethnicity and the New Jewish Politics"[32] and *The New Politics of American Jews: Identity, Status, and Power*[33]). For students, the best combination of readings is probably Feingold (n. 25), Elazar (n. 13), Medding (n. 32), and Cohen (n. 2). These allow for a discussion of internal organizational politics, American Jewry's foreign policy concerns, and patterns of Jewish political activity in terms of American domestic affairs.

The literature on Zionism and Israel is immense. Nevertheless, several recent and new books are particularly useful in putting it all into perspective: David Vital's history of the Zionist movement, *The Origins of Zionism*[34] and *Zionism: The Formative Years;*[35] Peter Medding, *The Founding of Israeli*

24. New York: Cambridge University Press, 1984.

25. New York: Twayne, 1974; repr. New York: Hippocrene, 1981.

26. In *Comparative Jewish Politics: Conflict and Consensus in Jewish Political Life,* ed. Stuart Cohen and Eliezer Don-Yehiya (Ramat Gan: Bar-Ilan University, 1986), pp. 101–17.

27. *American Jewish Archives* (April 1969): 57–83.

28. New York: Oxford University Press, 1987.

29. Philadelphia: Jewish Publication Society, 1973.

30. In *Comparative Jewish Politics: Public Life in Israel and the Diaspora,* ed. Sam Lehman-Wilzig and Bernard Susser (Ramat Gan: Bar-Ilan University Press, 1981), pp. 91–100.

31. Bloomington: Indiana University Press, 1986.

32. *Studies in Contemporary Jewry* 3 (1987): 26–48.

33. Forthcoming.

34. Oxford: Clarendon, 1975.

35. Oxford: Clarendon, 1982.

Democracy;[36] and the essays in *Israel: State and Society, 1948–1988.*[37] Another very useful tool is *Israel in the Middle East: Documents and Readings on Society, Politics, and Foreign Relations.*[38]

Jewish politics in Central and Western Europe involves studies of political orientations in the Imperial period (Jacob Toury, *Die politischen Orientierungen der Juden in Deutschland: von Jena bis Weimar*[39]); organized Jewish response to modern antisemitism and mass migration (Ismar Schorsch, *Jewish Reactions to German Antisemitism, 1870–1914*;[40] Jack Wertheimer, *Unwelcome Strangers: East European Jews in Imperial Germany*[41]); and the dilemmas posed by Emancipation and nationalism (Eugene C. Black, *The Social Politics of Anglo-Jewry 1880–1920*;[42] Stuart Cohen, *English Zionists and British Jews: The Communal Politics of Anglo-Jewry, 1895–1920*;[43] Paula Hyman, *From Dreyfus to Vichy: The Remaking of French Jewry, 1906–1939*;[44] Hillel J. Kieval, *The Making of Czech Jewry*;[45] Jehuda Reinharz, *Fatherland or Promised Land: The Dilemma of the German Jew, 1893–1914*;[46] Robert S. Wistrich, "The Clash of Ideologies in Jewish Vienna (1880–1918)"[47] and *The Jews of Vienna in the Age of Franz Joseph*[48]). *The Jew in the Modern World: A Documentary Reader*[49] includes selections pertinent to Jewish politics.

An alternative approach—which I have called the "political theory" approach—may consist of the following three topics: political theory and political philosophy in Judaic culture; power, leadership, organization, and goals; and Jews and the modern state (pre- and post-Zionism). The first of these is best addressed in essays by Daniel J. Elazar, "The Kehillah: From its Beginnings to the End of the Modern Epoch";[50] David Hartman, "Halakhah as a Ground for Creating a Shared Political Dialogue Among Contemporary

36. New York: Oxford University Press, 1990.
37. *Studies in Contemporary Jewry* 5 (1989), ed. Peter Y. Medding.
38. Ed. Itamar Rabinovich and Jehuda Reinharz (New York: Oxford University Press, 1984).
39. Tübingen: Mohr, 1966.
40. New York: Columbia University Press, 1972.
41. New York: Oxford University Press, 1987.
42. Oxford: Blackwell, 1988.
43. Princeton: Princeton University Press, 1982.
44. New York: Columbia University Press, 1979.
45. New York: Oxford University Press, 1988.
46. Ann Arbor: University of Michigan Press, 1975.
47. *Leo Baeck Institute Yearbook* 33 (1988): 201–30.
48. New York: Oxford University Press, 1989.
49. Ed. Paul Mendes-Flohr and Jehuda Reinharz (New York: Oxford University Press, 1980).
50. In Lehman-Wilzig and Susser (n. 30), pp. 23–63.

Jews";[51] Liebman (n. 30); Bernard Susser, "On the Reconstruction of Jewish Political Theory";[52] and others in Elazar (n. 14) and Lehman-Wilzig and Susser (n. 30). The second topic begins with the issue of power versus powerlessness and the Jews' political wisdom (Schorsch [n. 10], Biale [n. 11]) and goes on to examine how interests can be defined and articulated (Medding [nn. 16, 17, 32]). The third is dealt with by Eliezer Schweid, "The Attitude toward the State in Modern Jewish Thought before Zionism,"[53] Dan Segre, "The Jewish Political Tradition as a Vehicle for Jewish Auto-Emancipation,"[54] and Biale (n. 11).

The field has been enriched lately by the appearance of a new journal, *The Jewish Political Studies Review*. I can particularly recommend volume 1/3–4, devoted to *Jewish Political Studies in the University*. It includes, among others, useful essays on "Studying and Teaching Jewish Political Studies in the University," by Daniel Elazar;[55] "Israel's Democracy and Comparative Politics," by Benyamin Neuberger;[56] "Comparative Politics and the Jewish Political Experience," by Zvi Gitelman;[57] and "A Framework and Model for Studying and Teaching the Jewish Political Tradition," by Daniel Elazar and Stuart A. Cohen.[58]

Finally, there is the last approach to modern Jewish politics, one that abandons the survey method (whether historical–geographical or political-theoretical) to tackle topics that span a number of problems and political arenas. I will suggest several such topics.

One of these might be "the Jews and the Left," which might be treated as an issue in European, Israeli, and American Jewish politics (Frankel [n. 4]; Gitelman [n. 19]; Bernard K. Johnpoll, *The Politics of Futility: The General Jewish Workers' Bund of Poland, 1917–1943*;[59] Arthur Liebman, *Jews and the Left*;[60] Robert S. Wistrich, *Socialism and the Jews: The Dilemmas of Assimilation in Germany and Austria-Hungary*;[61] Mitchell Cohen, *Zion and State: Nation, Class, and the Shaping of Modern Israel*[62]).

51. In Elazar (n. 14), pp. 357–85.
52. In Lehman-Wlizig and Susser (n. 30), pp. 13–22.
53. In Elazar (n. 14), pp. 127–47.
54. In Elazar (n. 14), pp. 293–307.
55. Pp. 1–11.
56. Pp. 67–75.
57. Pp. 77–88.
58. Pp. 115–38.
59. Ithaca, N.Y.: Cornell University Press, 1967.
60. New York: Wiley, 1979.
61. Rutherford, N.J.: Fairleigh Dickinson University Press, 1982.
62. New York: Oxford University Press, 1987.

A second, along the same lines, might be "the politics of rescue," dealing with refugee policy during the Holocaust, in America (Henry Feingold, *The Politics of Rescue: The Roosevelt Administration and the Jews*;[63] David S. Wyman, *The Abandonment of the Jews: America and the Holocaust*[64]) as well as in Europe (Bernard Wasserstein, *Britain and the Jews of Europe, 1939–1945*[65]) and in the *yishuv* (Palestine), on which a comprehensive new study is available (Dalia Ofer, *Escaping the Holocaust: Illegal Immigration to the Land of Israel, 1939–44*[66]).

A third such unit could be done on the Jews and World War I, based on the essays in *The Jews and the European Crisis, 1914–1921*.[67]

Modern Jewish politics is a field of study that has come into its own. Today it is a requisite part of Jewish scholarship. However one decides to approach the topic, it is bound to enrich one's perspective on the Jews' interactions with their social environment and on the meaning of Jewish community today.

63. New Brunswick, N.J.: Rutgers University Press, 1970.
64. New York: Pantheon, 1984.
65. London: Institute of Jewish Affairs, 1979.
66. New York: Oxford University Press, 1990.
67. *Studies in Contemporary Jewry* 4 (1988), ed. Jonathan Frankel.

22. Zionist Ideology

Gideon Shimoni

Introductory Remarks

The purpose of this essay is to suggest outlines and bibliographical resources for teaching about "Zionist ideology" or, as some prefer it, "the Zionist idea." By far the greater part of the vast secondary as well as primary literature that has appeared on the history of Zionist ideology is in the Hebrew language. However, the proposals for university teaching that follow are predicated on the assumption that only readings in English may be set for the students. Fortunately, there is an ample basis for undergraduate teaching in the corpus of translated sources and research works available to the English reader as well as in the considerable number of original studies on Zionism written in English. It is further assumed that the university lecturer, although possessing a working knowledge of Hebrew, also prefers to use English translations in the preparation of the course. Accordingly, reference to works in Hebrew is made only where there is absolutely no equivalent material available in English. This is not to say, however, that some of the standard works on the history of Zionism fail to provide valuable discussions of the various ideological formulations that are an inseparable ingredient of the history of the Zionist movement. Preeminent among such histories of the Zionist movement are (1) the three volumes by David Vital: *The Origins of Zionism*,[1] *Zionism: The Formative Years*,[2] and *Zionism: The Crucial Phase*;[3] (2) Ben Halpern, *The*

1. Oxford: Clarendon, 1975.
2. Oxford: Clarendon, 1982.
3. Oxford: Clarendon, 1987.

Idea of the Jewish State;[4] and (3) Walter Laqueur, *A History of Zionism.*[5]

On Zionist ideology, as distinct from the history of the Zionist movement, two books are admirably suited to serve as basic prescribed texts for undergraduate teaching: Arthur Hertzberg, *The Zionist Idea: A Historical Analysis and Reader,*[6] and Shlomo Avineri, *The Making of Modern Zionism: The Intellectual Origins of the Jewish State.*[7] A third overview, geared to a more elementary level of knowledge, is Monty Penkower, *The Emergence of Zionist Thought.*[8] Also the *Encyclopaedia Judaica,* and more specifically, *The Encyclopedia of Zionism and Israel,*[9] may be put to good use in teaching on Zionist ideology. An updated revision of the latter encyclopedia is currently in press and should appear in 1992. Another major resource, especially useful for the bibliographies of students' assignments, is the annual annotated bibliography which forms a part of the quarterly journal *Studies in Zionism.*[10]

Finally, since a full discussion of the problematics involved in defining the term "ideology" is beyond the scope of this essay, it may be useful at the outset to state that my preferred definition of the term "ideology," in the context of the nationalist movement known as Zionism, is simply, an action-oriented system of ideas concerned with an entity known as the Jews. The historical parameters for the course framework under discussion are from approximately the mid-nineteenth century until the creation of the State of Israel in 1948.

Outline

An essential element of any discussion about Zionist ideology is an analysis of the historical context in which it emerged in the second half of the nineteenth century (or, as some historians might argue, in the last two decades of that century). This, of course, requires an explanation of the Emancipation process as it affected European Jewry. This ought to encompass the difference between the Jewish situation in West-Central Europe and that in the czarist

4. Cambridge: Harvard University Press, 2nd ed., 1969.
5. London: Weidenfeld and Nicolson, 1972.
6. New York: Atheneum, 1973.
7. London: Weidenfeld and Nicolson, 1981.
8. New York: Associated Faculty Press, 1986.
9. New York: McGraw-Hill and Herzl Press, 1971.
10. Published by the Institute for Research in the History of Zionism, Tel Aviv University (subscriptions available from Frank Cass & Co. Ltd., Gainsborough House, 11 Gainsborough Rd., London E11 1RS, England).This bibliography, cumulative from 1980, is also available on diskette to the journal's subscribers and has the advantage of specifying, as one of its bibliographical categories, works on Zionist ideology.

Russian empire; the changes undergone by the Jews as communities and as individuals in the course of their attempted integration into the various societies in which they were domiciled; and the reaction to these developments on the part of those majority societies, particularly the appearance of political antisemitism. Since the focus of our discussion is on ideology rather than on political history, major emphasis must be placed on the Jewish ideological underpinnings of Enlightenment (the Haskalah) and the aspiration toward integration into the civic, social, and national textures of European societies.

Almost every book on the history of Zionism has an introductory chapter that attempts to treat of these themes with varying degrees of detail. Shlomo Avineri's (n. 7) brief introduction (pp. 3–13) is useful for illustration of the problems of Jewish identity attendant upon Emancipation and in pointing to these as a formative factor in the emergence of Zionist ideology. Arthur Hertzberg's (n. 6) extensive introduction discusses (pp. 15–32) "the historical matrix within which modern Zionism was fashioned" in more complex terms involving a typology of Jewish responses to Emancipation and relating it to, and contrasting it with, Jewish messianism. It should be noted that Avineri includes chapters on the ideas of Nahman Krochmal and Heinrich Graetz. This may serve the teacher well in emphasizing that the core of Zionist ideology evolved out of a strongly ethnic self-affirmation, not only prevalent in the great mass of unemancipated Jewry in the czarist Russian empire, but also retained by important segments of the Jewish communities undergoing Emancipation in West-Central Europe. Although the return to Jewish ethnic self-affirmation, and thence to nationalism, exhibited by erstwhile believers in Emancipation and integration, such as Leo Pinsker and Theodor Herzl, was largely a reaction to the eruption of antisemitism, the main social bearers of the Zionist idea in its fully formed nationalist dimensions were those members of the Jewish intelligentsia who had never relinquished their Jewish ethnicity. Their thought patterns may be illustrated, in the West-Central European context, by examining the ideas of Krochmal and Graetz as Avineri does; and, in the czarist Russian context, by those of Peretz Smolenskin, as done by both Hertzberg and Avineri. The important point is that these thinkers, while favoring Emancipation, never waived their self-affirmation of Jewish ethnic distinctiveness. Moreover, they did so independently of the factor of antisemitism.

Perhaps the most serviceable and comprehensive introductory treatment is to be found in Halpern (n. 4), ch. 1, "The Setting of Modern Jewish History" (pp. 3–19), and ch. 3, "The Rise and Reception of Zionism in the Nineteenth Century" (pp. 55–94). Still lacking is the type of introduction to the subject that would place Zionism within the context of historical explanations for the rise of nationalist ideologies in general, although allusions to this question may be found in the abovementioned works (e.g., Halpern, pp. 20–23) and in general works on nationalism. An evaluation of the latter category is beyond the scope of this essay. However, students might be referred, for example, to Hugh Seton-Watson, *Nations and States*,[11] especially ch. 10, "Diaspora Nations" (pp. 383–416). See also Mitchell Cohen, *Zion and State: Nation, Class, and the Shaping of Modern Israel*,[12] pp. 17–41.

Another contextual desideratum for a course on the Zionist ideology is a discussion of the historical attachment of Judaism and Jews to Eretz Israel, in respect of traditional concepts of *galut* (exile) and Zion, as well as of the actual presence of Jews in Eretz Israel prior to the beginnings of Zionism. Once again, it is Halpern's work (n. 4) that provides the most serviceable overview (ch. 4, "Attachment to Zion: Traditional Bonds and Involvement of Jewish Organizations" [pp. 95–130]). A more ideologically focused analysis of "the meaning of the Land of Israel to the Jewish people, as it is reflected in Jewish thought," is Eliezer Schweid, *The Land of Israel: National Home or Land of Destiny*.[13] Parts 1, 2, and 3 survey the field up to the appearance of Zionism.

This leads to a complex question central to the history of Zionist ideology: Can one already discern formulations of Zionist ideology prior to the emergence of an organized movement of Zionism in the form of Hibbat Zion in the 1880s? The terms "proto-Zionist" or alternatively "precursors" or "forerunners" are generally applied to those persons who called for a return to Zion in one form or another. However, historians differ on the interpretation of such formulations or the significance to be attached to them and consequently on the answer to the question, Who were the first thinkers to formulate the Zionist idea?

The main ideas to be considered are those of Rabbis Yehuda Alkalai (1798–1878) and Zvi Hirsch Kalischer (1795–1874) and of the early socialist thinker Moses Hess (1812–1875). The most important contribution to the historians' debate over this question is that of Jacob Katz. An abbreviated English translation of some of Katz's essays is available in Jacob Katz, *Jewish Emancipation and Self-Emancipation*.[14] The most pertinent sections are ch. 8, "The Forerunners of Zionism" (pp. 104–15), and ch. 7, "The Jewish National Movement: A Sociological Analysis" (pp. 89–103). A version of his study of Kalischer is available as Jacob Katz, "Tsevi Hirsch Kalischer."[15] Halpern (n.

11. London: Methuen, 1977.
12. Oxford: Blackwell, 1987.
13. London: Associated University Presses, 1985.
14. Philadelphia: Jewish Publication Society, 1986.
15. In *Guardians of Our Heritage*, ed. Leo Jung (New York: Bloch, 1958), pp. 209–27.

4) follows Katz's interpretation but is very brief (pp. 89–103), and Hertzberg (n. 6) considers the question (pp. 32–40) and, more importantly, provides a selection of sources from the writings of Alkalai, Kalischer, and Hess.

Jacob Katz argues that the criteria for determining who were the precursors of Zionism are not only the similarity of ideas and proposals as compared with those associated with mature Zionist thought after 1880, but also evidence of the capacity of those ideas to generate an active social force. By these criteria he finds that the terms "forerunners" or "precursors" should be limited to a rather small circle of persons associated with the Hevrat Yishuv Eretz Israel (Colonization Association for Eretz Israel), which had a brief and inconsequential existence in the early 1860s. This incorporates the secularized messianic ideas of Moses Hess as well as the traditionalist messianic ideas of Rabbis Alkalai and Kalischer (also some others, notably Rabbi Joseph Natonek, on whom little is available in English). He suggests, however, that these manifestations be termed "precursors" of Zionism (or "proto-Zionism") rather than be designated as the first Zionist formulations proper, because there is only the most meager evidence of consequential development leading to the Zionist formulations of the 1880s. Katz also offers an explanation for the precursor phenomenon in terms of the geographical situations of Alkalai and Kalischer on the border between regions of Jewish emancipatory experience in Austria-Hungary and Germany on the one side, and the non-Emancipated condition of Russian Jewry on the other side. He further explains the social incapacity of these precursors' ideas in terms of the optimistic faith in Emancipation still prevalent among the enlightened Jewish intelligentsia in Europe. Only when this optimism was undermined by the antisemitic eruptions of the early 1880s did the social conditions become ripe for the formulation of a socially and politically productive nationalist ideology of Zionism. For a more comprehensive treatment of this subject than is available in English, the Hebrew-reading university teacher is referred to Jacob Katz, Toward Jewish Nationhood: Essays and Studies,[16] pp. 15–35, 263–356; and Josef Salmon, Religion and Zionism: First Confrontations,[17] pp. 11–111. One of Salmon's relevant articles was written in English, "Tradition and Modernity in Early Religious Zionist Thought."[18]

At this point in the discussion of Zionist ideology, the university teacher may choose between two obvious options: a chronologically ordered analysis of the thought of major Zionist thinkers, or a comparative–typological approach emphasizing various schools of thought. The former approach might

16. *Le-umiyut yehudit: masot u-mehkarim* (Jerusalem: Ha-sifriya ha-tzionit, 1979).
17. *Dat ve-tzionut: immutim rishonim* (Jerusalem: Ha-sifriya ha-tzionit, 1990).
18. *Tradition* 18 (Summer 1979): 79–98.

follow the order of Hertzberg (n. 6). For students' reading assignments, his succinct biographical introductions to each thinker in combination with the discussion of some of their ideas in his lengthy general introduction may be supplemented by equivalent chapters in Avineri (n. 7). Class discussion may be fruitfully conducted with reference to the fine selection of sources provided by Hertzberg. His part 1, "Precursors," will, of course, already have been discussed, as possibly also Peretz Smolenskin in part 2 (pp. 142–57). The following order of discussion suggests itself.

1. Hibbat Zion thinkers (Eliezer Ben-Yehudah, Moshe Leib Lilienblum, Leo Pinsker, with primary emphasis on the last-mentioned).
2. Theodor Herzl and, with lesser emphasis, Max Nordau.
3. Ahad Ha-Am, contrasting "cultural Zionism" as a school of thought with the "political Zionism" of Herzl.
4. Labor Zionism: (a) The non-Marxist or "constructivist" socialist school of thought illustrated by Nahman Syrkin and also by the nonsocialist, humanistic labor ideology of Aaron David Gordon. (b) The Marxist approach illustrated by the early thought of Ber Borochov: Both Avineri and Hertzberg include sections on Syrkin, Borochov, and A. D. Gordon, and a larger selection of Gordon's writings is available in English, *Selected Essays.*[19] On both Syrkin and Borochov the most authoritative additional references are Jonathan Frankel, *Prophecy and Politics: Socialism, Nationalism, and the Russian Jews 1862–1917,*[20] pp. 288–364. There are also authoritative works in English (or English translation) on the life and thought of key personalities such as Anita Shapira, *Berl: The Biography of a Socialist Zionist: Berl Katznelson 1887–1944;*[21] Shabtai Teveth, *Ben-Gurion: The Burning Ground 1886–1948;*[22] Shlomo Avineri, *Arlosoroff.*[23] There is, however, a dearth of authoritative works in English on other Labor Zionist ideologues of importance such as Meir Ya'ari of ha-Shomer ha-Tza'ir and Yitzhak Tabenkin of the ha-Kibbutz ha-Me'uhad movement and the Ahdut ha-Avodah party, and neither Hertzberg nor Avineri includes sources or discussions of these two personalities. A text that might enrich discussion of Labor Zionism and its clash with the Zionist Right is Cohen (n. 12), pp. 85–200. Also, Laqueur (n. 5) is serviceable for teaching on labor Zionist ideology and on the clash with Revisionist Zionism (part 2, pp. 209–383).

19. Trans. Frances Burnce (New York: League for Labor Palestine, 1938).
20. Cambridge: Cambridge University Press, 1981.
21. Cambridge: Cambridge University Press, 1984.
22. London: Robert Hale, 1987.
23. London: Peter Halban, 1989.

5. Orthodox Religious Zionism, its early phase illustrated by the thought of Rabbis Samuel Mohilever, Yehiel Michel Pines, and Yitzhak Yaakov Reines: Unfortunately, there is a dearth of recommendable works in English on Rabbi Reines, whose thought is vital for an understanding of the formative ideological position of Mizrahi, founded in 1902 (including the support it rendered to Herzl's controversial "Uganda scheme" proposal of 1903). Both Hertzberg and Avineri omit Reines. However, one might make use of Ehud Luz, *Parallels Meet: Religion and Nationalism in the Early Zionist Movement 1882–1904*,[24] ch. 9, "The Organization of Religious Zionism" (pp. 227–55); or Vital (n. 2), pp. 215–24. For the lecturer one may recommend Eliezer Don-Yehiya, "Ideology and Policy in Religious Zionism: The Zionist Thought of Rav Reines and 'Mizrahi' Policy under His Leadership" (in Hebrew).[25] Later phases of Orthodox Religious Zionism might be illustrated by using the sources in Hertzberg: Samuel Hayyim Landau for the accommodation of part of it (the ideology of Torah ve-Avodah) to the ideals of Labor Zionism, and Rabbi Abraham Isaac Kook for the infusion of a profoundly messianic dimension into Orthodox Religious Zionist thought. It should, however, be noted that this dimension only came to dominate the national-religious wing of Zionism some years after the creation of the State of Israel. Avineri's chapter on Rabbi Kook (pp. 18–97) might profitably be used. See also *Religious Zionism: An Anthology*.[26]

6. Ze'ev Jabotinsky and Revisionist Zionism: Hertzberg's treatment of this is inadequate. If Avineri's is used, it may be fruitful to add as counterpoint Israel Eldad, "Jabotinsky Distorted."[27] A far more comprehensive work and one that facilitates important distinctions between the thought of Jabotinsky, on the one hand, and extremist offshoots of the Zionist Right, on the other hand, is Yaacov Shavit, *Jabotinsky and the Revisionist Movement, 1925–1948*.[28]

A Comparative and Typological Approach

As an alternative to the above structure, one might use a comparative and typological approach. Although more complex, such an approach is certainly

24. Philadelphia: Jewish Publication Society, 1988.
25. *Ha-Tsionut* Studies in the History of the Zionist Movement and of the Jewish Community in Palestine, pub. Tel Aviv University 8 (1983): 103–46.
26. Ed. Yosef Tirosh (Jerusalem: World Zionist Organization, 1975).
27. *The Jerusalem Quarterly* 16 (Summer 1980): 27–37.
28. London: Frank Cass, 1988.

more intellectually stimulating and, in the final analysis, probably more instructive too. For an analysis using this approach see Gideon Shimoni, "Ideological Perspectives"[29] (this reference could be incorporated as a reading assignment for students).

The conceptual framework is as follows. An attempt is made to define the lowest common denominators of the Zionist ideology as a whole in the form of four propositions relating to, respectively, (1) definition of the Jewish entity, (2) diagnosis of the problematic situation to which the ideology addresses itself, (3) the solution envisaged, and (4) the means suggested for attaining the envisaged solution. This is done in class discussion on the basis of an analysis of the Zionist ideological formulations of Pinsker, Herzl, Ahad Ha-Am, and Rabbi Reines. The formulation extrapolated in this way might run roughly as follows: (1) The Jews are an entity with national and not only religious attributes; (2) The situation of the Jewish entity under conditions of dispersion is critically defective, not just in a messianic sense, but emphatically in a worldly sense; (3) The solution lies in territorial ingathering of Jews in Eretz Israel (or, failing that, transitionally in another territory) under conditions of autonomy at least, and sovereignty at best; (4) These purposes should be effected by political diplomacy, settlement activities, and the revival of Jewish national morale and culture.

This conceptual framework then lends itself to amplification by tracing the contours of divergence among Zionist thinkers in regard to each proposition. Thus, for example, political Zionists placed emphasis on the problem of Jewish distress resulting from the failures of Emancipation, whereas cultural Zionists emphasized "the problem of Judaism" (i.e., of retaining Jewish cultural individuality) rather than "the problem of the Jews," (i.e., of Jewish material distress). Socialist Zionists concurred with political Zionists in focusing on the problem of material distress but located its source in processes of class conflict. Similarly, the divergences in Zionist ideology over the dimension of "the ultimate vision" ranged over the demand for sovereignty modeled on the European liberal state (e.g., Herzl), visions of a socialist society, a society largely based on the Halakhah (Orthodox Religious Zionists), and the politically minimalist aspiration for a spiritual-cultural center (Ahad Ha-Am, followed by Judah Magnes and Martin Buber). In the same way, regarding the means and priorities to be adopted by Zionism, divergences of opinion over and above the common denominators can be demonstrated.

A useful source for student readings is Joseph Heller, *The Zionist Idea.*[30]

29. In *Zionism in Transition*, ed. Moshe Davis (New York: Arno, 1980), pp. 3–42.
30. New York: Schocken, 1949.

This was written in the 1940s by a Zionist for Zionists, originally in the form of a correspondence course. (Heller was an Anglo-Jewish Zionist of note and a devotee of Ahad Ha-Am.) As such, it is a documentary source illustrating the Western self-understanding of Zionist ideology on the eve of statehood. It contains concise expositions of the tenets underlying the major schools of thought in Zionism, namely, "Spiritual Zionism" (ch. 11), "Religious Zionism" (ch. 12), "Socialist Zionism," (ch. 13), and "General Zionism–Revisionism" (ch. 14). It also contains short expositions of the Zionist ideological response to "Objections to Zionism" (ch. 9), "Are the Jews a Nation" (ch. 3), and "The Arab Problem" (ch. 15). A supplementary source, also in the nature of partisan expositions, is *Struggle for Tomorrow: Modern Political Ideologies of the Jewish People*.[31] The advantage of this source is that it contains brief expositions of smaller schools of thought, such as Mapam (in which ha-Shomer ha-Tza'ir was the major constituent), Ihud (in which Judah Magnes, Martin Buber, and Ernst Simon were prominent), as well as other political ideologies ranging from Agudat Israel to that of Jewish Communists.

Central Ideological Issues

Having completed this comparative and typological survey, time permitting, one might proceed to focus more specifically on a few select issues of crucial ideological importance that cut across the entire spectrum of Zionist ideology. Of course, ideally speaking, each such issue could be the subject of an advanced seminar course open to students who have completed the above-outlined program. Two issues that call for special emphasis are "the implications of Zionism for Jewish cultural identity," and "the Arab question in Zionism."

The question of Jewish cultural identity as mediated by Zionism falls naturally into three parts: (1) Ahad Ha-Am's seminal thought on Jewish culture; (2) the inner conflict between Ahad Ha-Am's conceptions of normative secular Jewishness and the "free," nonnormative secular school of thought epitomized by Berdyczewski and Brenner; (3) the clash between secularized Jewishness and the orthodox rabbinate within Zionism.

In analyzing the thought of Ahad Ha-Am in this context, the emphasis shifts from his concept of a cultural center as counterpoint to Herzlian political Zionism, to his advocacy of a Zionist mode of Jewish identity that, although secularized, remained bound to certain cultural norms. These norms included not only the Hebrew language and literary heritage as cultural media and the association with the Land of Israel, but also putative Jewish moral

31. Ed. Basil J. Vlavianos and Feliks Gross (New York: Arts Incorporated, 1954).

norms as well as a respectful attitude toward the sancta of the Jewish religious heritage. Student readings might include Leon Simon, *Ahad Ha-Am: A Biography*,[32] especially ch. 9, "Jewish Humanism" (pp. 157–68), and ch. 15, "Philosophy of Judaism and the Spiritual Center" (pp. 279–98). More critical readings may be taken from *At the Crossroads: Essays on Ahad Ha-Am*,[33] especially Stanley Nash, "Ahad Ha-Am and 'Ahad Ha-Amism': The Onset of Crisis" (pp. 73–86). See also articles in *Jewish History* 4/2 (Fall 1990), especially Yaakov Shavit, "Ahad Ha-Am and Hebrew National Culture: Realist or Utopianist?"[34]

There is a dearth of works in English on the Zionist ideology of one particularly important thinker, Yehezkel Kaufmann. His incisive critique of both Ahad Ha-Am and the opposing views of Berdyczewski and others is available only in Hebrew. See his Between Paths[35] and, at greater length, his monumental Exile and Alienation,[36] especially section 9 (pp. 348–424). In English, use might be made of Laurence J. Silberstein, "Exile and Alienhood: Yehezkel Kaufmann on the Jewish Nation."[37] This section of the course is also an appropriate place for a discussion of the ideological formulations of Martin Buber, in the post-assimilationist context of German Jewry, and of Mordecai Kaplan, whose unique hybrid of secular assumptions and religious behavior may be considered an adaptation of Ahad Ha-Am's outlook to the American Jewish environment. Works in English on Buber and on Kaplan are plentiful.

The conflict between the secular Zionist intelligentsia, clustered (albeit controversially) around the seminal thought of Ahad Ha-Am, and the orthodox religious rabbinate which formed Mizrahi is admirably treated in Luz (n. 24). Select pages might serve as prescribed reading. Also Vital (n. 2), although essentially a political history and not a history of ideas, is serviceable in this respect. A good summary of the debates over culture in the Zionist organization that may serve for student reading is Moshe Rinott, "Religion and Education: The Cultural Question and the Zionist Movement 1897–1913."[38] See also Shmuel Almog, *Zionism and History: The Rise of a New Jewish Consciousness*,[39] ch. 2, "The Significance of Culture" (pp. 84–176).

The Arab question in Zionism is undoubtedly one that calls for special

32. Philadelphia: Jewish Publication Society, 1960.
33. Ed. Jacques Kornberg (Albany: State University of New York Press, 1983).
34. Pp. 71–87.
35. *Bein netivot* (Haifa: Reali School, 1952).
36. *Golah ve-nekhar*, 2 vols. (Tel Aviv: Dvir, 1954).
37. In *Texts and Responses: Studies Presented to Nahum N. Glatzer*, ed. Michael A. Fishbane and Paul R. Flohr (Leiden: Brill, 1975), pp. 239–55.
38. *Studies in Zionism* 5/1 (1984): 1–18.
39. New York: St. Martins; Jerusalem: Magnes, 1987.

attention in any discussion of Zionist ideology. In our present context the focus is, of course, not on political events and negotiations between Zionists and various Arab personalities, but rather on the fundamental ideological formulations of the Jewish right to national self-fulfillment in Eretz Israel and the implications of these formulations for the Zionist response to Arab counterclaims. Yosef Gorny, *Zionism and the Arabs 1882–1948: A Study of Ideology*,[40] might serve as a major resource, including select readings for students. Although much of this book deals with the operative aspects of the Jewish–Arab conflict in Eretz Israel, it also pays considerable attention to the ideological formulations of the main Jewish protagonists.

A conceptual and time framework that may be recommended for teaching is a typological analysis of the major Zionist positions adopted in the period from 1925, when both the Zionist Revisionist Organization and the diminutive Brit Shalom association came into existence, until 1937, when the Peel Commission's partition proposal in the wake of the Arab uprising in Palestine marked an important turning point. Within that time frame one may analyze comparatively the ideological formulations on the Zionist Right, of Jabotinsky and of the diminutive Brit ha-Biryonim (which diverged from Jabotinsky in important respects); the compromise for-the-sake-of-peace formulations of the small circle of intellectuals associated with Brit Shalom; and the positions, intermediate between these two extremes, prevalent in the Zionist Labor camp, particularly those of David Ben-Gurion.

A useful selection of sources may be found in one of a series of booklets published by the World Zionist Organization: *Sources: Anthology of Contemporary Jewish Thought*, no. 4.[41] It has an introduction by Eliezer Schweid and brief selections relating to the Arab question in Zionism from the writings of Ahad Ha-Am, Arthur Ruppin, David Ben-Gurion, Ze'ev Jabotinsky, A.D. Gordon, Martin Buber, and Berl Katznelson. Eliezer Schweid, *The Land of Israel: National Home or Land of Destiny*[42] is also relevant. Finally, an important reading on Ben-Gurion in this context is Shabtai Teveth, *Ben-Gurion and the Palestinian Arabs*.[43] Also, Martin Buber's ideological formulations call for discussion. Although Buber, still living in Germany, was only a sympathizer of the Brit Shalom association, he was a major participant in later metamorphoses of that phenomenon after settling in Eretz Israel in 1938. An important resource is *A Land of Two Peoples: Martin Buber on Jews and Arabs*.[44]

40. Oxford: Clarendon, 1987.
41. Ed. David Hardan (Jerusalem: World Zionist Organization, 1975).
42. Toronto: Associated University Presses and Herzl Press, 1985.
43. New York: Oxford University Press, 1983.
44. Ed. Paul R. Mendes-Flohr (New York: Oxford University Press, 1983).

Other major ideological themes that cut across all schools of Zionist thought may of course be chosen if time permits, or according to the preferences of the university lecturer. Examples are Negation of the Galut, for which Arnold M. Eisen, *Galut: Modern Jewish Reflection on Homeless and Homecoming*,[45] can provide a basis; and Zionist Ideology in the Context of American Jewry (or alternatively of English-speaking Jewries). The readings around which the latter theme might revolve are mainly interpretive essays such as Ben Halpern, "The Americanization of Zionism 1880–1930";[46] Melvin Urofsky, "Zionism: An American Experience";[47] and the symposium on "The Influence of Zionism on the American Jewish Community: An Assessment by Israeli and American Historians," with the participation of Evyatar Friesel, Henry L. Feingold, Allon Gal, and Melvin I. Urofsky.[48]

45. Bloomington: Indiana University Press, 1986.
46. *American Jewish History* 69/1 (September 1976): 15–33.
47. *American Jewish Historical Quarterly* 63/3 (March 1974): 215–43.
48. *American Jewish History* 75/2 (December 1985): 130–83.

23. Religious Culture and Politics in Israel

Chaim I. Waxman

The issue of religion in Israel should be seen within the context of the series of conflict settings within Israel referred to in my essay in this volume, "Israeli Society and Culture," in large part because of the challenges of blending traditional religion with modern national Jewish life. Especially in Israel, where the ideology of Zionism—a movement which, as Shmuel Eisenstadt pointed out in *The Transformation of Israeli Society: An Essay in Interpretation*,[1] is based on both rebellion and continuity—plays such a pivotal role, and where there is thus a highly intricate relationship between Israel and Diaspora Jewry, the challenges of such a blending are magnified and are reflected in almost every political conflict in the society. This essay highlights and clarifies the issues involved through a synthesis of contemporary works on the subject.

Most students of Israel agree that is not a theocracy. A notable exception is the Israeli philosopher, Gershon Weiler, *Jewish Theocracy*,[2] who argues that in effect the very notion of a Jewish state renders it a theocratic one. Although Weiler is unique, others readily agree that Israel is also not quite as secular as most modern societies. Religion, for example, plays a much greater role within the Israeli polity than within the American. The nature of religious conflict in Israel is thus much different than it is in other modern societies. Indeed, the basic conflict in Israel is over the limits of religion within the political sphere. A corollary to this is the tensions which emerge from the power struggles between religious and secular parties. But the impact and consequences of these conflicts are not then limited to specific Israeli political parties.

1. Boulder, Colo.: Westview, 1986.
2. Leiden: Brill, 1988.

Indeed, they have had major impact on relations between Israel and the Diaspora at various times in recent years and thus affect the entire modern Jewish experience.

In order to understand the background of these conflicts, one must go back to the early history of the Zionist Organization and the precarious relationship between the secular and religious Zionist organizations and movements, and the religious non-Zionist Agudat Israel movement as well. Ehud Luz, *Parallels Meet: Religion and Nationalism in the Early Zionist Movement, 1882–1904*,[3] provides the most complete analysis of the ideological and pragmatic issues involved. However, there was one segment of Orthodox Jewry, the Neturei Karta, which would have nothing to do with the Zionist movement, not only because it opposed the secularism of modern Zionism (which was the basis of the opposition of Agudat Israel), but because it defined all forms of Zionism, as well as any other human endeavors to end the Divinely decreed Exile, as inherently Satanic because the dispersion was ordained by God and the redemption could only come about through His intervention. The perspectives of the Neturei Karta are best presented in Emile Marmorstein, *Heaven at Bay: The Jewish Kulturkampf in the Holy Land*,[4] and I. Domb, *The Transformation: The Case of the Neturei Karta*.[5] A brief but cogent analysis of the major stream of Neturei Karta anti-Zionism can be found in Norman Lamm, "The Ideology of Neturei Karta—According to the Satmarer Version."[6]

With statehood, the Zionist (and non-Zionist) organizations became the political parties which constitute the Israeli Knesset (parliament). Anachronistic as it may appear to Americans, the religious organizations—both Zionist and non-Zionist—transformed themselves into political parties, and at least one religious bloc has served as a partner in every ruling coalition. The history and politics of Israel's religious political parties is analyzed by Gary S. Schiff, *Tradition and Politics: The Religious Parties of Israel*.[7] Somewhat early but still relevant analyses of the religious–secular conflicts in the political sphere are presented by S. Clement Leslie, *The Rift in Israel: Religious Authority and Secular Democracy*,[8] who labels the relationship a "rift," and by a lawyer and former Knesset member, S. Zalman Abramov, *Perpetual Dilemma: Jewish Religion in the Jewish State*,[9] who defines the relationship between Judaism

3. Trans. Lenn J. Schramm (Philadelphia: Jewish Publication Society, 1988).
4. London: Oxford University Press, 1969.
5. London: Hamadfis, 1958.
6. *Tradition* 12/1 (Fall 1971): 38–53.
7. Detroit: Wayne State University Press, 1977.
8. London: Routledge and Kegan Paul, 1971.
9. Rutherford, N.J.: Fairleigh Dickinson University Press, 1976.

and the state as a "perpetual dilemma." The best critical analysis of the broad range of religious issues in the political sphere is, not coincidentally, by two political scientists who are more sympathetic to traditional Judaism, Charles S. Liebman and Eliezer Don-Yehiya, *Civil Religion in Israel: Traditional Judaism and Political Culture in the Jewish State.*[10]

Some students of religion in Israel attribute the legal status of religion in Israel to the small but disproportionally powerful religious political parties within the Israeli parliamentary system. Although these parties represent only a small minority of the Israeli electorate, it is argued, they have held the balance of power in the efforts of both the major political blocs—Labor and Likud (Ma'arah and Gahal; Mapai and Herut, in the past)—to form coalitions. The power of the religious parties has been many times greater than the size of the electorate which those parties represent, and, it is often argued, they maintain an unfair stranglehold over the vast majority of the Israeli populace because of their political status. This view is reflected in such books as Ervin Birnbaum, *The Politics of Compromise*,[11] and Norman L. Zucker, *The Coming Crisis in Israel*,[12] among others.

However, religion in the State of Israel today is an issue of importance not only to those who vote for the religious parties, but to a very broad cross section of the Israeli electorate. As Liebman and Don-Yehiya found in their research, "What A Jewish State Means to Israeli Jews"[13] and *Religion and Politics in Israel*,[14]

93 percent of the Jewish population in Israel thought that Israel ought to be a Jewish state, 83 percent defined that to mean "a state whose population is predominantly Jewish"; according to 64 percent, "which lives in accordance with the values of Judaism"; and, according to 62 percent, "whose public image is in accord with the Jewish tradition." ... Seventy-six percent of the respondents felt that there ought to be some relationship between religion and state in Israel. ([n 13], p. 101)

Accordingly, the phenomenon of religious legislation in Israel exists largely not as the result of unethical and/or undemocratic political machinations, but because that is the will of the vast majority of Israelis. Liebman and Don-Yehiya do not suggest that the majority of the Israeli electorate supports each and every specific piece of religious legislation, even though it is somewhat

10. Berkeley and Los Angeles: University of California Press, 1983.
11. Rutherford, N.J.: Fairleigh Dickinson University Press, 1970.
12. Cambridge: MIT Press, 1973.
13. In *Comparative Jewish Politics: Public Life in Israel and the Diaspora*, ed. Sam N. Lehman-Wilzig and Bernard Susser (Ramat Gan: Bar Ilan University Press, 1981), pp. 101–109.
14. Bloomington: Indiana University Press, 1984, pp. 15–30.

difficult to envision the passage of any item in the Israeli Knesset against which there was strong opposition.

In any case, their data clearly indicate that religion plays a much greater role in Israeli society than simply serving as the raison d'être of the religious political parties. Israel was established as a Jewish state, and the vast majority of Israel's Jews—secular as well as religious—agree that Judaism is a basic and necessary component of being Jewish and, therefore, of Israel's society and its political culture. Indeed, as Liebman and Don-Yehiya demonstrate (n. 10), even the various versions of secular Zionism have incorporated Judaism into the civil religion of Israel.

One factor which exacerbates the religious–secular conflict is the interrelationship between religion and nationalism. Specifically, most of the religious parties are viewed as "hawkish" in general, and especially vis-à-vis Israel's retention of virtually all the Administered Territories, Judea and Samaria/the West Bank. Among secularists in particular, there is a prevalent image of religious Zionists as political messianists. This image stems, in large measure, from the strong religious Zionist influence in the settlement movement, Gush Emunim, as analyzed by Stewart Reiser, "The Religious Parties as a Support System for the Settler Movement."[15]

The literature on Gush Emunim is vast, compared to its size. And, as with any controversial subject, the quality varies. Among the major analyses, see Gideon Aran, "From Religious Zionism to Zionist Religion: The Roots of Gush Emunim";[16] Ian S. Lustick, *For the Land and the Lord: Jewish Fundamentalism in Israel*;[17] *The Impact of Gush Emunim: Politics and Settlement in the West Bank*;[18] Amnon Rubinstein, *The Zionist Dream Revisited*;[19] Ehud Sprinzak, *Gush Emunim: The Politics of Zionist Fundamentalism in Israel*;[20] and Janet Aviad, "The Messianism of Gush Emunim."[21] For a participant's account of the "Jewish underground," the group responsible for a number of physical crimes against Palestinian Arab leaders in the Territories, including assassination attempts which resulted in permanent physical injury to several

15. In *Israeli Politics in the 1990s: Key Domestic and Foreign Policy Factors*, ed. Bernard Reich and Gershon R. Kieval (Westport, Conn.: Greenwood, 1991), pp. 71–94.

16. In *Studies in Contemporary Jewry*, vol. 2, ed. Peter Y. Medding (Bloomington: Indiana University Press, 1986), pp. 116–43.

17. New York: Council on Foreign Relations, 1988.

18. Ed. David Newman (New York: St. Martin's, 1985).

19. New York: Schocken, 1984.

20. New York: American Jewish Committee, 1986.

21. In *Studies in Contemporary Jewry*, vol. 7, *Jews and Messianism in the Modern Era: Metaphor and Meaning*, ed. Jonathan Frankel (New York: Oxford University Press, 1991), pp. 197–213.

subjects, as well an attempt to blow up the Temple Mount in Jerusalem, see Haggai Segal, *Dear Brothers: The West Bank Jewish Underground.*[22]

The image of the religious as political messianists probably also stems from the ideology and actions of the late Meir Kahane and the extremist party which he founded and headed, Kach. There are no good biographical analyses of Meir Kahane. Virtually the only book-length portraits of Kahane are two highly sensationalist ones: Yair Kotler, *Heil Kahane*,[23] and Robert I. Friedman, *The False Prophet: Rabbi Meir Kahane—From FBI Informant to Knesset Member.*[24] Kahane himself was a prolific writer. Two of his latest books which contain the essence of his ideology as it relates to Israel are *They Must Go*[25] and *Uncomfortable Questions for Comfortable Jews.*[26] Much has been written on the social and political sources of Kahanism as well its implications for Israeli society, the most notable being Ehud Sprinzak, "Kach and Meir Kahane: The Emergence of Jewish Quasi-Fascism";[27] Aviezer Ravitzky, "Roots of Kahanism: Consciousness and Political Reality";[28] and Leon Wieseltier, "The Demons of the Jews."[29] The best analysis of the debate concerning Kahanism is Gerald Cromer, *The Debate About Kahanism in Israeli Society, 1984–1988.*[30] By contrast, there have been surprisingly few serious attempts to critically analyze the major ideas and conceptions of Kahane. One such attempt, by S. Dan Breslauer, *Meir Kahane: Ideologue, Hero, Thinker*,[31] deals primarily with Kahane's ideas and activities in the United States, prior to his migration to Israel.

However, the correlation between religion and nationalism is not limited solely to such immediate political issues as Israel's policies toward the Territories. Even more basically, there is a whole series of Israeli empirical studies which uniformly find a high correlation between religiosity and national Jewish identity and identification. The most significant among these are Simon N. Herman, *Israelis and Jews: The Continuity of an Identity*;[32] a series of surveys conducted in Israel in 1974 by Shlomit Levy and Louis E. Guttman[33] (part 4,

22. Woodmere, N.Y.: Beit Shammai, 1988.
23. New York: Adama Books, 1986.
24. Brooklyn: Lawrence Hill, 1990.
25. New York: Grosset and Dunlap, 1981.
26. Secaucus, N.J.: Lyle Stuart, 1987.
27. *Patterns of Prejudice* 19 (1985) no. 3: 15–21, no. 4: 3–13.
28. *The Jerusalem Quarterly* 39 (1986): 90–108.
29. *The New Republic* (11 November 1985): 15–25.
30. New York: Occasional Papers of the Frank Guggenheim Foundation, 1988.
31. Lewiston, N.Y.: Edwin Mellen, 1986.
32. New York: Random House, 1970.
33. 4 parts (Jerusalem: Israel Institute of Applied Social Research, 1974).

Values and Attitudes of Israeli High School Youth, contains an English summary); Eva Etzioni-Halevy and Rina Shapira, "Jewish Identification of Israeli Students: What Lies Ahead";[34] Simon N. Herman, *Jewish Identity: A Social Psychological Perspective;*[35] and Eva Etzioni-Halevy and Rina Shapira, *Political Culture in Israel: Cleavage and Integration Among Israeli Jews,*[36] pp. 157–78. The impact of the Arab–Israeli conflict on Judaism and religious Jewry in Israel is analyzed by Liebman and Don-Yehiya (n. 10). How the relationship between religion and nationalism contributes to the maintenance of a religio-political establishment in Israel are explored in Chaim I. Waxman, "Orthodox Judaism and Israeli Society."[37]

Religious Zionism is not monolithic, and since even before the formation of Mizrachi, the Religious Zionist Organization, in 1905, there were at least two factions within the Religious Zionist movement. Rabbi Yitzchak Yaakov Reines, the first president of the Mizrachi, stated on numerous occasions that he had an instrumental-political conception of Zionism, and he explicitly rejected the notion that Zionism was part of a messianic process. In fact, as Luz demonstrates (n. 3), he was a staunch supporter of Herzl's political Zionism within the World Zionist Organization, and he even persuaded the majority of the Mizrachi faction to vote for the Uganda Plan when it was first proposed. There is surprisingly little literature on Reines' thought in English. The best is Joseph Wanefsky, *Rabbi Isaac Jacob Reines: His Life and Thought,*[38] but it does not focus on his conception of Zionism.

By contrast, the other perspective, for whom Rabbi Abraham Isaac Kook, the Chief Rabbi of the Holy Land, was to become the spiritual leader, defined Zionism as part of the messianic process and proof that the contemporary era is "in the footsteps of the Messiah." Zionism, therefore, could only have meaning in Zion, and each new Jewish settlement in Zion was only helping to realize the arrival of the Messiah and total redemption of the Jewish people. Although Kook's voluminous writings are readily available in Hebrew, only a minute portion of his works have been translated in to English. The major ones are: Abraham Isaac Kook, *The Lights of Penitence, Lights of Holiness, The Moral Principles, Essays, Letters, and Poems,*[39] and Alter B. Z. Metzger, *Rabbi Kook's Philosophy of Penitence.*[40] A brief overview of his thought and

---

34. *Jewish Social Studies* 37/3–4 (July-October 1975): 251–66.
35. 2nd ed. (New Brunswick, N.J.: Transaction, 1989).
36. New York: Praeger, 1977.
37. *Midstream* (December 1991): 24–26.
38. New York: Philosophical Library, 1970.
39. Trans. and intro. Ben Zion Bokser (New York: Paulist Press, 1978).
40. New York: Bloch, 1968.

work is in Arthur Hertzberg, *The Zionist Idea*,[41] pp. 416–26. A bibliography of works in English on Rav Kook and selections of his writings in English translation appears in *Morasha*.[42] By far the most scholarly analysis of Kook written thus far has now been translated: Benjamin Ish-Shalom, *Rav Avraham Itzhak HaCohen Kook: Between Rationalism and Mysticism*.[43]

Until the Six Day War, the first perspective was the dominant one within the Religious Zionist Organization. This is not to say that messianism was totally absent from either religious or secular Zionism. On the contrary, a degree of messianism has long been a basic component within both Jewish tradition and Zionist ideology. On its role in Jewish tradition, see Chaim I. Waxman, *American Aliya: Portrait of an Innovative Migration Movement*,[44] pp. 39–49; on messianism in Zionism, see a number of the essays in Frankel (n. 21). However, in both those cases, it was a much more abstract and long-range messianism rather than a specific one with immediate political implications.

With the unanticipated victory, which many defined as miraculous, during the Six Day War, a wave of political messianism swept the country in general and Religious Zionism in particular. The son of Rabbi A.I. Kook, Rabbi Zvi Yehuda Kook, who was a teacher in the yeshiva founded by father, was a much more explicitly political messianist than his father had been. There is no book-length biography or analysis of Rabbi Z.Y. Kook. In the periodical literature, see Eliezer Don-Yehiya, "Messianic Theology and Radical Politics: Rav Kook, Father and Son, and Their Disciples"[45] and "Jewish Messianism, Religious Zionism, and Israeli Politics: The Impact and Origins of Gush Emunim."[46] As Don-Yehiya indicates, until the Six Day War, Kook's leadership was limited to a relatively small group of Religious Zionists who came under his tutelage in the yeshiva, Yeshivat Merkaz Harav. After that war, he came to be the dominant spiritual leader of Religious Zionism, and the movement became much more overtly nationalist. Thus, although there are more moderate elements within the National Religious Party, they could not muster sufficient support to gain a seat for Meimad, the Modern Orthodox Zionist movement which was expressly flexible on the issue of the Territories, in the 1988 Israeli elections for the twelfth Knesset. In the 1992 elections, the NRP adopted an explicit right-wing stance: "*Ha mafdal le-yeminhu*" (The NRP is

41. Garden City, N.Y.: Doubleday, 1959.
42. 2/1 (Fall–Winter 1985): 35–37.
43. Trans. Ora Wiskind Elper (Albany: State University of New York Press, 1993).
44. Detroit: Wayne State University Press, 1989.
45. *Morasha: A Journal of Religious Zionism* 3/2 (Spring–Summer 1988): 39–47.
46. *Middle Eastern Studies* 23/2 (April 1987): 215–34.

on your right)—and there was virtually no moderate Modern Orthodox voice.

A variety of factors contributed to Meimad's lack of success. Samuel C. Heilman and Menachem Friedman, for example, in their pamphlet *The Haredim in Israel: Who Are They and What Do They Want?*,[47] p. 23, n. 10, claim that in part it was due to Meimad's refusal to publicly pronounce that it would never join a coalition led by Likud. Be that as it may, the loss was probably due at least as much to the fact there there is a strong traditional Jewish attachment to Judea and Samaria and a fairly widespread feeling, even among those who may otherwise eschew right-wing politics, that Jews also have a right to settle in those parts of Eretz Israel. The issues of the Territories and the traditional Jewish attachment to Judea and Samaria are examined in Chaim I. Waxman, "The Israeli-Jewish Presence in the Territories."[48]

The much more basic arena of religious–secular strife, however, has virtually nothing to do with the Territories, and the conflict is primarily not between the Religious Zionist and secular elements in Israeli society. Rather, as Heilman and Friedman (n. 47) elucidate, it is between the secular and the much more sectarian, "ultra-orthodox," non-Zionist elements known as Haredim. In recent years, the major political advances have been made by Haredi parties, including Agudat Israel, the Sephardic Shas party, and Degel Hatorah. Many complex issues are involved in the strife, including the fact that while, on the one hand, many Haredim do not serve in the military, the Haredi parties make major demands for government economic support of their institutions. Also, in some cities, particularly Jerusalem, the Haredim are growing rapidly and increasing numbers of areas are becoming Haredi neighborhoods, in which non-Haredim feel overtly alienated. Heilman and Friedman offer a good summary and analysis of the growing potential for conflict between the Haredim and the rest of Israeli society. A fascinating ethnography of the Haredim is found in Samuel C. Heilman, *Defenders of the Faith: Inside Ultra-Orthodox Jewry.*[49] A more detailed study of the relationship between the Haredim, Religious Zionists, and many other aspects of religious developments in Israel and their impact on both Israeli society and Israel–American Jewish relations is found in Charles S. Liebman and Steven M. Cohen, *Two Worlds of Judaism.*[50] In brief, they suggest that Israeli Judaism is becoming increasingly particularistic while American Judaism is becoming increasingly universalistic, and they raise the question as to whether there are not developing two separate and distinct types of Judaism. In a much more extreme and

47. New York: American Jewish Committee, 1991.
48. In Reich and Kieval (n. 15), pp. 95–109.
49. New York: Schocken, 1992.
50. New Haven: Yale University Press, 1990.

highly polemical style, Uri Huppert decries what he views in Israel as a turn *Back to the Ghetto: Zionism in Retreat*,[51] particularly because of the growing strength of the Haredim and the heightened nationalism of the Religious Zionists.

On the other hand, despite what appears to be the growing rift between the religious and secular, there are some indications of an awareness and concern about these issues on both sides of the conflict, and attempts have been undertaken to resolve the sources of conflict. A number of such attempts are analyzed and discussed in a useful collection of essays, *Religious and Secular: Conflict and Accommodation between Jews in Israel*,[52] a book which also highlights the variety of religious types in Israel. For another collection in which that theme is even more central, see *Tradition, Innovation, Conflict: Jewishness and Judaism in Contemporary Israel*.[53]

There are many ways in which the subject of religion in Israel can be incorporated into a survey course on the Modern Jewish Experience. Probably the most obvious way is, after a discussion of the characteristics of modernity, to present the case of Israel as a manifestation of the conflict between traditional society and modern society, or at least between traditional and modern segments within a society. Within the context of a sociology of religion and Halakhah perspective, it would be particularly illuminating to examine the role of religion and the nature and types of religious conflicts which develop in different types of Jewish societies. Were the structure and function of religion in Medieval European Jewish communities substantively different from those of modern societies? Compare the religious issues of representative nineteenth-century East European Jewish communities with those of contemporary Diaspora communities, and then compare the latter with those which characterize Israel today. Background material for this type of analysis might include, among others, David Ellenson, *Tradition in Transition: Orthodoxy, Halakhah, and the Boundaries of Modern Jewish Identity*;[54] Menachem Friedman, "Life Tradition and Book Tradition in the Development of Ultraorthodox Judaism";[55] and Chaim I. Waxman, "Toward a Sociology of *Psak*."[56]

Looking at the issue from another angle, it is worthwhile to compare the

51. Buffalo: Prometheus, 1988.

52. Ed. Charles S. Liebman (Jerusalem: Keter, 1990).

53. Ed. Zvi Sobel and Benjamin Beit-Hallahmi (Albany: State University of New York Press, 1991).

54. Lanham, Md.: University Press of America, 1989.

55. In *Judaism Viewed from Within and from Without: Anthropological Perspectives*, ed. Harvey E. Goldberg (Albany: State University of New York Press, 1987), pp. 235–55.

56. *Tradition* 25/3 (Spring 1991): 12–25.

developments of Reform and Conservative Judaism in the West with their development in Israel. For the West, Michael A. Meyer, *Response to Modernity: A History of the Reform Movement in Judaism*,[57] and Marshall Sklare, *Conservative Judaism: An American Religious Movement*,[58] are basic. Ephraim Tabory has extensively researched the development of those movements. See, among others, his articles "Reform and Conservative Judaism in Israel: Aims and Platforms"[59] and "The Identity Dilemma of Non-Orthodox Religious Movements: Reform and Conservative Judaism in Israel."[60]

Another way is to contrast modern Western views of the relationship between religion and society and then look at the case of Israel. It might then be interesting to discuss with the students their own views concerning the place of religion in Israel. Do they hold the same views concerning separation of religion and state for Israel as they do for the United States? There is evidence that a significant portion of America's Jews do not. For an analysis of this phenomenon, see Chaim I. Waxman, "Religion and State in Israel: The Perspective of American Jewry."[61]

There are two major problems in presenting the subject. For one, it is a real challenge to the instructor to present perspectives in what is, essentially, a clash of ideologies in a nonideological and objective manner. Virtually anyone familiar with the issues has strong opinions about them and must therefore be very careful not to present them an unfairly. This, of course, is familiar to anyone with experience in presenting controversial material.

In addition, American undergraduates frequently have very limited knowledge and understanding of cultures other than their own, and they may therefore have difficulty grasping the depth of the significance of the issues of religion in Israel to all parties involved. At least within a semester-long course on the subject, there is room to expect that the students will be able to read and absorb enough to gain some real understanding of the subject. However, the problem is compounded in a survey course in which this subject is only one of many covered in the survey and, therefore, much less time is spent on it. Nevertheless, with careful selection of the clearest and most pertinent readings, this challenge, too, can be met and the students can gain new insight into the complexity of Israel as well as Jews and Judaism.

57. New York: Oxford University Press, 1988.

58. Augmented ed. (Lanham, Md.: University Press of America, 1985).

59. *Judaism* 31/4 (Fall 1982): 390–400.

60. In Sobel and Beit-Hallahmi (n. 53), pp. 135–52.

61. In *Israel and Diaspora Jewry: Ideological and Political Perspectives*, ed. Eliezer Don-Yehiya (Ramat Gan: Bar Ilan University Press, 1991), pp. 97–107.

Disciplinary Perspectives

24. Modern Jewish Literature

David G. Roskies

A Bird's Eye View of the Field

The very term "Jewish literature," suggesting an internally coherent, multilingual body of writing, already carries a great deal of polemical weight. In his pathbreaking essay of 1818, "Etwas über die rabbinische Literatur,"[1] German-Jewish scholar Leopold Zunz defined all of postbiblical Jewish writing until the advent of Emancipation as "Rabbinic Literature." Henceforth, cultured Jews would write in German, not in Hebrew; as scholars, poets, and playwrights, not as rabbis. Meanwhile, back in Eastern Europe, the purveyors of Enlightenment were just beginning to write works of philosophy, natural science, philology, criticism, and belles lettres in the very language that Zunz considered dead. As modern Jews became more fragmented—ideologically, geographically, linguistically—so too did their "literature." And no sooner did they adopt the term *sifrut* or *literatur* than the battle lines were drawn: between sacred and secular; Hebrew and Yiddish; Jewish and non-Jewish; highbrow and popular.

Thus it is all the more stunning to consider the accomplishment of Israel Zinberg's twelve-volume *History of Jewish Literature*.[2] Zinberg's encyclopedic embrace of all of Jewish culture, from the Golden Age of Spain until the late nineteenth century, and his enthusiastic treatment of all great Jews, whether mystics or apostates, reformers or fundamentalists, bespoke the

---

1. In *Studies in Jewish Thought: An Anthology of German Jewish Scholarship*, excerpted, trans., ed. Alfred Jospe (Detroit: Wayne State University Press, 1981), pp. 19–25.

2. Trans. and ed. Bernard Martin (Cleveland: Press of Case Western Reserve University; New York: Ktav, 1972–78).

humanistic outlook of the Russian-Jewish intelligentsia. That and his multilingual approach to Jewish creativity ran afoul of the Bolsheviks, forcing Zinberg to recast his magnum opus into Yiddish, the "official" language of the Jewish proletariat, and to publish it outside the Soviet Union (Vilna, 1929–37). Despite Zinberg's pariah status, volumes 6–12 of his *History* are still the best general introduction to Old Yiddish Literature and to the manifold expressions of the Jewish Enlightenment (the Haskalah) in German, Hebrew, Yiddish, Russian, and Polish.

Zinberg, who perished in the Gulag, had but a single heir, the late Dov Sadan (1902–1989). Inspired by the Ingathering of the Exiles to the nascent State of Israel, Sadan formulated the concept of *sifrut Yisrael* (Jewish literature). A lifelong Zionist, Sadan privileged Hebrew as the timeless repository of Jewish creativity but saw Yiddish as the Jewish Diaspora language par excellence. In Sadan's scheme, a writer's greatness could be measured by the degree of interplay between Hebrew and Yiddish, the religious and secular traditions, the Jewish and the non-Jewish realms. Sadan also coined the term *la' az* to denote a third possibility: when a Jew wrote in a non-Jewish language for the sake of addressing a Jewish audience. Sadan claimed that when a Jew (like Moses Mendelssohn in his celebrated German translation of the Pentateuch) wrote for other Jews, he used a distinct and distinguishable literary language. The only sample of Sadan's vast literary critical output in English is his influential essay on Sholem Aleichem, "Three Foundations."[3] Sadan's baroque style of writing, in Hebrew as in Yiddish, has become an almost insurmountable barrier for modern readers.

Sadan was the last integrationist, both because no one else possessed his knowledge of languages and cultures and because no one else shared his politics. The field of Jewish literary studies was dominated instead by the German-born critic Baruch Kurzweil (1907–1972). With typical bravado, Kurzweil set forth the problem as one of Our New Literature: Continuity or Revolt? (in Hebrew).[4] Kurzweil saw the birth of Zionism and of modern Jewish culture as apocalyptic signs of the tragic break with Jewish Tradition. The greatest writers, in his view, were S.Y. Agnon and Uri Zvi Greenberg, because their work was assembled from the detritus of that metaphysical disaster. The new Israeli literature, in contrast, merely replicated an absurd and godless reality. See James S. Diamond, *Barukh Kurzweil and Modern Hebrew Literature*.[5]

3. *Prooftexts* 6 (1986): 55–63.

4. *Sifrutenu ha-hadashah: hemshekh o mahapekhah?* (Jerusalem and Tel Aviv: Schocken, 1959).

5. Brown Judaic Studies 39 (Chico, Calif.: Scholars Press, 1983).

For the generation of Israeli-trained scholars, who have lived to see a linguistically self-sufficient and secular Hebrew literature produced on native soil, Sadan's and Kurzweil's schemes are useful only as foils. In a brief, provocative essay, "Modern Hebrew Literature: Zionist Perspectives and Israeli Realities,"[6] scholar and critic Dan Miron placed them both in a distinguished line of false visionaries that began with Ahad Ha-Am. In his own critical writings, Miron has advanced the careers of the hardnosed secular writers, the ones who refused to make Jewishness central to their art, like nineteenth-century satirist Abramovitsh–Mendele, modernist prose writer Uri Nissan Gnessin, and modernist poet Natan Alterman (*A Traveler Disguised: A Study in the Rise of Modern Yiddish Fiction in the Nineteenth Century,*[7] "Hooks in the Nose of Eternity" [in Hebrew],[8] and Parts into a Whole: Structure, Genre, and Ideas in Natan Alterman's Poetry [in Hebrew][9]). Gershon Shaked, in his multivolume history Hebrew Narrative Fiction, 1880–1970 (in Hebrew),[10] has made Yosef Hayyim Brenner's existentialism out to be the central value of modern Hebrew culture.

The rejection of Zionism and of any other ideological criterion for the judging of a literary work underlay the founding of *Hasifrut*, the first Hebrew journal devoted to the "science of literature" (1968–86). For a brief moment, the Tel Aviv School of Poetry and Poetics was at the international cutting edge of literary theory, and in this way the study of Hebrew literature was finally "emancipated" from any particularist claims; see Alan Mintz, "On the Tel Aviv School of Poetics."[11] Yet in a country still under seige four decades after its founding, the escape from politics was a luxury that neither writers nor literary scholars could afford. And so the role of Zionist politics and Zionist history has begun to preoccupy Miron, Shaked, and their many students; for some recent examples of this (re)turn to politics, see Nurit Gertz, "To Caesar What Is Caesar's: Ideology versus Literature in the Stories of Hazaz,"[12] and Hannan Hever, "Minority Discourse of a National Minority: Israeli Fiction of

6. *Prooftexts* 4 (1984): 49–69.

7. New York: Schocken, 1973.

8. In *Uri Nissan Gnessin: mehkarim u-te'udot* (U.N. Gnessin: Studies and Documents), ed. Dan Miron and Dan Laor (Jerusalem: Mosad Bialik, 1986), pp. 231–368.

9. *Mipperat el 'ikkar Mivneh, ze'aner, ve-hagut beshirato shel Natan Alterman* (Tel Aviv: Sifriat Poalim, 1981).

10. *Ha-sipporet ha-'ivrit 1880–1970* (Tel Aviv: Ha-otsate keter ve-ha-kibbutz ha-meyuhad), vol. 1, *Ba-golah* (In Exile, 1977); vol. 2, *Ba-'arets uva-tefutsot* (In the Land of Israel and the Diaspora, 1983); vol. 3, *Ha-moderna bein shtei milhamot* (The *moderna* between the Two World Wars, 1988). An English translation of the projected four volumes is in preparation.

11. *Prooftexts* 4 (1984): 215–35.

12. *Prooftexts* 8 (1988): 183–96.

the Early Sixties."[13] The writings of Brenner and Alterman, for example, are being reexamined in the light of their politics, not only their poetics.

The clearest sign of a new integration between literature and life, the sacred and the secular, is the emerging consensus on who occupies the center of the Hebrew literary canon, and why. Shaked, who "rescued" Agnon from the clutches of Kurzweil & Co. by stressing the narrative complexity of Agnon's stories, has now returned to the Master with a new formulation: *Shmuel Yosef Agnon: Revolutionary Traditionalist.*[14] Miron has made the identical claim about Bialik, Berdyczewski, and Gnessin in a series of monographic studies (Come, Night: Hebrew Literature between the Rational and Irrational at the Turn of the Twentieth Century [in Hebrew];[15] [n. 8]), the point being that the great writers are both the sum and the subversion of all that came before them. Of contemporary writers, it is clear that poet Yehudah Amichai already occupies this pedestal; see Glenda Abramson, *The Writing of Yehuda Amichai: A Thematic Approach.*[16]

To make this kind of claim, of course, requires a way, not only a will. Scholars who never opened a Talmud will not recognize rabbinic resonances in a satire by Abramovitsh or a poem by Bialik, no matter how ideologically predisposed they might be to find them. American Jewish literary studies have therefore been fortunate to have its critical agenda set by Robert Alter. Since the early 1960s, Alter has introduced English readers to the full scope of Jewish imaginative writing—in poetry, prose, memoir, and scholarship; in Hebrew, English, Yiddish, German, French, and Russian—against a permanent backdrop of Bible and rabbinics. In succinct and eminently readable essays, Alter has stressed the ongoing tension between language and history, with "language" as the abode of symbolism, holiness, the artistic imagination, and "history" as the vehicle of crisis, destruction, loss of faith. Where he feels a writer has been "kidnapped" by exaggerated historical claims, Alter sets out to rescue that writer's artistry and playfulness; see especially "The Kidnapping of Bialik and Tchernichovsky"[17] and "Jewish Humor and the Domestication of Myth."[18] Conversely, he exposes the serious historical and existential

13. *Prooftexts* 10 (1990): 109–28.

14. New York: New York University Press, 1989.

15. *Bo'ah, laylah: Ha-sifrut ha-'ivrit bein higayon le-'i-gayon bimifneh ha-me'ah ha-'esrim* (Tel Aviv: Dvir, 1987).

16. Albany: State University of New York Press, 1989.

17. In *After the Tradition: Essays on Modern Jewish Writing* (New York: Dutton, 1971), pp. 226–40.

18. In *Defenses of the Imagination: Jewish Writers and Historical Crisis* (Philadelphia: Jewish Publication Society, 1977), pp. 155–67.

concerns of those writers who might seem overly fastidious and self-reflexive. In much the same spirit as the "revolutionary–traditionalist" formulation of his Israeli colleagues, Alter confers highest honors upon those authors, like Agnon, who engage the historical reality on the outside and are concerned about the art of writing: see his essay on Agnon's *Shirah*, "A Novel of the Post-Tragic World,"[19] and his introduction to Agnon's "At the Outset of the Day."[20] Alter has also written a whole book on the subject, *Partial Magic: The Novel as a Self-Conscious Genre.*[21]

The apparent ease with which Alter moves from one literature to another, using English to erase the linguistic barriers, should not obscure the poignant questions that lie at the heart of his work: Is language governed by history? Does the culture one lives in determine one's destiny? Those who write in and about Yiddish have discovered that the answer to both questions is yes. All the efforts to make Yiddish culture self-sufficient, or to "emancipate" the writer from the claims of the collective, were doomed to fail. What remains unanswered is whether this represented a triumph or a tragic failure. The abiding interest in Sholem Aleichem seems to suggest that when Solomon Rabinovitsh of Kiev became the folk presence "How-Do-You-Do," it was a formula for instant success; see Dan Miron, *Sholem Aleykhem: Person, Persona, Presence.*[22] The most convenient guide to Sholem Aleichem criticism is the issue of *Prooftexts*[23] devoted to the subject. The Nobel Prize for Literature awarded ninety years later to Isaac Bashevis Singer proves that nothing much has changed: Yiddish is now valued as a mirror of a vanished world.

The fate of Yiddish writing, then, was intimately bound up with the fate of its speakers. Recent scholarship has examined how Yiddish writers confronted the ever-growing cycles of violence, from the pogroms of the 1880s until the Holocaust, and concluded that their very protest against history became a source of meaning for the survivors (David G. Roskies, *Against the Apocalypse: Responses to Catastrophe in Modern Jewish Culture*[24]). In *A Little Love in Big Manhattan: Two Yiddish Poets,*[25] her biography of the two leading American-Yiddish poets, Moyshe-Leib Halpern and Mani Leib, Ruth Wisse has shown that the predicament of Yiddish became the substance of their art—Halpern through constant self-parody; Mani Leib through self-tran-

---

19. In (n. 18), pp. 169–86.
20. In *Modern Hebrew Literature*, ed. Robert Alter (New York: Behrman, 1971).
21. Berkeley and Los Angeles: University of California Press, 1975.
22. New York: YIVO, 1972.
23. 6/1 (January 1986).
24. Cambridge: Harvard University Press, 1984.
25. Cambridge: Harvard University Press, 1987.

scendence.The selection of poets and poems in *The Penguin Book of Modern Yiddish Verse*[26] is likewise predicated on seeing Yiddish as a unique expression of *yiddishkayt*.

Happily, there is one dissenting voice, that of Benjamin Harshav, who has assembled a counteranthology of American Yiddish poetry.[27] Here the most modern and "difficult" poets rub shoulders with American graphic artists of East European Jewish extraction to drive home the Americanness of the whole Jewish cultural enterprise. Were it not for the language barrier, Harshav argues, the Yiddish poets would be as much a part of American modernism as Ben Shahn and Raphael Soyer. Similarly, in *The Meaning of Yiddish*,[28] Harshav insists on the modernity of such writers as Sholem Aleichem, on their "deconstruction" of Jewish folklore and folkspeech.

If Harshav's effort has little support within the tiny Yiddish studies establishment, it has even less chance of making a dent in the burgeoning field of American Jewish studies. That is because there are competing mythologies at work in which Yiddish occupies a very different place. The dominant myth, first advanced by Irving Howe in *World of Our Fathers*,[29] is this: In the beginning was the Lower East Side, home and haven for the Yiddish-speaking masses. From there, the brightest, the best, and the most politically committed among the second generation made their way a few blocks north to Greenwich Village, and founded *The Partisan Review*. All the rest was history: how the "New York Jewish Intellectuals" redefined the very meaning of America and how Saul Bellow went on to win the Nobel Prize—see, for instance, Marcus Klein, *Foreigners: The Making of American Literature 1900–1940*,[30] and Mark Schechner, *After the Revolution: Studies in the Contemporary Jewish-American Imagination*.[31] In this scheme, Yiddish exists only to be superseded by a secular-progressive-urbane-existentialist-and-psychoanalytic sensibility. Thus Howe's anthology of *Jewish-American Stories*[32] begins with three Founding Fathers of the Old World: Sholem Aleichem, Isaac Babel, and Isaac Bashevis Singer. Why not Kafka, considering that his portrait hangs above the desk where Cynthia Ozick writes? Because Kafka and German Jewry are too modern to measure the distance traveled by former fellow travelers.

26. New York: Viking, 1987.
27. *American Yiddish Poetry: A Bilingual Anthology*, ed. Benjamin and Barbara Harshav (Berkeley and Los Angeles: University of California Press, 1986).
28. Berkeley and Los Angeles: University of California Press, 1990.
29. New York: Harcourt Brace Jovanovich, 1976.
30. Chicago: University of Chicago Press, 1981.
31. Bloomington: Indiana University Press, 1987.
32. New York: New American Library, 1977.

For all that Howe and his school stress the working-class origins of American-Jewish writing, they share the intellectuals' disdain for popular culture. Yet others have argued that the three most creative and critical points on the map of Jewish America are Second Avenue, the home of Yiddish vaudeville; East Broadway, the former domain of the popular Yiddish press; and Hollywood, the greatest dream factory the world has ever seen. For the rehabilitation of Yiddish popular culture in America, see Nahma Sandrow, *Vagabond Stars: A World History of Yiddish Theater;*[33] Mark Slobin, *Tenement Songs: The Popular Music of the Jewish Immigrants;*[34] and *From Hester Street to Hollywood: The Jewish-American Stage and Screen,*[35] especially Sarah Blacher Cohen's manifesto "Yiddish Origins and Jewish-American Transformations" (pp. 1–17). Where Woody Allen shares the limelight with Yiddish vaudeville star Aaron Lebedev, café radicals are left out in the cold. The current revival of American-Jewish klezmer music bears irreverent testimony to the continued vigor of the Yiddish underside.

There is yet a third possible reading of American Jewish culture, in which Yiddish, radical politics, and lowbrow theatrics play no structural role whatsoever. In his institutional history of the Jewish Publication Society, Jonathan D. Sarna charts *The Americanization of Jewish Culture*[36] beginning with such Baltimore Brahmins as Henrietta Szold and culminating with the elite havurot that produced the countercultural *Jewish Catalogues.*[37] That American Jewish culture may indeed be rooted in a middle class and elite circle of academics who took religion and Zionism seriously is further strengthened by other early examples of English-language creativity. If instead of beginning the story in Yiddish with the (Social Democratic) *Jewish Daily Forward* or the (Anarchist) *Free Voice of Labor*, Jewish cultural historians begin it a priori in English with the extraordinary *Jewish Encyclopedia*[38] (1898–1906) or with the campus-based *Menorah Journal*[39] (1915–62), then it justifies the price of linguistic assimilation and *embourgeoisement* and looks ahead to a vibrant future.

The debate over origins and endings is important because it defines who's

33. New York: Harper and Row, 1977.
34. Urbana: University of Illinois Press, 1982.
35. Ed. Sarah Blacher Cohen (Bloomington: Indiana University Press, 1983).
36. *JPS: The Americanization of Jewish Culture 1888–1988* (Philadelphia: Jewish Publication Society, 1989).
37. Philadelphia: Jewish Publication Society, 1973—80.
38. Isidore Singer, Managing Editor (New York: Funk & Wagnalls).
39. On which see Elinor Grumer, "The Apprenticeship of Lionel Trilling," *Prooftexts* 4 (1984): 153–73.

in and who's out. Alternatively, critics and scholars writing in English look to the issues that shape Jewish self-perception as a way of legitimating Jewish creative writing. This explains the current preoccupation with the Holocaust and Jewish responses to catastrophe. The earliest works in the field— Lawrence L. Langer, *The Holocaust and the Literary Imagination*;[40] Edward Alexander, *The Resonance of Dust*;[41] Alvin Rosenfeld, *A Double Dying*;[42] and Sidra DeKoven Ezrahi, *By Words Alone*[43]—cast a very wide net indeed, so that in recent years the countertrend has been to isolate different cultural traditions and critical issues within the vast body of imaginative writing in and about the Holocaust in every European language. Those critics who speak of a "literature of destruction" that originated in the Bible necessarily stress the continuities of Jewish and human response to catastrophe: Roskies (n. 24); Alan Mintz, *Hurban: Responses to Catastrophe in Hebrew Literature*.[44] Those who focus exclusively on the Holocaust begin with Anne Frank and Elie Wiesel and see the destruction of European Jewry as the end-point of Jewish history.

At the other pole of Jewish self-perception is the State of Israel. Surprisingly few books have as yet been written in English on Israeli literature, and what little there is tends to focus on rather marginal subjects such as the image of the Arab in Israeli fiction, Israeli responses to the Holocaust (as opposed to its own and ongoing life-and-death struggle for survival), or on feminist issues: *Facing the Holocaust: Selected Israeli Fiction*;[45] Gila Ramras-Rauch, *The Arab in Israeli Literature*.[46] Because gender has replaced class as the decisive measure of "continuity and revolt"—at least among academics— feminist criticism has finally been brought to bear on Jewish prose fiction and poetry. Israeli literature—still caught between its European past and its myth of the Sabra as the New Macho Jew—is especially fertile ground for this line of inquiry. Why is it, the critics want to know, that Israeli women writers have taken so long to break into the novel form? Why don't they write autobiographically, the way their Anglo-Saxon counterparts have been doing for two centuries? If Zionism celebrated "mother earth," then why do women fare so poorly in male-authored fiction? (Nehama Aschkenasy, *Eve's Journey: Femi-*

---

40. New Haven: Yale University Press, 1975.
41. Columbus: Ohio State University Press, 1979.
42. Bloomington: Indiana University Press, 1980.
43. Chicago: University of Chcago Press, 1980.
44. New York: Columbia Univerity Press, 1984.
45. Ed. Gila Ramras-Rauch and Joseph Michman-Melkman (Philadelphia: Jewish Publication Society, 1985).
46. Bloomington: Indiana University Press; London: I.B. Tauris, 1989.

nine Images in Hebraic Literary Tradition;[47] Esther Fuchs, *Israeli Mythogynies: Women in Contemporary Hebrew Fiction;*[48] *The Representation of Women in Jewish Literature.*[49]

Which brings us finally to the writers themselves—male and female. Fitting them into these grand metahistorical schemes of destruction and redemption, continuity and revolt is no easy matter, for Jewish literary biographies scarcely exist. The one notable exception is Ernst Pawel, *The Nightmare of Reason: A Life of Franz Kafka,*[50] which goes a long way toward situating this great writer within his particular historical and cultural context. Kafka is in fact an excellent figure to begin with, for the lives of modern Jewish writers are characterized by competing loyalties, major breaks in midcareer, or total breakdown. Almost in every writer's life one can find a major fault line that represents a crisis of faith (in God, in the Enlightenment, in Socialism, Communism, Zionism); a forced or voluntary move to a new and hostile environment (America, Palestine, the Soviet Union); or a psychological crisis.

A good place to begin is Alan Mintz, *"Banished from Their Father's Table" : Loss of Faith and Hebrew Autobiography,*[51] and Michael Stanislawski, *For Whom Do I Toil? Judah Leib Gordon and the Crisis of Russian Jewry.*[52] Completing the group portrait of the great nineteenth-century pioneers would be Sholem Yankev Abramovitsh, the Founding Father of both modern Hebrew and Yiddish literature. Unfortunately, his biography has not yet been written.

Nor indeed has the biography of any major twentieth-century Hebrew or Yiddish writer. Their autobiographies are often the best available substitute, so long as one keeps in mind that every autobiography is a fiction and some are clearly more fiction that fact. The latter is certainly true of Hayyim Nahman Bialik's Aftergrowth (in Hebrew),[53] an idyllic tale of paradise lost, or Sholem Aleichem's *From the Fair,*[54] which merges the life cycles of a traditional storyteller with that of his fictional characters. I. L. Peretz's *My Memoirs,*[55] in contrast, reveal in a starkly modern idiom the unresolved conflict between heart and mind that have plagued the author from earliest childhood. Perhaps

47. Philadelphia: University of Pennsylvania Press, 1986.
48. Albany: State University of New York Press, 1987.
49. *Prooftexts* 8/1 (January 1988).
50. New York: Farrar, Straus and Giroux, 1984.
51. Bloomington: Indiana University Press, 1989.
52. New York: Oxford University Press, 1988.
53. *Safiah*, trans. I. H. Lask (Philadelphia: Jewish Publication Society, 1939).
54. Trans. Curt Leviant (New York: Viking, 1985).
55. Trans. Seymour Levitan, in *The I. L.Peretz Reader*, ed. Ruth R. Wisse (New York: Schocken, 1990, pp. 267–359.

because his own life was riven in half, between Poland and America, and then again, between Yiddish and English, it was possible for Isaac Bashevis Singer to completely cover his tracks, all the while producing autobiographical fictions for children as well as for adults (including *In My Father's Court*[56] and *Love and Exile*[57]). For recent scholarship, see the special issues of *Studies in American Jewish Literature*[58] and *Prooftexts*;[59] Chone Shmeruk and Leonard Wolf are writing full-scale biographies of Singer.

For reasons not yet explained or even explored, many Jewish-American writers experienced profound breaks in their careers despite their staying in the same place and writing in the same language. From Anzia Yezierska, who was catapulted to fame and fortune by MGM, to Henry Roth and Delmore Schwartz, who fashioned a modernist Jewish prose style, to A. M. Klein, the first distinctive Jewish voice in English poetry, there is a recurrent pattern of failure and unrealized potential (see Anzia Yezierska, *Red Ribbon on a White Horse*;[60] James Atlas, *Delmore Schwartz: The Life of an American Poet*;[61] Elisa New, "Reconsidering Delmore Schwartz";[62] Henry Roth, *Shifting Landscape*;[63] and Usher Kaplan, *Like One That Dreamed: A Portrait of A.M. Klein*[64]). It might therefore be useful to compare how American-Yiddish writers, like Mani Leib, Jacob Glatstein, and even Singer himself found creative solutions for the historical and personal upheavals they faced.

Compensating for a dearth of full-scale biographies, the field of Jewish literature is rich in biobibliographical guides. Though very uneven in its quality, *The Blackwell Companion to Jewish Culture*[65] may serve as the all-purpose compendium. For American-Jewish studies see *Twentieth-Century American-Jewish Fiction Writers*[66] and *Jewish Writers of North America*.[67] The most important serials are *Hebrew Annual Review* (1977–), *Prooftexts: A Journal of Jewish Literary History* (1981–), and *Studies in American Jewish Literature* (1981–).

56. New York: Farrar, Straus & Giroux, 1966.
57. Garden City, N.Y.: Doubleday, 1984.
58. Vol. 1 (1981).
59. 9/1 (January 1989).
60. 1950; New York: Persea Books, 1981.
61. New York: New Directions, 1977.
62. *Prooftexts* 5 (1985): 245–62.
63. Ed. Mario Materassi (Philadelphia: Jewish Publication Society, 1987).
64. New York: McGraw-Hill Ryerson, 1982.
65. Ed. Glenda Abramson (New York: Blackwell Reference, 1989).
66. *Dictionary of Literary Biography*, vol. 28, ed. Daniel Walden (Detroit: Gale, 1984).
67. *American Studies Information Guide Series*, vol. 8, ed. Ira Bruce Nadel (Detroit: Gale, 1981).

Some Classroom Ideas

Teaching literature in the context of the Modern Jewish Experience can be extremely rewarding because literature is nothing if not experiential. Teaching Jewish literature in English translation can also have its advantages insofar as the teacher can more easily point to shared experiences and structural similarities across space and time. The teacher of such a course may walk with confidence where most literature professionals fear to tread.

- Exploit the best available anthologies. Individual titles, usually your personal favorites, have a way of going out of print.
- In an introductory survey course such as this, prose may be easier to work with than poetry. Even if students fail to grasp the artistry of the fiction, they can respond to its social or psychological setting. Also, prose suffers less from translation.
- These are the four prose anthologies in English that I use with greatest frequency:

    JAS: *Jewish American Stories*, ed. Irving Howe (n. 32)

    LoD: *The Literature of Destruction: Jewish Responses to Catastrophe*, ed. David G. Roskies[68]

    MHL: *Modern Hebrew Literature*, ed. Robert Alter (n. 20)

    TYS: *Treasury of Yiddish Stories*, ed. Irving Howe and Eliezer Greenberg[69]

- Try to mix and match: Western and Eastern Europe; male and female writers; adult and child perspectives. Since you will find that women writers are underrepresented, you will either have to: (a) do your own sleuthing; (b) explain why Jewish women write more (personal) poetry than prose; or (c) ignore the whole issue.
- Even as you blur the linguistic boundaries by using only English (or French, or Spanish) translations, ask yourself and your students if the language in any way shapes the nature of the experience described. How is it, you may ask, that Yiddish writers stress the life of the collective? Why and when does the psychological hero enter into Yiddish and Hebrew writing? How do socialism and Zionism color the writer's perspective? Is there such a thing as *la'az*, a distinguishable body of Jewish writing written in a non-Jewish language? Who really determines whether a work is "Jewish" or not—the author or the reader?

---

68. Philadelphia: Jewish Publication Society, 1989.
69. New York: Schocken, 1954; expanded ed., New York: Viking, 1989.

Let's take a look at what can be done with some of the modern masters.

1. S.Y. Abramovitsh (Mendele Moykher-Sforim, or Mendele the Book-
    seller), "Shem and Japheth on the Train" (1890; *LoD*, *MHL*)
    This is a brilliant sermonic text that plays the Russian-Jewish reality off
    the biblical and rabbinic traditions. Abramovitsh's message will surprise
    most students. He believes that a rapprochement is possible between the
    Jews and their Slavic neighbors—as long as the State does not interfere.
    As a true heir of the Jewish Enlightenment, Abramovitsh reserves his
    most trenchant criticism for the Jews themselves. But for the first time he
    creates a truly sympathetic character in the person of Reb Moshe
    ("Shem" of the title), who steals the show from the caustic Mendele.
    Other issues raised by the story are:

    - the train as a vehicle of change
    - the rise of political antisemitism
    - East meets West; Jew meets gentile
    - the politics of self-reliance in Eastern Europe
    - the use of allegory in the face of political censorship

2. I.L. Peretz, "Bontshe the Silent" (1894; *TYS*)
    Possibly the most misread of all Yiddish stories, "Bontshe the Silent" rep-
    resents Peretz at his most radical. It is a call to social revolution, as the
    ending makes unequivocally clear. Other issues:

    - pacifism versus passivity: the modern assault on traditional Jewish val-
      ues
    - the theme of heavenly justice: can there be any recompense for such
      human degradation?
    - the place of parody in modern Jewish culture

3. I.L. Peretz, "The Dead Town" (ca. 1895; *TYS*)
    This and the next story by Sholem Aleichem provide mirror images of the
    shtetl. While Peretz lays out a panorama of utter decay—religious, social,
    and especially economic—Sholem Aleichem turns the shtetl's weakness
    into its source of strength. The town of Kasrilevke is so isolated from the
    outside world that it can cut all events down to manageable size. Other
    issues:

    - who is mad and who is dead: between psychological realism and alle-
      gorical fantasy
    - comparison with Gogol's *Dead Souls*
    - the shtetl as abandoned wife/*agunah*/"grass widow"

4. Sholem Aleichem, "Dreyfus in Kasrilevke" (1902; *TYS*)
   Drawing on Yiddish folk humor about the foolstown of Chelm, Sholem
   Aleichem creates an ironic community of faith. As the town vacillates
   between ecstasy and despair, the naive townsfolk must confront the
   enemy within in the person of Yarmo the Janitor. But their real anger gets
   directed at one of their own: the rationalist Zeydl, the only man in town
   who reads a newspaper (the Hebrew *Hazefirah*). Other issues:

   • the schlemiel as victor-in-defeat
   • the Dreyfus Affair in the Jewish imagination

5. Hayyim Nahman Bialik, "In the City of Slaughter" (1903; *LoD*)
   Bialik's monumental Hebrew poem may have done more to shape Jewish
   perceptions of catastrophe and to steel Jewish resolve in the face of
   enemy attack than either of the proclamations (by the Jewish Labor Bund
   and The Hebrew Writers' Union) that accompany the text. Bialik also
   translated the poem into Yiddish. By withholding evidence of Jewish self-
   defense, by focusing on the ruined and desecrated landscape, on silence
   and emptiness, the poet turns the pogrom in Kishinev into a symbol of
   God's powerlessness. Other issues:

   • the Kishinev pogrom as international catalyst
   • the poet as prophet; Hebrew poetry as secular scripture
   • liturgy and the Law versus Jewish self-determination

6. Sholem Aleichem, "Hodl" (1905; *TYS*)
   This famous chapter of Sholem Aleichem's masterpiece *Tevye the Dairy-
   man* depicts the seduction of one of Tevye's daughters by the dream of
   social revolution. (The new translation by Hillel Halkin[70] captures
   Tevye's performance far more successfully.) Unlike the writers of the
   Enlightenment who depicted the struggle between fathers and sons from
   the perspective of the younger generation, it is Tevye who wins the reader's sympathy. Or at least that is what he is meant to do. Other issues:

   • Tevye's use of Scripture
   • Tevye as a modern Job
   • Tevye as the patriarch without sons

7. Isaac Babel, "The Rabbi's Son" (1925); "And Then There Were None"
   (1923; *LoD*)
   Babel is recognized as a master of the short story. In *Red Cavalry*, from

---

70. New York: Schocken, 1987.

which the first story is drawn, he treats the experience of revolution from the inside. He also does so in Russian. The struggle of young Jews between their rabbinic sensibilities and the cruel demands of revolutionary terror is brilliantly captured in this story. In the second story, told against the backdrop of World War I, the struggle intensifies when the Russian-Jewish soldier is confronted by a Jewish POW who is about to be executed. This story was never published in book form in the Soviet Union.

- the role of the Jew in uniform
- violence as a source of moral purgation or, Red Calvary

8. Hayyim Hazaz, "Rahamim" (1933; *MHL*)
    A different kind of binary opposition gets played out in this story set in Palestine. Here the two main character types in modern Jewish fiction, the *Talush* and *Ba'al-guf*, are forced to interact with one another. The first is an intellectual "dangling man" too caught up in his own psyche to act in history. The second is a kind of noble savage, fiercely loyal to the tribe, who is all brawn and no brains. Alternatively, they are Don Quixote and Sancho Panza representing two different actors in the Zionist drama. Other issues:

    - the new Sephardic mystique of the the Zionist movement
    - the redemptive return to the soil

9. Delmore Schwartz, "America! America!" (1940; *JAS*)
    Schwartz, a first-rate critic and poet, is valued today primarily as a writer of short stories. By filtering the mother's monologue through the consciousness of her son, Schwartz succeeds in fusing the two generations into one—despite the vast differences in their experience. The failure of the son to do more than mimic and mock his own mother is a sobering measure of his own paralysis, just as shoes become a fetish for parents and children alike. Other issues:

    - the use of monologue in Yiddish and in English
    - the Great Depression
    - the New York Intellectuals and their social responsibility

10. S. Y. Agnon, "The Lady and the Peddler" (1943; *MHL*)
    Agnon return us once again to the allegorical tale, this time with no holds barred. The lady's blood lust is a horrific shorthand for the events unfolding in Europe, while the Jewish peddler's gradual capitulation to animal desires is the chilling price of assimilation. Even as he demonizes the

Gentile in this story, Agnon pays minute attention to the psychology, the anatomy, and the gastronomy of demented love. Food and sex are interdependent. Despite the miracle that saves the day (or rather, the night), the ending, too, subverts the reader's pious expectations. Other issues:

- the technique of indirection in the response to the Holocaust
- the implacable hatred of the goyim: from Abramovitsh to Agnon

11. Bernard Malamud, "The Magic Barrel" (1954; *JAS*)
    This delightful parody on the tale of the star-crossed lovers (the heroine's name is Stella) has a serious side to it as well. Malamud here develops his lifelong theme of Jewish suffering as redemptive. Inevitably, it is the wizened East European Jew—whether as penniless matchmaker or as persecuted Jewbird—who awakens the moral sensibilities of young and callous American Jews. Other issues:

- in search of a Jewish-American style
- the American rabbi as antihero

12. Tillie Olsen, "Tell Me a Riddle" (1961; *JAS*)
    The Jewish Labor Movement, invented in America, is considered by some to be the main legacy of the immigrant generation to its comfortable sons and daughters. Tillie Olsen adds a feminist twist to this proposition. Other issues:

- the domestic battleground of the Jewish home: only in America?
- the role of Jews in the American Labor Movement
- the search for a usable past

25. Jewish Art in the Modern Era

Richard I. Cohen

As Jewish civilization has accorded central importance to the literary tradition, the visual dimension is often overlooked in the study of Jewish society, past and present. Jewish education in the traditional framework, unlike Medieval Christian society, shied away from instruction by visual images and established a clear hierarchy that regarded the written text as the supreme source of knowledge and truth. Nevertheless, visual images were present in Jewish life since classical times in texts and in synagogues, and it would appear that the rabbinic opposition was not as pronounced or fervent as is commonly assumed. Indeed in certain periods and communities artistic expressions became an integral part of Jewish life, and as one passes into the Modern period, advocates and patrons of Jewish artistic creativity—in both its traditional and secular form—flourished. Yet inquiry into and study of this cultural domain lagged far behind. Leopold Zunz, one of the founding fathers of the "Science of Judaism," had appealed in his general call for the study of the Jewish past, "Etwas über die rabbinische Literatur" (1818),[1] for the inclusion of art as well, but generations would pass before any serious attention was given to any aspect of the visual realm.

The parameters of "Jewish art" prior to the Modern period—from the age of Absolutism in the seventeenth century—were rather clear and defined: it included all art relating to Jewish ritual behavior (tombstones included) as well as illuminated manuscripts, synagogue decorations—mosaics, frescoes, portals, and so on—Jewish symbols, and archeological remains. With the

---

1. *Gesammelte Schriften*, vol. 1 (Berlin, 1875), pp. 1–31.

coming of the Modern period and the gradual involvement of Jews in the visual arts, beyond the normative religious perspective, the field of "Jewish art" was greatly extended. The present discussion relates to visual aspects ranging from synagogal art of the Modern period to creators of modern art, ranging from Moritz Oppenheim to R. B. Kitaj. Within this wide scope fall many other forms of visual material that can highlight or illuminate a particular area of the Jewish experience. Thus the premise of this essay is that Jewish art, in the widest sense, is an integral facet of the Jewish cultural world, and as such its integration into the teaching of Jewish civilization can only enrich and broaden our understanding.

The appreciation and study of these areas have developed slowly and are still very much in their infancy. In the middle of the nineteenth century, as a result of the increasing interest in Palestine among European powers, archeological investigations into Palestine's past inspired the imagination of European scholars. Their interest was of course the Classical period, and in one work by de Saulcy,[2] Jewish art was treated independently. This book and those to follow at the end of the nineteenth century concentrated on classical Judaism, Medieval synagogues, and illuminated manuscripts.

However, the study of synagogue architecture in the Modern period was not totally ignored. Mathias Bersohn, a Polish Jew and himself a collector of Judaica, wrote in Polish at the end of the nineteenth century an extensive work on the wooden synagogues in Poland that illuminated the apogee of that style in the eighteenth century;[3] several decades later, Alfred Grotte published in 1915 a survey in German on the German, Bohemian, and Polish synagogues from the eleventh to the nineteenth century.[4] However, the extensive treatment of modern synagogues would have to wait for more than a few decades before the first serious synthetic treatments of the topic were penned by Rachel Wischnitzer, in her book on American synagogues[5] in 1955 and later in her study of European synagogues.[6] Recently interest in the study of synagogue architecture has grown among scholars in the United States and Germany and several important works have appeared (see nn. 48, 49, 50).

2. Louis Félicien Joseph Caignart de Saulcy, *Voyage autour de la mer Morte et dans les terres bibliques exécuté de decembre 1850 à zvril 1851* (Paris: Gide & J. Baudry, 1853–54).
3. Mathias Bersohn, *Kilka słów o dawniejszych bóżnicach drewnianych w Polsce*, 3 vols. (Cracow: Wakładem autora, 1895–1903).
4. *Deutsche, böhmische und polnische Synagogentypen vom XI. bis Anfang des XIX. Jahrhunderts* (Leipzig: Spamer, 1915).
5. *Synagogue Architecture in the United States: History and Interpretation* (Philadelphia: Jewish Publication Society, 1955).
6. *The Architecture of the European Synagogue* (Philadelphia: Jewish Publication Society, 1964).

Following several exhibitions of Jewish artists at the beginning of the twentieth century, attention was directed to the appearance of a Jewish school of modern art. Actively encouraged by certain Zionist intellectuals, in particular Martin Buber and Berthold Feiwel, and by the Russian art critic and archeologist Vladimir Stasov, these artists (Hermann Struck, Jehuda Epstein, Lesser Ury, to name but a few) became the center of attention in various Zionist publications, and special issues displaying their works were published. Eventually, evaluations and analyses of Jewish artists were published in two journals devoted to literary and artistic issues (*Rimon* in Hebrew and *Milgroim* in Yiddish) that appeared in Berlin in 1922–24, under the editorship of Mark Wischnitzer. Rachel Wischnitzer (then under the name Wischnitzer-Bernstein), the art editor, emerged as one of the important art critics and scholars, publishing in those journals various essays on Jewish art, including modern Jewish artists. These essays, like those of Buber and Feiwel, were not scholarship in the rigorous sense but were the first serious treatment of Jewish artists in the context of their Jewishness. Wischnitzer continued for many decades to write on these themes, though she never made them her central focus of attention. (See Rochelle Weinstein's bibliography of Wischnitzer's writings in Rachel Wischnitzer, *From Dura to Rembrandt: Studies in the History of Art*,[7] pp. 180–88).

Sporadic treatment of these modern issues was included in several synthetic works on Jewish art (as was the case of Grotte's work on the synagogues) published in German in the twenties and thirties. See Karl Schwarz, *Die Juden in der Kunst*;[8] Ernst Cohn-Wiener, *Die jüdische Kunst: Ihre Geschichte von den Anfängen bis zur Gegenwart*;[9] and Franz Landsberger, *Einführung in die jüdische Kunst*.[10] Landsberger, who was the curator of the Berlin Jewish museum from 1935 and was to become one of the deans of Jewish art historians, later published several seminal essays on Jewish ceremonial art that laid the foundation of research in this area. After the demise of German Jewry, serious discussion on modern Jewish art would occasionally be addressed by scholars, but not in a systematic and rigorous way until the present generation. Avram Kampf, Ziva Amishai-Maisels, Alfred Werner, and others have contributed important monographic studies on Jewish artists, providing new iconographical and social insights into their work. These works are no longer presented in the framework of broad studies on Jewish art since classical days but concentrate on modern art and view their subjects accord-

7. Milwaukee, Vienna, and Jerusalem: Center for Jewish Art, 1990.

8. Vienna and Jerusalem: Löwit, 1936.

9. Berlin: Wasservogel, 1929.

10. Berlin: Philo, 1935.

ingly. (Several works by these authors are discussed at one point or another in this survey.)

Toward the end of the nineteenth century, and in conjunction with the burgeoning interest in the collection and preservation of Jewish ceremonial objects, attention also shifted to their description and study. Following the original impetus of Heinrich Frauberger in the *Mitteilungen der Gesellschaft zur Erforschung jüdischer Kunstdenkmäler*, the study of Jewish ceremonial art slowly evolved. Not until the appearance of Rudolf Hallo (1896–1933) in the twenties could one speak of an heir to Frauberger. Hallo, who became a curator of the state museum in Kassel, where he inaugurated a department of Jewish art, began to systematically identify, describe, and date objects, bringing a high level of connoisseurship to the field. His essays and thoroughly researched catalogues and books, published in the late twenties and early thirties in Germany, remain excellent sources for the history of Jewish ceremonial art in Germany in the Modern period. Hallo's orientation was pursued in Palestine by Mordecai Narkiss, the acting director of the Bezalel National Museum in Jerusalem from 1932, whose seminal study The Hanukkah Lamp (in Hebrew)[11] remains to this day the only comprehensive study of a particular type of ceremonial object. Narkiss's many other studies of ceremonial art deepened our knowledge of the interrelationship between Jewish objects and Christian art, while pointing out Christian influences on Jewish art.

Following World War II, research in ceremonial art was pursued by several scholars, who each brought an academic tradition to bear on their work. Some of the most prominent of these scholars were Stephen Kayser, Franz Landsberger, Cecil Roth, Guido Schoenberger, and Isaiah Shachar. Today, institutions for the preservation and study of modern Jewish ceremonial art flourish and a new cadre of curators and scholars is emerging. Several individuals who have significantly contributed to furthering the nature of the discipline deserve special mention: Joseph Gutmann, Bezalel Narkiss, and Vivian Mann.

Some Important English-Language Books and Articles

As mentioned, this area of study, still very much in its infancy, has hardly been assimilated into other disciplines. The following selected English bibliography identifies research carried out during this century, particularly in the last generation. It includes catalogues which are rarely accompanied by scholarly articles yet are indispensable for any treatment of the subject. The list

11. *Menorat ha-hanukkah* (Jerusalem: Bnei Bezalel, 1939).

assembled here is divided into sections according to themes of Jewish art discussed. It provides the instructor an opportunity to choose those issues that are most appropriate to the course taught; though books of a general nature need to be consulted to cover the various themes, they have not been included in these sections.

An important bibliographical work covering all areas of Jewish art, in all languages, was published in 1967 and is of much help for the interested reader and researcher: L. A. Mayer, *Bibliography of Jewish Art*.[12] For more up-to-date bibliography see also the lists of current publications that appear in the *Journal of Jewish Art*—from 1986/87 *Jewish Art*—the only periodical exclusively devoted to Jewish art.

Jewish Ceremonial Art in the Modern Era

The following works offer general overviews of the major aspects of Jewish ceremonial art. They are important for the instructor as basic guides to connecting the objects to their ritualistic function and sources. However, they do not provide the reader with a sufficient socio-historical context to make them easy reading for the student who is a complete neophyte to the area. For a course on Jewish customs and rituals, one could supplement, in the case of Ahkenazic traditions, with the last volume in the list: Isaiah Shachar, *The Jewish Year*;[13] Joseph Gutmann, *The Jewish Sanctuary*;[14] Joseph Gutmann, *The Jewish Life Cycle*;[15] and *Beauty in Holiness*.[16] Unlike the others, the last is an important collection of essays on different ceremonial objects. Though somewhat outdated, these essays still serve as a valuable introduction to research on Jewish ceremonial art. In *The Precious Legacy: Judaic Treasures from the Czechoslovak State Collections*,[17] essays by Vivian Mann offer a good overview of ceremonial art within the context of the Prague collection, one of the most important of Jewish ceremonial art. Isaiah Shachar, *Jewish Tradition in Art: The Feuchtwanger Collection of Judaica*,[18] is an example of an important catalogue of ceremonial art; it does not include essays but can be used as a sourcebook.

Yosef Hayim Yerushalmi, *Haggadah and History*,[19] is a valuable and encompassing survey of the evolution of the publishing history of the Hag-

12. Jerusalem: Magnes, 1967.
13. (Iconography of Religions, Section 23: Judaism 3) Leiden: Brill, 1975.
14. (Iconography of Religions, Section 23: Judaism 1) Leiden: Brill, 1983.
15. (Iconography of Religions, Section 23: Judaism 4) Leiden: Brill, 1987.
16. Ed. J. Gutmann (New York: Ktav, 1970).
17. Ed. David Altshuler (New York: Summit, 1983).
18. Rev. and trans. R. Grafman (Jerusalem: Israel Museum, 1981).
19. Philadelphia: Jewish Publication Society, 1975.

gadah since the sixteenth century. It includes illustrations from the most cele-
brated Haggadahs with instructive texts. Shalom Sabar, *Ketubbah: Jewish
Marriage Contracts of Hebrew Union College Skirball Museum and Klau
Library*,[20] one of the finest (and most handsome) catalogues of Jewish ceremonial art, offers the reader a perceptive overview of the development of the
Jewish marriage contract while pointing to unique characteristics stemming
from geographical origins. Herman Pollack, *Jewish Folkways in Germanic
Lands (1648–1806): Studies in Aspects of Daily Life*:[21] this pathfinding work
illuminates cultural and ritualistic practices of German Jewry during the
period of Absolutism. Based on responsa literature, community minute-books,
travel literature, and so on, it often illustrates the practices with material culled
from Christian discussions of Jewish ceremonies from the seventeenth and
eighteenth centuries.

Modern Jewish Artists and Modern Jewish Society

Avram Kampf, *Jewish Experience in the Art of the Twentieth Century*:[22] in
less than one hundred pages of text, Kampf covers the course of Jewish art in
the major centers of Jewish creativity from a totally new and provocative
viewpoint. Never mundane in his choice of artists, and writing in a prophetic
tone, Kampf has provided a serious thesis on the manner in which the Jewish
artist makes sense of his Jewish experience and how he fuses that past into the
creative process. *Chagall To Kitaj: Jewish Experience in 20th Century Art*[23] is
a revised edition of this book.

   K. E. Silver and R. Golan, *The Circle of Montparnasse: Jewish Artists in
Paris, 1909–1945*:[24] this fine catalogue traces the activity of Jewish artists in
Paris in the twentieth century. As this area is not well treated in the Kampf
volume, this catalogue serves as a complement, though it is written from a
very different perspective. *Tradition and Revolution: The Jewish Renaissance
in Russian Avant-Garde Art 1912–1928*[25] contains some very fine essays on
Jewish artists in Russia. As this was a formative period for Jewish art, the catalogue and essays are central to the issues at hand. Mirjam Rajner, "The
Awakening of Jewish National Art in Russia,"[26] covers material not discussed
in the above publication and offers a perceptive sociocultural examination of

   20. Philadelphia: Jewish Publication Society, 1990.
   21. Cambridge: MIT Press, 1971.
   22. South Hadley, Mass.: Bergin and Garvey, 1984; 240 pp., 16 color plates, 177 black and
white illus.
   23. London: Lund Humphries and Barbican Art Gallery, 1990.
   24. New York: The Jewish Museum, 1985.
   25. Ed. Ruth Apter-Gabriel (Jerusalem: The Israel Museum, 1987).
   26. *Jewish Art* 16–17 (1990–91): 98–121.

the origins of the rise of Jewish national art in Russia at the turn of the century. Antokolsky is the central figure discussed. In *Art and Its Uses: The Visual Image and Modern Jewish Society,*[27] several authors examine the ways in which modern Jewish artists confronted Jewish society; see the essays by M. Heyd, Z. Amishai-Maisels, I. Rogoff, and V. Barsky. Ismar Schorsch, "Art as Social History: Moritz Oppenheim and the German Jewish Vision of Emancipation,"[28] is a significant methodological contribution to Jewish cultural history treating Oppenheim from the perspective of German-Jewish society's confrontation with integration and modernity in the nineteenth century. In *Painting a Place in America: Jewish Artists in New York 1900–1945,*[29] several essays deal with the complex acculturation of East European Jewish artists in New York. The book is especially valuable in courses that deal with twentieth-century American society. Richard I. Cohen, "Nostalgia and 'Return to the Ghetto': A Cultural Phenomenon in Western and Central Europe,"[30] discusses Oppenheim and other Jewish artists in the nineteenth century within the context of individual Jewish efforts to mediate between modernity and the Jewish past.

Art and Political Events in Jewish Life in Modern Society

An interesting and original study by Emily Braun, "From Risorgimento to the Resistance: A Century of Jewish Artists in Italy,"[31] examines Italian Jewish artists against the background of dramatic changes in Italian society during the last century. Several essays in *The Dreyfus Affair: Art, Truth, and Justice*[32] treat the antisemitic caricatures of the period. They shed light on the visual struggle of the *dreyfusards* and their opponents. The volume is both an excellent catalogue and an important didactic instrument for any course that touches on late nineteenth century French history and antisemitism. In this regard see also "The Visual Dreyfus Affair—A New Text?"[33] by Richard I.

27. Ed. Richard I. Cohen; vol. 6 of *Studies in Contemporary Jewry*, ed. Ezra Mendelsohn (New York: Oxford University Press, 1990).

28. In *Moritz Oppenheim: The First Jewish Painter*, ed. Elisheva Cohen (Jerusalem: The Israel Museum, 1983), pp. 31–61; repr. in *Danzig between East and West: Aspects of Modern Jewish History*, ed. Isadore Twersky (Cambridge: Harvard University Press, 1985), pp. 139–72.

29. Ed. Norman L. Kleeblatt and Susan Chevlowe (Bloomington: Indiana University Press, 1992), pp. 130–55.

30. In *Assimilation and Community: The Jews in Nineteenth-Century Europe*, ed. Jonathan Frankel and Steven J. Zipperstein (Cambridge: Cambridge University Press, 1989), pp. 137–90.

31. In *Gardens and Ghettos: The Art of Jewish Life in Italy*, ed. Vivian B. Mann (Berkeley and Los Angeles: University of California Press, 1989), pp. 137–90.

32. Ed. Norman L. Kleeblatt (Berkeley and Los Angeles: University of California Press, 1987).

33. In Cohen (n. 27), pp. 71–90.

Cohen. Michael Berkowitz, "Art in Zionist Popular Culture and Jewish National Self-Consciousness,"[34] is an original treatment of popular visual material, ranging from postcards to covers of cigarette packs, generated by the development of Zionism. Berkowitz is interested in showing how this visual dimension helped generate a national self-consciousness. Haya Friedberg, "The Unwritten Message: Visual Commentary in Twentieth-Century Haggadah Illustrations,"[35] attempts to show how modern interpreters of the Haggadah have utilized recent historical events to visually represent freedom, oppression, and the longing for peace. She also highlights the ways in which artists are "in a constant dialogue both with their traditional iconographical sources and with the contemporary meaning of the text they illustrate" (p. 171). Milly Heyd, "The Uses of Primitivism: Reuven Rubin in Palestine,"[36] deals with an early period in Rubin's artistic career in Palestine. She is concerned with the way in which he interpreted the Zionist vision and reality and how he integrated memories of his home country, Romania, in certain works. Gideon Ofrat, "The Lost Pioneer,"[37] portrays the ways in which the pioneer was treated in Jewish art in Palestine in the pre-State period. *Bezalel 1906–1929*,[38] a catalogue and book of essays on the history of Bezalel, is a major contribution to understanding the interplay between nationalism and the arts. The conceptions and orientations of Boris Schatz, Bezalel's founder, are studied in depth through dozens of illustrations.

Other Recommended Books

Y. L. Bialer, *Jewish Life in Art and Tradition*,[39] is an introduction to Jewish ceremonial art in the Judaica collection of the Wolfson Museum, Hechal Shlomo, Jerusalem. Written by its former curator, it is a very readable volume. *Jewish Art: An Illustrated History*[40] contains several general essays that relate to the Modern period and provides a good overview. Wischnitzer (n. 7) is a collection of Wischnitzer's classic articles on Jewish art. Though many do not relate to the Modern period, they offer an important introduction to the work of a pioneering scholar of Jewish art and to the issues that concerned scholars in this field from the beginning of the century. Bezalel Narkiss provides a biographical sketch of Wischnitzer's life, "Rachel Wischnitzer, Doyenne of His-

34. In Cohen (n. 27), pp. 9–42.
35. *Jewish Art* 16–17 (1990–91): 157–71.
36. In Cohen (n. 27), pp. 43–70.
37. *Ariel: A Review of Arts and Letters in Israel* 62 (1985): 25–42.
38. Ed. Nurit Shilo-Cohen (Jerusalem: The Israel Museum, 1983).
39. Jerusalem: Hechal Shlomo, 1980.
40. Ed. Bezalel Narkiss (Greenwich, Conn.: New York Graphic Society, 2nd ed., 1971).

torians of Jewish Art,"[41] covering the range of her scholarly interests and inter alia discusses the strides taken in research on Jewish art through the century.

Central Themes

The gradual integration of Jews into the fabric of European and American societies opened many new avenues for Jewish cultural and social expression. These became apparent already in the early part of the nineteenth century when Jews took an active interest in the fields of music, literature, and the visual arts, assuming an important role both as entrepreneurs and creators of modern culture. Unfortunately, little has been written specifically about this important process, though the names of Jewish figures tend to crop up in discussions of the topic. An overall theme that deserves attention in a historical course on the Modern period is the penetration of Jews into these new professional disciplines. Within that perspective it would be worthwhile to reflect on whether a particular Jewish outlook played a role in this process and to assess the significance of Jewish participation in the arts as an aspect of Jewish integration into the surrounding society. An example of this can be deduced from the recent spate of books on Jews in Vienna and the pathbreaking work of Carl Schorske, *Fin-de-Siècle Vienna: Politics and Culture*;[42] see for further reading a review essay of these new works: Robert S. Wistrich, "Vienna, the Habsburg Empire, and the Jews."[43]

A more specific theme that lies at the heart of these issues is the way in which modern Jewish artists appropriate the Jewish past, memory, and tradition. Through attention to the iconographic precedents and symbolic meanings of a work of art, one can decipher the levels of association that a Jewish artist is trying to establish and thereby open another window into the dialectic process of Jewish integration into modern society. Explicit or implicit references to images of the Jewish world serve as codes to decipher ways in which Jews utilize elements of their past in confronting modernity. (See, for example, Z. Amishai-Maisels, "Ben Shahn and the Problem of Jewish Identity";[44] this essay treats Ben Shahn's struggle with his identity as an American artist and as a Jew in the wake of World War II. See also these articles on the contemporary artist R. B. Kitaj: Vivianne Barsky, "'Home Is Where the Heart Is': Jewish

41. In Wischnitzer (n. 7), pp. 9–25.

42. New York: Knopf, 1980.

43. In *Studies in Contemporary Jewry*, vol. 7, *Jews and Messianism in the Modern Era: Metaphor and Meaning*, ed. Jonathan Frankel (New York: Oxford University Press, 1991), pp. 317–27.

44. *Jewish Art* 13–14 (1986–87): 304–19.

Themes in the Art of R. B. Kitaj,"[45] and Carol Salus, "R.B. Kitaj's *The Murder of Rosa Luxemburg:* A Personal Metaphor."[46]) By studying artists from multiple vantage points, one can comprehend how Jewish symbols are transferred into the modern context and the manner in which the Jewish past presses itself upon the modern Jewish consciousness; see, for example, Milly Heyd, "King David Modernized: Ivan Schwebel and Contemporary Sources."[47]

Jewish aesthetic taste is obviously not a dimension easily determined and is by no means of a uniform nature, but it should not be ignored in determining the cultural ethos of Jewish society. Though the notion of *hiddur mitzvah* (performance of rituals in a handsome fashion) was a traditional norm, its applicability to tangible objects was not always affirmed. In the Modern period, followers of the Enlightenment employed aesthetic considerations and reproached those elements of Jewish society which denied the value of aesthetics. The gradual *embourgeoisement* of Jewish life in the last centuries contributed to a reevaluation of aesthetic attitudes. Thus, in studying how Jews integrated their changing values and status with their religious sensibilities, one can turn to the visual dimension. By analyzing the architecture of modern synagogues, patronage of ceremonial art, private art collectors, and Jewish museums, one can perceive how certain Jews tried to develop a new Jewish aesthetic, consciously or unconsciously, and how they merged their modern sensitivities with their sense of Jewish tradition. For example, how did Reform and Conservative Jews assimilate their ideological visions when building their synagogues? How did middle class Jewish society appropriate bourgeois attitudes and apply them to the context of Jewish life in the visual dimension? What were the implications for Orthodox Jewry? As these issues often relate to a changing public image of Jewish society, it is worthwhile to consider them in conjunction with literary sources.

Specific studies have already illuminated some of these issues. In the area of synagogue architecture, scholars have explored the connections between the community's sense of belonging in a European context and its internal Jewish pursuits. For example, Carol H. Krinsky, "Hector Guimard's *Art Nouveau* Synagogue in Paris,"[48] elucidates how architectural decisions were influenced by social patterns and conflict. This was the case of a synagogue built by East European immigrants in Paris at the beginning of the twentieth century. The article provides a unique perspective on the communal conflict in

45. In Cohen (n. 27), pp. 149–85.
46. *Jewish Art* 16–17 (1990–91): 130–38.
47. *Jewish Art* 13–14 (1986–87): 327–46.
48. *Journal of Jewish Art* 6 (1979): 105–11.

Parisian Jewry during that period. Further insights of this sort can be found in Carol H. Krinsky, *Synagogues of Europe: Architecture, History, Meaning*,[49] pp. 59–90, and in Wischnitzer (n. 6), pp. 171–218. For German readers, Harold Hammer-Schenk's two volumes on German synagogues in the nineteenth and twentieth centuries[50] offer the social and cultural historian a wealth of insights into the interplay between self-perception and public representation among modern German Jews. In the latter works the interest to the social historian lies in the ways in which Jews in the nineteenth and twentieth centuries decided on a particular style of architecture for their synagogues. By seeing the synagogue as the public and external expression of the community's internal identity, one gains another perspective on patterns of Jewish integration into European society.

Issues of Major Debate

As the field we are discussing has yet to penetrate into many academic institutions, few issues engender much sustained controversy. One recurring debate revolves around the definition of a Jewish artist and whether one can attribute Jewish influences to his or her other work. In a sense, and this has been a major concern for the historian of modern Jewry, this issue parallels problems of interpretation of modern Jewish writers and thinkers whose language is neither Hebrew nor Yiddish, and whose audience and subject matter extend far beyond the communal experience. Such, for example, is the case of Chagall, where art historians offer conflicting interpretations of the sources of his oeuvre. Chagall has inspired extensive scholarship and has been the center of several recent exhibitions. For a look at several views on these questions see the essays in *Tradition and Revolution* (n. 25); *Chagall To Kitaj* (n. 23); *Marc Chagall: The Russian Years 1906–1922*,[51] which includes interesting essays on Chagall's Russian period, insightful letters from the artist to various officials involved in the State Jewish Theatre, and Chagall's drypoint engravings for Gogol's novel *Dead Souls*; and *The Circle of Montparnasse* (n. 24).

Other essays of interest include Mira Friedman, "The Tree of Jesse and the Tree of Life in Chagall,"[52] which continues her work on various aspects of Chagall's activity. In this context special attention should be given to the excellent essays of Ziva Amishai-Maisels; see especially "Chagall's Jewish

49. Cambridge: MIT Press, 1985.
50. *Synagogen in Deutschland*, 2 vols. (Hamburg: Christians, 1981).
51. Ed. Christoph Vitali (Frankfurt: Schirn Kunsthalle Frankfurt, 1991).
52. *Jewish Art* 15 (1989): 61–80.

In-Jokes"[53] and "The Jewish Jesus."[54] Her contributions have been informed with profound insights into the ways in which Chagall transmits historical, personal, and religious themes.

Related to this problem is the continuing question of whether there is such a thing as "Jewish art" at all. Within such discussions, efforts are made to distinguish the parameters and foci of Jewish art. In this case, the discussions revolve around aspects of Jewish art in all periods and in relationship to all forms of art. Such a discussion in the context of an overall course in Jewish history does not seem to be the most vital and pressing issue; but, were one to desire to foray into that arena, one could consult the following items: Bezalel Narkiss, "Jewish Peoples, Arts of: Visual Arts";[55] *The Seminar on Jewish Art (January–September 1984): Proceedings,*[56] a slim volume discussing the theme of Jewish art and including a bibliography of several items that present contrasting views on the definition of Jewish art; and Elliott Horowitz, "The Way We Were: *Jewish Life in the Middle Ages.*"[57] Though Horowitz's review essay on Thérèse and Mendel Metzger, *Jewish Life in the Middle Ages: Illuminated Hebrew Manuscripts of the Thirteenth to the Sixteenth Centuries,*[58] deals with premodern material, it illuminates the ways in which a social historian interprets aspects of Jewish art and, as such, is an important call for the integration of visual material into the study of Jewish history, through an interdisciplinary approach.

Bibliography for Class Sessions

Artists and Society

The following bibliography relates to the interrelationship between Jewish artists and modern Jewish society. This theme has been dealt with in several contexts, historical and art historical, and one can focus either on the methodological issues that appear or on their relevance to the particular historical phenomenon under study. Thus the list relates to different artists at different periods, though a common theme—art and its relation to society—unites the various essays.

---

53. *Journal of Jewish Art* 5 (1978): 76–93.
54. *Journal of Jewish Art* 9 (1982): 84–104.
55. *Encyclopaedia Britannica,* 15th ed. (1974), *Macropaedia,* vol. 10: 202–205 [omitted from the 1985 rearrangment of the encyclopedia].
56. Ed. Vivian B. Mann and Gordon Tucker (New York: Jewish Theological Seminary, 1985).
57. *Jewish History* 1 (1986): 75–90.
58. New York: Chartwell, 1982.

Schorsch (n. 28), one of the prominent historians of modern German-Jewish history, presents a most convincing evaluation of Moritz Oppenheim's paintings for an understanding of modern German-Jewish history. Norman L. Kleeblatt, "Illustrating Jewish Lifestyles on Opposite Banks of the Rhine: Alphonse Lévy's Alsatian Peasants and Moritz Daniel Oppenheim's Frankfurt Burghers,"[59] offers a different perspective from Schorsch and compares Oppenheim's work with that of Alphonse Lévy, bringing to light some of the social issues that lay behind their respective works. Irit Rogoff, "Max Liebermann and the Painting of the Public Sphere,"[60] claims that certain paintings of Max Liebermann, not ostensibly on Jewish themes, should be seen in the light of social and political tensions current in Wilhelmian Germany. The author builds creatively on J. Habermas's theory of the "public sphere." Avram Kampf (n. 22), pp. 14–47, or (n. 23), explores the interplay between Russian Jewish artists at the beginning of the twentieth century and the quest for the development of a particular Jewish artistic style. He relates inter alia to the works of Chagall, Lissitzky, Ryback, Aronson, and Altmann. Though the concern of Milly Heyd in "Lilien and Beardsley: 'To the pure all things are pure'"[61] is to show the influence of Beardsley on Lilien, her interpretations of Lilien's work provide an interesting insight into the way the artist interpreted the Zionist movement in its infancy. This article could be used in conjunction with Berkowitz (n. 34). Berkowitz treats "popular culture" and shows how it was mobilized to serve the purposes of the Zionist movement.

Ceremonial Art

The following bibliography relates to Jewish ceremonial art in the Modern period; the essays chosen show how a close study of ceremonial art can be illuminating to certain aspects of the interrelationship between Jews and non-Jews in the Modern period, and how it also provides a clue to internal developments of the Jewish community. One should not assume that these pieces reveal "information" that cannot be reached through other means, but rather, they provide a visceral understanding of those phenomena.

Milly Heyd, "Illustrations in Early Editions of the Tsene-U'rene: Jewish Adaptations of Christian Sources,"[62] deftly shows the ways in which Jewish books adapted Christian sources and integrated them into their context. In this particular case, a popular book , oriented to women and children, reveals a

59. *Jewish Art* 16–17 (1990–91): 53–63.
60. In Cohen (n. 27), pp. 91–110.
61. *Journal of Jewish Art* 7 (1980): 58-69.
62. *Journal of Jewish Art* 10 (1984): 64–86.

certain openness to the surrounding society. By examining a Torah shield, Franz Landsberger, "A German Torah Ornamentation,"[63] shows how the patron of the object, through his choice of certain symbols, brought to bear his ideological orientation to the German–Jewish symbiosis.

Vivian Mann, "The Golden Age of Jewish Ceremonial Art in Frankfurt— Metalwork of the Eighteenth Century,"[64] treats ceremonial art from the perspective of a particular school that developed in Frankfurt in the eighteenth century. It raises issues of a socioeconomic nature that relate to the rise of a Jewish economic elite in that period. Bezalel Narkiss has written encompassing introductions to several facsimile editions of important printed Haggadahs of the Modern period. These introductions show iconographical influences on the Jewish prints while also paying special attention to the Midrashic influences on the iconography. See, for example, *The Illustrations of the Amsterdam Haggadah and Its Place in the History of Hebrew Printing*[65] and *The Passover Haggadah Venice 1609.*[66]

Shalom Sabar, "The Use and Meaning of Christian Motifs in Illustrations of Jewish Marriage Contracts in Italy,"[67] shows how the ghetto setting in Italian Jewish society did not impede Christian influence on Jewish ceremonial objects. The article can lead to a discussion of the nature of ghetto life and the openness of Jewish society in Italy to external influences. See also his "The Beginnings of *Ketubbah* Decorations in Italy: Venice in the Late Sixteenth to the Early Seventeenth Centuries,"[68] and (n. 20), pp. 3–32. The author's precision in describing marriage contracts provides the historian with much material from which to work.

Nancy M. Berman, *Moshe Zabari: A Twenty-Five Year Retrospective. Hallelujah*[69] presents the work of an important contemporary Jewish silversmith and illustrates the ways in which he incorporates innovative style and design with Jewish symbolism and content.

63. In *Beauty and Holiness*, ed. J. Gutmann (New York: Ktav, 1970), pp. 106–21.
64. *Leo Baeck Institute Yearbook* 31 (1986): 389–403.
65. Jerusalem: Makor, 1972.
66. Jerusalem: Makor, 1974.
67. *Journal of Jewish Art* 10 (1984): 47–63.
68. *Jewish Art* 13–14 (1986–87): 96–110.
69. New York: The Jewish Museum; Los Angeles: The Skirball Museum, 1986.

26. Jewish Music in the Modern Era

Neil W. Levin

Jewish music came forward to meet modernity bearing a diverse and deeply rooted musical trousseau. If generically uneven by the measure of Western musical standards and forms, it was nonetheless a legacy that embraced in the aggregate a wide geographical spectrum of local and regional traditions and practices—with some of its underpinnings in ancient Israel, and other foundations in both Arabic and European cultures. Its contents comprised a complex liturgical *melos*—born in antiquity, fleshed out in the formative years of the Medieval European Jewish experience, and augmented during succeeding centuries; a rich and spiritually as well as socially reflective secular folk music tradition that encompassed several languages; and virtually no art music, neither sacred nor secular, the relatively few isolated and historically anomalous instances notwithstanding. Both sacred and folk genres had already enjoyed a long and continuous history by the dawn of the modern era. Art music, however, on the model of the developed West European expressive forms, awaited conception until the first decade of the twentieth century.

Jewish musical scholarship—historical, analytical, or ethnological—is a quite recent thing altogether. It has been both a beneficiary and a product of the Jewish encounter with modern historical conceptions, comparative cultural studies, and the overall universal outlook or world view which modern Western scholarship embraced in general. Until the modern era, serious Jewish writings on music pertained mostly to the realms of philosophy or theology, apart from older anecdotal references in rabbinic literature. Virtually all premodern musical scholarship concerning Judaically related music was the exclusive domain of Christian scholars, whose interest in the subject often derived from their theological agendas.

242

In the nineteenth century, educated Jews began for the first time to evince serious academic interest in their own musical practices, history, and traditions. This was consistent with the new prevailing emphasis on the historical continuity of music within national-cultural groups, an approach whose basic foundation lay in the sometimes naive romantic-nationalist thinking of that era, which in turn had been stimulated by German folklore scholars such as Johann Gottfried Herder. In time, a more mature concept of historical continuity emerged, which derived in part from theories of evolution in the scientific world: musical forms came to be understood as living organisms in a cyclical progression, in relation to other cultural forces, as opposed to the eighteeth-century linear view. The emergence of *Wissenschaft des Judentums* further encouraged the analytical and scientific critical evaluation of music, as part of its broader research agenda. Initially, attention was focused on musical notations of previously orally transmitted synagogue traditions and the accounts of cantors about their practices. Later in the nineteenth century, under the influence of the Haskalah, cantor-writers in Eastern as well as Central Europe began to concern themselves with the nature of sacred music and its historical foundations.

One of the most influential instigators of modern historical awareness of Jewish music and its roots was himself neither a musical nor a Judaic scholar, but a highly cultured cantor and synagogue composer. Salomon Sulzer (1804–1890)—the first truly modern cantor, the first Oberkantor of Vienna, and the acknowledged "father of modern *hazzanut*" both as an art form and as an institution—spearheaded the rescue of musical *minhag Ashkenaz* from its centuries-long decay. His approach was to effect a lasting synthesis between that oral tradition and the established Western musical art of European high culture. It was the first real and successful musical reconciliation of past with present in the cultural experience of European Jews. Yet it was no mere pragmatic compromise, but rather a recognition of the potential artistic value in Jewish tradition. Moreover, Sulzer perceived a conceptual difference between genuine tradition and its artificial mask in much of the synagogal music practice that had come down to his generation. In calling for the sifting of the former from the latter, he adumbrated an important musicological emphasis that later would characterize the study of all traditional music. He insisted on the objective examination of the accumulated composite repertoire:

The necessary refinement of the synagogue service had to proceed by way of restoration ... to remain on historical ground in order to recapture the original noble form. ... In so doing the [Vienna] Synagogue was careful to establish the historical continuity of its liturgy.[1]

1. *Denkschrift* (Vienna, 1876).

Sulzer addressed only the realm of liturgical music, and exclusively its Ashkenazi form. His legacy resides in his compositions and arrangements, not in scholarly writings. But his ideals were to have significant repercussions for the entire direction of scholarship on Jewish music.

That the preponderance of modern Jewish music scholarship and research has neglected the musical experience of the modern era itself is demonstrated by the existence of only one (quite recent) volume in English about Sulzer, *Salomon Sulzer: Cantor, Composer, Innovator.*[2] Only partially biographical, these essays by a group of Austrian scholars treat Sulzer and the so-called "Sulzer Phenomenon" within the context of the first stages of Emancipation and the Jewish encounter with modern European culture in Vienna. Especially illuminating is the discussion of his broad influence in East as well as West European cosmopolitan communities and the resultant emergence of the modern cantor. Yet, this can only be considered a preliminary study, not an interpretive biography. Hanoch Avenary, *Kantor Salomon Sulzer und seine Zeit,*[3] must also be mentioned, even in the absence of an English translation, since it remains unique. This annotated assemblage of original documents pertaining to Sulzer's career (letters, communal records, memoranda, registers, and other papers) is indispensable to an understanding of his impact on modern Jewish musical experience, his complex relationships with Viennese society, and the role of Viennese social and political forces. A comprehensive interdisciplinary study of Sulzer and the wider significance of his contributions, the proceedings of the recent international Sulzer conference (1991–92) held serially in London, Vienna, Jerusalem, New York, and Los Angeles, is in preparation.

Of Sulzer's many pupils and disciples, Eduard Birnbaum (1855–1922) was the one most profoundly inspired toward actual Jewish music research. Birnbaum, who was almost entirely self-trained in musicological investigation (he was also a prominent cantor, and Oberkantor of the Neue Synagoge in Königsberg), commanded the respect and admiration of some of the leading scholars of his day in both Judaic and general musicological disciplines. He may be considered the first modern Jewish music scholar—in many ways the "grandfather" of the field. He is most remembered today for the unprecedented (in both size and scope) collection of Jewish musical manuscripts, historical documents, printed music, books, and all manner of related material that reposes at Hebrew Union College, Cincinnati, under his name. That collection reflects the full range of liturgical music expression in practically all

2. Ed. Bernard Purin (Bregenz, Austria: Land Vorlberg, 1990); trans. under supervision of and ed. Neil Levin (Bregenz: Land Vorlberg, 1991).

3. Sigmaringen, Germany: Thorbecke, 1985.

parts of Europe, both before and during the modern experience. It forms a database which is still heavily relied on by researchers in many related fields.

Birnbaum's annotated thematic catalogue of all prayer texts sung in Ashkenazi synagogues up to the first decade of the twentieth century contains a wealth of bibliographical and historical information. His contributions and their ramifications for subsequent historical study are discussed in Eric Werner, "Manuscripts of Jewish Music in the Eduard Birnbaum Collection,"[4] which is of value and accessible to the general reader.

Just as we may consider Birnbaum the "grandfather" of the modern scholarly study of Jewish music, so the honor of that discipline's immediate parentage belongs unquestionably to Abraham Zvi Idelsohn (1882–1938). Idelsohn has been called the "father of Jewish music research"—a title that is wholly justified not only by virtue of the extraordinary volume of his writings, their erudition and imagination, the sheer quantity of knowledge he unearthed and contributed, and the still unmatched geographical and multigeneric scope of his work; but also in view of his having laid basic foundations for the infrastructure of the entire field. For, despite all the subsequent changes in perception, shifts in emphasis, methodological advances, benefits of technology, and even contradictory findings, Idelsohn's work remains the model for the systematic and scientific exploration of Jewish music.

Idelsohn relied extensively (and with full acknowledgement) on Birnbaum's research—and to some extent on his methods—for his own studies of Ashkenazi liturgical music, especially in the historical realm. His "Songs and Singers of the Synagogue in the 18th Century"[5] is still considered a classic study. It offers a well-balanced survey and description of Ashkenazi cantorial art and practice (including choral and instrumental precedents) in Central Europe during the two centuries prior to Emancipation, together with rabbinic responsa and a good account of the manuscript evidence itself. Idelsohn produced a multitude of writings on Jewish music in Europe—some more historical and others more theoretical. In general, he combined technical analysis with an examination of historical derivation. He ventured far beyond Birnbaum's (or anyone else's) boundaries of time, space, or subject matter; and he made extraliturgical excursions into secular Yiddish and Hasidic music. In addition, he delved deeply into the music of Yemenite, Persian, Sephardi (Mediterranean, North African, and Near Eastern), Babylonian, and many other non-European Jewish cultures—always stressing the interrelationships between liturgy and music.

4. *Hebrew Union College Annual* 18 (1944): 397–428.
5. *Hebrew Union College Annual, Jubilee Volume* (1925): 397–424.

The list of Idelsohn's writings itself indicates that there was hardly any topic even tangentially related to Jewish music that eluded his attention. He viewed Jewish music (the first to do so) as a complex field of study in its full breadth—an organic whole with many branches and tributaries. By so perceiving it from the perspective of that broad world outlook, he succeeded in bringing the entire field into the mainstream of European humanistic studies—a significant departure from the parochialism of premodern conceptions.

Idelsohn discerned for the first time that oral musical traditions and the written historical dimensions are of equal value to scholarship. This manifestly modern idea stood in sharp contrast to the previously accepted notion that traditional or orally transmitted music is qualitatively inferior to—and thus less worthy of serious study than—academically developed music with a theoretical basis and notated history. He took strong exception to the perception of European synagogue music as an essentially diluted imitation of Western church styles, pointing instead to an organic relationship between cantorial chant and Near Eastern music. He identified two complementary strata in the Ashkenazi tradition: an older Eastern or "Oriental" one, which contains basic motives; and a more recent one that exhibits the influence of post-Exilic host cultures. This discovery of the importance of Eastern Jewish communities to a balanced understanding of Jewish music as a whole was one of Idelsohn's trailblazing achievements. He championed the ethnographic approach, which was quite new at that time and revolutionary in the field of Jewish music in particular. This involved the amassing of data by audio recording in the field (viz., within the living environment of each transplanted community among Jews in Palestine); he then transcribed the results by means of musical notation, for which he refined methods to accomodate to non-Western musical features. Idelsohn, through his comparative evaluations of this amassed data, became the acknowledged pioneer in Jewish ethnomusicology (some four decades before the term for the discipline was coined by Jaap Kunst in 1950): he examined living music within, and as an inextricable part of, its total cultural and societal framework (sometimes defined simply as "music in culture"); and he studied that music in relation to all social, economic, anthropological, religious, ceremonial, and cross-cultural—not only historical—forces.

Such an approach to the study as well as the appreciation of Jewish music implies a world view that arose out of the modern nexus between Jewish and European historical-cultural paths. That world view is a distinct outgrowth of European high culture's transcendental perspectives and European high art's aspirations to the universal. So born as an inherently Western venture, this ethnomusicological view became the modus operandi for the study of all traditional Jewish music, whether a Yiddish lullaby, a Yemenite bridal song, a Hasidic *niggun* (wordless melody), or a Moroccan *pizmon* (liturgical poem with a refrain). In this sense the work not only of Idelsohn, but of the successive wave of music scholars, embodies the intellectual mandate of the modern Jewish experience. So, for example, authentic Yemenite music may not itself be representative of modernity—in terms of its typology and substance. But its study, its application of the tools and perspectives provided by European cultural and scholastic development, its invitation to expand our musical-cultural awareness, and ultimately its auditory appreciation, all render it a profoundly modern experience.

Idlesohn's magum opus is his ten-volume *Thesaurus of Hebrew-Oriental Melodies* (HOM), a lifelong work that was compiled and published in stages (1914–32). It is a monument to the living musical traditions of Diaspora Jewries still extant in the early part of this century, and, in most cases, up to World War II. These volumes provide his musical notations from field recordings by informants, along with some material reproduced from eighteenth- and nineteenth-century cantorial notebooks. The organization of entries in itself represents one of Idelsohn's chief accomplishments: the development of a classification system for this body of music, for which there was no precedent. Each volume contains an elaborate interpretive apparatus, in which are discussed in detail all possible comparative, analytical, historical, linguistic, and literary issues that pertain to the music—often together with descriptions of social and liturgical customs. Although much of the contents is technical in nature, there are nonetheless descriptive parts that are accessible and valuable to the nonmusical historian.

Apart from the methodological impact, HOM has served multiple purposes to both scholars and laity. First, it has stimulated a general awareness of the music of the Eastern communities and made the wealth of their repertories available for the first time well beyond their geographical and cultural confines. Second, it has served as a critical vehicle for preservation, since at the time the specimens were recorded there was still a reasonable expectation of authenticity. The entire matter of preservation has now become a major part— almost a division in itself—of Jewish music scholarship. Especially since the material as well as human destruction of the Holocaust, this has applied to written—even published—music as well. Ironically, however, music actually produced or created during the modern Jewish experience has often received the least attention. (Some printed music of Sulzer, for example, remains unrecovered; even some music written or notated by early twentieth century European cantors has not yet been retrieved.)

By the time of the many later and admittedly more sophisticated field recordings by others, there was already much greater danger of musical, linguistic, and cross-cultural blurring—especially in the era of easy exposure to mass media, popular entertainment, and other forces of acculturation. Thus the value of the materials in the HOM volumes remains significant despite vast technological improvements in methods and field procedures for collecting and recording since Idelsohn's time. No organized continuation of the HOM project has yet been ventured on anywhere near so broad a scale—namely, addressing the entire repertoire of whole communities. Emphasis in recent Jewish music scholarship has moved gradually toward a more specific, microscopic orientation, resulting in many more single-issue studies. Over the years there have been a number of musicologically oriented anthologies, either wholly or partly devoted to orally transmitted music and containing at least some historical-analytical discussion. But these are usually less comprehensive, reflecting a single category or even subcategory. Examples are Yehiel Adaqi and Uri Sharvit, A Treasury of Yemenite Jewish Chants (in Hebrew);[6] Chemjo Vinaver, *Anthology of Hassidic Music*;[7] Samuel G. Armistead and Joseph H. Silverman (with musical transcriptions and studies by Israel J. Katz), *Judeo-Spanish Ballads from Oral Tradition*, vol. 1, *Epic Ballads*;[8] and Neil W. Levin, *Zemirot Anthology*.[9] In the current climate, all-encompassing anthologies on Idelsohn's scale—addressing complete communal repertoires in full cultural perspective—appear to inspire less scholarly interest than do more finite topics.

The egregious absence of general accounts of Jewish music and its history is frequently lamented. Idelsohn's one English-language attempt at such an all-inclusive overview book, *Jewish Music in its Historical Development*[10]— no doubt his most widely read work—comes closest to narrowing the gap. Despite its limitations as seen now at the end of the twentieth century (which could not now be adequately ameliorated in any single volume anyway), it remains a classic of the field. Indeed, even after more than sixty years, and even after the emergence of entire new fields and subfields within Jewish music scholarship, it is still the only survey volume of its type and scope that can be taken seriously. It is relied on as a basic text for courses on Jewish music, whether in specialized contexts (cantorial training programs and the

6. *Me otzar neimot yehudei teiman* (Jerusalem: Israeli Institute of Religious Music, 1981).
7. Ed. Eliyahu Schleifer (Jerusalem: Hebrew University, Jewish Music Resource Center, 1985).
8. Folk Literature of the Sephardic Jews 2 (Berkeley and Los Angeles: University of California Press, 1986).
9. Cedarhurst, N.Y.: Tara Publications, 1981.
10. New York: Holt, 1929; numerous reprints.

like) or within university survey courses. Yet it is not a textbook in either format or approach; and in addition to the want of issues, trends, developments, information, personalities, and music itself that could not have been known or written about in 1929, some of its conclusions are today understandably obsolete. "But what else is there?" is a commonly voiced response of those outside the scholarly community who wish either to familiarize themselves with the field or to prepare course presentations or curricula.

Most of the basic models in *Jewish Music* are still accepted, and much of the historical information on *hazzanim* and other folk musicians is still of merit. But the contemporary reader will find it disconcerting to encounter characterizations such as "Semitic–Oriental," "racial propensities," and references to "masculine" versus "feminine" musical features. Another problem with the book is that Idelsohn attempted to tread a middle ground between scholarly writing and a simpler, popular exposition—to appeal at the same time to musicians with some technical background and an educated laity (Jewish and non-Jewish). That dual purpose simply does not always work, any more than it has yet found success in the continual attempts in the literature on general (Western) music. Here we face the perpetual and as yet unresolved problem of dealing with the history or nature of so abstract an expressive form as music without resort to some technical sophistication—the challenge of explaining music without music.

Idelsohn's approach to the liturgical music traditions extant among modern Jewry centered around the principle of historical continuity in the ongoing development and generational transmission of synagogal music over many centuries. His overall thesis further included his perception of an underlying, almost primeval interconnection—geographical as well as time-related—among all the various forms and expressions of Hebrew sacred song. Thus he discerned and identified relationships between the chants, modes, and many of the tunes which he found employed by European Jewry in the nineteenth and twentieth centuries (many of which still flourish in liturgical practice at the end of the twentieth century) and those both of earlier periods in the West and of contemporaneous non-European communities. Moreover, he concluded that many of those inherited musical traditions of modern Jewry exhibit the effect of "foreign" or host environmental influences, but that these have fused over time with older, more specifically "Jewish" characteristics (dating, at least in some cases, to antiquity) to form an organic whole. While subsequent scholarship has questioned whether there is some endemic, pre-exilic, and almost culturally congenital *melos* that is somehow inherently reflective of "the spiritual (and emotional) life of the Jewish people," and while his belief that all the varieties of scriptural cantillation in the Modern era are traceable to a common source has been refuted, Idelsohn's basic concept of historical continuity has been generally accepted by most reliable scholars.

Eric Werner (1901–1988), one of the very few other titans in the field of Judaically related musicology, in a very real sense was the heir to Idelsohn and his role. He dealt more narrowly (and more scientifically), however, with the issue of continuity as it pertained to sacred traditions in the modern era, focusing entirely on the Ashkenazi realm and emphasizing the inextricable relationship between liturgical melodies and the liturgy (text) itself and their frequently corresponding developments. A product and an advocate of a rigorous and more strictly historical European school of musicology of the Berlin–Vienna academic axis, Werner reached further back in time than had Idelsohn, in order to test both the continuity and the identity of these traditions at an earlier pivotal point in Judeo-Christian liturgical history. *A Voice Still Heard*[11] is his major contribution to the comprehensive study of the Ashkenazi liturgical music tradition. It represents decades of careful, systematic examination of that evolved labyrinth in all its manifestations and ramifications. Werner's goal was the identification of genuine tradition and continuity as vital, living forces. Many of the melodies and musical customs in use throughout the modern era are discussed in detail, with special reference to regional variants, origins, and comparisons with secular and even non-Jewish sources. The last four chapters cover the Modern era, treating it almost completely from a nontechnical angle, so that the book will be highly useful to general considerations of modern Jewish culture.

Throughout his writings, Werner distinguishes between genuine and "pseudo" traditions. The distinction is particularly applicable to the consideration of Jewish music in the modern era, from both historical and esthetic perspectives. Ultimately, it pertains directly to the contemporary invocation of "tradition" as an apology for the banal and faddish, a lament Werner often voiced. For him, the entrenched status of musical habit in a particular region was not sufficient to warrant investing it with the authority of musical tradition. Rather, that appellation evoked for him an earlier patrician definition as "hallowed by literary and rabbinic testimony"; see also his "The Role of Tradition in the Music of the Synagogue."[12]

Another of Werner's important themes is actually a paraphrase of an idea of the neo-Kantian philosopher, Hermann Cohen: the distinction between "active" and "passive" assimilation. Werner applied this principle to the absorption of non-Jewish or "foreign" musical elements and the actual way in

11. University Park: Pennsylvania State University Press, 1976.
12. *Judaism* 8 1964): 156–63.

which they have been assimilated into Ashkenazi tradition. The passive form coincides with our contemporary negative connotation of "assimilation"—for music, the passive surrender of established tradition to foreign musical environments by wholesale imitation or adoption, or even by combination, but where the identity and integrity of the tradition becomes completely absorbed and dominated by the host culture. The active form suggests a conscious borrowing of host cultural elements for the stylization of tradition—ideally, insofar as the former serves the latter esthetically and artistically. It may involve, for example, the selected use of Western musical structural forms and harmonizations for settings of traditional chants or melodies.

Yiddish folk music, now considered a legitimate part of East European folklore in general, has become a significant area of current scholarly focus—especially in a climate of ethnic interest. Apart from Idelsohn's limited studies on this subject, however, the field was largely dominated prior to World War II by the activities of Russian and (later) Soviet ethnologists and historians. There, and in surrounding regions of the former Russian empire, serious study of Jewish folk music and lore was just coming into its own and beginning to yield valuable results when the Holocaust, together with the Stalinist purges, destroyed much of the accumulated archival evidence as well as many of its students and terminated the living folk culture itself. Fortunately, at the same time a good deal of documentation survived—some hidden and suppressed by Soviet authorities, some salvaged and brought to Israel or the United States. Popular interest in Yiddish culture (transcending immigrant generations) is currently at a zenith in America and has most recently begun to spread to Western Europe—even among non-Jewish audiences. A number of sophisticated ethnomusicologists, however, have delved into the musical evidence with the full force of scientific historical evaluation and comparative analysis, combined with intercultural considerations. The contemporary study of Yiddish folk music goes far deeper than nostalgic ethnic revival movements. It not only scrutinizes the actual musical features and their evolution, but also views the repertoire in the aggregate as a means by which to understand social and behavioral patterns, sociopolitical movements, urbanization, industrialization, internecine religious conflicts, changing mores and values, and the overall ramifications of modernity for East European Jewry.

Systematic attention to Yiddish folk music began only at the end of the nineteenth century, primarily as a pursuit of the Russian-Jewish intelligentsia. (The few obscure earlier compilations in Western Europe—with Judeo-German texts for Western Rococo style tunes—do not represent Yiddish folksong in this context as an ethnic genre, especially from the musical perspective.) Its first bloom showed with the publication of Saul Ginsburg and Pesah Marek, Yiddish Folksongs in Russia (in Russian),[13] which has recently been reissued in facsimile with additional historical background material and annotations by the Israeli folklorist, Dov Noy.[14] Its breadth and scope are reflected in 376 songs from Lithuania, Kurland, Poltava, and Podolia—with contributors' identities and locales, variants, and extensive introduction and bibliography. Unfortunately, no musical notations were included. Nor did Ginsburg and Marek presage the field methods of later ethnomusicologists: the songs were not transcribed directly from oral tradition "in the field"—within their natural habitats. Rather, they were sent in by collectors and aficionados from various urban communities—in response to advertised requests in several intellectually oriented journals. The internal organization of the material also reflects a leaning toward literary and historical rather than musical concerns. Nonetheless, it helped to acquire for Jewish folksong a new measure of approbation in intellectual circles as a legitimate cultural expression.

This interest was further spurred by the founding of the *Gesellschaft für jüdische Volksmusik* in St. Petersburg in 1908 and the organization of the Music Division of the Jewish Ethnographic Expedition (1911–14), through the offices of the Jewish Historico-Ethnographic Society in St. Petersburg, in the name of Baron Horace Guinzbourg. The latter venture involved collecting every form and type of Jewish musical evidence (other divisions addressed other ethnological and cultural documentation and artifacts) first-hand from visits to sixty-six cities and villages throughout the Pale of Settlement (and a further expedition to the Caucasus)—originally with the intention (never realized) of creating a national Jewish museum. The 1917 Bolshevik Revolution altered those plans, and the results (those that have survived) repose now in a variety of places—some known, some only suspected or hoped. It is anticipated that much of the material—including writings and studies—will surface in the next few years. The story of the expedition is told in a fascinating article (of the same title) by Albert Weisser.[15]

The *Gesellschaft* was tantamount to a "cultural movement," with nationalistic and Zionistic overtones—very much a product of modern experience. Its most important contribution was its outright establishment of a Jewish art music—imposed in a short time frame by conscious design, somewhat after the manner of the so-called Russian nationalist composers, rather than evolved over centuries as with Western art music. This is essentially the inter-

13. *Evreiskiya narodnyia piesni v Rossii* (St. Petersburg: Voschod, 1901).
14. Ramat Gan: Bar Ilan University, 1991.
15. *Musica Judaica* 4 1981/82): 1–7.

pretation espoused by Albert Weisser, *The Modern Renaissance of Jewish Music* ,[16] the definitive study of this unique and fascinating chapter in Jewish cultural history and the only reliable volume devoted to the subject of Jewish art music in the modern era. (Weisser had collected a substantial amount of additional information in the decades following the book's publication and was planning a revised and updated version at the time of his death in 1982. With the availability of his archives and his copious notes on the project, it is hoped that one will appear eventually. Meanwhile, the relaxation of restrictions and access to archives in Russia and Ukraine will no doubt yield precious additional fruit and many long-awaited answers. The first serious research in this area since Weisser's work is now under way in Israel, with the assistance of Russian immigrant students.) Weisser treats the entire *Gesellschaft* episode and the development of the art music genre in relation to a confluence of forces at the turn of the century: Herzlian Zionism; the continuing vitality of the Haskalah; the pervasive influence of late nineteenth century nationalist music currents, not only in Russia, but in other East Central European areas and even in France and England as well; and the Russo-Jewish intelligentsia outside and inside the Pale, whose ethnic cohesiveness provided the musical elite with the raw folkloric ingredients to draw on.

Weisser's book stresses that this art music movement should not be seen exclusively or even specifically as a Yiddish language or folklore phenomenon per se—and especially not in terms of the connotations of social and political agendas attached to musical expression of the "secular Yiddishists" in America. Nor was it merely a romantic worship of the shtetl, as was often later the case in America (and, most recently, in Western Europe). For the *Gesellschaft* composers Yiddish was one indigenous part of European Jewish culture that could find elevated expression in art. Hence, their equal interest in Modern Hebrew as a language of Jewish ethnic as well as high cultural expression, and their creation of Hebrew *Lieder* as a legitimate vocal genre. Their collective opus contains numerous settings of Hebrew poetry by Bialik and Tchernikovsky, as well as other, lesser known Hebrew poets; biblical texts used as secular lyrics; and both Yiddish and Hebrew translations of Russian poetry.

These considerations of Jewish art music in the Diaspora define a principal theme of cultural expression in the modern experience. That theme can form the basis for a class session within any historical survey, which can be divided into two parts: one devoted to the folklore foundations of art music, and the other addressing the art music movement itself and the creative results. The

16. New York: Bloch, 1954; repr. New York: Da Capo, 1983.

Weisser volume will serve admirably as the preparatory source, preferably supplemented by selections from the limited number of available recordings.

By contrast, Soviet Jewish folk music scholarship assumed a more strictly ethnomusicological perspective. Both vocal and instrumental folk repertoires were studied for their intrinsic modern value as a living expressive culture in the aggregate, rather than either as nostalgia-provoking premodern relic or as a reservoir of potential source material for artistic creativity along the lines of the earlier *Gesellschaft* endeavors. Unlike the nineteenth-century romantic-nationalist camp of folklorists who viewed the *shtetl* as the autonomous quintessence of an inherent "folk soul" or spirit, Soviet ethnologists stressed the interethnicity of Jewish folk music and its interrelatedness with other indigenous, non-Jewish East European traditions. They emphasized the urban and the developed over the rural/small village and the backward, "old order" contexts of Yiddish folksong, seeing it as one component of a wider, socially conscious ethnic music network that reflected a constellation of modern events and social, political, and economic forces. The Soviet school made far-ranging advances in technical procedures and methods for collection and transcription.

One of the most significant and visionary (and, until recently, neglected) of those Soviet scholars was Moshe Beregovsky (1892–1961), whose studies lifted Jewish folk music scholarship out of its previous parochial confines and into the mainstream of modern ethnomusicology. Three of his watershed essays have been translated in *Old Jewish Folk Music: The Collections and Writings of Moshe Beregovsky*.[17] These are prefaced by the editor's incisive interpretation and followed by reproductions of major portions of Beregovsky's musical transcriptions, with English translations of the highly revealing song texts. The book is indispensable to any general consideration of Jewish folk music in the Modern era.

Beregovsky's work betrays the "internationalist" proletarian orientation of his intellectual milieu, for whom the validity and authenticity of Jewish folk music resided in its expression of universal working class aspirations and mores, rather than primarily in its evocation of specifically "Jewish" sentiments. Hence, the particular interest in Yiddish song texts on themes of urbanization, industrialization, exploitation, and political class concerns. Consistent with that world view, there is an aggressive anti-nationalist—and thus anti-Zionist—frame of reference. But that ideological inclination must be understood within its historical context. The deeper significance of Beregovsky's work lies in his keen demonstration that assimilated "foreign" musical elements do not necessarily negate the viable identity or validity of a particular

17. Ed. Mark Slobin (Philadelphia: University of Pennsylvania Press, 1982).

ethnic music. He thus affirmed East European Jewish folk music as a full-fledged and relevant expression of modern Jewish experience.

Little information is available about Jewish art music activity in Russia following the Revolution, or even concerning the whereabouts of certain music known to have been written there but which has never surfaced beyond its borders. Here too, we can now be hopeful that information will soon begin to emerge in the aftermath of the Soviet experience. It is also as yet too early to know what if any work may have been done by Soviet musicologists in the postwar period (especially through the 1970s and 1980s) on Jewish-related art music.

With the waves of East European immigration to America between the 1880s and the 1930s, a rich Yiddish musical culture developed here as well. Imported European repertories were greatly augmented by the creativity of many American-Yiddish songwriters, especially in response to social and political movements and events. At the same time, altogether new Yiddish musical categories emerged, such as patriotic expressions and songs about American historical figures. A good deal of this material entered the folk repertoire of American Jews. And, of course, both the early Yiddish vaudeville medium and the subsequent American-Yiddish theater hatched a new genre of popular Yiddish song. During that immigrant period some studies on Jewish folksong were produced in America, but mostly in Yiddish.

In the second half of the twentieth century, American scholars produced a few significant works on this topic in English. Ruth Rubin, *Voice of a People: The Story of Yiddish Folksong*,[18] the only survey to address the entire gamut of Yiddish folksong, is eminently accessible to the lay reader. It deals, however, exclusively with the texts—their significance vis-à-vis historical, social, political, and cultural issues; their origins and literary parallels; and their variants. Included in the topical breakdown are the various song categories pertaining to the life cycle, religious customs, Hasidism and the response it generated (including the special group of critical, anti-Hasidic songs), the Haskalah, literary influences, the American experience, Zionism, revolutionary movements in Russia both before and during the Soviet experience, collective agriculture, social struggle, the Holocaust and partisan movements, ghetto uprisings and the German occupation, and even the phenomenon of a Jewish "underworld." Of special historical value are the discussions of Yiddish song references to such incidents and personalities as the Dreyfus affair, Baron Rothschild, Hirsch Leckert, Boruch Shulman, particular pogroms and European wars, military conscription, and propaganda.

18. New York: Yoseloff, 1963.

There is as yet no full-length book in any language devoted to a systematic investigation of the musical features of Yiddish folksongs. Nor, for that matter, is there any such work concerning the full range of musical issues pertaining to modern Hebrew folksong (notwithstanding Michal Smoira-Cohen's monograph, *Folksong in Israel—An Analysis Attempted*,[19] which is too musicologically sophisticated for consideration here, and which does not pretend to be a comprehensive musical survey). Once again, we observe the scholarly emphasis on older, premodern musical genres and forms. Regarding the folksong that falls strictly within the purview of the modern era, we possess no contemporary parallels to the erudite and detailed musical studies on Ladino ballads by Israel Katz,[20] for example, or on Iraqi traditions by Amonon Shiloah.[21]

The popular Yiddish music culture of Jewish-American immigrants—theatre, radio, and other commercial types as reflected in published sheet music and recordings—is discussed at length in Mark Slobin, *Tenement Songs.*[22] Here we have a literary and a sociological consideration of popular music's role in the life of the Yiddish-speaking immigrant community and of how that music both reflected and aided the processes of assimilation and adjustment to the new society. The book also presents interesting insights into the process of folklorization of popular or theater music, and it excels in treating the iconography (cover illustrations, sheet music design, posters, etc.) as an indicator of popular culture and its transmission. In assessing that popular culture as a de facto musical tradition, Slobin relies upon a multidiscipline approach—interweaving the areas of sociology, popular music history, folkloristics, urban studies, and theater history.

I have thus far considered Jewish music in the modern era according to its generic divisions: liturgical, folk, art, and popular forms. But we may further broaden our understanding by approaching the subject from a different angle—by charting the course of Jewish musical culture in terms of specific institutions and institutionalized vehicles of its transmission and expression. The composite phenomenon of the modern cantor—seen in its various stages and in its generational and regional variations—offers an important plane of perspective that intersects many of the other religious, sociological, cultural,

19. Tel Aviv: Israel Music Institute, 1963.

20. *Judeo-Spanish Traditional Ballads from Jerusalem: An Ethnomusicological Study* (Brooklyn: Institute of Medieval Music, 1972).

21. *The Musical Traditions of Iraqi Jews: Selection of Piyyutim and Songs* (Or Yehuda: Institute for Research on Iraqi Jewry, Iraqi Jews' Traditional Cultural Center, 1983).

22. Urbana: University of Illinois Press, 1982.

and economic considerations. The art and the institution of the cantor provide a prism through which both musical history itself and a broad spectrum of other related cultural issues and value systems may be refracted. The perception of the cantor as folk hero among certain American and European social groups in the nineteenth and early twentieth centuries is of special sociological significance and has begun to attract scholarly attention.

Notwithstanding a reasonable journal literature on technical aspects of cantorial art, we still lack a comprehensive overview study (in any language) of cantorial/synagogal choral music and its development in the modern era; we also do not have an adequate literature on the biographies of cantors. Some basic information may be gleaned from a few nonmusicological publications. Leo Landman's well-documented monograph *The Cantor*[23] is limited for the most part to the cantor's social status. *Legendary Voices*[24] by Samuel Vigoda (1892–1990)—himself one of the virtuoso luminaries from the European scene—presents an array of stories, anecdotes, and only partially fact-based narrative accounts of some of the giants of the so-called "Golden Age of *Hazzanut*." Although disjointed and completely lacking in documentation, it offers valuable insights into the cantor's stellar role within modern European Jewish culture prior to World War II. Akiva Zimmermann, With One Song: Essays, Research, and Notes on Hazzanut and Jewish Music (in Hebrew),[25] is both a broader and more concisely written collection of information on cantors and related subjects. It is mainly a potpourri of cantorial accounts and vignettes gathered from numerous, often obscure, periodical sources as well as personal interviews, but without historical interpretation.

Mark Slobin, *Chosen Voices: The Story of the American Cantorate*,[26] provides an interesting study of the institutional and role changes that have occurred within the American context. A "story" rather than a history, the book's greatest strength lies in the sociological considerations and data on professional dynamics, which do not appear in standard studies of American Jewish history.

The Holocaust and its significance for the course of Jewish music has begun recently to attract scholarly attention. It is a complex subject, requiring controlled sensitivity in order not to trivialize the events. We may divide a consideration of the Holocaust into three principal areas: the nature and extent of the musical culture that was destroyed—in particular, that which flourished

23. New York: Yeshiva University Press, 1972.

24. New York: Vigoda, 1981.

25. *Be-ron yahad: Meolam ha-hazzanut veha-muzika ha-yehudit* (Tel Aviv: Arkhiyon ha-hazanut ha-merkazi, 1988).

26. Urbana: University of Illinois Press, 1989.

just prior to the Nazi era; musical life in Germany under the Nazi restrictions and persecutions, between 1933 and 1938; and the musical expression actually generated by the Holocaust, as a response to its horrors.

Little has been written concerning the musical activities and contributions of German-speaking Jewry during the early years of the twentieth century prior to the Nazi onslaught. The first three chapters of Philip Bohlman, *The Land Where Two Streams Flow: Music in the German-Jewish Community of Israel*[27] offer a capsule description of that now-extinct communal culture, especially with reference to the sphere of art music; See also his informative "The Resurgence of Jewish Musical Life in an Urban German Community: Mannheim on the Eve of World War II."[28] Issachar Fater, *Jewish Music in Poland between the Two World Wars* (in Yiddish),[29] must be cited here because it is the only book to cover that subject at length. Despite its numerous inaccuracies, it nonetheless presents a balanced picture of the aggregate Jewish musical life in Poland prior to the Nazi invasion. Much of its information—including illustrations, biographical data, and program accounts—is not readily available elsewhere, except in archives.

The music composed, adapted, sung, and played by Jews in the Nazi-created ghettos, within partisan Resistance movements, and even in concentration camps is the most painful to confront. The most thorough study to date deals with one particular repertoire: *Singing for Survival: Songs of the Lodz Ghetto, 1940–1945*, by Gila Flam.[30] The author availed herself of archival materials as well as interviews with survivors, in order to present the full context within which that repertoire functioned. It offers a novel interpretive approach to understanding the psychological and sociological dimensions of the ghetto existence. We can expect similar studies of other ghettos in coming years.

David Bloch, an American-Israeli musicologist, has done extensive work in unearthing and documenting the art music composed and performed in the Terezin concentration camp. Thus far his attention has been directed at reconstructed performances and recordings with historical documentation, which include solo, chamber and symphonic works, and two operas. This is an ongoing project, which should eventually result in published literature.

The rich art music culture of modern Israel provides perhaps the most explicit artistic expression of the modern experience. There, more than any-

27. Urbana: University of Illinois Press, 1989.

28. *Musica Judaica* 7 (1985/86): 34–53.

29. *Yiddishe musik in Poyln tsvishn beide velt-milchoymes* (Tel Aviv: Velt federatzia fun poylishe yidn, 1970).

30. Urbana: University of Illinois Press, 1992.

where else, the forces of modernity have converged, intertwined with each other, and blended with extant non-European, premodern elements to shape a collective creativity.

An all-inclusive historical study of Israeli music, covering the variety of approaches and probing systematically the repertoire itself as well as the intercultural factors, would be a welcome addition to our musicological literature. Existing studies of a selective and finite nature are: Peter Gradenwitz, *Music and Musicians in Israel*,[31] a basic information resource that does not extend its sights very far to historical interpretation or analysis of musicological issues; and Alexander Ringer, "Musical Composition in Modern Israel,"[32] which brings to the subject a more profound perspective of a leading historical musicologist. Zvi Keren, *Contemporary Israeli Music*,[33] may also be consulted.

The unique phenomenon of the kibbutz has had a direct impact on music in Israel—especially in terms of choral practice. Together with numerous other factors, this is discussed in Natan Shahar, Musical Life and the Composer in the Kibbutz: Historical and Socio-Musical Aspects (in Hebrew).[34] The same author has written a study of the history of Israeli (and Palestinian) folksong,[35] whose publication would add immeasurably to our breadth of understanding.

Jehoash Hirshberg, "The 'Israeli' in Israeli Music: The Audience Responds,"[36] lays groundwork for addressing the issue of musical identity (Jewish as well as specifically Israeli). Similar issues pertaining to Jewish composers in the Diaspora as well as in Israel were debated and discussed at length at the 1989 Counter-Harmonies conference in New York, which explored the interdependence between the musical cultures of America and Israel. Deliberations such as "Jewish Identity and Contemporary Music," "Jewish Emigré Composers,"and "The Jewish Composer in a Secular Culture" revealed cultural interrelationships and a number of other concerns not probed elsewhere in any printed format. The publication of these papers will contribute to our awareness of this key dimension of modern Jewish expression.

31. 3rd ed. (Tel Aviv: Israeli Music Publications, 1978).
32. In *Contemporary Music in Europe: A Comprehensive Survey*, ed. Paul Henry Lang (New York: G. Schirmer, 1965), pp. 282–97.
33. Ramat Gan: Bar Ilan University Press, 1980.
34. M.A. thesis, Bar Ilan University, 1978.
35. "Ha-shir ha-erets isra'eli 1920–1950: Ha-yivatim sotsiomusikaliim u-musicaliim" (The Eretz-Israeli Song 1920–1950: Sociomusical and Musical Aspects) (Ph.D. dissertation, Hebrew University, 1989).
36. *Israel Studies in Musicology* 1 (1978): 159–73.

260   *Neil W. Levin*

Although conceived primarily as a detailed biographical study, *Paul Ben-Haim: His Life and Work*,[37] also by Jehoash Hirshberg, examines that pioneer Israeli composer in the context of the *yishuv* and its ramifications for the evolution of Israeli musical life. While parts of it engage in musical analysis, the work is not exclusively technical. It presents a vivid picture of the environment that nurtured not only Ben-Haim but so many others, and that sowed the seeds of an Israeli national school. As such it expands our appreciation both of Israeli cultural history generally, and of musical sociology within modern immigrant communities.

Bohlman (n. 27) explores at length the nexus between Central European and Israeli musical culture and considers that relationship and its cultural progeny from an ethnological as well as a historical perspective. The author examines the musical benefits to Israeli high music culture, which accrued in great measure as a result of German-Jewish (and other German-speaking Central European) settlement in Palestine in the 1930s and 1940s. Although many of those immigrant composers attempted to adopt a new style that would incorporate some of the native musical features they encountered in the eastern Mediterranean region, Bohlman nonetheless observes very little real preservation of authentic non-European material within their music. To the contrary, he sees the introduction of eastern Mediterranean elements into an essentially Western or Central European music as a form of exaggeration, therefore preserving very little of the Middle Eastern tradition from which it drew.

Bohlman (n. 27) is also notable for its allusions to another general theme of the modern Jewish experience: the issue of Jewish identity in relation to Jewish participation in host cultures and societies. Moreover, there is the implied question of whether that identity can remain viable in the face of cultural duality. The issue has obvious implications for Jewish life in the modern era (even in Israel), well beyond music per se or even art in general. In part, Bohlman's study serves as a model study of culture and ethnicity which focuses on the ever-perplexing question of identity. As has been observed by Samuel Adler, a prominent German-Jewish emigré composer (in America) whose own range of work embodies such a duality, some German Jews forged an identity based on German and Jewish components that were not deemed mutually exclusive. Even on European soil, and then within the environments of the *yishuv* and the State, those German-Jewish composers, performers, and audiences did not see their adherence to German or Middle European cultural identity as impinging negatively on active Jewish life. Nor did they find objective scientific study necessarily incompatible with personal and religious belief or communal reli-

37. Tel Aviv: Am Oved, 1990.

gious practice. That self-secure outlook was instrumental in molding the musical life of modern Israel.

A final topic of perennial interest concerns the role of Jews in the composition and performance of Western art or so-called classical music, a topic worthy in itself of a full session within a consideration of modern Jewish history. Several recent works treat the subject within the contexts both of European and Jewish musical cultures; some address as well the inner psychological and artistic conflicts generated by the modern Jewish experience. Among such works are Eric Werner, "Felix Mendelssohn – Gustav Mahler: Two Borderline Cases of Assimilation";[38] Peter Gradenwitz, "Gustav Mahler and Arnold Schoenberg";[39] Alexander Ringer, *Arnold Schoenberg: The Composer as Jew*;[40] and Alexander Knapp's forthcoming volume on Ernest Bloch. Numerous other prominent Jewish composers within the general Western musical framework could also be considered in such deliberations—especially those whose creativity has to some degree encompassed works of Jewish relevance (sacred or secular): Samuel Adler, Aaron Copland, Jacques Halévy, Darius Milhaud, Hugo Weisgall, Kurt Weill, and Stefan Wolpe, to name only a few, as well as a host of modern Israeli composers. Also intriguing is the twentieth-century phenomenon of extensive but numerically disproportionate representation of Jews among performing artists—especially in America and Russia. Serious studies of such instances of cross-cultural or bi-cultural participation would significantly enrich our overall understanding of the modern Jewish experience—of its cultural climate and of the ways in which Jews have benefited from and contributed to Western culture during this extraordinary chapter in Jewish history.

38. *Yuval* 4 (1982): 240–64.
39. *Leo Baeck Institute Yearbook* 5 1960): 262–84.
40. Oxford: Clarendon, 1991.

27. Modern Jewish Thought

Neil Gillman

The Field

"Jewish thought" is a convenient umbrella term which delineates the inquiry into the broad intellectual assumptions underlying the varied forms of Jewish expression. It avoids the more technical connotations of "Jewish philosophy" and "Jewish theology" and hence includes both of these. It can also refer to both secular and religious forms of expression, for example, in our period to both political Zionism and Holocaust theology. When approached from a historical perspective, it becomes "Jewish intellectual history" or "history of Jewish thought."

The Period

Historical periodization is somewhat arbitrary, and the determination of precisely when Judaism entered its "Modern" period is no exception to this rule. If there is a consensus on the issue, it focuses on the last half of the eighteenth century as the terminus a quo largely because these decades mark Judaism's initial encounter with the two movements that to a significant extent set the Jewish agenda to our very day: the political Emancipation of Western Jewry, and its intellectual counterpart, the Jewish Enlightenment (or Haskalah). From this approach, then, the first noteworthy modern Jewish thinker is Moses Mendelssohn (1726–1789), whose life and writings exhibit a striking awareness of the potential impact of these two issues.

But this consensus should not blind us to significant anticipations of modernity in the work of much earlier thinkers such as the Italian historian Azariah dei Rossi (1511–1578) and the Dutch philosopher Baruch Spinoza (1632–1667). Some thinkers have viewed the apostasy of Sabbatai Zevi in 1667 as marking the end of the Jewish Middle Ages. We should understand, then, that Jewish modernity was preceded by an extended transitional era, the "Premodern" period, as it has been dubbed, in which new themes, ideas, and methodologies begin to filter into the Jewish material in a tentative, preliminary way.

But in light of the limitations of time in a typical semester course and in view of the richness of the later material, this essay uses the late eighteenth century date as denoting the first appearance of modern Jewish thought.

Bibliography

I begin with one masterful overview of the intellectual history of the period as a whole and one generous anthology of sources. The overview is the extended essay "The Modern Age" by the premier Jewish historian of our century, Salo W. Baron, included in *Great Ages and Ideas of the Jewish People*.[1] This volume, a compilation of six essays by six eminent authorities, each writing on his field, can be recommended as a superb, inexpensive text on Jewish intellectual history as a whole. The anthology is *The Jew in the Modern World: A Documentary History*.[2] Baron captures both the main impulses and the ambiguities of the period with grace and precision; the bibliography appended to the essay is rich but dated. The Mendes-Flohr and Reinharz selections range from the "Harbingers of Political and Economic Change" in the late seventeenth century through to the Holocaust. The editors provide brief but pointed introductions to each selection, and the demographical tables appended to the volume supply significant background data. Together, these two inexpensive volumes are simply indispensable and should be acquired by all students.

Note also the encyclopedic *Contemporary Jewish Religious Thought: Original Essays on Critical Concepts, Movements, and Beliefs*.[3] This collection of 140 short essays is bulky, uneven, and limited in its scope (as indicated by the title). Despite this, it remains a useful reference tool.

On Mendelssohn, see in particular his *Jerusalem; or, On Religious Power and Judaism*.[4] Altmann's introduction and commentary, in particular, distin-

1. Ed. Leo W. Schwarz (New York: Random House, 1956), pp. 315–484.
2. Ed. Paul R. Mendes-Flohr and Jehuda Reinharz (New York: Oxford University Press, 1980).
3. Ed. Arthur A. Cohen and Paul Mendes-Flohr (New York: Scribners, 1987).
4. Trans. Allan Arkush, intro. and commentary Alexander Altmann (Hanover, N.H.: University Presses of New England, 1983).

guish this edition of this landmark statement by tracing the underlying assumptions and impulses that mark the dawn of Jewish modernity. Altmann's book-length biography of Mendelssohn, *Moses Mendelssohn: A Biographical Study*,[5] is definitive.

Anticipations of modernity in sixteenth- and seventeenth-century Jewish historiography are traced in the anthology *Ideas of Jewish History*.[6] The full impact of modern Jewish historiographies on Judaism is described in Yosef Hayim Yerushalmi's slim but powerful *Zakhor: Jewish History and Jewish Memory*.[7]

Spinoza's "premodern" critical temper, as applied specifically to Jewish religion, is best exemplified in his *Theologico-Political Treatise* (to date, available in English only in the 1883 translation by R. H. M. Elwes).[8] The thesis that Spinoza's work marks the dawn of modern Jewish secularism is advanced in Yirmiyahu Yovel's comprehensive but tendentious *Spinoza and Other Heretics*.[9] The thesis that Spinoza's *Ethics* marks him as "the first modern philosopher" is argued in the classic *The Philosophy of Spinoza: Unfolding the Latent Processes of his Reasoning*, by Harry Austryn Wolfson.[10] The thesis is discussed in Seymour Feldman's Introduction to Spinoza's *The Ethics and Selected Letters*.[11]

Finally, on the impact of Sabbatianism, see ch. 8 of Gershom Scholem, *Major Trends in Jewish Mysticism*,[12] still the most accessible gateway into the study of Jewish mysticism. Scholem's *Sabbatai Sevi: The Mystical Messiah*,[13] is long, technical, and endlessly fascinating.

Emancipation and Enlightenment

For the Jewish community, modernity meant Emancipation and Enlightenment. Emancipation was the movement that sought the integration of Jews into the political, socioeconomic, and cultural structures of the emerging national states in Europe and in America. Enlightenment was the parallel movement which sought the integration of Judaism into the new intellectual

5. University: University of Alabama Press, 1973.
6. Ed. Michael A. Meyer (Detroit: Wayne State University Press, 1987).
7. Seattle: University of Washington Press, 1982.
8. London: Bell, 1883; repr. New York: Dover, 1951.
9. 2 vols. to date, vol. 3 forthcoming (Princeton: Princeton University Press, 1989).
10. Cambridge: Harvard University Press, 1934.
11. Trans. Samuel Shirley (Indianapolis: Hackett, 1982).
12. Jerusalem: Schocken, 1941.
13. Princeton: Princeton University Press, 1973.

currents of the West—the critical temper, rationalism, and the new historical awareness. In brief, Emancipation meant the collapse of the Jewish political ghetto; Enlightenment meant the collapse of its intellectual ghetto.

The ultimate impact of these two movements was to force a redefinition of the terms of Jewish identity. From antiquity, Jewish identity had been understood as a nexus of religion and peoplehood. Ruth 1:16 said it all: "Your people shall be my people, and your God my God." With the rise of the new national states, however, that nexus was irreparably shattered. Broadly speaking, Jews had to choose between one of these two forms of identity. They could become citizens of the emerging national states, hence sacrifice their national identity and understand themselves as a religious community on the model of Christianity; or they could reject Emancipation and define themselves as a national entity on the model of the other national states, but then they would have to seek their own national home in some other part of the world. The initial Jewish response to this dilemma, through much of the nineteenth century, was to accept Emancipation and to work on the redefinition of Jewish identity in religious terms alone. That response is captured in the Declaration of the Assembly of French Jewish Notables of 1806, who identify themselves as "Frenchmen professing the religion of Moses." The anti-Emancipation reaction to that response led to the emergence of political Zionism as a nationalist solution to the dilemma toward the end of that century. It was not until the early decades of the twentieth century that some possible reintegration of these two impulses is explored.

But if the initial impulse was to accept the terms of Emancipation and define Jewish identity in terms of religion alone, that new definition then had to deal with the further impact of the Enlightenment. It became clear that Jewish religion itself would have to be radically redefined if the goals of the emancipatory impulse were to be achieved. If Jews were to be integrated into modern society, Judaism too would have to be shown to belong. All forms of Jewish religious expression—its distinctive ways of thinking, ritual forms, the Hebrew language, and the methods used for the study of Jewish texts and institutions—would have to be looked at anew in terms of the reigning spirit of the age.

Particularly the *Wissenschaft des Judentums* (Science of Judaism) school understood that for Judaism, the ticket of admission into modern Europe would be the subjecting of Jewish religion to the very same canons of scholarly inquiry that were used for the study of any culture. Factual accuracy, normative neutrality, the emancipation of scholarship from belief, the quest for truth whatever that truth might be and whatever its source or its implications—these became the guiding principles for the study of Judaism as well.

This alone would dispel the anti-Jewish animus that pervaded European culture, would engender Jewish self-respect, and would legitimatize the integration of the Jewish community into European life. The ultimate impact of this impulse, then, was an inevitable secularization of Jewish thought. Thus, though the terms of Jewish identity were already diluted by the splitting off of its national dimension, the religious dimension that remained was further strained by the Jewish Enlightenment.

In Western Europe, the religious redefinition of Jewish identity took three forms, depending on the extent to which the secularizing impact was acknowledged and accepted. The earliest of these responses was the Reform movement in Germany toward the end of the second decade of the century. In this early guise, exemplified in the writings of Abraham Geiger (1810–1874), Reform advocated an increasingly radical redefinition of all forms of Jewish religious life. The reaction to Reform took two forms: a Neo-Orthodox movement, led by Samson Raphael Hirsch (1808–1888), which attempted to reaffirm traditional forms of belief and practice as a conscious and deliberate reaction to modernity; and the Positive-Historical (later, in its American incarnation, to be dubbed "Conservative") school, led by Zechariah Frankel (1801–1875), which sought a middle ground, combining modern scholarship with the attempt to retain much of traditional Jewish practice. By the middle of the century each of these movements was well established in Europe, and toward the end of the century each found itself recreated in the new American setting.

But the impact of the Jewish Enlightenment went far beyond the religious institutions. It prompted a revival of the Hebrew language and of a new, secularized belletristic movement both in Hebrew and in Yiddish. It led to new understandings of the dynamics of Jewish history and historiography. It propelled Jews into the fields of Western learning. In the end, it served as a transition from the insulated, Jewish world of the Early Modern period to the more frankly assimilated model of the late nineteenth century. Finally, it led also to significant reactions. In Eastern Europe, these took the form of the popular revivalist Hasidic movement, the moralist Musar movement, and the revival of talmudic learning as a new model of piety in the Lithuanian academies.

Bibliography

The Declaration of The Assembly of French Notables can be found in part 3 of Mendes-Flohr and Reinharz (n. 2). Part 4 of the volume deals with the patterns of religious adjustment in Reform, Conservative, and Neo-Orthodox Judaisms, and part 5 with the Science of Judaism school. The documentary material assembled here is particularly rich.

For a more complete treatment of these latter developments, see: on Reform, *Abraham Geiger and Liberal Judaism: The Challenge of the Nineteenth Century*;[14] on Neo-Orthodoxy, Samson Raphael Hirsch, *The Nineteen Letters of Ben Uziel*.[15] There is no single comparable study of Frankel and the Positive-Historical school in English, but ch. 4 of *The Rise of Reform Judaism: A Sourcebook of its European Origins*[16] traces Frankel's break with the growing radicalization of European Reform. This volume is also particularly strong on original documents. See also the material on nineteenth-century Jewish historiography collected in Meyer (n. 6), particularly the material on Nahman Krochmal and Heinrich Graetz and on the Science of Judaism school. For a book-length study of Hirsch, see Noah H. Rosenbloom, *Tradition in an Age of Reform: The Religious Philosophy of Samson Raphael Hirsch*.[17]

On the East European experience, there is little in English beyond the material collected in part 8 of Mendes-Flohr and Reinharz (n. 2) and the relevent pages in Baron (n. 1). The most influential historian of this particular transitional period in Jewish history is Jacob Katz. His *Out of the Ghetto: The Social Background of Jewish Emancipation 1770–1870*[18] is particularly insightful. Shalom Spiegel, *Hebrew Reborn*,[19] is a series of elegantly crafted sketches of the leading figures in the Jewish Enlightenment.

The Nationalist Reaction

If the pro-Emancipation movement dominated the first half of the nineteenth century, the second half was dominated by the increasingly articulate voices of Jewish nationalists. Moses Hess, *Rome and Jerusalem*,[20] in Western Europe, and Leo Pinsker, *Auto-Emancipation*,[21] in Eastern Europe, were precursors to what is arguably the single most influential book of the entire period, Theodor Herzl, *The Jewish State*,[22] which effectively launched the Zionist movement.

In these early guises, Zionism provided a preeminently secular format for

14. Ed. Max Wiener (Cincinnati: Hebrew Union College Press, 1981).
15. Trans. Rabbi Dr. Bernard Drachman, ed. Jacob Breuer (New York: Feldheim, 1960)
16. Ed. W. Gunther Plaut (New York: World Union for Progressive Judaism, 1963).
17. Philadelphia: Jewish Publication Society, 1976.
18. Cambridge: Harvard University Press, 1973.
19. New York: Meridian, 1957.
20. 1862; repr. New York: Philosphical Library, 1958.
21. 1882; repr. New York: Zionist Organization of America, 1948.
22. 1896; repr. Tel Aviv: Newman, 1954.

Jewish identity. Its subsequent history revolves around its attempt to struggle with giving that identity a sufficiently weighty Jewish dimension, all the while avoiding any explicit religious referent. The major contribution to that inquiry was provided by Ahad Ha-Am (pen name for Asher Zvi Ginsberg, 1856–1927), Herzl's most formidable opponent in the early Zionist Congresses. Ahad Ha-Am viewed Zionism as the solution to the problem, not of the Jews as Herzl did, but rather of Judaism. Zionism would be the force that would revitalize Jewish cultural creativity, all in a secular vein. Ahad Ha-Am, then, remains the father of all forms of secular or cultural Judaism to this day.

Bibliography

On Zionism in all its expressions, we are blessed with a superb anthology, *The Zionist Idea: A Historical Analysis and Reader.*[23] Hertzberg's introduction is long and masterful and the selections, ranging from the eighteenth-century precursors through the twentieth-century architects of the State of Israel, are comprehensive and generous. This volume is indispensable and should be acquired by all students. A recent book-length biography of Herzl is Ernst Pawel, *The Labyrinth of Exile: A Life of Theodor Herzl.*[24]

The overriding issue for modern Jewish thought, then, throughout the nineteenth century and even to this day, has been the question of the Jewishness of Jewish identity in an age where Jews have found it increasingly easy to integrate into the variety of political and intellectual "outside worlds" in which they found themselves. How is it possible to infuse that self-definition with sufficient Jewish weight to balance out the seductions and accommodations required of those who seek to be fully in tune with modernity as well? Much of the agenda of modern Jewish thought revolves around various attempts to resolve that tension.

Theological Resolution

The more theological resolution of that issue in early twentieth century Europe found its expression in the work of two major thinkers, Martin Buber (1878–1965) and his friend and colleague, Franz Rosenzweig (1886–1929). Both identified personally with the marginal quality of German-Jewish identity—indeed, Rosenzweig himself briefly flirted with apostasy. Both grappled with the various resolutions to that set of dilemmas, and both became paradig-

---

23. Ed. Arthur Hertzberg (Garden City, N.Y.: Doubleday, 1959).
24. New York: Farrar, Straus and Giroux, 1989.

matic figures for their generation and also for American Jews in the years following World War II. Together, they served as the founding fathers of Jewish existentialism, which remains one of the main currents of Jewish philosophical/theological inquiry in our century.

Bibliography

Buber's *I and Thou* remains one of the most influential books of the century. It should be studied in the Walter Kaufmann translation with prologue and notes.[25] Equally important, at least for Buber's contribution to Jewish thought, is the anthology of early (1909–1918) and later (1939–1951) addresses, *On Judaism*.[26] A useful anthology of Buber's writings on a wide range of theological, social, political, and educational issues is *The Writings of Martin Buber*.[27] Herberg's introduction is a superb, concise summary of Buber's thought. Maurice S. Friedman has devoted his career to studying Buber. His *Encounter on the Narrow Ridge: A Life of Martin Buber*,[28] a one-volume condensation of his massive three-volume biography, *Martin Buber's Life and Work*,[29] tends to be overly eulogistic, but Friedman's summaries of Buber's writings are insightful.

Indispensable for Rosenzweig is *Franz Rosenzweig: His Life and Thought*,[30] which introduced both the man and the thought to the English-speaking public. The first half of the book is the story of his tragically short life, told largely through his own writings, and the second is a generous anthology of his thought. In the case of Rosenzweig, the life and the thought are inseparable. A second valuable anthology, also edited by Glatzer, is *On Jewish Learning*.[31] It contains, among other items, a celebrated exchange of letters with Buber on Jewish law. An excellent discussion of Rosenzweig's thought, particularly of his gradual movement from German idealism to existentialism, is the concluding chapter of Julius Guttmann, *Philosophies of Judaism*.[32] The reworking of Buberian and Rosenzweigian thought by their American disciples is discussed below.

25. New York: Scribners, 1970.
26. Ed. Nahum N. Glatzer (New York: Schocken, 1967).
27. Ed. Will Herberg (New York: Meridian, 1956).
28. New York: Paragon, 1991.
29. New York: Dutton, 1981–83.
30. Ed. Nahum N. Glatzer (New York: Schocken, 1953).
31. New York: Schocken, 1955.
32. Trans. David W. Silverman (Philadelphia: Jewish Publication Society, 1964).

The American Experience

The twentieth century saw the gradual shift of the center of Jewish life and thought from the Continent to America. The broad agenda of nineteenth-century Jewish thought—the redefinition of the terms of Jewish identity in the light of a politically and intellectually open society—remains the same, but the very nature of American culture added its own distinctive coloration to the enterprise. On one hand, the constitutional barrier between church and state worked to insulate the Jewish world and allow its innate richness to emerge. But from another perspective, the very power and energy of this new "outside" world, the blatant secularism, openness, and individualism of American life, were extraordinarily seductive.

The most significant new contribution to the discussion of this issue was provided by Mordecai Kaplan (1880–1981), in many ways the most influential American Jewish thinker in the first half of the century. Kaplan was a religious and theological naturalist. This perspective led him to cut through the religion/peoplehood dilemma and redefine Judaism as a "civilization"—to be precise, as "the evolving religious civilization of the Jewish people." This conceptualization enabled Kaplan to address the full range of issues confronting modern American Jewry, and though some of his theology has become anachronistic, many of his proposals have now become main-line Jewish thinking.

Bibliography

American Jewish thought cannot be studied apart from its broader context in the sociology of American Jewish life. A particularly useful compendium is the anthology *American Jews: A Reader*.[33] This volume also contains studies of Reform, Conservative, and Orthodox Jewries in their American setting. Two of these movements have issued ideological platforms that merit close study. In fact, American Reform has issued three of these: The Pittsburgh Platform of 1885, the Columbus Platform of 1936, and the Centennial Perspective of 1976. The evolution of Reform ideology over the century, as reflected in these statements, is fascinating to observe. They are grouped together and discussed in Eugene Borowitz, *Reform Judaism Today*.[34] *Emet ve-emunah: Statement of Principles of Conservative Judaism*[35] was published in 1988.

33. Ed. Marshall Sklare (New York: Behrman, 1983).
34. New York: Behrman, 1983.
35. Available through the United Synagogue Book Service, 155 Fifth Avenue, New York, NY 10010.

Kaplan's classic statement of his position is his *Judaism as a Civilization: Toward a Reconstruction of American-Jewish Life.*[36] Much more accessible is his *The Future of the American Jew.*[37] For class purposes, the anthology *Dynamic Judaism: The Essential Writings of Mordecai Kaplan*[38] is recommended. Equally valuable as a point of entry into the various dimensions of Kaplan's thought is his *Questions Jews Ask: Reconstructionist Answers.*[39] The *American Judaism of Mordecai M. Kaplan*[40] is a rich anthology of studies on the full range of Kaplan's work.

American Jewish Thought

The twentieth century also saw two marker events in Jewish history, the Holocaust and the creation of the State of Israel. Like all events of this magnitude, these generated a sense of crisis regarding the existing paradigms and stimulated a reassessment of the substance of Jewish thinking. The Holocaust inevitably cast much of classical Jewish theology into question, and the creation of the State of Israel has generated a new interest in Jewish political theory as Jewish ideologues have struggled with the implications of Jewish power and political authority, both radically new experiences for the Jewish community. It has also generated one further issue, of necessity totally unanticipated in the past: the question of the very legitimacy of a Jewish Diaspora existence, or of the relationship between Diaspora Jewry and the new State.

Of these two, the new political thinking is still in its infancy. But the encounter with modernity in its American setting served to stimulate a major revival of Jewish theological inquiry, particularly after World War II. If Mordecai Kaplan dominated American Jewish thought in the first half of the century, the second half saw the emergence of the neo-Hasidic thought of Abraham Joshua Heschel and also of a group of Jewish existentialists such as the late Will Herberg and, still among us, Eugene Borowitz and Emil Fackenheim, who reworked the thought of Buber and Rosenzweig in a more native, American idiom. American Jewish thinkers have delved into the theological implications of the Holocaust. More recently, a group of Neo-Orthodox theo-

36. New York: Macmillan, 1934; repr, Philadelphia: Jewish Publication Society; New York: Reconstructionist Press, 1981.

37. New York: Macmillan, 1958.

38. Ed. Emmanuel S. Goldsmith and Mel Scult (New York: Schocken, 1985).

39. New York: The Jewish Reconstructionist Foundation, 1956.

40. Ed. Emanuel S. Goldsmith, Mel Scult, and Robert M. Seltzer (New York: New York University Press, 1990).

logians—preeminently David Hartman—have attempted to give new life to classical (i.e., biblical, rabbinic/talmudic, and Maimonidean) theological categories as an authentically Jewish response to modernity. Their mentor in this work has been Rabbi Joseph Baer Soloveitchik, arguably the most eminent Orthodox rabbinic authority of the past generation, who also exerted a great deal of influence in shaping the Modern Orthodox philosophical response to modernity.

Bibliography

In the fledgling field of Jewish political theory, see the seminal *The Jewish Polity: Jewish Political Organization from Biblical Times to the Present*,[41] by Daniel J. Elazar and Stuart A. Cohen. On the range of responses to the new reality created for Israeli and Diaspora Jews alike by the establishment of the State of Israel, see Arnold M. Eisen, *Galut: Modern Jewish Reflections on Homelessness and Homecoming*.[42]

The most accessible entree into Heschel's thought is through the anthology *Between God and Man: An Interpretation of Judaism from the Writings of Abraham Joshua Heschel*.[43] Rothschild's introduction is a superb summary of the thought of this singularly elusive thinker.

Robert G. Goldy, *The Emergence of Jewish Theology in America*,[44] traces the transmission of European Jewish thought to America. A central role in this process was played by Will Herberg, whose *Judaism and Modern Man*[45] had a major impact on the first generation of Jews following the War. *The Jewish Thought of Emil Fackenheim: A Reader*[46] is a rich anthology of selections from the work of this Buberian thinker, much of it inspired by reflections on the implications of the Holocaust. Equally prolific is Eugene Borowitz, whose *Renewing the Covenant: A Theology for the Postmodern Jew*[47] is the most recent of this prolific author's restatements of the main currents in the field and a compelling argument in favor of the author's own "liberal" position.

Apart from Fackenheim, on the enterprise of Holocaust theology, attention must be paid to Richard Rubenstein's controversial Jewish version of Christian "death of God" theology in his *After Auschwitz: Radical Theology and Contemporary Judaism*.[48] In a more traditionalist vein, Eliezer Berkovits,

41. Bloomington: Indiana University Press, 1987.
42. Bloomington: Indiana University Press, 1986.
43. Ed. Fritz A. Rothschild (New York: Free Press, 1959).
44. Bloomington: Indiana University Press, 1990.
45. New York: Farrar, Straus and Young, 1951.
46. Ed. Michael L. Morgan (Detroit: Wayne State University Press, 1987).
47. Philadelphia: Jewish Publication Society, 1991.
48. Indianapolis: Bobbs Merrill, 1966.

Faith after the Holocaust,[49] argues for a much more classical response to the events of our century. Richard Rubenstein and John K. Roth have also authored *Approaches to Auschwitz: The Holocaust and its Legacy,*[50] an interdisciplinary text bringing together historical, literary, theological, and religious material designed specifically for college courses on the Holocaust. Steven T. Katz, *Post Holocaust Dialogues: Critical Studies in Modern Jewish Thought,*[51] is a sympathetic yet critical survey of the range of options espoused by various Jewish thinkers. Finally, it is well-nigh impossible to reflect on the Holocaust without reading Elie Wiesel. To this writer, his very first published volume, *Night,*[52] remains his most compelling statement.

Among the new traditionalists, David Hartman, *A Living Covenant: The Innovative Spirit in Traditional Judaism,*[53] is a restatement in very contemporary terms of what the author calls Judaism's "covenantal anthropology." It also makes a powerful case for the fact that only in the Jewish state can the full range of issues involved in Judaism's engagement with modernity be explored. Soloveitchik's philosophical writings have only recently appeared in English, but his *Halakhic Man*[54] has been particularly influential.

Spirituality and Religion

This return to tradition has also stimulated a renewed interest in Jewish mysticism. This rich body of Jewish expression was largely debunked by nineteenth-century Jewish scholars who found it totally alien to the more rational spirit of the age. But largely under the guidance of Gershom Scholem, longtime Professor of Jewish Mysticism at the Hebrew University, who literally created the field as a modern scholarly discipline, and his student and critic, Moshe Idell, Jewish mysticism and its modern offshoot, Hasidism, have found their place on the agenda of Jewish scholarship. Even more, mysticism has proven to be a singularly attractive form of Jewish religious expression for young Jews today.

Equally new, and also striking in its contrast to the rational–critical temper of the nineteenth century, has been the emergence of Jewish religion as a field of scholarly inquiry by Jewish academicians. This field—the phenomenology of religion—was created at the turn of the century by social scientists and by

49. New York: Ktav, 1973.
50. Atlanta: John Knox Press, 1987.
51. New York: New York University Press, 1983.
52. New York: Hill and Wang, 1960.
53. New York: Free Press, 1985.
54. Trans. Lawrence Kaplan (Philadelphia: Jewish Publication Society, 1983).

students of primitive religions. It gradually penetrated the world of Christian scholarship, and even more recently, Jewish studies as well. It has, for example, prompted a spate of works on Jewish ritual, liturgy, and the mythic structure of biblical and talmudic religion.

Bibliography

Scholem (n. 12) remains the most accessible gateway into the complex world of Jewish mysticism. The last chapter of this volume deals with the modern transformation of this tradition in Hasidism. Moshe Idel's revisionist view of the material, of interest to the more serious and advanced student, is in his *Kabbalah: New Perspectives*.[55] Louis Jacobs, *Jewish Mystical Testimonies*,[56] collects a number of representative texts from the the writings of earlier mystics and from the Hasidic masters as well, and Jacobs' commentaries are always enlightening. David R. Blumenthal, *God at the Center: Meditations on Jewish Spirituality*,[57] is a particularly attractive presentation of Hasidic themes structured around the Jewish liturgical year.

Jacob Neusner has pioneered in the application of the methods of the phenomenology of religion to the study of Judaism. He has written extensively on talmudic religion but his *The Enchantments of Judaism: Rites of Transformation From Birth Through Death*[58] is a striking illumination of the Jewish rites of passage. Two other scholars, Jon D. Levenson and Jonathan Z. Smith, have published extensively in the field. Levenson, *Sinai and Zion: An Entry into the Jewish Bible*,[59] and Smith, *To Take Place: Toward Theory in Ritual*,[60] are imaginative explorations of the Jewish material. The single most comprehensive study of the relationship of liturgy and ritual in Judaism is Lawrence A. Hoffman, *Beyond the Text: A Holistic Approach to Liturgy*.[61] Finally, Neil Gillman, *Sacred Fragments: Recovering Theology for the Modern Jew*,[62] deals with the interrelationship of theology and religion in Judaism.

55. New Haven: Yale University Press, 1988.
56. New York: Schocken, 1977.
57. San Francisco: Harper and Row, 1988.
58. New York: Basic Books, 1987.
59. New York: Harper and Row, 1985.
60. Chicago: University of Chicago Press, 1987.
61. Bloomington: Indiana University Press, 1987.
62. Philadelphia: Jewish Publication Society, 1990.

28. Modern Jewish Demography
Sergio DellaPergola

The scientific study of Jewish population, sometimes referred to as Jewish demography, focuses on the changing size and composition of Jewish populations, and on the determinants and consequences of such changes. It should be clearly indicated from the outset that variations in Jewish population size and composition reflect the action of both biological and demographic variables— as in the case of populations in general—and of identificational-cultural variables—as in the case of most other minority groups or subpopulations. The following statement most concisely identifies the main area of interest of Jewish population studies. For any given region or territory, the size of Jewish population at a given time reflects the size of the same Jewish population at an earlier time plus the number of Jewish births less Jewish deaths, plus the number of Jewish immigrants less emigrants, plus the number of new accessions to Judaism (through formal conversion or otherwise) less secessions during the same time interval. Looking at world Jewry's population size, migrations can be ignored.

These same factors of change in population size also determine continuous changes in the composition of the Jewish population according to a variety of characteristics such as age, sex, place of origin, seniority in the community of residence, and so on. Further changes of no less importance for the overall composition of Jewish populations, and of populations in general, derive from sociodemographic processes which do not directly touch on population size. Examples include marriage and other changes in marital status, geographical mobility within a given country and territorial division or internationally, educational and occupational changes, and other forms of social mobility. Of special interest for Jewish populations are any intervening changes in Jewish identity, attitudes, and behaviors. Population composition within each of these variables will affect each of the direct determinants of change in population size, thus exerting an indirect influence on the latter.

The study of Jewish demography is concerned with the analysis of each of the many structural and dynamic aspects of population size and composition, their mutual interactions, and their final outcomes. Moreover, population studies often consider how demographic trends are affected by, or affect other, nondemographic processes (political, institutional, economic, biological, etc.).

The main rationale for the study of Jewish populations rests with the substantial and growing scientific interest in understanding the demography of religious, ethnic, and cultural groups and minorities. Such insights are being increasingly perceived as a fundamental element in the analysis of population and societal processes in general. Jewish demography therefore provides a valuable contribution to the general progress of social scientific knowledge. At the same time, demographic changes provide an important if not indispensable background for the appreciation of the Jewish historical and cultural experience. Hence, Jewish demography organically contributes to the development of Jewish studies.

As a more applicable and practical outcome, Jewish population studies may provide Jewish communal bodies and institutions with the database they need in relation to the daily running and future planning of Jewish community services. Many relevant examples can be provided of how Jewish population trends may interact with the supply and functioning of Jewish community services. Understanding these trends is a prerequisite for any serious attempt to develop Jewish community planning and policies.

Methodological Issues

Basic Concepts and Definitions

The very definition of the target population, embodied in the paradigmatic "Who is a Jew?" question, constitutes a major and ever elusive issue in the field of Jewish population studies—in an extended time perspective, and particularly in the Contemporary period. As a general rule, the study of modern and contemporary Jewish populations tends to rely more on operative than on normative definitions of the target population. Halakhah (Jewish rabbinic law) provides a clear and authoritative definition of "who is a Jew." However, for empirical research purposes, it is usually impossible to undertake the stringent legal controls involved in ascertaining the Jewish identity of each individual according to Halakhah. Therefore, the Jewish population is usually defined according to subjective criteria, such as self-identification, or based on the more or less accurate proxies offered by easily categorized variables, such as religion or ethnic origin in population censuses.

Feudal society may have provided an environment in which social categories, including religion, tended to be relatively stable. Identification of individuals with specific sectors of society, including religious groups, usually followed clear rules. So did passages, where feasible, from one population group to another, including accessions to or (more likely) secessions from the Jewish community. In modern and contemporary societies, on the other hand, patterns of identification between individual self and a meaningful collective frame of reference (such as religion or ethnic or cultural group) have tended to become more complicated, reflecting the diffusion of subtle processes of cultural, ideological, and psychosocial change. Contemporary patterns of Jewish identity have been especially affected.

One significant complicating factor in contemporary societies is the increasing frequency of intermarriage. Intermarriage provides the major context for the growing number of individuals whose Jewish identification may be the object of controversy between different religious or legal authorities. More significantly, in the context of the same process, many more "marginal" individuals prefer not, or do not know whether or when, to identify with the Jewish group—whether or not they might be entitled to do so according to some objective rule. While instances of partial, segmented, or dual Jewish identity have become more frequent, the sociodemographic boundary of Jewish populations has become increasingly flexible, porous, and blurred.

Following these trends, at least two distinct definitions should become standard requirements in the analysis of Jewish populations: the core and the enlarged Jewish population. The core approaches a conventional concept of a Jewish population. It includes all those who are ready to identify with the Jewish group, and those of actual Jewish origin who are now indifferent or agnostic but do not formally identify with another religious group. The enlarged Jewish population also includes those individuals of Jewish origin who currently identify with another religious group, as well as all the non-Jewish members of mixed households. Ideally, sociodemographic processes should be analyzed with respect to both core and enlarged Jewish populations, each of which provides a meaningful, albeit different, framework for analysis. Unfortunately, much recent research has confused these two concepts. It should be noted that growth in an enlarged Jewish population may be accompanied by decline in the associated core Jewish population.

Some would argue that the highly fluid and voluntaristic patterns of identification of contemporary Jewish populations make unfeasible any attempt to quantify the number of Jews locally or globally. Even if one rejects this position, Jewish population figures and estimates should always be taken as orders of magnitude, surrounded by variable and sometimes significant margins of error.

Sources of Data

The study of Jewish population has no definite time framework. It overlaps with Jewish history from the origins to our days and beyond. Clearly, quite different situations characterize the documentary basis of Jewish demography in different historical periods. The types and quality of available sources of data have determined the more or less reliable or speculative character of Jewish population studies and have deeply affected the character and direction of research in the field over time.

Where direct and unequivocal information is lacking, three different approaches combined may usefully assist in the attempt to posit at least basic orders of magnitude of a Jewish population, or to outline the likely direction of major intervening changes. First, information of demographic relevance as transmitted by early Jewish tradition can provide a chronology of the major events affecting the rhythm of evolution of the Jewish population in the past, or even a typological sense of the quantities involved. Second, verified historical evidence relating to neighboring or similar populations may provide yardsticks to infer parallel changes that may have affected Jewish populations. Third, judicious use of mathematical models which describe expected patterns of population dynamics and structure under given assumptions may assist in the critical assessment of what might have been possible or impossible under known circumstances.

In the course of time, and especially since the beginning of the modern era, the amount of reliable information concerning demographic processes of the Jews has tended to grow. Yet, even in the Contemporary period, the scientific study of Jewish populations is hindered by exacting methodological problems. A primary difficulty concerns the availability and quality of data. Relevant sources may be numerous, but sociodemographic data were and continue to be very scattered, often not very reliable, and lacking altogether in certain regards. Hence, the possibility of developing systematic comparisons between different places and over extended periods of time—an imperative research need given the character of the Jewish experience—is rather limited.

The wide geographic dispersion of world Jewry implies exposure in the past and present to many different political regimes and legal arrangements.

This in turn affects two basic aspects of modern and contemporary data sources on Jewish populations: (1) whether or not the Jews are classified as one among other religious or ethnic groups in census or civil register statistics collected and released by official state or local authorities; (2) the degree of institutional centralization of the Jewish community in a certain place, and the proportion of Jewish population formally affiliated with any Jewish institutions.

Official population censuses and/or registers, where available, can provide good sources of information on the characteristics of Jewish populations as well as of other religio-ethnic groups. Over the last hundred years, though, major international migrations tended to flow from countries with Jewish population statistics to countries lacking such statistics. One of the side effects of the Holocaust was the destruction of large Jewish populations for which detailed demographic data were routinely collected. Nowadays, about three-fourths of Diaspora Jews live in countries where no official data on religious groups are available due to the separation between Church and State or other reasons. In this context, the State of Israel today constitutes the major exception, with detailed and reliable sociodemographic data constantly supplied by its Central Bureau of Statistics.

Centralized listings of Jewish households kept by Jewish community organizations, where available, provide a useful database for research purposes. Demographic data are sometimes available from registers of Jewish vital events, such as marriages, births, and burials. Based on these sources, trends can sometimes be reconstructed over extended time periods. But most large contemporary Jewish communities in the Diaspora have no such central listings or recordkeeping.

Thus the study of Jewish demography has come to depend mostly on a variety of private or public research initiatives. General social surveys sometimes include a question on religion or ethnic origin. But Jews usually are scant minorities in such surveys, leaving little margin for meaningful analyses of Jewish population characteristics. Jewish-sponsored sample surveys involving larger numbers of Jewish households have been undertaken in several countries, and even more often in selected local communities, through specially designed questionnaires and direct interviewing. Such studies have provided detailed sociodemographic and attitudinal profiles of the selected Jewries—beyond the limited array of topics covered by the typical official census. Unfortunately, lack of uniformity regarding basic concepts, definitions, survey techniques, questionnaire contents, and format of analysis has detracted from the scientific and practical value of many of these studies.

Following the 1987 Jerusalem Conference on Jewish Population, some important new steps were taken toward greater coordination of research initiatives and concepts. An International Scientific Advisory Committee was formed, and a new round of Jewish population surveys based on common concepts and the same core questionnaire was launched in several countries. The leading initiative was the 1989–90 United States National Jewish Population Survey, whose first results were released in 1990. It can be hoped that the database for a systematic study of Jewish population worldwide will improve substantially during the 1990s.

Research Resources and Prospects

The global dispersion of the Jews has had deep implications for the possibility of developing effective research facilities and undertaking systematic projects in the field of Jewish population studies. In a less recent past, the Bureau für Demographie und Statistik der Juden (Berlin, 1905–1931, with a few interruptions) did provide such a central research facility, including publication of the *Zeitschrift für Demographie und Statistik der Juden* and several monographs.

After World War II, the Hebrew University of Jerusalem has become one of the major centers stimulating research on Jewish population globally, mainly through the Division of Jewish Demography and Statistics at the Institute of Contemporary Jewry (founded in 1959). The Division holds extensive documentation and bibliographic files and from 1970 to 1991 has published twenty-four volumes in the series Jewish Population Studies (JPS). It organizes sessions on Jewish Demography in the framework of the quadrennial World Congress of Jewish Studies.

In the United States, since the 1980s important research activities have been carried out at the Center for Modern Jewish Studies at Brandeis University and the North American Jewish Data Bank sponsored by the Council of Jewish Federations at the Graduate Center of the City University of New York. Each of these centers is a depository for large amounts of documentation on Jewish populations. Research units operate at the central Jewish community institutions in the United Kingdom (the Board of Deputies) and Argentina (Asociación Mutual Israelita Argentina).

Much remains to be done to improve coordination and the quality of research internationally. One persisting challenge is the need to create the basis for systematic and periodic updating of the data that exist nationally and internationally, instead of the sporadic efforts that have been typical of the past. Better documentation is the necessary baseline for improvements at the conceptual-theoretical level, which in turn are necessary if Jewish population studies are to become a standard area of research and teaching in institutions of higher learning, both in the social sciences and in Judaic studies. The data collection efforts of recent years, the intensive and rather intriguing Jewish population trends they reveal, and the debate—academic and public—they generate augur well for the continuing expansion of further research and analysis in the field of Jewish demography and for the improved quality of the outcome.

Substantive Issues

Major Population Trends

While the actual patterns of change of modern and contemporary Jewish populations are beyond the scope of this essay, it is worth at least mentioning some of the fundamental processes. After remaining comparatively small and stable across the Middle Ages and the Early Modern period around an estimated level of one million or fewer, world Jewish population started growing toward the end of the seventeenth century. It reached maximum growth rates during the nineteenth century, and was still growing globally after World War I. The all-time peak of about 16.5 million Jews was reached on the eve of World War II and the Holocaust. Jewish population growth was particularly concentrated in Eastern Europe, whose Jewish communities were the largest regional component of world Jewry; rapid growth also created the pool for the large intercontinental migration that, mainly from the 1880s, was to develop the newer centers of Jewish settlement in North America, in other overseas countries, and in Palestine.

The main determinant of the rapid Jewish demographic increase was the comparatively early transition from higher to lower mortality levels, which anticipated by several decades similar trends among the total population of the same countries. At a later stage, Jewish birth rates declined too, once again anticipating by several decades similar developments among the general population. Similar distinctive Jewish population trends can be observed in a variety of regional environments, though substantial time lags separate the onset and tempo of these changes in the more modernized communities in Europe versus the more traditional ones in Asia and Africa. Among the direct and indirect consequences (via international migration) of these population trends of the nineteenth and early twentieth centuries was a radical change in the geography and internal cultural balance of world Jewry.

Since the loss of over one third of its global size through the Holocaust and World War II, Jewish population has been following two distinct courses. That of Israel is characterized by continued intensive immigration, the process of absorption and integration of heterogeneous migration, and an overall convergence of the diverse demographic behaviors of immigrants and their children. This has created a comparatively young population, displaying a persisting family orientation, with moderately high fertility levels and growth rates. Jews in the Diaspora, on the other hand, with some local variation tended to display low or very low fertility rates, growing rates of singlehood, divorce, and mixed marriage, a negative balance of new accessions versus secessions (including children of mixed marriages), population aging, and, finally, numerical decline caused by a negative balance between Jewish births and Jewish deaths.

Toward the last quarter of the twentieth century, the two quite different Jewish population patterns of Israel and the Diaspora have tended to produce zero population growth among a world Jewry estimated at less than thirteen million globally. Jews were once again the forerunners in anticipating the slowdown of population growth in the more developed countries and, eventually, the world. The most likely implication of recent Jewish population trends is that decline in the Diaspora would overcome increase in Israel, resulting in a numerically diminishing Jewish people toward the beginning of the twenty-first century.

Several major analytic issues emerge from the substantive Jewish population trends just outlined, some of which have stimulated controversy among observers. Some of these issues are now reviewed, with a critical eye to the relevant literature of the last decades.

Analytic Approaches

The in-depth study of one specific group or community, in this case the Jews, calls for a comparative frame of reference. Three major types of relevant comparisons in the study of Jewish populations could be: (1) the same Jewish population observed at repeated points in time, (2) different Jewish populations observed at the same time, and (3) Jews and relevant non-Jewish populations observed at the same time. There are at least three major parameters for judging the validity of approaches in available Jewish demographic research. First, one may relate to the possible range between all-inclusiveness versus time–place–issue specificity. Thinking again of the great complexity of the Jewish sociohistorical experience, one can hardly hope to reach any definitive conclusions about the Jews of a given country, let alone an entire continent or the whole world, without a deep command of historical change, geographical variation, and thematic richness. Second is the apparent contradiction between essentially fact-oriented, descriptive versus theoretically oriented, analytic work. Here we risk opposing extremes: the intense accumulation of facts and figures without a clear indication of sociohistorical direction and meaning, or sweeping generalizations based on databases that are narrow in terms of time perspective, geographical coverage, or thematic complexity. Third, there is the dialectic between general disciplinary and particularistic communal concerns: the ultimate evaluation of Jewish population studies must be based on criteria laid down by the disciplines of general demography and sociology. At the same time, the final relevance of research should also take into account its benefits for societal applicability and human welfare, for the Jewish community and generally.

Explanatory Frameworks

As already noted, one of the major aims of research is to bring about understanding of empirically observed facts in the light of some broader conceptual framework. One framework quite popular in the past was that of race versus environment, emerging from the interest of nineteenth-century science in physical anthropology. The infamous exploitation of the concept of human race for political purposes has rendered this approach obsolete and disreputable. It should be noted, though, that the genetics of isolated and migrant populations continues to be a serious and relevant aspect of contemporary scholarship dealing with the Jews and similar groups.

Another major paradigm focuses on the differences between Jews and other groups in the light of their respective minority versus majority status. Minority status—a long-standing feature for most Jews in the world—played a significant role in determining differences between Jews and non-Jews. These differences related to legal, economic, social, psychological, and other individual and collective patterns. The same differences, in turn, may have been directly or indirectly tied to population trends. Members of a minority group generally tend to be exposed to a different set of constraints and incentives than members of the majority (and most often, dominant) group. Usually the minority's range of options is more limited, which leads to a comparatively smaller degree of differentiation in its compositional characteristics, to concentration in certain sectors of society, and to sharing various socioeconomic and psychological traits with other members of the same minority. These features may have related to the more concentrated timing and faster rhythm of change observed in the demographic evolution of Jewish populations. Some of these mechanisms can be also hypothesized to stand behind the significant sociodemographic differences which exist between Jews in the Diaspora, where they constitute small minorities of the total population, and in Israel, where they constitute the majority.

Finally, Jewish population trends can be associated with the changing equilibrium between the two major categories of structural versus cultural determinants. Structural determinants may be posited to play an important role in determining rational behaviors aimed at maximizing one's own material welfare; cultural determinants may be seen at work mainly in relation to emotional or spiritual fulfillment not necessarily connected with utilitarian reward. Neither type of variable seems to be sufficient, though both are necessary to provide a full and balanced understanding of Jewish population trends, or of population trends in general. Of particular interest here is the scrutiny of what traditional Jewish culture and communal institutions have to say and to do with attitudes and behaviors whose ultimate effect can be measured demographically. The changing demographic dynamics of Jewish populations can be interpreted as a reflection of both structural and cultural change among the Jews.

Characterization of Observed Trends

Various attempts to characterize the main thrust of modern and contemporary Jewish sociodemographic trends have emerged from recent research. Such alternative characterizations have sparked recurring debates about the ultimate policy implications of Jewish demography. Without elaborating here on the merit and substance of such debates, some of the major distinctions are worth mentioning.

One often-debated issue is that of distinctiveness versus conformity, that is, whether in the final analysis the apparent peculiarities of Jewish population trends reflect a unique and original blend of patterns, or merely can be attributed to a slightly modified version of the experience of other populations. The question is not only whether the general level or frequency of features such as mortality, marriage, fertility, or geographic mobility is different among Jews and non-Jews. One would like to ascertain whether the same peculiarities persist after controlling for an adequate number of further sociodemographic variables—in other words, whether the modes of interaction between different sociodemographic variables are significantly different between Jews and control groups. In the light of what was said above about the possible role of cultural and structural factors in the explanation of population trends, judgment seems to tend strongly toward distinctiveness, even when—as often in the present time—the absolute size of demographic differentials between Jews and non-Jews may be modest.

Another debate, sometimes imbued with value judgment, has involved those who mostly read in the recent Jewish population trends a pattern of continuity versus erosion. The failure of Jewish populations in the Diaspora to replace themselves demographically, because of low fertility rates, and the growing incidence of assimilation and out-marriage accompanied by declining frequencies of conversion to Judaism, have provided evidence for the erosion hypothesis. The persistence of large masses of Jews in numerous urban metropolitan areas in the Western countries, and the distinctive social and professional environments which continue to characterize the daily life of many of them, have offered the main basis for the continuity tenet. The most recent research findings, such as those from the 1990 National Jewish Population Survey in the United States, suggest new and sharper terms of reference for this ongoing debate. The new data indicate that the complex of biodemographic and identificational factors of Jewish continuity is now experiencing unprecedented challenge. It is not only a matter of maintaining a Jewish community locally. This may be and still is achieved, in spite of the possible weakening of Jewish cultural life. It is rather the global sense of peoplehood and the universal meaning of Jewish solidarity that are at stake. So is the ability to produce the population of a new generation and to transmit to it a sense of Jewish identity that it will pass on to the next generation.

The further attempt to distinguish between the quantitative versus qualitative correlates and implications of Jewish population trends sometimes carries the suggestion that the total number of Jews, including those who identify more and those who identify less, has lesser societal meaning than the intellectual and spiritual quality of those who choose to be actively involved with the Jewish community. On the other hand, quantity can be shown to be strictly related to quality, as it affects a variety of fundamental processes for the viability of a Jewish community. These range from the extension of marriage markets and the amount of effort required to find a compatible spouse within the group, to the ability of local communities to support an articulated network of Jewish cultural and recreative activities and thus offer a meaningful collective frame of reference to the individual Jew.

Finally, the already mentioned different demographic course taken in recent decades by Israel versus Diaspora Jewries leads toward a changing quantitative balance between these two components of world Jewry. While at the beginning of the 1990s Israel represented barely thirty percent of the world total, current family trends, reinforced by international migration, might lead in the early twenty-first century to Israel being not only the largest Jewish community on earth, but the one holding a majority of the world Jewish population. That time is even closer when we observe only the population of Jewish children. The presence of a majority of all Jews in Israel would obviously constitute a revolutionary step in a Jewish history which has been fundamentally Diaspora-oriented for the past two thousand years.

Whether such change will actually take place depends greatly on the further assessment of the respective roles of Israel and the Diaspora (especially America and the other more developed countries) on a world scale of core versus periphery. In many respects, Israel does now constitute the ethnocultural core of the global Jewish people, whose peripheral fringes are declining or fading away. Those fringes are mostly located in the Diaspora, where they coexist with the more strongly identified sections of the respective Jewish communities. As such, Israel may attract some ideologically motivated immigration. But Israel's future viability on the international scene, its capacity to attract further large-scale migration and to keep a hold on its own population, will depend essentially on its ability to join the core of more developed countries, escaping the economic and political semi-periphery where it belongs now. Demographic trends, together with nondemographic processes such as the general state of world and regional economic, political, and military affairs, may determine the future size and geographic distribution of the Jewish population in Israel and elsewhere—and hence for the broader Jewish experience worldwide.

Teaching Jewish Demography

Jewish population studies may be taught as a separate topic in the framework of a Judaic Studies or a general sociology program. However, the discussion of demographic issues may usefully highlight other major junctures of the modern Jewish experience in the framework of a Modern Jewish History course. The Jews' early demographic transition may provide an exemplary case study within a general discussion of the broader concept of modernization. A deeper analysis of the demographic trends of the nineteenth and early twentieth centuries will usefully be associated with an examination of the social significance of traditional Jewish culture for Jewish population and community.

Mass international migrations will be dealt with as a central chapter in the modern Jewish experience. Migration is both a consequence of the demographic and social transformations of the nineteenth century and a cause of the dramatic shift of Jewish centers of gravity in the contemporary world. This entails several crucial transitions among the Jews, among others from an economically and culturally marginalized entity to one standing much closer to the core of global decision-making; and from a traditional and rather segregated to an open and much more secular environment. Discussion of Jewish migrations offers the necessary introduction to understanding the emergence and growth of American Jewry to the status of one of the numerically largest and economically most successful Jewish communities in history.

Any survey of the emergence of the modern *yishuv* in Palestine, during the late Ottoman period and especially during the interwar British Mandate, and of the evolution of the State of Israel as a new major center of Jewish life must consider the demographic aspects of immigration and immigrant absorption. The contemporary balance between the conflicitng demographic trends in Israel and throughout the world can be put in the wider perspective of the different cultural and social constraints and opportunities available to Jews in the context of statehood versus as a minority community.

Those beginning their exploration of the field of Jewish demography will find the following to be among the most helpful readings. Wide sociohistorical perspectives on demographic trends among world Jewry are provided in Roberto Bachi, *Population Trends of World Jewry*;[1] U. O. Schmelz, "Jewish Survival: The Demographic Factors";[2] and Sergio DellaPergola, "Changing Patterns of Jewish Demography in the Modern World."[3] See also U. O. Schmelz and Sergio DellaPergola, "World Jewish Population, 1990,"[4] for the most recent update on the current global situation.

Among the rapidly growing literature on American Jewish population trends, see first of all Sidney Goldstein, "Jews in the United States: Perspectives from Demography"[5] and "Profile of American Jewry: Insights from the 1990 National Jewish Population Survey."[6] Further standard reading is the 1990 National Jewish Population Survey outline released by Barry A. Kosmin and colleagues.[7] I also recommend comparison of the quite different interpretations of recent trends suggested by Calvin Goldscheider, especially *The American Jewish Community: Social Science Research and Policy Implications*;[8] Steven M. Cohen, *American Assimilation or Jewish Revival?*;[9] and U. O. Schmelz and Sergio DellaPergola, *Basic Trends in American Jewish Demography*.[10]

1. Jewish Population Studies 9 (Jerusalem: Hebrew University, Institute of Contemporary Jewry, 1976).

2. *American Jewish Yearbook* 81 (1981): 61–117.

3. *Studia Rosenthaliana*, special issue published together with vol. 23/2 (Fall 1989), pp. 154–74.

4. *American Jewish Year Book* 92 (1992): 484–512.

5. *American Jewish Year Book* 81 (1981): 3–59.

6 *American Jewish Year Book* 92 (1992): 77–173.

7. B.A. Kosmin, Sidney Goldstein, J. Waksberg, N. Lerer, A. Keysar, and J. Scheckner, *Highlights of the CJF National Jewish Population Survey* (New York: Council of Jewish Federations, 1991).

8. Atlanta: Scholars Press, 1986.

9. Bloomington: Indiana University Press, 1988.

10. New York: American Jewish Committee, Institute of Human Relations, 1988.

The most important work on the Jewish population of Israel is Roberto Bachi, *The Population of Israel*.[11] Other useful books are Dov Friedlander and Calvin Goldscheider, *The Population of Israel*,[12] and U. O. Schmelz, Sergio DellaPergola, and Uri Avner, *Ethnic Differences among Israeli Jews: A New Look*.[13]

Additional Selected Bibliography

Altshuler, M. 1987. *Soviet Jewry since the Second World War: Population and Social Structure*. Westport, Conn.: Greenwood Press.

Bachi, Roberto, F. Massarik, B. Lazerwitz, Sidney Goldstein, and U. O. Schmelz. 1973. *Papers in Jewish Demography 1970* (Jewish Population Studies 5). Jerusalem: Hebrew University, Institute of Contemporary Jewry.

Baron, Salo W. 1971. "Population." *Encyclopaedia Judaica* 13, cols. 866–903.

Bloch, B. 1980. "Vital Events Among the Jews in European Russia towards the End of the XIX Century," in *Papers in Jewish Demography 1977*, ed. U. O. Schmelz, P. Glikson, and Sergio DellaPergola. Jerusalem: Hebrew University, Institute of Contemporary Jewry, pp. 69–81.

Cohen, R. 1983. "Recent Trends in Jewish Historical Demography," in *Papers in Jewish Demography 1981*, ed. U.O. Schmelz, P. Glikson, and Sergio DellaPergola. Jerusalem: Hebrew University, Institute of Contemporary Jewry, pp. 43–48.

Cohen, S. M. 1983. *American Modernity and Jewish Identity*. New York: Tavistock.

Cohen, S. M., J. S. Woocher, and B. A. Phillips. 1984. *Perspectives in Jewish Population Research*. Boulder, Colo.: Westview.

DellaPergola, Sergio. 1980. "Patterns of American Jewish Fertility." *Demography* 17/3: 261–73.

———. 1989a. "Marriage, Conversion, Children, and Jewish Continuity: Some Demographic Aspects of 'Who is a Jew?'" in *Survey of Jewish Affairs 1989*, ed. W. Frankel. Oxford: Blackwell for the Institute of Jewish Affairs, pp. 171–87.

———. 1989b. *Recent Trends in Jewish Marriage* (Occasional Paper 1989-07). Jerusalem: Hebrew University, Institute of Contemporary Jewry.

———. 1992. "Major Demographic Trends of World Jewry: The Last Hundred Years," in *Genetic Diversity among Jews: Diseases and Markers at the DNA Level*, ed. B. Bonné-Tamir and A. Adam. New York: Oxford University Press, pp. 3–30.

DellaPergola, Sergio, and Leah Cohen. 1992. *World Jewish Population: Trends and Policies* (Jewish Population Studies 23). Jerusalem: Hebrew University, Institute of Contemporary Jewry and Association for Demographic Policy of the Jewish People.

11. Jewish Population Studies 11 (Jerusalem: Hebrew University, Institute of Contemporary Jewry; and Prime Minister's Office, Demographic Center, 1977).

12. New York: Columbia University Press, 1979.

13. Jewish Population Studies 22 (Jerusalem: Hebrew University, Institute of Contemporary Jewry, and American Jewish Committee, 1991).

DellaPergola, Sergio, and A. A. Dubb. 1988. "South African Jewry: A Sociodemographic Profile." *American Jewish Yearbook* 88: 59–140.

DellaPergola, Sergio, and U. O. Schmelz. 1989. "Demographic Transformations of American Jewry: Marriage and Mixed Marriage in the 1980s." *Studies in Contemporary Jewry* 5: 169–200.

Goldscheider, C. 1986a. *Jewish Continuity and Change: Emerging Patterns in America*. Bloomington: Indiana University Press.

———. 1986b. *American Jewish Fertility: Trends and Differentials in the Providence Metropolitan Area*. Atlanta: Scholars Press.

Goldscheider, C., and Sidney Goldstein. 1988. *The Jewish Community of Rhode Island: A Social and Demographic Study 1987*. Providence: Jewish Federation of Rhode Island.

Himmelfarb, H. S., and Sergio DellaPergola. 1989. *Jewish Education Worldwide: Cross-cultural Perspectives* (Jewish Population Studies 21). Lanham, Md.: University Press of America with Hebrew University, Institute of Contemporary Jewry.

Kuznets, S. 1960. "Economic Structure and Life of the Jews," in *The Jews: Their History, Culture, and Religion*, ed. Louis Finkelstein. New York: Harper, vol. 2, pp. 1597–1666.

———. 1975. "Immigration of Russian Jews to the United States: Background and Structure." *Perspectives in American History* 9: 35–124.

Lestchinsky, J. 1960. "Jewish Migrations, 1840–1946," in *The Jews: Their History, Culture, and Religion*, ed. Louis Finkelstein. New York: Harper, vol. 2, pp. 1536–96.

Massarik, F., and A. Chenkin. 1974. "United States National Jewish Population Study: A First Report." *American Jewish Yearbook* 73: 264–306.

Mayer, E. 1987. *Love and Tradition: Marriage between Jews and Christians*. New York: Schocken.

McEvedy, Colin, and Richard Jones. 1978. *Atlas of World Population History*. Harmondsworth: Penguin.

Peritz, Eric, and Mario Baras. 1992. *Studies in the Fertility of Israel* (Jewish Population Studies 24). Jerusalem: Hebrew University, Institute of Contemporary Jewry and Association for Demographic Policy of the Jewish People.

Phillips, B. A. 1986. "Los Angeles Jewry: A Demographic Portrait." *American Jewish Yearbook* 86: 126–95.

Ritterband, P. 1981. *Modern Jewish Fertility*. Leiden: Brill.

Ritterband, P., and S. M. Cohen. 1984. "The Social Characteristics of the New York Area Jewish Community, 1981." *American Jewish Yearbook* 84: 61–117.

Robison, S. M., with J. Starr. 1943. *Jewish Population Studies*. New York: Conference on Jewish Relations.

Ruppin, A. 1940. *The Jewish Fate and Future*. London: Macmillan.

Schmelz, U. O. 1981. *World Jewish Population: Regional Estimates and Projections* (Jewish Population Studies 13). Jerusalem: Hebrew University, Institute of Contemporary Jewry.

————. 1984. *Aging of World Jewry* (Jewish Population Studies 15). Jerusalem: Hebrew University, Institute of Contemporary Jewry; and JDC–Brookdale Institute of Gerontology and Adult Human Development.

————. 1989. *World Jewish Population in the 1980s: A Short Outline* (Occasional Paper 1989-06). Jerusalem: Hebrew University, Institute of Contemporary Jewry.

Schmelz, U. O., and G. Nathan. 1986. *Studies in the Population of Israel in Honor of Roberto Bachi* (Scripta Hierosolymitana 30). Jerusalem: Magnes.

Stampfer, S. 1988a. "Remarriage among Jews and Christians in Nineteenth-Century Eastern Europe." *Jewish History* 3/2: 85–114.

————. 1988b. "The 1764 Census of Polish Jewry." *Bar Ilan* 24–25: 41–147.

Tobin, G. A. 1989. "A Sociodemographic Profile of the Jews in the United States in the 1980s," in *Papers in Jewish Demography 1985*, ed. U. O. Schmelz and Sergio DellaPergola. Jerusalem: Hebrew University, Institute of Contemporary Jewry, pp. 43–65.

United Nations 1991. *World Population Prospects 1990* (Population Studies 120). New York: United Nations, Department of International Economic and Social Affairs.

van Praag, P. 1976. *Demography of the Jews in the Netherlands* (Jewish Population Studies 8). Jerusalem: Hebrew University, Institute of Contemporary Jewry.

Waterman, S., and B. Kosmin. 1986. *British Jewry in the Eighties: A Statistical and Geographical Guide*. London: Board of Deputies of British Jews.

Winter, J. A., and L. I. Levin. 1984. *Advancing the State of the Art: Colloquium on Jewish Population Studies*, 2 vols. New York: Council of Jewish Federations.

29. American and Canadian Jewish Sociology

Stuart Schoenfeld

The Development of the Literature in the Field

The sociology and anthropology of American and Canadian Jews is primarily a post–World War II phenomenon. There were far fewer sociologists and anthropologists before the war than there are now; few were Jewish; fewer studied Jews. Louis Wirth—a member of the influential "Chicago School" of American sociology—devoted a volume, *The Ghetto*,[1] to the Jewish immigrant experience. Louis Rosenberg, *Canada's Jews*,[2] compiled detailed data based on the Canadian censuses. Such analysis was, and still is, possible because Canada, unlike the United States, enumerates Jews on the census— twice, in fact: as an "ethnic group" and as a religious group.

Within the past forty years the social scientific study of the Jews has developed substantially. It is possible to identify two reasons for the volume and diversity of the literature which we now have. First, Jewish organizations decided to sponsor research, although it should be noted that communal sponsorship of research has been much more developed in the United States than in Canada. *The Authoritarian Personality*, by Theodore Adorno,[3] a study conducted and published under the sponsorship of the American Jewish Committee, was a landmark in the history of social psychology. The AJC–sponsored studies of the suburb of "Lakeville" in the 1950s, Marshall Sklare and Joseph Greenblum, *Jewish Identity on the Suburban Frontier*,[4] and Benjamin Ringer,

---

1. Chicago: University of Chicago Press, 1928; repr. 1965.
2. Montreal: Canadian Jewish Congress, 1939.
3. New York: Harper, 1950.
4. Chicago: University of Chicago Press, 1959; 2nd ed., 1979.

The Edge of Friendliness: A Study of Jewish–Gentile Relations,[5] marked an emerging shift in communal concern to the question of Jewish survival in an open society and a corresponding interest in applying the perspectives and methods of sociology. An impressive range of social scientific studies sponsored by the AJC has continued.

The Jewish community survey pioneered in the Lakeville study was adopted as a research tool by scores of Jewish federations across the United States and Canada. The Council of Jewish Federations conducted a National Jewish Population Survey in 1970–71 and in 1990. Initial results of the latter are reported in Barry A. Kosmin, Sidney Goldstein, Joseph Waksberg, Nava Lerer, Ariella Keysar, and Jeffrey Scheckner, *Highlights of the CJF National Jewish Population Survey.*[6] A series of monographs based on the 1990 NJPS is being written. The Conservative and Reform movements have also sponsored research, as have a variety of other Jewish organizations. The Jerusalem Center for Public Affairs has undertaken major projects in Israel and in the Diaspora. The recent work of the Commission on Jewish Education in North America had an important research component. Communally sponsored research has been eclectic in perspective. Sociologists are perhaps the most often involved, but political scientists, social workers, psychologists, economists, educational researchers, independent market researchers, and anthropologists also take part.

A second source of the growth in the sociology and anthropology of the Jews in the United States and Canada has been the growth of interest among those who hold academic appointments. The disciplines of sociology and anthropology have expanded, and the fields of ethnic and religious studies along with them. Academic researchers on contemporary Jewish life are scattered among the hundreds of sociology and anthropology departments in North American universities. The development of university programs in Jewish Studies has made academic appointments available to many others. A sociologist or anthropologist is normally considered desirable, and most of the programs in Jewish Studies of any size have one, sometimes more. The gradual evolution of a handful of teacher-training – adult education institutes into postsecondary degree-granting institutions has provided another home for those who do research on the Jews of the United States and Canada. Numerous academic studies of North American Jewry have been published by scholarly presses and presses specializing in Judaica. The establishment in the 1970s of the Association for the Social Scientific Study of Jewry, which pub-

---

5. New York: Basic Books, 1967.
6. N.p.: Council of Jewish Federations, 1991.

lishes the journal *Contemporary Jewry*, was an indicator that the study of North American Jewry had emerged as a field of inquiry within the academic structure of North American social science.

There are some differences between the research which is organizationally sponsored and that which is driven by an academic agenda. The organizationally sponsored study is often a survey which gives a statistical overview of the population in which the organization is interested. The academically oriented research is often more interested in pursuing a theoretical issue within the discipline, complete with a substantial literature review and references to other populations. The policy implications of the work are not highlighted, and the desire to reflect what is "up to date" in the discipline may be pronounced. Needless to say, these differences are tendencies rather than rigid divisions. The sociologists that Jewish organizations call on to conduct research are most often university-based scholars, who consequently write for both communal and academic audiences.

The ethnographic literature on North American Jews in particular has been, with few exceptions, an academic enterprise. Articles in the *Jewish Folklore and Ethnological Review* approach the study of North American Jews in ways unlike most of the studies under organizational sponsorship. Selections of ethnographic studies are found in *Judaism Viewed from Within and Without: Anthropological Studies*;[7] *Persistence and Flexibility: Anthropological Perspectives on the American Jewish Experience*;[8] and *Between Two Worlds: Ethnographic Essays on American Jewry*.[9]

As well as existing within a disciplinary framework, the sociology and anthropology of North American Jews is informed by the work done by social and cultural historians, political scientists, literary critics, and psychologists. While the focus of this essay is on what has been done by sociologists and anthropologists, it also refers to work done by scholars in these associated fields. It is also noteworthy that on some topics that would reveal much about contemporary Jewish life in the United States and Canada, very little has been written.

Issues in the Field and Major Works: Continuity and Ambivalence

The academic discussion of the Jews of North America goes on in the context of an underlying theme. This theme used to be known as "assimilation." By a

7. Ed. Harvey Goldberg (Albany: State University of New York Press, 1987).
8. Ed. Walter Zenner (Albany: State University of New York Press, 1988).
9. Ed. Jack Kugelmass (Ithaca: Cornell University Press, 1988).

public relations sleight of hand, it is now more commonly referred to as "Jewish continuity." Same issue, same literature, but a more upbeat label. Those who do research sponsored by Jewish organizations tend to be more preoccupied with this theme, but it is in the background of most work.

There was a continuing debate during the late 1980s. Charles Silberman, *A Certain People*,[10] collected an impressive amount of positive anecdotal evidence, while Calvin Goldscheider, *Jewish Continuity and Change*,[11] presented statistical evidence of continuing Jewish distinctiveness, and Jonathan Woocher, *Sacred Survival: the Civil Religion of American Jews*,[12] identified a consistent if only partly institutionalized value system shared by the leadership in Jewish federations. The optimism characteristic of these studies contested the widespread opinion, based on considerable data, that with every generation American Jews, in general, have become less Jewish; on this issue see Steven M. Cohen, *American Modernity and Jewish Identity*,[13] *American Assimilation or Jewish Revival?*,[14] and *Content or Continuity? Alternative Basis for Commitment: The 1989 National Survey of American Jews*;[15] and Chaim Waxman, *America's Jews in Transition*.[16]

Nathan Glazer, "New Perspectives in American Jewish Sociology,"[17] and Rela Geffen Monson, *Jewish Campus Life: a Survey of Student Attitudes towards Marriage and Family*,[18] give succinct accounts of the literature most often cited on "Jewish continuity." Steven M. Cohen and Charles Liebman, *The Quality of American Jewish Life—Two Views*,[19] present different readings of the situation although they are both expert in the same literature. Calvin Goldscheider's policy-oriented review of the literature, *The American Jewish Community: Social Science Research and Policy Implications*,[20] is a rare case of a sociologist taking the risk of making specific recommendation to the American Jewish leadership and publishing responses along with his proposals. Leonard Fein, *Where Are We?*,[21] appeared well into the debate, taking a position supporting Jewish continuity not so much as a prediction, but as a

10. New York: Summit, 1985.
11. Bloomington: Indiana University Press, 1986.
12. Bloomington: Indiana University Press, 1986.
13. New York: Tavistock, 1983.
14. Bloomington: Indiana University Press, 1988.
15. New York: American Jewish Committee, 1991.
16. Philadelphia: Temple University Press, 1983.
17. *American Jewish Year Book* 87 (1987) 3–19.
18. New York: American Jewish Committee, 1984.
19. New York: American Jewish Committee, 1987.
20. Atlanta: Scholars Press, 1986.
21. New York: Harper and Row, 1988.

moral choice. As a committed Jew and a liberal, Fein argued that American Jews have a future as a moral community that nurtures its members even as it promotes righteousness in the broader society.

The results of the 1990 National Jewish Population Study, Kosmin et al. (n. 6), do indicate that there is strong evidence supporting the pessimistic view. The optimists are likely to prove resilient, finding in some of the studies mentioned below grounds for expecting subsequent generations of Jews to continue to choose to be Jewish. Silberman, after all, wasn't making things up, and there remains a large infrastructure committed on a range of ideological bases to promoting Jewish continuity.

In Canada, there has not yet been a scholarly monograph on Jewish continuity. The folklore among Canadian Jews holds that they are a generation behind the Americans, and much of the discourse on Jewish continuity in Canada borrows freely from American sources. However, there is evidence that in addition to the generational lag, Canada is structurally different from the United States in ways that promote the maintenance of ethnoreligious identities; see Stuart Schoenfeld, "The Jewish Religion in North America: Canadian and American Comparisons;"[22] Morton Weinfeld, "Canadian Jews and Canadian Pluralism."[23] For a detailed historical study on the cultural identity of Canadian Jewry, see Michael Brown, *Jew or Juif? Jews, French Canadians, and Anglo-Canadians, 1759–1914.*[24] Canada, moreover, is going through a major constitutional crisis and no one is sure what structural arrangements and social attitudes will emerge over the next decade. Irving Abella's recent history, *A Coat of Many Colours: Two Centuries of Jewish Life in Canada,*[25] poses the issue of Jewish continuity but does not aim to be an exhaustive discussion of it. While the focus of Daniel Elazar and Harold Waller's detailed study, *Maintaining Consensus: the Canadian Jewish Polity in the Postwar World,*[26] is on the structure, processes, and agenda of the organized Jewish community, issues related to Jewish continuity receive considerable attention. Raymond Breton, Wsevolod Isajiw, Warren Kalbach, and Jeffrey Reitz's analysis of a 1978–79 survey in Toronto, *Ethnic Identity and Inequality,*[27] places the data on Jews in relationship to that for other groups, showing that Jews were more likely to be high in ethnic group identity, residentially concen-

22. *Canadian Journal of Sociology* 3 (1978): 209–31.

23. In *American Pluralism and the Jewish Community*, ed. Seymour Martin Lipset (New Brunswick, N.J.: Transaction, 1990), pp. 87–106.

24. Philadelphia: Jewish Publication Society, 1986.

25. Toronto: Lester and Orpen Dennys, 1990.

26. Lanham, Md.: University Press of America, 1990.

27. Toronto: University of Toronto Press, 1990.

trated, have high occupational status, and be organizationally affiliated than others. There are sociological studies of a couple of small communities: Sheva Medjuck, *The Jews of Atlantic Canada*;[28] Marion Meyer, *The Jews of Kingston: A Microcosm of Canadian Jewry?*.[29] The Toronto Jewish Community Federation has recently published results of its 1990 survey, as Jay Brodbar-Nemzer, *Greater Toronto Jewish Community Study: A First Look*.[30] The *Canadian Jewish Mosaic*[31] and *Canadian Jewry Today*[32] contain some of the detailed studies necessary, but there is clearly much more to be done.

This essay acknowledges the high profile of the debate on "Jewish continuity," but it also points to a broader body of literature and suggests how some of that literature may be used with students. There are studies of the immigration experience (including recent immigration), demography, social mobility, antisemitism, Jewish identity, family life, intermarriage, community organization, religiosity, education, and intellectual life. In the course of reviewing research on these topics, this essay suggests that ambivalence—being attracted to two things which appear to be contradictory and which may in fact be contradictory—provides a unifying focus which supplements the theme of "continuity." Charles Liebman, in his thematic use of ambivalence as a perspective on American Jewish life, wrote that Jews are "torn" with unusual intensity "between two forces: the desire for acceptance by the gentile society and the attraction of non-Jewish values and attitudes, and the desire for group identity and survival as a distinct community" (*The Ambivalent American Jew*,[33] p. 23). The focus on ambivalence draws attention past the statistical indicators of generational change to the qualitative assessment of the life experience of different generations of North American Jews.

The Immigrant Experience

There are many studies of the nineteenth- and early twentieth century waves of Jewish immigration to the United States and Canada. For a contemporary account that approaches Jewish immigration in the style of what was to become early twentieth century sociology, see Hutchins Hapgood, *The Spirit of the Ghetto*.[34] For recent work which picks up the current social science interest in the construction of consciousness and probes Jewish ambivalence, see Stephan F. Brumberg, *Going to America, Going to School: The Jewish*

28. St. John's, Nfld.: Breakwater Books, 1986.
29. Kingston, Ont.: Limestone Press, 1983.
30. Toronto: Toronto Jewish Community Federation, 1991.
31. Ed. Irwin Cotler, Morton Weinfeld, and William Shaffir (Toronto: Wiley, 1980).
32. Ed. Edmond Y. Lipsitz (Downsview, Ont.: JESL, 1989).
33. Philadelphia: Jewish Publication Society, 1973.
34. Cambridge, Mass.: Belknap, 1967.

Immigrant Public School Encounter in Turn-of-the-Century New York City,[35] on the meaning of public education, and Andrew Heinze, *Adapting to Abundance: Jewish Immigrants, Mass Consumption, and the Search for American Identity*,[36] on learning to participate in a culture of consumption.

The extensive literature on refugees in the 1930s and 1940s and on Holocaust survivors has two major emphases—the politics of exclusion and postwar immigration, and the psychological consequences of surviving a campaign of mass murder and brutalization. The study of economic, cultural, and political integration of refugees and survivors into the North American Jewish community, on the other hand, has gotten little systematic attention. It is nevertheless clear that those who fled Europe at midcentury significantly changed North American Jewry. For example, the yeshiva-oriented Orthodox rabbis revived a more insular, uncompromising Orthodoxy. William B. Helmreich, *The World of the Yeshiva: An Intimate Portrait of Orthodox Jewry*,[37] looks at the internal dynamics of this community; it deserves another study examining its relationship to the rest of North American Jewry. Refugee scholars became some, if not most, of the outstanding academic authorities in the United States from the 1950s through the 1970s; the Jewish communal agenda in both the United States and Canada has been influenced by refugees and survivors who have built up considerable fortunes in the New World. The importance of this wave of immigrants for Holocaust remembrance activities and the campaign to identify war criminals may seem self-evident, but it has received little scholarly study; see Harold Troper and Morton Weinfeld, *Old Wounds: Jews, Ukrainians, and the Hunt for Nazi War Criminals in Canada*.[38]

The North American Jewish population cannot be properly understood without some examination of recent immigrants. Fortunately there are some fine studies. See, on Israelis, Moshe Shokeid, *Children of Circumstance: Israeli Emigrants in New York*;[39] on Soviet Jews, Fran Markowitz, "Rituals as the Key to Soviet Immigrants' Jewish Identity"[40] and "Jewish in the USSR, Russian in the USA;"[41] on North African Jewish migrants to Montreal, Marie Berdugo-Cohen, Yolande Cohen, and Joseph Levy, *Juifs Marocains à Montréal: Témoignages d'une immigration moderne*.[42]

35. New York: Praeger, 1986.
36. New York: Columbia University Press, 1990.
37. New York: Free Press, 1982.
38. Markham, Ont.: Viking, 1989.
39. Ithaca: Cornell University Press, 1988.
40. In Kugelmass (n. 9), pp. 128–47.
41. In Zenner (n. 8), pp. 79–95.
42. Montreal: VLB, 1987.

Demography

In general sociology, demography is the study of population characteristics—with typical emphasis on population size as influenced by fertility, mortality, and migration. Among those who do research on Jews, the word has taken on a broader meaning. The community studies commissioned by local federations and the CJF have become known as "demographic" studies because they present a statistical portrait of the Jewish population in a particular region.

The questionnaire used in the Lakeville study in the 1950s (n. 4) has been refined and expanded. The volume *Perspectives in Jewish Population Research*[43] is a valuable source on community surveys. Demographic studies have asked about household composition, synagogue attendance, ritual behaviors, synagogue membership, attitudes toward Israel, financial support for Israel, visits to Israel, Jewish organizational membership, friendships, Jewish education of children, attitudes toward intermarriage, migration, political attitudes, support for the United Jewish Appeal, knowledge of the local federation, anticipated need for social services, and the desire for those needs to be met through Jewish communal organizations.

Demographic surveys appear as technical reports for federation staff and other insiders, with less technical summaries broadly available to members of the Jewish community and other interested parties, and are used as raw data for academic analysis. The study of other issues in North American Jewish life is often conducted with the demographic studies in the background. Particularly in such areas as Jewish identity and intermarriage, the demographic statistics provide the context and often also the major source of data.

Jewish Identity

Demographic studies have included many indicators of the extent to which Jews self-consciously think and behave in distinctive ways. Some of these data were used by Sklare and Greenblum (n. 4) and Cohen (n. 13) as the basis for books on Jewish identity. Harold Himmelfarb, "Research on American Jewish Identity and Identification: Progress, Pitfalls, and Prospects,"[44] pointed out the limitations of this approach, suggesting that the studies of behavior be called studies of "identification," while studies of attitudes, feelings, and their development examine what is closer to the social-psychological usage of "identity." Goldscheider's study (n. 11) used the same database as Cohen (n. 13), but with an emphasis on the data on "social cohesion" rather

---

43. Ed. Steven M. Cohen, Jonathan S. Woocher, and Bruce Phillips (Boulder: Westview, 1984).

44. In *Understanding American Jewry*, ed. Marshall Sklare (New Brunswick, N.J.: Transaction, 1982), pp. 56–95.

than Cohen's focus on "Jewish identification." Goldscheider's contrast of "cohesion" with "identity" has helped to clarify the social and the cultural dimensions of ethnicity, even though most of his colleagues find his conclusions too optimistic. The social dimension of ethnicity consists of those attributes—secular educational level, occupational distribution, residential concentration, friendship networks, consumption styles—which correlate with ethnicity. The cultural dimension of ethnicity consists of those things which self-consciously make up distinctive values and their associated behaviors—religious practices, attitudes toward Israel, attitudes toward intermarriage. Indicators of Jewish "identity" often mix the two dimensions. The two, as Milton Gordon pointed out some years ago in *Assimilation in American Life*,[45] don't have to go together although they often do. Goldscheider's focus on "cohesion" gives primary attention to the social dimension—the extent to which Jews are statistically exceptional and the implications of that exceptionality for the continuation of a distinctive group.

Cohen's 1988 study (n. 14), using 1981 New York community survey data, reviews the options which exists about what data are important for projecting Jewish continuity (pp. 3–8), notes that the data available from community surveys are not far from fully adequate (p. 119), and tentatively concludes that stability rather than revival or decline is the most likely interpretation of the available evidence. Cohen's subsequent national survey (n. 15) asked a range of attitudinal questions not included in the demographic studies, including one on the qualities of a "good Jew" which was used in the Lakeville research.

A second approach to Jewish identity, influenced by the theories and methods of anthropology, has produced a substantial body of ethnographic studies. These studies reflect the broader growth of interpretive social science (see Paul Rabinow and William Sullivan, *Interpretive Social Science*[46] and *Interpretive Social Science: A Second Look*[47]). This approach is concerned with understanding purposeful action rather than establishing causal relationships between variables. The interpretive literature looks on Jewish identity as emergent, situational, and strategic. Zenner (n. 8) contains a good sampling of this literature. Kugelmass (n. 9) contains thoughtful methodological as well as substantive pieces. Goldberg (n. 7) contains Israeli and American studies. Frida Kerner Furman, *Beyond Yiddishkeit: the Struggle for Jewish Identity in a Reform Synagogue*,[48] Riv-Ellen Prell, *Prayer and Community*;[49] David

---

45. New York: Oxford University Press, 1964.
46. Berkeley and Los Angeles: University of California Press, 1979.
47. Berkeley and Los Angeles: University of California Press, 1987.
48. Albany: State University of New York Press, 1987.
49. Detroit: Wayne State University Press, 1989.

Schoem, *Ethnic Survival in America: an Ethnography of a Jewish Afternoon School*;[50] William Shaffir, *Life in a Religious Community*;[51] and Shokeid (n. 39) are also interesting and informative ethnographies of North American Jewish identity. The ethnographic studies by Barbara Meyerhoff, *Number Our Days*,[52] and Samuel Heilman, *Synagogue Life: a Study in Symbolic Interaction*[53] and *The People of the Book: Drama, Fellowship, and Religion*[54] are not overtly about identity but are relevant.

Manning Nash's recent *The Cauldron of Ethnicity in the Modern World*[55] is interesting for the perspective it brings to Jewish identity although it is undoubtedly disturbing to the scholars who have specialized expertise in this area. Nash is writing for a scholarly audience on an important theoretical topic—the variety of ways in which ethnic identity can be understood in contemporary societies. He develops his argument by using ethnicity in Malaysia, Mayan identity in Guatemala, and Jewish identity in the United States as case studies. His knowledge of Malayasia and Guatemala is that of an expert who has done his own fieldwork and has been involved in the development of the literature. His knowledge of American Jews is based on his insider status and knowledge of some of the literature. It is fascinating to watch him use data about Jews as grist for his theoretical mill. Specialized scholars will find his evaluation of issues provocative. Yet it is a little disturbing to think that his one chapter on Jews in the United States will likely be widely read and cited as authoritative when it doesn't direct the reader to some of the important work that has been done.

Social Mobility

Among general sociologists, perhaps the best known source on Jewish mobility in the United States is Stephen Steinberg, *The Ethnic Myth: Race, Ethnicity, and Class in America*.[56] This is a general study of ethnicity and social mobility in the United States written for scholars and students in American ethnic relations rather than for Jewish organizational leaders and students in Jewish studies. Of its ten chapters, four deal in whole or in part with Jews, and the question of why Jews have been more successful than other groups is in the background throughout the book. Steinberg resolutely marshals the evi-

50. Atlanta: Scholars Press. 1989.
51. Toronto: Holt, Rinehart and Winston of Canada, 1974.
52. New York: Dutton, 1978.
53. Chicago: University of Chicago Press, 1976.
54. Chicago: University of Chicago Press, 1983.
55. Chicago: University of Chicago Press, 1989.
56. Boston: Beacon, 1981; 2nd ed. 1989.

dence for social-structural explanations of ethnic mobility in contrast to cultural explanations. Jews were not successful because they carried traditional cultural values such as hard work, respect for learning, and familial support for children's achievements; rather, the situation in which they found themselves in the United States elicited and rewarded these values. Other groups who have achieved less were in different situations which elicited different attitudinal and behavioral responses.

Contrast this with Seymour Martin Lipset's essay on Jewish exceptionalism, "A Unique People in an Exceptional Country,"[57] in a specialized volume which will most likely be read by a narrower, more Jewish audience than Steinberg's. Lipset introduces his essay with reference to a variety of studies that show exceptional Jewish achievement and goes on to cite studies that relate that achievement to Jewish values. There is no citation to Steinberg's position; nor does Steinberg for his part show a thorough command of the literature, especially the studies of the Jewish family, which gives some insight into how values are shaped and become part of a life strategy. There is something distressing about this gap between the discourse on Jews which is part of the general discourse in sociology and the discourse found in the subfield of scholars who write on the contemporary Jewish community. It is obviously a challenge to future academic work.

In Canada the place of Jews in the occupational structure compared to various ethnic groups is studied by Jeffrey Reitz, "Ethnic Concentration in Labour Markets and Their Implications for Ethnic Equality";[58] Evelyn Kallen and M. J. Kellner, "Jewish Entrepreneurs: Factors Effecting Minority Success,"[59] analyze entrepreneurial careers.

Family Life

The literature on the Jewish family has various types of authors and audiences. Much of it appears in *The Journal of Jewish Communal Service*, which has a primary audience of the thousands of social workers employed by Jewish agencies across North America. A social-work orientation is also pronounced in the bibliographies and literature reviews of Gerald Bubis, *Saving the Jewish Family: Myths and Realities in the Diaspora, Strategies for the Future*,[60] and Benjamin Schlesinger, *Jewish Family Issues: A Resource*

57. In Lipset (n. 23), pp. 3–29.
58. In Breton et al. (n. 27), pp. 135–95.
59. In *The Changing Jewish Community*, ed. Stuart Schoenfeld (Toronto: York University Institute for Behavioral Research, 1983), pp. 138–53.
60. Lanham, Md.: University Press of America, 1987.

Guide;[61] Norman Linzer, *The Jewish Family: Authority and Tradition in Modern Perspective*,[62] presents the perspective of an Orthodox social worker. The series on the Jewish family published by the American Jewish Committee gives priority to the question of continuity. Among these are the ongoing studies on intermarriage, which is treated separately below. The readers *The Jewish Family: Metaphor and Memory*[63] and *The Jewish Family: Myths and Realities*[64] reflect a primarily academic agenda; much of the material in these readers is not about North America, but it is nevertheless relevant.

For studies of Jewish family life which place the issues of continuity and ambivalence in different contexts see Zena Smith Blau's pre-feminist essay "The Strategy of the Jewish Mother"[65] on the mother as a partner in her children's later success; the findings of Richard L. Zweigenhaft and G. William Domhoff, *Jews in the Protestant Establishment*,[66] on the family relationships of Jews at the very highest corporate and social levels of American society; Thomas J. Cottle, *Divorce and the Jewish Child*,[67] on the effects of divorce; Monson (n. 18) on attitudes toward marriage and family of Jewish university students; Paula Hyman's feminist analysis of the Jewish discourse about the family, "The Modern Jewish Family";[68] Jay Brodbar-Nemzer, "Marital Relations and Self-Esteem: How Jewish Families Are Different,"[69] on the Jewish valuing of family stability and nurturance; and Myrna Silverman's study of the relationship between opportunity structure, kinship networks, and economic success over three generations, "Family, Kinship, and Ethnicity: Strategies for Upward Mobility."[70]

Intermarriage

The series of studies by Egon Mayer and associates have carefully documented many dimensions of this topic. *Love and Tradition*[71] brings many smaller studies together, but more recent ones—which the American Jewish Committee publishes on a regular basis—continue to monitor what has

61. New York: Garland, 1987.

62. New York: Human Sciences Press, 1984.

63. Ed. David Kraemer (New York: Oxford University Press, 1989).

64. Ed. Steven M. Cohen and Paula E. Hyman (New York: Holmes and Meier, 1986).

65. In *The Jew in American Society*, ed. Marshall Sklare (New York: Berman, 1974), pp. 165–87.

66. New York: Praeger, 1982.

67. New York: American Jewish Committee, 1981.

68. In Kraemer (n. 63), pp. 179–93.

69. *Journal of Marriage and the Family* 48 (1986): 89–98.

70. In Zenner (n. 8), pp. 165–82.

71. Ed. Egon Mayer (New York: Schocken, 1987).

become a major preoccupation of the organized Jewish community. There is also literature addressed directly to those living in intermarriages or thinking about it. Paul Cowan and Rachel Cowan, *Mixed Blessings: Marriage between Christians and Jews*,[72] respects the autonomy of the individuals about whom and for whom the book is written. The Reform movement, whose synagogues are in touch with many mixed as well as conversionary marriages, produces much material about working with these families. An older, anecdotal and judgmental literature on intermarriage worries about intermarriage as a Jewish and personal problem. A newer, anecdotal and judgmental literature celebrates intermarriage. On Canada see Stuart Schoenfeld, *An Invitation to a Discussion: Assimilation, Intermarriage, and Jewish Identity in Ontario.*[73]

The Changing Status of Women

The assertion of a feminist challenge to received gender definitions and expectations has been building for the past few hundred years in all aspects of Western society. Jewish feminists have articulated this challenge within the North American Jewish community. They have understandably been especially interested in an intellectual agenda which allows Jewish women to understand and redefine their place in the community. For some, feminism has been part of the movement out of a self-conscious commitment to Jewish values and Jewish social networks. For others, it is a resource for invigorating a backward but beloved community and culture. For others, the encounter between feminism and Judaism is the setting for the self-conscious expression of the ambivalence which is latent in all of North American Jewish life. The social consequences of feminism for the structure and experience of Jewish life are only now beginning to be explored; see Sylvia Barak Fishman, "Impact of Feminism on American Jewish Life."[74] See also *Lillith* magazine.

Community Organization

Jews in the Diaspora have a tradition of membership in a corporate body which defends their interests vis a vis the larger society, provides for their own institutions, and finances itself through taxation and contributions. In North America, Jewish organizational affiliation is voluntary, raising the issues of membership recruitment and retention, interorganizational rivalry and cooperation, the extent to which organizations represent or should represent the

72. New York: Doubleday, 1987.
73. Toronto: Canadian Jewish Congress, Ontario Region, 1987.
74. *American Jewish Year Book* 89 (1989): 3–62.

views of unaffiliated Jews as well as the affiliated, dissent from "official" organizational positions, and the continuing need to engage in fund-raising. Daniel Elazar's thorough study *Community and Polity*[75] is now in the process of revision and may be out by the time this chapter is in print. Meanwhile, the chapters in Lipset (n. 23) by Elazar, "Developments in Jewish Community Organization in the Second Postwar Generation";[76] Lawrence Rubin, "The Emerging Jewish Public-Affairs Culture";[77] and Arnold Dashevsky, "Sources of Jewish Charitable Giving: Incentives and Barriers,"[78] are readable, up to date, and informative, and present much to stimulate class discussion. On Canada, Elazar and Waller (n. 26) is indispensable. J. Alan Winter, "Keeping the Costs of Living Jewishly Affordable,"[79] is one of several studies of the cost of affiliation.

Organizations, as mentioned above, are major sponsors of research. The selection by David Rosenham, "Jewish Identity and Policy Research,"[80] with the response by Roy Feldman[81] and comments on the role of policy research by Marshall Sklare, "Reflections on the Establishment of the Wilstein Institute,"[82] give some idea of the relationship of Jewish organizations to the research agenda on North American Jewish life.

Religious Life

Studies of religious life are usually concerned, one way or another, with ambivalence about value and lifestyle choices. Despite the widespread scholarly adherence to the secularization thesis, religion remains a lively topic in public affairs and private life. Much the same situation applies to Jews as to the rest of humanity. Statistical evidence confirms everyone's personal impression—that there has been a marked decline in ritual observance over the past hundred years. Yet Jews are more likely to understand their identity in terms of religious affiliation than in any other way; synagogue attendance (usually infrequent) and home observance provide the routines around which Jewish identity is acted out; and the single best indicator of other indicators of Jewish identity is denominational affiliation. The community surveys nor-

75. Philadelphia: Jewish Publication Society, 1976.
76. In Lipset (n. 23), pp. 173–92.
77. In Lipset (n. 23), pp. 193–201.
78. In Lipset (n. 23), pp. 203–25.
79. In *Jewish Identity in America*, ed. David M. Gordis and Yoav Ben-Horin (Los Angeles: Wilstein Institute, 1990), pp. 253–66.
80. In Gordis and Ben-Horin (n. 79), pp. 279–81.
81. In Gordis and Ben-Horin (n. 79), pp. 283–86.
82. In Gordis and Ben-Horin (n. 79), pp. 287–94.

mally include questions about denominational preference and affiliation, and about ritual observance. For a survey of recent trends, developments, and unresolved debates, see Jack Wertheimer, "Recent Trends in American Judaism."[83]

There are also now a number of ethnographic studies which examine Jewish religious participation: Heilman's studies of a modern Orthodox congregation (n. 53) and of Talmud study groups (n. 54); Helmreich's portrait of the yeshiva world (n. 37); Prell's exploration of a havura (n. 49); Shifra Epstein's analysis of a Hasidic Purim play, "Drama on the Table: the Bobover Hasidim Piremshpiyl";[84] Markowitz's study of the use of ritual by immigrants from the U.S.S.R. (n. 40); Shaffir's ethnography of Lubavitch Hasidim (n. 51); and the studies of bar and bat mitzvah by Judith Davis, "Mazel Tov: The Bar Mitzvah as a Multigenerational Ritual of Change and Continuity,"[85] and Stuart Schoenfeld, "Folk Religion, Elite Religion, and the Role of Bar Mitzvah in the Development of the Synagogue and Jewish School in America,"[86] "Integration into the Group and Sacred Uniqueness: An Analysis of Adult Bat Mitzvah,"[87] "Some Aspects of the Social Significance of Bar and Bat Mitzvah Celebrations,"[88] and "Ritual and Role Transition: Adult Bat Mitzvah as a Successful Rite of Passage."[89] The ethnographic studies typically probe the personal relevance of religious participation—how it fits, or does not fit, into other aspects of identity; its rewards and its costs. Samuel Heilman's memoir, *The Gate behind the Wall*,[90] is, like Fein's book (n. 21), an informed study of his religious ambivalence.

Education

There is a flourishing industry in the general sociology of education, but very little in the sociology of Jewish education. The literature that does exist fits, not surprisingly, into the broad theme of North American Jewish ambivalence. One of David Schoem's articles on his ethnography of a congregational after-

83. *American Jewish Year Book* 89 (1989): 63–162.

84. In Goldberg (n. 7), pp. 195–217.

85. In *Rituals in Families and Family Therapies*, ed. E. Imber-Black, J. Roberts, and R. A. Whiting (New York: Norton, 1990), pp. 177–208.

86. *Contemporary Judaism* 9/1 (1987): 67–85.

87. In Zenner (n. 8), pp. 117–35.

88. In *Essays in the Social Scientific Study of Judaism and Jewish Life*, ed. Jack Lightstone and Simcha Fishbane (Montreal: Concordia University, Department of Religion, 1990), pp. 277–304.

89. In *The Uses of Tradition: Jewish Continuity in the Modern Era*, ed. Jack Wertheimer (Cambridge: Harvard University Press, 1992), pp 349–76.

90. New York: Summit Books, 1984.

noon school is entitled "Learning to Be a Part-Time Jew,"[91] indicating that one of the ways of responding to ambivalence is compartmentalization. This piece, like his book (n. 50), indicates that the strategy of compartmentalization is neither well thought out nor effectively delivered. The ambivalence of American Jews about the significance of their Jewish identity is also found in Alvin Schiff's analysis of the problems of the supplementary schools in Greater New York, *Jewish Supplementary Schooling: An Educational System in Need of Change*,[92] which relates his findings to the literature on "effective" schools. The very first criterion cited for an effective school is "a clear focus and institutional mission and a clearly defined curriculum" (p. 41), which Schiff concludes that the supplementary schools studied do not have (p. 118).

Day schools are growing in all the branches of Judaism, even as supplementary school enrollment declines. In Canada, day school enrollment has passed that of supplementary schools. While there are statistical data and institutional studies of day schools, the ways in which days schools handle— through their curriculum, staffing, teaching practices, and ambiance—the ambivalence of North American Jewish life remains to be studied; see, for example, Charles Grysman, "The Orthodox Day School and Its Non-observant Population."[93] Bernard Cooperman's comments on the institutionalization of university-level courses in Jewish Studies, "Jewish Studies in the University,"[94] notes that they have been inserted into a central arena of North American Jewish ambivalence, and the implications of that context have not yet been worked out. The Commission on Jewish Education in North America, *A Time to Act*,[95] sponsored a series of research studies. They are inevitably partial and do not consider some relevant topics, but they lay the ground for additional, more probing research into supplementary schools, day schools, yeshivas, university Jewish Studies programs, and adult Jewish education. Research sponsored by the Commission's successor, the Council for Initiatives in Jewish Education, is now under way.

Antisemitism and the Holocaust

The largest wave of Jewish migration to North America was a response to both deeping poverty and a revived wave of antisemitic violence in Eastern Europe. The Jews who came in this wave, as did the other Jewish immigrants

91. In Zenner (n. 8), pp. 96–116.
92. New York: Board of Jewish Education of Greater New York, 1988.
93. *Jewish Education* 57/2–4 (1989): 32–38.
94. In Gordis and Ben-Horin (n. 79), pp. 195–206.
95. Lanham, Md.: University Press of America, 1990.

to North America, carried with them centuries of memories of persecution. When they found that the American and Canadian reception of large numbers of Jewish immigrants was itself ambivalent, the drive to ensure that the United States and Canada make good on the liberal promise of legal equality and ideological tolerance became a major part of their collective agenda. The racism they encountered and the campaigns to outlaw discrimination, repeal restrictive immigration legislation, and foster a climate of opinion in which Jews were recognized as fully legitimate members of society are remembered as a collective saga of ultimately succesful integration. These topics have been the concern not of sociologists, but primarily of historians, whose extensive writings on these topics have been part of the process of constructing this collective memory. Antisemitism has not disappeared; Jewish organizations continue to act against the lingering elements of old-fashioned racism and the newer antisemitism which vilifies Israel and Zionism. Some who write about contemporary Jewish life (Fein [n. 21], Silberman [n. 10]) remark about the preoccupation with antisemitism in public Jewish discourse.

This preoccupation is, of course, a legacy of the mass murder of European Jewry. The Holocaust is one of the basic points of reference of modern Western historical consciousness. The literature—both scholarly and popular—is voluminous; fiction, memoirs, and magazine articles continue to be published; movies and television shows continue to be made about it; and its images have been appropriated into the symbolism of contemporary iconography. As an aspect of the debate over Jewish continuity and ambivalence, historians, theologians, philosophers, novelists, and poets have probed its significance more than sociologists or anthropologists. Linking the Holocaust to the establishment of the State of Israel as a modern version of the myth of death and rebirth has been noted, for example, by Jacob Neusner, *The Death and Birth of Judaism: The Impact of Christianity, Secularism, and the Holocaust on Jewish Faith*[96]; the moral imperatives placed on the Jews who have survived have been investigated by Elie Wiesel, Emil Fackenheim, Irving Greenberg, and others; the circumstances behind the selection of the Jews for victimization has been a concern of Jewish and non-Jewish intellectuals. Beside these fundamental issues, there are obvious consequences of immense significance for the ways in which North American Jews see themselves in the world—the destruction of the world's largest geographical concentration of Jews, a modernizing Yiddish culture, and the major source of Jewish immigration to North America.

There are a number of studies that highlight the importance of antisemitism

96. New York: Basic Books, 1987.

as a motivation to Jewish organizational affiliation and participation: for the United States, see Leonard Dinnerstein, *Uneasy at Home: Antisemitism and the American Jewish Experience*;[97] for Canada, Irving Abella and Harold Troper, *None Is Too Many: Canada and the Jews of Europe 1933–1948*;[98] Troper and Weinfeld (n. 38); Cyril Levitt and William Shaffir, *The Riot at Christie Pits*;[99] and Yaacov Glickman, "Anti-Semitism and Jewish Social Cohesion in Canada."[100] There have been studies of the personal characteristics of survivors of the Holocaust who immigrated to North America, but their impact on the Jewish community as a whole, while acknowledged, has not been systematically studied. Their impact is likely to be more profound in Canada, where they constitute a larger proportion of the Jewish population than in the United States. The impact of the cultural image of the Jew as victim has undoubtedly had major consequences for Jewish self-awareness, but this topic has been explored more by cultural critics (e.g., Sander Gilman, *Jewish Self-Hatred: Anti-Semitism and the Hidden Language of the Jews*[101]) than by sociologists or anthropologists.

Intellectual Life

Intellectuals, like feminists, are a group where the ambivalence about Jewish identity which is latent in North American Jewish life is self-consciously expressed and acted on. Many of the extraordinary group of Jewish intellectuals who had an immense impact on North American culture, particularly through their contributions in the humanities and social sciences, are now aging or deceased. Their world views were formed during the period of Nazi antisemitism and the mass murder of European Jewry, and many were personally affected. As members of the North American intellectual elite, they were role models or direct mentors of many other Jewish intellectuals. The stances they took toward Jewish community and culture varied. For many, childhood in a Jewish community and the experience of antisemitism made them part of the Jewish community, even if their public ideologies were cosmopolitan. They did not deny that they were part of a shared community of fate, and they participated to some extent in the institutions of the Jewish community; however, in their writing many showed no particular commitment to Jewish continuity. Some, like Erich Fromm, while socially marginal to the Jewish

97. New York: Columbia University Press, 1987.
98. Toronto: Lester and Orpen Dennys, 1986.
99. Toronto: Lester and Orpen Dennys, 1987.
100. In *Ethnicity and Ethnic Relations in Canada,* ed. Rita M. Bienvenue and Jay E. Goldstein, 2nd ed. (Toronto: Butterworth's, 1985), pp. 263–84.
101. Baltimore: Johns Hopkins University Press, 1986.

community, were able to write books like *You Shall Be as Gods*,[102] in which the traditional Jewish perspective is treated with respect and affection. Others, like Walter Kaufmann, "The Future of Jewish Identity" and "The Future of the Jews in the Diaspora,"[103] were able to identify a secular Jewish tradition worthy of conservation and development in the future. Leslie Fiedler's recent essay *Fiedler on the Roof: Essays on Jewish Identity*[104] is the personal statement of a Jewish intellectual who is intermarried and has intermarried children, which acknowledges the impact of antisemitism on his life but fails to find that reason enough (contra Fackenheim) to insist on the preservation of the Jews as a distinct group in the contemporary world. Although there are numerous articles and books on the Jewish identity of intellectuals, the impact of Jewish intellectuals on Jewish life in North America has not yet been studied. For biographies and some discussion of the identity of Jewish intellectuals as a distinct group, see Alexander Bloom, *Prodigal Sons: The New York Intellectuals and Their World*;[105] Bernard Rosenberg and Ernest Goldstein, *Creators and Disturbers: Reminiscences by Jewish Intellectuals of New York*;[106] and Lewis A. Coser, *Refugee Scholars in America: Their Impact and Their Experiences*.[107] On the Jewish identity of university professors, see Albert G. Crawford and Rela Geffen Monson, *Academy and Community: A Study of the Jewish Identity and Involvement of Professors*.[108]

A Note on Identifying Ambivalance as a Parallel Theme to Continuity

It is not possible to review in an essay of this length all the work on contemporary Jewish life in North America. Nor in the scope of this essay is it possible to work out a full account of Jewish ambivalence. Some of the poles of ambivalence which would need to be explored are tradition versus innovation, individual autonomy versus group obligations, particularism versus universalism, status in the Jewish community versus status in the broader society, and Jewish culture versus mass culture. Various strategies for living with ambiva-

102. New York: Holt, Rinehart and Winston, 1966.
103. In *Existentialism, Religion, and Death* (New York. New American Library, 1976), pp. 164–89.
104. New York: Oxford University Press, 1991.
105. New York: Oxford University Press, 1986.
106. New York: Columbia University Press, 1982.
107. New Haven: Yale University Press, 1984.
108. New York: American Jewish Committee, 1982.

lence would also require some systematic discussion. Studies such as Elliot Orring, "Rechnitzer Rejects: a Humor of Modern Orthodoxy"[109] suggest future areas of research. As well there are methodological and policy implications. The focus on "continuity/assimilation" frames the discussion of Jewish life in North America in a predictive model, which ultimately may not be the most useful for either social analysis or policy planning. The focus on "ambivalence" frames the discussion in a voluntaristic model, directing attention toward understanding values and lifestyle dilemmas and the processes of making decisions in these areas.

A Three-Session Unit on American and Canadian Jews

In the context of a substantial, interesting body of literature, the choice of readings for a three-session unit means leaving out some favorite studies. In order to convey something of the richness of the field, two readers—Gordis and Ben Horin (n. 79) and Zenner (n. 8)—are chosen as required reading, along with the recent National Jewish Population Study (n. 6) and the report of the Commission on Jewish Education (n. 95). Lipset (n. 23) also has a number of excellent articles, and some instructors may want to use it as required reading. There was more freedom in compiling the recommended reading list, but even here, self-restraint was reluctantly exercised. The unit is organized around the issues of Jewish continuity and ambivalence. It is suggested that the instructor stress at the beginning that continuity has two dimensions— first, Will there continue to be an identifiable group of Jews in North America? and second, What will this identity mean to them? The second question leads naturally into the topic of ambivalence.

1. Social-historical and Statistical Profile

The first session gives the student numbers. The issue for class discussion is, What questions about Jewish continuity come out of these numbers and what kinds of evidence are useful for exploring them? Basic texts: Kosmin et al. (n. 6) and Cohen (n. 14), chs. 1 and 8—ch. 1 contains a useful section on alternative criteria used to measure the likelihood of continuity, and ch. 8, a summary evaluation of the evidence. Recommended: Goldscheider (n. 11), and the balance of Cohen (n. 14). Canada: Brodbar-Nemzer (n. 30).

---

109. In Kugelmass (n. 9), pp. 148–61.

2. Jewish Identity

The second session is designed to make the methodological point that there is a variety of ways to gather and interpret the data on Jewish identity. (a) Quantitative research. Required: Bruce A. Phillips, "Sociological Analysis of Jewish Identity."[110] Recommended: Cohen (n. 15) and Winter (n. 79). Canada: Wsevolod Isajiw, "Ethnic Identity Retention."[111] (b). Qualitative research. Required: Walter Zenner and Belcove-Shalin, "The Cultural Anthropology of American Jewry";[112] Markowitz (n. 41); Schoem (n. 91); Schoenfeld (n. 87); Hannah Kliger, "A Home Away from Home: Participation in Jewish Immigrant Associations in America";[113] and Silverman (n. 70). Recommended: remaining articles in Zenner (n. 8), Furman (n. 48), Heilman (n. 53), Helmreich (n. 37), Shokeid (n. 39). (c) Other recommended reading: Henry Feingold, "The American Component of American Jewish Identity";[114] Jonathan Sarna, "Jewish Identity in the Changing World of American Religion";[115] Stuart E. Eisenstadt, "American Jews and Israel in the Bush Era";[116] Arnold J. Band, "Popular Fiction and the Shaping of Jewish Identity";[117] Alan J. Berger, "Job's Children: Post-Holocaust Jewish Identity in Second Generation Literature";[118] Bernard D. Cooperman (n. 94); and the "Panel Discussion: The Role of the Synagogue in Jewish Identity," with contributions by Harold Shulweiss,[119] Richard N. Levy,[120] and Daniel Landes;[121] Arnold Eisen, "The Rhetoric of Choseness and the Fabrication of American Jewish Identity";[122] Weinfeld (n. 23); Edward Shapiro, "The Jewishness of New York Intellectuals: Sydney Hook, a Case Study";[123] Fishman (n. 74); Wertheimer (n. 83); Woocher (n. 12); and Cowan and Cowan (n. 72). Personal statements: Heilman (n. 90) and Fein (n. 21) as documents of ambivalence/biculturalism; Paul Cowan, *An Orphan in History*;[124] and Annie Roiphe, *Generation without*

110. In Gordis and Ben-Horin (n. 79), pp. 3–26.
111. In Breton, Isajiw, Kalbach, and Reitz (n. 27), pp. 34–91.
112. In Zenner (n. 8), pp. 3–41.
113. In Zenner (n. 8), pp. 143–64.
114. In Gordis and Ben-Horin (n. 79), pp. 69–80.
115. In Gordis and Ben-Horin (n. 79), pp. 91–103.
116. In Gordis and Ben-Horin (n. 79), pp. 139–55.
117. In Gordis and Ben-Horin (n. 79), pp. 215–26.
118. In Gordis and Ben-Horin (n. 79), pp. 227 49.
119. In Gordis and Ben-Horin (n. 79), pp. 159–65.
120. In Gordis and Ben-Horin (n. 79), pp. 167–72.
121. In Gordis and Ben-Horin (n. 79), pp. 173–80.
122. In Lipset (n. 23), pp. 53–70.
123. In Lipset (n. 23), pp. 153–71.
124. Garden City, N.Y.: Doubleday, 1982.

Memory: A Jewish Journey in Christian America.[125] On intellectuals: Fromm (n. 102), Kaufmann (n. 103), and Fiedler (n. 104).

3. Organizational Structures and Strategies of Continuity

The third session is designed to indicate to students that the issues of continuity and ambivalence are not just ones that millions of Jews address as individuals, but ones that are also addressed by the words and deeds of Jewish organizations. Required: Cooperman (n. 94), Rosenham (n. 80), Feldman, (n. 81), Sklare, (n. 82), and Commission on Jewish Education in North America (n. 95). Recommended: on communal organizations: Elazar (n. 76) and Dashevsky (n. 78). On the synagogue: Wertheimer (n. 83) and Goldscheider (n. 20).

4. Recommended Overviews

Shorter readings: Nathan Glazer, "American Jewry or American Judaism,"[126] perceptively sketches the ambivalence of North American Jews, although without actually using the word. See also Rela Geffen Monson, "The Sociology of the American Jewish Community";[127] Glazer (n. 17); Cohen and Liebman (n. 19); and Lipset (n. 57). Books: Silberman (n. 10), Goldscheider (n. 11) and Fein (n. 21). On Canada: Abella (n. 25) and Elazar and Waller (n. 26).

125. New York: Simon and Schuster, 1981.
126. In Lipset (n. 23), pp. 31–41.
127. *Modern Judaism* 11/1 (1990): 147–56.

Part II

TEACHING RESOURCES

An Annotated Guide to Major Reference Works

Jack Wertheimer

Annotated Bibliographies

1. Yonah Alexander, Miriam Alexander, and Mordecai S. Chertoff, *A Bibliography of Israel* (New York: Herzl, 1981).
   Listings are organized according to subject: History, Geography, Archaeology, Biography, Religion and Philosophies, Literature, Nationalism, Israel and the Arab Middle East, Contemporary Israel, Israel among the Nations, and Israel and World Jewry. This work includes a comprehensive annotated list of books and articles important for the study of both contemporary Israel and the span of Jewish history which preceded the establishment of the State of Israel. Includes author and title indexes.
2. William W. Brickman, *The Jewish Community in America: An Annotated and Classified Bibliographical Guide* (New York: Burt Franklin, 1977).
   This is a guide to scholarly works written in several languages. The focus is on the American Jewish experience from colonial times to the present, especially the adjustment of different immigrating groups to the American way of life. Listings are organized according to broad subjects, including: General Histories, Regional and Local History, Biographies, Religious Life, etc. Includes appendixes and index.
3. David M. Bunis, *Sephardic Studies: A Research Bibliography* (New York: Garland, 1981).
   This work contains multilingual listings which are organized according to subject: General Works, Judezmo Language, Judezmo Literature, Judezmo Folklore and Folklife, and Historical Background. The entries

on Sephardic history are classified under Pre-Expulsion and Post-Expulsion Periods, and they are categorized by subject within those classifications. Includes an index of institutions and organizations concerned with Sephardic studies. As one of the few comprehensive bibliographies devoted to the study of Sephardic Jewry, this work is an essential resource. It may also prove useful to students of general linguistics and literature. Includes indexes of authors and subjects.

4. Susan S. Cohen, *Antisemitism: An Annotated Bibliography* (New York: Garland, 1987).

    For the Modern period (1789–1985), listings are organized according to geographic locations. Particularly noteworthy are the extensive listings for the period from 1945 to 1985, as well as a section on Antisemitism in Literature and the Arts. Includes subject and author indexes.

5. Charles Cutter and Micha Falk Oppenheim, *Jewish Reference Sources: A Selective, Annotated Bibliographic Guide* (New York: Garland, 1982).

    Listings are organized as General Reference or Subject Reference materials. Pertinent subject areas include: Anti-Semitism, History, Literature, Socialism, Folklore, etc. This work is comprehensive and wide-ranging, and it includes references to many different resource media. Includes author and title indexes.

6. Abraham Edelheit and Hershel Edelheit, *The Jewish World in Modern Times: A Selected, Annotated Bibliography* (Boulder, Colo.: Westview, 1988).

    Listings are organized according to subject, such as: General History, Religious Trends, Antisemitism, The Holocaust, Zionism, etc. Additional listings are organized according to geographic regions, such as: Central Europe, Eastern Europe, U.S.S.R., Americas, etc. The focus of this work is world Jewry in general, as well as specific Jewish communities. The book includes a brief outline of modern Jewish history, a glossary, indexes, and cross references.

7. Ruth Frank and William Wollheim, *The Book of Jewish Books: A Reader's Guide to Judaism* (San Francisco: Harper and Row, 1986).

    Listings are annotated and organized according to subject: Bible, Children's Books, History, Holocaust, Israel and Zionism, Jewish Living, Jewish Thought, Literature and the Arts, Periodicals, Prayer Books, References, and Women. This work is especially useful for the general reader or the beginner. Includes glossary and index of names and titles.

8. Isaac Goldberg, *Bibliography of Modern Hebrew Literature in Translation* (Ramat-Gan: Institute for the Translation of Hebrew Literature, 1979–).

Published annually, these volumes arrange listings by language, and within each language, by genre. English-language entries include: Book Reviews, Criticism, Drama, Essays, Novels, Humor and Satire, Juvenilia, Poetry, Short Stories, Interviews, and Novellas. Includes Hebrew titles. The primary focus of this work is on nonscholarly literary works. Includes indexes of authors, translators, book reviewers, and subjects.

9. David B. Griffiths, *A Critical Bibliography of Writings on Judaism*, part 2 (Lewiston, N.Y.: Edwin Mellen, 1988).

    Listings are organized according to subject: The Holocaust, Zionism, and Modernity and Modern Thought. This is an excellent comprehensive resource for scholars. The section devoted to works on Zionism is especially complete and useful.

10. Jeffrey Gurock, *American Jewish History: A Bibliographical Guide* (New York: Anti-Defamation League, 1983).

    The most sophisticated and comprehensive annotated bibliography of work on American Jewry, this volume is primarily organized by historical eras: Colonial and Early National Period (1654– ca. 1840), The Era of German Migration (ca.1840–1880), The Era of East European Migration (ca.1880–1924), and From the Close of East European Immigration to the Present. Within each section there are subdivisions according to topics pertinent to the particular historical era. There is a very useful section entitled Special Topics, which provides reference to works on a wide range of subjects, including: American Zionism, American Jews and Liberalism, American Jewry and the Holocaust, etc. Included are extensive notes and bibliography, and author and title indexes.

11. Julius Guttmann, *Philosophies of Judaism* (New York: Holt, Rinehart and Winston, 1964).

    Appended to this study is an extensive multilingual bibliography of works related to the study of Jewish philosophy. Listings are organized according to subject: Fundamentals and First Influences, Jewish Religious Philosophy in the Middle Ages, and Jewish Philosophy of Religion in the Modern Era. The latter is particularly useful because there is such a paucity of bibliographic listings on Jewish thought in the modern era. This is the standard resource for students of Jewish philosophy.

12. Ora Hamelsdorf and Sandra Adelsberg, *Jewish Women and Jewish Law: A Bibliography* (Fresh Meadows, N.Y.: Biblio, 1980).

    Entries in this bibliography attempt to address important aspects of the contemporary discussion of the Jewish woman's role and status within the family, in Jewish courts, and in the synagogue, as well as women's religious identity and obligatory rituals. Also addressed is the Jewish woman's legal status as daughter, mother, wife, and divorcee. Literature from all American Jewish movements is included. This is a somewhat terse, nevertheless helpful, resource for the study of the legal status of the contemporary Jewish woman.

13. Hebrew Union College – Jewish Institute of Religion Library, *Dictionary Catalog of the Klau Library, Cincinnati*, 32 vols. (Boston: G.K. Hall, 1964).

    The Klau Library of Hebrew Union College houses one of the largest collections of Hebraica and Judaica in the world. This catalogue is useful even to readers without immediate access to the Klau library in that it apprises one of the scope and breadth of literature in a given area.

14. *The Schocken Guide to Jewish Books: Where to Start Reading about Jewish History, Literature, Culture, and Religion*, ed. Barry W. Holtz (New York: Schocken, 1992).

    Though not limited to the modern Jewish experience, this volume provides many excellent introductions to the state of fields in modern Jewish studies: pertinent essays cover European and American Jewry, Hebrew, Yiddish and American Jewish Literature, The Holocaust, Israel, and Jewish Women's Studies.Essays also offer suggestions for further reading,

15. Gershon Hundert and Gershon Bacon, *The Jews in Poland and Russia: Bibliographical Essays* (Bloomington: Indiana University Press, 1984).

    For students of the modern era, the book's second section is pertinent as it covers East European Jewry from the First Partition of Poland to the present. Subdivisions within each major heading are defined by both historical periods and pertinent contemporary themes, such as Anti-Semitism and The Holocaust. The title of the work is somewhat misleading, as the scope is broad — generally addressing the Jewish experience in the unfolding of East European history.

16. *The Jewish Experience in America: A Historical Bibliography* (Santa Barbara, Calif.: ABC–Clio, 1983).

    Listings are arranged alphabetically by author. This work primarily contains references to material of scholarly interest published in scholarly journals between 1973 and 1979. Included are over 800 annotated entries which refer to articles written in 42 languages. Includes a subject index.

17. Jonathan Kaplan, *2000 Books and More: An Annotated and Selected Bibliography of Jewish History and Thought* (Jerusalem: Magnes, 1983).

    This is a collection of multilingual listings organized according to broad subject headings, including historical eras and phenomena. This work is especially suited to the study of Jewish nationalism and Zionism. Many entries are in Hebrew.

18. Sylvia Orenstein, *Source Book on Soviet Jewry: An Annotated Bibliography* (American Jewish Committee, 1981).
    Listings are for articles and books written between 1974 and 1980 which address all aspects of Russian Jewish life, history, and culture. Included is a brief list of books on general Russian history, as well as the overarching problems of religion and nationality in the Soviet Union. There is also material which addresses human rights struggles in the Soviet Union, including Jewish activism. This is a good resource, though it does not address the important developments in the Soviet Union since 1980. Includes index.
19. Jacob Robinson and Philip Friedman, *Yad Washem*, 14 vols., some in Hebrew (New York: YIVO Institute for Jewish Research, 1960–77).
    This collection contains multilingual listings which are categorized according to broad subjects, such as: The Jewish Catastrophe in Historical Perspective, Reference Tools, and Research. This work is especially concerned with the fate of Jews under the impact of Nazism. Includes index.
20. Inger M. Ruud, *Women and Judaism: A Select Annotated Bibliography* (New York: Garland, 1988).
    There are entries for a broad range of topics, ranging from religion to family, education to politics in various historical periods. Listings are multilingual and are arranged alphabetically by author. The majority of the entries are concerned with the status of women in the United States and Israel. Includes indexes of countries, subjects, and authors.
21. Martin H. Sable, *Holocaust Studies: A Directory and Bibliography of Bibliographies* (Greenwood, Fla.: Penkevill, 1987).
    Listings refer to bibliographies that address some aspect of the Holocaust. Most of the bibliographies treat the Holocaust as a whole, but there are some with more specific foci, such as the Warsaw Ghetto Uprising of 1943, or one of many specific concentration camps. Listings are primarily organized according to language. The work also includes directories of Holocaust studies associations, survivors' organizations, Holocaust museums and memorials, and subject and author indexes. This is an indispensable work for any student of the Holocaust.
22. Benjamin Schlesinger, *Jewish Family Issues: A Resource Guide* (New York: Garland, 1987).
    This work consists of two main parts: (1) a bibliographical discussion of three major aspects of Jewish family life (The Jewish Family in Retrospect, Jewish One-Parent Families, The Jewish Woman); (2) an annotated bibliography, 1960–86, with over 500 entries. The bibliography com-

prises many subjects, including: Adoption, Divorce, Intermarriage, Poverty, Sexuality, etc. This work is timely and up to date, and it represents one of the few bibliographies addressing Jewish family issues. The scope of the entries is international. Includes index.

23. John Sherman, *The Arab–Israeli Conflict, 1945–1971* (New York: Garland, 1978).

Listings are organized according to specific years from 1945 to 1971. Special attention is given to the impact of the United States and the Soviet Union in the conflict. Because of its publication date, it does not address the many important developments in the Arab–Israeli Conflict since the onset of the Intifada. Includes author and subject indexes.

24. Michael Shermis, *Jewish–Christian Relations: An Annotated Bibliography and Resource Guide* (Bloomington: Indiana University Press, 1988).

This work is intended to serve as both a scholarly and a practical resource guide for the study of Jewish–Christian relations, especially as they have developed during the past twenty-five years. Listings are organized according to subject, including: the Holocaust, Israel, Vatican Council II, Intermarriage, Mission, etc. Includes descriptions of journals and organizations devoted to the promotion and/or study of Jewish–Christian relations. Also included are sample class syllabi for university-level course work. Includes index. This is an excellent resource.

25. Shlomo Shunami, *Bibliography of Jewish Bibliographies*, 2nd ed. (Jerusalem: Hebrew University, 1970); *Supplement to 2nd ed.* (1975).

Listings are multilingual (and especially highlight Hebrew works) and are categorized according to broad subjects, including: General Bibliographies, Literature, Religion, Sects, Zionism, History, etc. Includes indexes. This is an exhaustive and comprehensive work and is considered to be the standard bibliography of Judaica. It is an essential resource for the student of the modern Jewish experience. It is most suited to researchers who know the specific topic or subject area they wish to examine.

26. Robert Singerman, *Antisemitic Propaganda: An Annotated Bibliography and Research Guide* (New York: Garland, 1982).

Bibliography listings are organized according to year, covering the period 1871–1981. The Research Guide is organized according to subject, such as: General Survey, Christianity and Antisemitism, etc. The unifying motif of this work is the alleged international conspiracy of Jews to gain control of world governance. Includes listings organized according to country. This is an unusual and useful work. Includes index.

27. Esther M. Snyder, *World Bibliographical Series,* Vol. 58: *Israel* (Santa Barbara, Calif.: Clio, 1985).

Listings are organized according to subject, including: History, Arab–Israeli Conflict, Religion, Education, Politics, etc. Includes lists of guides to libraries, museums, mass media, periodicals, etc. This work is especially useful as a general introduction to the study of Israel.

28. Sheila Spector, *Jewish Mysticism: An Annotated Bibliography on the Kabbalah in English* (New York: Garland, 1984).

    Listings are annotated and are organized by subject: General Reference works, Introductory Surveys, Topics in Jewish Mysticism, The History of Kabbalah, Major Scholars, and Non-Jewish Kabbalah. Includes both primary and secondary sources. This is as comprehensive and current a bibliography of kabbalah in English as can be found.

29. Norman A. Stillman, *The Jews of Arab Lands in Modern Times* (Philadelphia: Jewish Publication Society, 1991).

    The focus of this work is the history of Jews living in Arab lands during the past two centuries. The work is divided into two parts: (1) a synthetic history of the period; (2) excerpts from primary sources which correspond to each of the historical phases previously described. The bulk of the work consists of the sources in part 2. This is an excellent sourcebook of primary materials and is especially valuable for its extensive bibliography.

30. David S. Zubatsky, *Jewish Autobiographies and Biographies* (New York: Garland, 1989).

    This work comprehensively lists Jews from all walks of life and many different countries. It includes books, dissertations, and theses regarding Jews from the 1st century C.E. to the present. Includes a subject index.

Guides to Periodicals

31. *Articles of Interest in Current Periodicals* (New York: American Jewish Committee, 1949–).

    The guides are issued irregularly (usually bimonthly). Listings are arranged according to subject, such as Abortion, Black–Jewish Relations, Church and State, etc. Includes items of both a general and scholarly nature.

32. Bitya Ben-Shammai, *Index of Articles on Jewish Studies (RAMBI)* (in Hebrew) (Jerusalem: Jewish National and University Library, 1966–), Annual.

    This guide to journal articles provides a selective bibliography for various fields of Jewish study and the study of Eretz Israel. Entries are arranged according to subject (Philosophy and Religion, Literature, History, the State of Israel, etc.) and are compiled from thousands of periodicals which have articles in Hebrew, Yiddish, and European languages. Most of the entries reflect holdings of the Jewish National and University Library in Jerusalem. This resource is particularly helpful for locating scholarly articles written outside North America.

33. Daniel Feibel, *Current Contents of Periodicals on the Middle East* (Tel Aviv: Tel Aviv University, Shiloah Center for Middle East Studies, 1980–), Bimonthly.

    Contains references to more than 60 periodicals, most of them in English, but some in Hebrew or Arabic. Includes copies of tables of contents.

34. *Index to Jewish Periodicals* (Cleveland Heights, Ohio: Index to Jewish Periodicals, 1963–), Semiannual.

    Listing are organized alphabetically, with subjects and authors inter-mixed. Includes a list of the periodicals cited in the particular issue and cross references.

35. Robert Singerman, *Jewish Serials of the World: A Research Bibliography of Secondary Sources* (New York: Greenwood, 1986).

    This work identifies source materials for the study of the history of the Jewish press between 1675 and mid-1985. Listings are organized accord-ing to country, with subdivisions determined by language where neces-sary. Listings are multilingual and can be located in most American university libraries. Includes chapters on the history of Jewish serials and on multinational serials. Includes author and subject indexes.

Guides to Film, Music, and the Arts

36. *Art in Jewish Life: Bibliography and Resources* (New York: National Council on Art in Jewish Life, 1972).

    This resource is a compilation of materials pertaining to the various roles of the visual arts in Jewish life. Included are lists of slide sets which depict Jewish ceremonial art and architecture, archeology, and Jews in the fine arts. Slide sets are provided for a variety of topics, including Judaic Art and Architecture, Jews as Artists, and Scenes from the Bible in West-ern Art. Also included is a section entitled Slide Lecture Series, which provides information on topics for which the researcher may use both slides and a prepared text. Topics include Passover in Jewish Art, The Hanukkah Lamp, The Jewish Theater, etc. This resource also includes a bibliography of available films and filmstrips related to Jewish artistic achievements and interests. This resource is limited in scope, but it provides a helpful visual introduction to the role of art in Jewish life.

37. *Catalogue of Jewish Films in Israel* (Jerusalem: Hebrew University, A.F. Rad Jewish Films Archives, 1972).

   This is an annotated catalogue of films regarding Israel and Zionism. Includes information about film length, language, subject matter, etc.

38. Stuart Fox, *Jewish Films in the United States: A Comprehensive Survey and Descriptive Filmography* (Boston: G.K. Hall, 1976).

   This resource is the result of the collective efforts of the Institute of Contemporary Jewry of the Hebrew University in Jerusalem and the Division of Cinema at the University of Southern California in Los Angeles. It describes films and television programs which in any way pertain to Jews and Judaism. Included are films made and/or released in the United States from the early twentieth century to the date of publication. Approximately 4000 titles are included, primarily organized chronologically. This work is comprehensive and of value to students of the Jewish experience in the twentieth century.

39. Hannah Grad Goodman, *Aspects of Jewish Life: A Select and Annotated Bibliography of Books and Multimedia Materials* (New York: Jewish Book Council, 1974).

   Listings are organized according to wide-ranging subjects, including: American Jewish History, Ben Gurion, Buber, Hasidism, The Holocaust, Holidays, Talmud, Yiddish Literature, etc. Within each subject area are listed multimedia resources, including books, films, filmstrips, dramatizations, musical and dramatic works, songs, cassettes, etc.

40. Irene Heskes, *The Resource Book of Jewish Music* (Westport, Conn.: Greenwood, 1985).

   This work is an annotated bibliographical resource for the study of Jewish music. Entries are organized according to the form of the item: Reference Works, Books, Articles, Periodicals, etc. Selection of materials for inclusion was based upon a broad overview of Jewish music: Bible, History, Religion, Folk Expression, Scholarship, Musicianship, Education, and Sociological Developments. This is a good, up-to-date resource. Includes both musical compositions and works on the study of Jewish music. Includes indexes.

41. Albert Weisser, *Bibliography of Publications and Other Resources in Jewish Music* (New York: National Jewish Music Council, 1969).

   Includes lists of books and articles regarding Jewish music, based in part on J. Yasser's *Bibliography of Books and Articles on Jewish Music* (1955).

Guides to Collections

42. Shimeon Brisman, *A History and Guide to Judaic Encyclopedias and Lexicons* (Cincinnati: Hebrew Union College Press, 1987).
    Listings are organized according to subject, such as: General Encyclopedias/Lexicons of Judaica, Modern Jewish Authors, Arts and Sciences, Diaspora Communities, etc. Includes index.

43. *Directory of Archives and Manuscript Repositories in the United States* (Phoenix: Oryx, 1988).
    This is a general reference work of archival and manuscript repositories in the United States. There is a subject index at the back of the work which includes many references under the general category of "Jews," both according to the state in which the collection is found and by various topic headings, such as: Education, Labor Movements, Immigration, etc. Annotated entries for each collection include address, access information, materials solicited, and scope and content of holdings. Includes many cross references.

44. *Directory of World Jewish Press and Publications* (Jerusalem: Directory of World Jewish Press and Publications, 1984).
    Listings are for some 900 Jewish publications throughout the world, including bulletins and newsletters, newspapers, journals, and magazines. Entries are organized according to continent, then according to country, and then according to title. Information for entries includes name and address of publisher, frequency of issue, circulation, principal contributors, etc. Includes entries of both general and scholarly interest and title and country indexes.

45. Geula Gilat, *Directory of Special Libraries in Israel* (Tel Aviv: National Center of Scientific and Technological Information, 1985).
    Listings are in English and Hebrew. Specialized libraries are listed alphabetically. Includes library name, address, telephone number, librarian's name, and subjects of collections. Includes alphabetized special subject index.

46. *A Guide to Libraries of Judaica and Hebraica in Europe* (Copenhagen: Association of Libraries of Judaica and Hebraica in Europe, 1985).
    Includes a country-by-country listing of libraries with their addresses and holdings. Includes an appendix of Hebrew manuscript collections in Europe on microfilm, country by country.

47. Philip P. Mason, *Directory of Jewish Archival Institutions* (Detroit: Wayne State University Press, 1975).
    Includes information on the following archives in the United States:

American Jewish Archives, American Jewish Historical Society, Leo Baeck Institute, Bund Archives of the Jewish Labor Movement, The Dropsie University, Hebrew Union College – Jewish Institute of Religion, Library of the Jewish Theological Seminary of America, and YIVO Institute for Jewish Research. Includes archive's address, hours, scope and content, types of records, major collections, etc. This work is somewhat dated.

48. Jacob Robinson and Yehuda Bauer, *Guide to Unpublished Materials of the Holocaust Period*, 6 vols. (Jerusalem: Hebrew University, Institute of Contemporary Jewry, 1970–81).

Listings include: Collections, Documents, Manuscripts, Museum Pieces, Photographs, Papers, Clippings, and Drawings. Material is described according to the name of the archives, the period, character and size of the collection, and files of special interest.

49. William L. Shulman, *Association of Holocaust Organizations* (Bayside, N.Y: Holocaust Resource Center and Archives, 1990–), Annual.

This directory provides information regarding institutions and organizations in the United States and Canada that provide services and resources related to the study of the Holocaust. Listings are organized alphabetically. Each entry provides information regarding the type of services the organization offers. Includes a membership list of the Association of Holocaust Organizations. Includes a geographical index.

Databases

50. *America: History and Life (*1964–).

This database indexes and abstracts articles, monographs, and dissertations that address all aspects of North American history. Examples of online searches in this database might include Black–Jewish Relations in the American South, The Jews of New York City, Jewish Women in the Feminist Movement, etc.

51. *Art and Humanities Search* (1980–).

This database indexes over 1300 journals which contain a wide variety of material, as diverse as archeology, classics, history, literature, music, philosophy, and religion. Material can be accessed by author, subject, title, or motif.

52. *DIALOG.*

This online system draws on hundreds of databases including many related to the study of Judaica. This system can be utilized effectively to locate bibliographic material in diverse fields of learning. The limitation of this tool is determined only by the number of databases to which it has access. *DIALOG* currently contains very little Hebrew-language material.

53. *Historical Abstracts* (1973–).

This database contains material related to the study of world history from 1450 to the present, excluding that of the United States and Canada. Articles are abstracted from over 2000 journals in 30 languages. *Historical Abstracts* could be very useful for locating material about Jews in Israel, Europe, and other parts of the world.

54. *Mideast File* (1979–).

This database contains materials which address all aspects of the contemporary Middle East. Fields such as current affairs, economics, history, sociology, etc. can be readily accessed. Included are over 340 journals, as well as research reports, government publications, books, interviews, etc.

55. *OCLC* (On-line Computer Library Center).

This is a very widely used and voluminous database cataloging system which includes over 17 million items of interest to researchers. Material can be accessed by a variety of search keys, including author, title, date, date range, etc. *OCLC* provides the researcher with information regarding the location of the material sought, which may then make the item accessible by way of interlibrary loan programs.

56. *Religious Index* (1975–).

This database indexes and abstracts more than 500 journals and multiauthor works. Included are references to the history of religions, theology, biblical literature, the sociology and psychology of religion, etc. Most of the materials included are English-language publications. This is a good resource for anyone interested in some religious aspect of the Jewish experience.

57. *RLIN* (Research Libraries Information Network).

This database cataloguing system provides rapid online access to a vast amount of bibliographical material. Records are grouped according to the type of material sought, including books, journals, maps, musical scores, etc. The researcher can find various kinds of material catalogued and cross-referenced with this tool, including manuscript collections, archives' holdings, etc. *RLIN* has the ability to search Hebrew and Yiddish titles online. It provides the researcher with information regarding the location of the material sought, which allows for the possibility of acquiring it by way of interlibrary loan programs.

58. *YIVO Database* (New York).

This is a locally created and maintained database which catalogs the

YIVO collection of photographs from Eastern Europe of towns, schools, camps, cemeteries, political organizations, etc. Material can be accessed by place names, occupations, names of people, etc. The disadvantage of databases like this one is that the researcher can only access the material sought if he engages his search on the institution's premises. Access from other institutions is not possible in locally maintained databases.

Atlases

59. Evyatar Friesel, *Atlas of Modern Jewish History* (New York: Oxford University Press, 1990).

    Maps serve as the primary source of information in this very useful work. The subject matter is classified in seven broad categories: Jewish Demography, Europe: Seventeenth Century to World War I, Major Themes in Modern Jewish History, Muslim Countries, Europe: Interwar Years, Europe: 1940–1980s, and The New Centers of Jewry. The extensive use of maps, diagrams, and graphics provides for a visually enhanced perspective on the demographic aspects of Jewish history. This is a very useful learning tool. Includes index.

60. Martin Gilbert, *Jewish History Atlas* (New York: Macmillan, 1977; repr. New York: Dorset, 1985).

    This atlas traces the unfolding of Jewish history from ancient Mesopotamia to modern Israel. Included are maps of traders, philosophers, financiers, settlers, and sages, as well as persecution and forced migrations. This work contains over 120 maps, approximately three-quarters of which concern modern Jewish history.

61. Martin Gilbert, *The Macmillan Atlas of the Holocaust* (New York: Macmillan, 1982).

    This work contains 314 maps, which depict chronologically the destruction of each of the main Jewish communities of Europe during the course of the Holocaust, as well as acts of resistance and revolt, and the fate of individuals. Each map is accompanied by a descriptive narrative. Many photographs are also included in this work. This is a first-rate resource for the study of the Holocaust. Includes bibliography and index.

Sample Syllabi for Survey Courses on the
Modern Jewish Experience Taught in
Diverse Linguistic and National Settings

1. The Modern Jewish Experience

Compiled by the American Team for a Course Taught in the U.S.

Suggested Background Readings

1.* Robert Seltzer, *Jewish People, Jewish Thought* (New York: Macmillan, 1980).
2. *Great Ages and Ideas of the Jewish People*, ed. Leo W. Schwarz (New York: Random House, 1956).
3. *History of the Jewish People*, ed. H.H. Ben Sasson and Shmuel Ettinger (Cambridge: Harvard University Press, 1976).
4. A survey of modern history.

COURSE OUTLINE

I. Introduction

Session 1: Jewish Life on the Eve of the Modern Age

    a. The autonomous Jewish community in Europe and in Sephardic lands
    b. The nature of Jewish law
    c. The institutional and social structure of Jewish life
    d. Communal leadership

---

*For ease of reference in the Index of Authors, each item in the Syllabi is numbered; subsequent mentions of the same item are cited in brief and provided with the same number.

5. Jacob Katz, *Tradition and Crisis* (New York: Free Press, 1961), chs. 1–5, 9–19.
6. Shlomo Deshen, *The Mellah Society: Jewish Community Life in Sherifian Morocco* (Chicago: University of Chicago Press, 1989), chs. 2, 3, 7–Conclusion.

Session 2: The Transition to Jewish Modernity

    a. The geography of Jewish dispersal
    b. Resettlement in the West
    c. Piety and wealth
    d. The Court Jews

7. Evyatar Freisel, *Atlas of Jewish History* (New York: Oxford Univesity Press, 1990) maps 1, 2, 15–18.
8. *The Memoirs of Glueckel of Hameln*, ed. Marvin Lowenthal (New York: Schocken, 1977), pp. 1–129.
3. *History of the Jewish People*, ed. H.H. Ben Sasson and Shmuel Ettinger, pp. 727–40.

II. Enlightenment and Emancipation

Session 3: Moses Mendelssohn and the Emergence of Modern Judaism

    a. Mendelssohn as a figure
    b. His thought: theology of revelation; the nature of Jewish law; straddling cultures; religious coercion and kehillah autonomy

9. Michael Meyer, *The Origins of the Modern Jew* (Detroit: Wayne State University Press, 1967), chs. 1–2.
10. *The Jew in the Modern World*, ed. Paul Mendes-Flohr and Jehuda Reinharz (New York: Oxford University Press, 1980), 2/14–19.†

Session 4: The Absolutist State and the Haskalah

    a. The policies of Absolutist states and their seeming tolerance
    b. The program and major personalities of the Jewish Enlightenment movement
    c. The Haskalah and the reshaping of Jewish culture

†This reader serves as the major collection of primary sources on the syllabus. All references to this book herein read: Mendes-Flohr and Reinharz and then the part and document numbers in that part—e.g., part 3 documents 1–5 is given as 3/1–5.

11. Raphael Mahler, *History of Modern Jewry* (New York: Schocken , 1971) chs. 3A, 7A, 8
10. Mendes-Flohr and Reinharz, 1/6, 8–11; 2/8, 20, 21

Session 5: "Liberty, Fraternity, Equality"—The Revolution

   a. The debate over the Jews in pre-Revolutionary France
   b. The emergence of new forms of antisemitism
   c. Emancipation in France

10. Mendes-Flohr and Reinharz, 3/1–6; 7/1–3.
12. Arthur Hertzberg, *The French Enlightenment and the Jews* (New York: Columbia University Press, 1968), chs. 9–10.

Session 6: The Fate of Emancipation

   a. The Assembly of Notables convened by Napoleon
   b. The revocation of Emancipation in Germany
   c. The Congress of Vienna and the Age of Reaction

10. Mendes-Flohr and Reinharz, 3/7–20.
13. Simon Dubnow, *History of the Jews*, vol. 4: *From Cromwell's Commonwealth to the Napoleonic Era* (South Brunswick, N.J.: Thomas Yoseloff, 1971), part 2, ch. 1 (pp. 505–66).

III. Responses to Emancipation

Session 7: Reform Judaism

   a. The genesis of Reform
   b. The nature of synagogue reforms
   c. Debates among rabbis concerning permissible reforms
   d. The ideology of reformers and its relationship to the Emancipation struggle

10. Mendes-Flohr and Reinharz, 4/1–8.
14. Michael Meyer, *Response to Modernity* (New York: Oxford University Press, 1988), prologue and chs. 1 2.

Session 8: Orthodoxy

   a. What is Orthodoxy?
   b. Official responses to reforms

　　c. The leaders of Neo-Orthodoxy
　　d. The separatist program of some Orthodox leaders
　　e. Modern and traditional elements in varieties of Orthodoxy

15. S. R. Hirsch, *The Nineteen Letters of Ben Uziel* (New York: Feldheim, 1960).
16. Jacob Katz, "Orthodoxy in Historical Perspective," *Studies in Contemporary Jewry* 2 (1986): 3–17.
10. Mendes-Flohr and Reinharz, 4/3.

Session 9: Positive-Historical Judaism and the New Jewish Learning

　　a. The program of Zacharias Frankel and the Breslau seminary
　　b. Frankel's critique of Orthodoxy and Reform
　　c. The nature of *Wissenschaft des Judentums*; and its relationship to religious reform, the internal needs of German Jewry, the critique of antisemites

17. Ismar Schorsch, "Zacharias Frankel and the European Origins of Conservative Judaism," *Judaism* 30 (Summer 1981): 344–54.
10. Mendes-Flohr and Reinharz, 4/11; 5/2, 4–6.
18. Heinrich Graetz, *The Structure of Jewish History and Other Essays*, ed. and trans. Ismar Schorsch (New York: Jewish Theological Seminary, 1975), ch. 7, pp. 191–258.

Session 10: The Social and Economic Transformation of the Jews of Western Europe

　　a. An introduction to Jewish social history and its concerns
　　b. The experience of Jewish women
　　c. Jewish participation in European culture, Heine as an exemplar
　　d. The phenomenon of conversion to Christianity
　　e. Peripheral Jews

19. Todd Endelman, *The Jews of Georgian England, 1714–1830: Tradition and Change in a Liberal Society* (Philadelphia: Jewish Publication Society, 1979), ch. 4.
20. Deborah Hertz, "Seductive Conversion in Berlin, 1770–1809," in *Jewish Apostasy in the Modern World*, ed. Todd Endelman (New York: Holmes and Meier, 1987), pp. 48–82.
21. Marion A. Kaplan, *The Making of the Jewish Middle Class: Women, Family, and Identity in Imperial Germany* (New York: Oxford University Press, 1991), chs. 2–3.

10. Mendes-Flohr and Reinharz, 6/4–7.

Session 11: Antisemitic Reactions to Emancipation

    a. Political Antisemitism
    b. New ideologies
    c. Continuity and discontinuity in nineteenth-century antisemitism
    d. What is modern about modern antisemitism?

10. Mendes-Flohr and Reinharz, 7/9–19.
3. *History of the Jewish People*, ed. Shmuel Ettinger and H.H. Ben Sasson, pp. 870–89.
22. *The Dreyfus Affair: Art, Truth, and Justice*, ed. Norman L. Kleeblatt (Berkeley: University of California Press, 1987), pp. 1–116.

Session 12: The Transformation of United States Jewry

    a. The recapitulation of Emancipation themes through the distinctive experience of Jews in the United States
    b. The growth and development of United States Jewry in the Sephardic and German periods
    c. The emergence of classical Reform Judaism

23. *History of the Jews in the United States, 1790–1840*, ed. Joseph L. Blau and Salo W. Baron (New York: Columbia University Press, 1963), vol. 1, documents 22–29, 34; vol. 2, documents 196–209.
24. Leon A. Jick, *The Americanization of the Synagogue* (Hanover, N.H.: University Presses of New England, 1976), chs. 4–8, 11.

IV. Traditional Jewries and Their Transformation

Session 13: Jews in the Muslim World

    a. Continuity and change in Jewish societies
    b. Varying degrees of contact with colonial powers
    c. Montefiore and the Alliance Israélite Universelle
    d. The legal status of Jews in Muslim lands
    e. The nature of Muslim attitudes toward Jews

25. Norman Stillman, *The Jews of Arab Lands in Modern Times* (Philadelphia: Jewish Publication Society, 1991), pp. 3–64, 183–224.
6. Shlomo Deshen, *The Mellah Society*, chs. 4–6.

Session 14: The Internal Life of East European Jewry

    a. Economic and social life in the eighteenth century
    b. The emergence of Hasidism
    c. The nature of Mitnaggedism
    d. Haskalah—the new challenge

26. *In Praise of the Besht*, ed. Dan Ben Amos and Jerome Mintz (Bloomington: Indiana University Press, 1970), documents 1–39.
27. *The Jew in the Medieval World: A Source Book, 315–1791*, ed. Jacob Rader Marcus (New York: Athencum, 1975), document 55, pp. 276–78.
10. Mendes-Flohr and Reinharz, 8/7.
28. *The Golden Tradition*, ed. Lucy Dawidowicz (Northvale, N.J.: Aronson, 1989, reprint), part 1.
29. Simon Dubnow, *History of the Jews in Poland and Russia from the Earliest Times until the Present Day* (New York: Ktav, 1975, reprint), vol. 1, ch. 4, "The Inner Life of Polish Jewry at Its Zenith," pp. 103–38.

Session 15: The Legal Status of Russian Jewry

    a. The partitions of Poland
    b. The policies of successive czars—e.g., the Pale of Settlement, conscription, treatment of Judaism and the organized community
    c. Official Haskalah
    d. Reforms
    e. Pogroms

30. Salo Baron, *The Russian Jews under Tsars and Soviets* (New York: Macmillan, 1964), chs. 2–4.
10. Mendes-Flohr and Reinharz, 8/1–6.
31. David G. Roskies, *The Literature of Destruction* (Philadelphia: Jewish Publication Society, 1989), document 38.

Part V: Whither?

Session 16: The New Jewish Politics

    a. Jewish Socialism
    b. Diaspora Nationalism
    c. Hibbat Zion—Lovers of Zion

28. *The Golden Tradition*, part 10.

32. Simon Dubnow, *Nationalism and History* (Philadelphia: Jewish Publication Society, 1958), fourth letter, pp. 131–42.
33. *The Zionist Idea*, ed. Arthur Hertzberg (Garden City, N.Y.: Doubleday, 1959), pp. 101–15.
30. Salo Baron, *The Russian Jews Under Tsars and Soviets*, ch. 9.

Session 17: The Rise of the Zionist Movement

   a. Herzlian Zionism
   b. The first congresses
   c. Conflicting Zionist ideas

34. Amos Elon, *Herzl* (New York: Holt, Rinehart and Winston, 1975), chs. 8–10.
33. *The Zionist Idea*, selections on Herzl, pp. 200–30; Ahad Ha-Am, pp. 247–77; and Syrkin, pp. 330–50.

Session 18: Jewish Literary Creativity in Hebrew and Yiddish

   a. Responses to catastrophe
   b. Revisions of the Jewish past

35. Sholem Aleichem, "Dreyfus in Kasrilevke"; Peretz, "Bontsha the Silent" and "If Not Higher," in *Treasury of Yiddish Literature*, ed. Irving Howe and E. Greenberg (New York: Viking, 1953), pp. 187–92, 231–34.
31. David Roskies, *Literature of Destruction*, pp. 160–68 ("In the City of Slaughter")

Session 19: Migration

   a. Internal migration and urbanization
   b. Transcontinental movement
   c. The aliyahs

7. Evyatar Freisel, *Atlas of Modern Jewish History*, maps 3, 4, 28, 30, 33.
10. Mendes-Flohr and Reinharz, Appendix: "The Demography of Modern Jewish History," pp. 525–42.
36. Zalman Shazar, *Morningstars* (Philadelpia: Jewish Publication Society, 1967), pp. 171–234.
37. Mary Antin, *The Promised Land*, excerpted in *Modern Jewish History: A Source Reader*, ed. Robert Chazan and Marc Lee Raphael (New York: Schocken, 1974), pp. 129–41.

Session 20: Jewish Life in the United States, 1881–1924

    a. Immigration from Eastern Europe
    b. United States government policies
    c. Uptown and Downtown Jews
    d. Agencies of Americanization
    e. The second generation

38. Irving Howe, *World of Our Fathers* (New York: Harcourt, Brace Jovanovich, 1976), chs. 6, 14.
39. *The Bintel Brief I*, ed. Isaac Metzger (New York: Behrman, 1971), pp. 93–111, 162–63.
40. Kenneth Libo, *We Lived There Too* (New York: St. Martin's, 1984), chs. 2, 11.

VI. World Jewry on the Eve of the Holocaust

Session 21: The Jews of Central Europe and Poland in the Interwar Period

    a. Major challenges facing German, Austrian, Polish, and Hungarian Jewries
    b. Socioeconomic transformations
    c. Comparisons of these Jewries

41. Ezra Mendelsohn, *The Jews of East Central Europe between the World Wars* (Bloomington: Indiana University Press, 1983), ch. 1 ("Poland").
10. Mendes-Flohr and Reinharz, 6/3, 11–14.
42. Nahum N. Glatzer, *Franz Rosenzweig: His Life and Thought* (New York: Schocken, 2nd ed., 1970), pp. 214–47.
43. Martin Buber, *On Judaism* (New York: Schocken, 1967), pp. 214–47.

Session 22: The Holocaust

    a. Nazi antisemitism
    b. Legislation against Jews
    c. The Final Solution
    d. Jewish responses

10. Mendes-Flohr and Reinharz, 11/1–28.
31. David Roskies, *The Literature of Destruction*, document 93 and others.
44. Lucy Dawidowicz, *The War against the Jews* (New York: Holt, Rinehart and Winston, 1975), chs. 1, 3, 6, 7, 10.

Session 23: Soviet Jewry

    a. Legal Emancipation
    b. Social and economic transformations
    c. Jewish culture

45. Isaac Babel, "The Rabbi's Son," "Gedali," "Story of My Dovecot," in *Isaac Babel: the Collected Stories*, trans. Walter Morison (New York: Meridian, 1960).
10. Mendes-Flohr and Reinharz, 8/29–32.
46. Zvi Gitelman, *A Century of Ambivalence: The Jews of Russia and the Soviet Union 1881 to the Present Day* (New York: Schocken, 1988), chs. 2, 3, 5, 6.

Session 24: The Yishuv—From Balfour to Statehood

    a. Political relations with England
    b. Conflict with the Arab world
    c. Diplomacy

10. Mendes-Flohr and Reinharz, 10/19–29.
47. Hayim Hazzaz, "The Sermon," in *Modern Hebrew Literature*, ed. Robert Alter (New York: Behrman, 1975), pp. 267–87.
48. Walter Laqueur, *History of Zionism* (New York: Schocken, 1972), chs. 6, 7, 9, 11.

VII. Jewish Life in The Postwar World

Session 25: Israel—Politics and Culture

    a. The absorption of new immigrants
    b. Ben Gurion's conception of statism
    c. The Israeli political system and the major parties
    d. Cultural life

49. A. B. Yehoshua, "Facing the Forest," in *Modern Hebrew Literature*, ed. Robert Alter, pp. 353–92.
50. Howard M. Sachar, *A History of Israel: From the Rise of Zionism to Our Time* (New York: Knopf, 1976), chs. 14, 15.

Session 26: Sephardic Jews in the Twentieth Century

    a. False emancipation and the breakdown of traditional communities

   b. Absorption in Israel
   c. Alternatives in France
   d. The transplantation of Sephardic culture in Israel

25. Norman Stillman, *The Jews of Arab Lands in Modern Times*, pp. 65–182.
51. Yehoram Bilu, "Dreams and the Works of the Saint," in *Judaism Viewed from Within and Without*, ed. Harvey E. Goldberg (Albany: State University of New York Press, 1987), pp. 285–326.

Session 27: American Jewry since 1945

   a. Suburbanization and anomie
   b. Economic mobility
   c. Impact on American culture
   d. Religious innovations
   e. The impact of feminism

52. *Dynamic Judaism: The Essential Writings of Mordecai M. Kaplan*, ed. Emanuel Goldsmith and Mel Scult (New York: Schocken, 1985), parts 1, 3, 7, 11.
53. Philip Roth, "Eli the Fanatic," in *Goodbye, Columbus* (Boston: Houghton Mifflin, 1959), pp. 249–98.
54. Sylvia Barack Fishman, "The Impact of Feminism on American Jewish Life," *American Jewish Yearbook* 89 (1989) 3–62.
55. Jack Wertheimer, "Recent Trends in American Judaism," *American Jewish Yearbook* 89 (1989): 63–162.

Session 28: Israel and the Diaspora

   a. The 1967 war and Jewish responses
   b. The exodus of Soviet Jewry
   c. Israel

50. Howard M. Sachar, *A History of Israel*, chs. 21–23.
56. Charles S. Liebman and Steven M. Cohen, *Two Worlds of Judaism: The Israeli and American Experiences* (New Haven: Yale University Press, 1990), chs. 2, 4, 6.

2. The Modern Jewish Experience

Compiled by Milton Shain for a Course Taught in South Africa

Single semester option (13 weeks, three lectures per week, fortnightly tutorials)

The course is a first year undergraduate semester elective. It is assumed that students have no prior knowledge of the modern Jewish experience. Knowledge of Hebrew or a European language is not a prerequisite and course readings are therefore limited to English.

Recommended Background Readings

1. Robert M Seltzer, *Jewish People, Jewish Thought: The Jewish Experience in History* (New York: Macmillan, 1980).
2. Howard M Sachar, *The Course of Modern Jewish History*, rev. ed. (New York: Vintage, 1990).

LECTURE THEMES

Week 1. European Jewry in the Mercantile Age

  a. European Jewry 1500–1648: an overview
  b. Community and polity

I wish to thank Professor Bernard Steinberg for his comments and suggestions.

    c. The Sabbetai Sevi episode

3. Jacob Katz, *Tradition and Crisis* (New York: Free Press of Glencoe, 1971), pp. 79–134.

1. R. M. Seltzer, *Jewish People, Jewish Thought* (1980), pp. 454–74.

4. Harry C. Schnur, *Mystic Rebels* (New York: Beechhurst, 1949), pp. 159–236.

Week 2: Hasidism

    a. The origins of Hasidism
    b. The Baal Shem Tov and his disciples
    c. The Hasidic dynasties

1. R. M. Seltzer, *Jewish People, Jewish Thought*, pp. 474–96.

5. Martin Buber, *Hasidism and Modern Man* (New York: Horizon, 1958), pp. 21–43, 47–69.

6. Jacob S. Minkin, *The Romance of Hassidism* (New York: Macmillan, 1955), pp. 60–151.

7. Louis I. Newman, *The Hasidic Anthology* (New York: Bloch, 1963), Introduction.

Week 3: Enlightenment and Emancipation

    a. Enlightenment and the Jews
    b. Understanding Emancipation
    c. The Process of Emancipation

8. Salo W. Baron, "Newer Approaches to Emancipation," *Diogenes* 29 (Spring 1960): 56–81.

9. Jacob Katz, *Out of the Ghetto* (New York: Schocken, 1978), pp. 28–41.

10. Reinhard Rürup, "Jewish Emancipation and Bourgeois Society," *Leo Baeck Institute Yearbook* 14 (1969): 67–91.

2. H. M. Sachar, *The Course of Modern Jewish History*, pp. 38–61 and 94–119.

1. R. M. Seltzer, *Jewish People, Jewish Thought*, pp. 512–33.

Week 4: Jewish Responses to Modernity in the Nineteenth Century

    a. The Haskalah: an overview
    b. The rise of Reform and the Science of Judaism
    c. S. R. Hirsch: Neo-Orthodoxy

11. Paul Mendes-Flohr and Jehuda Reinharz, *The Jew in the Modern World* (New York: Oxford University Press, 1980), pp. 140–210.
12. David Rudavsky, *Modern Jewish Religious Movements* (New York: Behrman, 1967), pp. 34–94.
2. H. M. Sachar, *The Course of Modern Jewish History*, pp. 159–72.
1. R. M. Seltzer, *Jewish People, Jewish Thought*, pp. 580–625.

Week 5: The Rise of Modern Antisemitism to 1914

a. The foundations of modern antisemitism
b. Nationalism, racism, and Social Darwinism
c. A case study: the Dreyfus Affair

13. Samuel Ettinger, "The Origins of Modern Anti-Semitism," in *Dispersion and Unity* 9 (1969): 17–37.
14. Jacob Katz, *From Prejudice to Destruction* (Cambridge: Harvard University Press, 1980), pp. 1–10.
2. H. M. Sachar, *The Course of Modern Jewish History*, pp. 261–76.
1. R. M. Seltzer, *Jewish People, Jewish Thought*, pp. 626–34.

Week 6: Jewish Migration and the Making of South African Jewry

a. The great migrations 1881–1914
b. The making of South African Jewry I
c. The making of South African Jewry II

15. Steven Cohen, "Historical Background," in Marcus Arkin, *South African Jewry: A Contemporary Survey* (Cape Town: Oxford University Press, 1984), pp. 1–22.
16. Lloyd P. Gartner, "The Great Migration 1881–1914; Myths and Realities," *Kaplan Centre Papers* 3 (1984):
17. Gustav Saron, "The Making of South African Jewry," in *South African Jewry 1965*, ed. L Feldberg (Johannesburg: Fieldhill, n.d.), pp. 9–49.

Week 7: Germany and the Jews 1918–1945

a. German antisemitism 1918–1933
b. The Nazi era and the Holocaust
c. Perspectives on the Holocaust

18. Yehuda Bauer, "The Place of the Holocaust in Contemporary History," in *Studies in Contemporary Jewry*, vol. 1, ed. J. Frankel (1984): 201–24.

19. Lucy S. Dawidowicz, *The War against the Jews* (New York: Holt, Reinhart and Winston, 1975), pp. 50–77.
2. H. M. Sachar, *The Course of Modern Jewish History*, pp. 511–44.
1. R. M. Seltzer, *Jewish People, Jewish Thought*, pp. 661–71.

Week 8: The Rise of Zionism

    a. The historical roots of Zionism
    b. The rise of Zionism to 1917
    c. Major trends in Zionist thought

20. Shlomo Avineri, *The Making of Modern Zionism* (New York: Basic Books, 1981), pp. 3–13.
21. *The Zionist Idea,* ed. Arthur Hertzberg (New York: Atheneum, 1984), pp. 15–100.
22. Jacob Katz, "The Jewish National Movement," in *Jewish Society through the Ages*, ed. Haim H. Ben-Sasson and Samuel Ettinger, pp. 267–83.
2. H. M. Sachar, *The Course of Modern Jewish History*, pp. 303–26.
1. R. M. Seltzer, *Jewish People, Jewish Thought*, pp. 634–42, 655–58.

Week 9: Twentieth-Century Jewish Thought

    a. Twentieth-century Jewish thought: an overview
    b. Abraham Kook
    c. Franz Rosenzweig

23. Shmuel H. Bergman, *Faith and Reason* (Washington: B'nai B'rith Hillel Foundations, 1961), Introduction.
1. R. M. Seltzer, *Jewish People, Jewish Thought*, pp. 720–66.

Week 10: Twentieth-Century Jewish Thought

    a. Martin Buber
    b. Mordecai Kaplan
    c. Abraham Heschel

23. S. H. Bergman, *Faith and Reason*, pp. 55–97.
1. R. M. Seltzer, *Jewish People, Jewish Thought*, pp. 720–66.

Week 11: Contemporary Jewry

    a. Profile of world Jewry: demographic issues
    b. Contemporary Jewish identity
    c. Israel and the Diaspora

24. Steven M. Cohen, *American Modernity and Jewish Identity* (New York: Travistock, 1983), pp. 171–79.
25. Daniel J. Elazar, *People and Polity. The Organizational Dynamics of World Jewry* (Detroit: Wayne State University Press, 1989), pp. 94–111.
26. Simon N. Herman, *Jewish Identity: A Psychological Perspective* (Beverly Hills, Calif.: Sage, 1977), pp. 39–61.
27. U. O. Schmelz and Sergio DellaPergola, "World Jewish Population 1986," Jerusalem: Hebrew University, Institute of Contemporary Jewry, Division of Jewish Demography and Statistics, Occasional Papers.

Week 12: South African Jewry

    a. Structures and polity
    b. Demography
    c. Sources of cohesion and cleavage

28. Antony Arkin, "Economic Activities," in M. Arkin, *South African Jewry: A Contemporary Survey*, pp. 57–79.
29. Sergio DellaPergola and Allie A. Dubb, "South African Jewry: A Sociodemographic Profile," in *American Jewish Year Book* (1988): 59–140.

Week 13: South African Jewry: Issues

    a. Antisemitism
    b. Jews and Zionism/Jews and apartheid
    c. Jews and political transition

30. Marcus Arkin, "The Zionist Dimension," in M. Arkin, *South African Jewry: A Contemporary Survey*, pp. 79–93.
31. Milton Shain, "From Pariah to Parvenu: The Anti-Jewish Stereotype in South Africa, 1880–1910," in *Jewish Journal of Sociology* 26/2 (December 1984): 111–27.
32. Milton Shain and Sally Frankenthal, "South African Jewry, Apartheid, and the Transition," in *Patterns of Prejudice* 25/1 (1991).
33. Gideon Shimoni, *Jews and Zionism: The South African Experience 1910–1967* (Cape Town: Oxford University Press, 1980), pp. 97–136.
34. Gideon Shimoni, "South African Jews and the Apartheid Crisis," in *American Jewish Year Book* 88 (1988): 3–58.

3. The Modern Jewish Experience

Compiled by Nancy L. Green for a Course Taught in France

The seminar meets once a week for three hours. Students will be responsible for (1) presenting an oral introduction to one of the week's readings; and (2) writing a 20–25-page research paper on a topic of their choice.

Recommended general texts

1. Salomon Grayzel, *Histoire des Juifs: époque moderne et contemporaine*, 2 vols. (Paris: Service technique pour l'éducation, 1967–69).
2. Abraham Leon Sachar, *Histoire des Juifs* (Paris: Flammarion, 1973).

SEMINAR OUTLINE

Week 1: Questions in Jewish Historiography

3. *Yosef Hayim Yerushalmi, *Zakhor* (Paris: La Découverte, 1984).
4. Salo Baron, *History and Jewish Historians* (Philadelphia: Jewish Publication Society, 1964).

*Items marked with an asterisk are required readings, others are recommended.

Week 2: From Tradition to Reform

5. *Jacob Katz, *Hors du Ghetto* (Paris: Hachette, 1984), chs. 1–4 (pp. 7–63).
6. *Moses Mendelssohn, *Jérusalem* (Paris: Presses d'Aujourd'hui, 1982).
7. *S. R. Hirsch, *19 épîtres sur le judaïsme* (Paris: Cerf, 1987), pp. 17–79 (introduction and first two epistles).

Week 3: Paths to Assimilation

8. *Hannah Arendt, *Rahel Varnhagen* (Paris: Tierce, 1986).
9. Michael Marrus, *Les Juifs de France à l'époque de l'affaire Dreyfus* (Paris: Calmann-Lévy, 1972).

Week 4: Political Emancipation—The French Revolution

10. *André Chouraqui, Nancy L. Green, et al., *La Révolution française et l'émancipation des Juifs de France* (Paris: Hamoré, 1989), pp. 13–75.
11. *Abbé Grégoire, *Essai sur la régénération physique, morale et politique des Juifs* (Paris: Flammarion, 1988).

Week 5: Nineteenth-Century Social and Economic Change

5. *Jacob Katz, *Hors du Ghetto*, chs. 7, 11 (pp. 113–33, 191–206).
12. *Patrick Girard, *Les Juifs en France de 1789 à 1860* (Paris: Calmann-Lévy, 1976), chs. 3–4 (pp. 99–167).
13. Phyllis Albert, *The Modernization of French Jewry: Consistory and Community in the Nineteenth Century* (Hanover, N.H.: University Presses of New England, 1977).

Week 6: Antisemitism

14. *Léon Poliakov, *Histoire de l'antisémitisme* (Paris: Le livre de poche, coll. Pluriel, 1981), Tome 2, Livre 2, "L'Europe suicidaire," pp. 263–354 (1870–1914), pp. 357–469 (1914–1933).
15. *Jean-Paul Sartre, *Réflexions sur la question juive* (Paris: Gallimard, 1985).

Week 7: Emigration 1: The Old World

16. *Rachel Ertel, *Le Shtetl* (Paris: Payot, 1982), pp. 1–172.
17. *Pavel Korzec, *Juifs en Pologne* (Paris: Presses de la Fondation Nationale des Sciences Politiques, 1980), pp. 25–67.

Week 8: Emigration 2: From East to West

18. *Nancy Green, *Les travailleurs immigrés juifs à la Belle Epoque* (Paris: Fayard, 1985), ch. 1 (pp. 19–60).
19. *Paula Hyman, *De Dreyfus à Vichy* (Paris: Fayard, 1985), pp. 99–136.
20. *Nathan Glazer, *Les Juifs américains* (Paris: Calmann-Lévy, 1972), pp. 45–72, 95–119.

Week 9: Jews in Europe between the Wars

16. *Rachel Ertel, *Le Shtetl*, pp. 173–242.
21. *Charlotte Roland, D*u Ghetto à l'Occident* (Paris: Editions du Minuit, 1962), pp. 217–92.
22. David Weinberg, *Les Juifs à Paris de 1933 à 1939* (Paris: Calmann-Lévy, 1974).
23. Karl Löwith, *Ma vie en allemagne avant et après 1933* (Paris: Hachette, 1988).

Week 10: Holocaust

24. *Hannah Arendt, *Eichmann à Jérusalem* (Paris: Gallimard, 1966).
25. *Gershom Scholem, *Fidelité et utopie* (Paris: Calmann-Lévy, 1978), pp. 213–28.
26. Raul Hilberg, *La déstruction des Juifs d'Europe* (Paris: Fayard, 1988).
27. Michael Marrus and Robert Paxton, *Vichy et les Juifs* (Paris: Calmann-Lévy, 1981).

Week 11: Jews in the French-Speaking Colonies

28. *André Chouraqui, *Histoire des Juifs en Afrique du Nord* (Paris: Hachette, 1985), pp. 281–448.
28. André Chouraqui, *Histoire des Juifs en Afrique du Nord*, pp. 449–514, "Exodes et Retour en Israël."

Week 12: Zionism

29. *Ben Gourion, *Du rêve à la réalité: choix de textes* (Paris: Stock, 1986), pp. 49–170.
30. *Mitchell Cohen, *Du rêve sioniste à la réalité israélienne* (Paris: La Découverte, 1990), pp. 31–110.
31. Theodor Herzl, *L'État des Juifs*, Paris: La Découverte, 1990).

Week 13: Soviet Jewry

32. **Les Juifs en Union soviétique depuis 1917*, ed. Lionel Kochan (Paris: Calmann-Lévy, 1971), pp. 25–174, 387–457.

Week 14: American Jewry

20. *Nathan Glazer, *Les Juifs américains*, pp. 73–94, 121–262.
33. Rachel Ertel, *Le roman juif américain* (Paris: Payot, 1980), pp. 167–302.

4. The Modern Jewish Experience

Compiled by Uri Kaufmann for a Course Taught in Germany

Background reading

Brief overviews

1. Friedrich Battenberg, *Das Europäische Zeitalter der Juden* (Darmstadt: Wissenschaftliche Buchgesellschaft, 1990), vol. 2, pp. 34–310.
2. *Geschichte des jüd. Volkes*, ed. Haim Hillel Ben-Sasson, vols. 2–3 (München: Beck, 1979–80).
3. Heinz Mosche Graupe, *Die Entstehung des modernen Judentums (...) 1650–1942* (Hamburg: Leibniz, 1969).
4. Monika Richarz, *Jüd. Leben in Deutschland in Selbstzeugnissen 1780–1945*, vols. 1–3 (Stuttgart: Deutsche Verlagsanstalt, 1976–82), "Einleitungen" und "Selbstzeugnisse."
5. Bernard Lewis, *Die Juden in der islamischen Welt* (München: Beck, 1987).

More advanced studies

6. Ismar Elbogen, *Ein Jahrhundert jüdischen Lebens: Die Geschichte des neuzeitlichen Judentums* (Frankfurt: Europ. Verlagsanstalt, 1967).
7. Ismar Elbogen, *Die Geschichte der Juden in Deutschland* (repr. Wiesbaden: Fourier, 1982).
8. Heinrich Graetz, *Geschichte der Juden von den ältesten Zeiten bis auf die Gegenwart,* vols. 9–11 (Leipzig: Leiner, 1900–   ).

9. Simon Dubnow, *Weltgeschichte des jüd. Volkes*, vol. 6–10 (Berlin: Jüdischer Verlag, 1927–29).
10. Hermann Greive, *Die Juden: Grundzüge ihrer Geschichte im mittelalterlichen und neuzeitlichen Europa* (Darmstadt: Wissenschaftliche Buchgesellschaft, 1982).
11. Martin Philippson, *Neueste Geschichte des jüdischen Volkes*, 3 vols. (Leipzig: Bei Fock, 1907–11).
12. Leon Poliakov, *Geschichte des Antisemitismus*, vols. 4–8 (Worms: G.Heintz; Frankfurt: Athenäum, 1981–88).
13. Gershom Scholem, *Die jüd. Mystik in ihren Hauptströmungen* (Frankfurt: Suhrkamp, 1967), pp. 267–314.

OUTLINE

Topic 1. Introduction

The expulsion of Jews from the German imperial cities, their settlement in rural areas and in Eastern Europe, the new Sephardic communities, attempts at reorganization (Shulhan Arukh), Sabbetai Sevi, the legal situation of the Jews in Europe and the Ottoman empire around 1700–1750, the struggle over rabbinic authority (Emden/Eybeschütz), rural Jews

2. *Geschichte des jüd. Volkes*, vol. 2, pp. 9–30, 65–80.
14. Riccardo Calimani, *Die Kaufleute von Venedig: die Geschichte der Juden in der Löwenrepublik* (Düsseldorf: Claassen, 1988).
9. Simon Dubnow, *Weltgeschichte*, vol. 7, pp. 11–263 (Osteuropa 1648–1789), pp. 436–506 (Italien, Holland, Türkei).
15. Frantisek Graus, *Pest – Geissler – Judenmorde: Das 14. Jh. als Krisenzeit* (Göttingen: Vandenhoeck & Ruprecht, 1987).
16. Henry Kamen, *Die spanische Inquisition* (München: Deutscher Taschenbuchverlag, 1969).
17. Alfred Landau, *Jüdische Privatbriefe aus dem Jahre 1619* (Wien: Braumüller, 1911).
18. Beatrice Leroy, *Die Sephardim: Geschichte des iberischen Judentums* (München: Beck, 1987).
19. Heiko A. Oberman, *Wurzeln des Antisemitismus* (Berlin: Severin und Siedler, 1981).
13. Gershom Scholem, *Die jüd. Mystik*, pp. 315–55.
20. Selma Stern, *Josel von Rosheim* (Stuttgart: Deutsche Verlagsanstalt, 1959).
21. Markus Wenninger, *Man bedarf keiner Juden mehr* (Wien: Böhlau, 1981).

Topic 2. Transition to Modernity

Westward migration, the social stratification of Jewish society, forerunners of Enlightenment

9. Simon Dubnow, *Weltgeschichte*, vol. 7, pp. 325–39.
22. Rudolf Glanz, *Geschichte des niederen jüdischen Volkes* (New York: Selbstverlag, 1968).
23. Wladimir Kaplan-Kogan, *Die Wanderbewegungen der Juden* (Bonn: Marcus & Webers, 1913).
24. Franz Kobler, *Jüdische Geschichte in Briefen aus Ost und West (...)* (Wien: Saturnverlag, 1938).

Topic 3. Enlightenment

Mendelssohn and his disciples, the *me'assefim*, especially I. Euchel, Friedlaender, Ben David and Saul Ascher; East European Jewish dissidents: Salkind Hurwitz and Salomon Maimon

Source
25. Salomon Maimon, *Geschichte des eigenen Lebens*, (Berlin: Schocken, 1935).

Studies
26. Jacob Allerhand, *Das Judentum in der Aufklärung* (Stuttgart: Frommann-Holzboog, 1980).
27. Hanna Emmrich, *Das Judentum bei Voltaire* (Breslau: Priebatsch, 1930).
28. *Deutsche Aufklärung und Judenemanzipation*, ed. Walter Grab (Tel Aviv: Universität Tel Aviv, 1980).
29. Walter Grab, Gegenseitige *Einflüsse deutscher und jüdischer Kultur* (Tel Aviv: Universität Tel Aviv, 1982).
30. Jacob Katz, *Aus dem Ghetto in die bürgerliche Gesellschaft* (Frankfurt: Athenäum, 1986).
12. Leon Poliakov, *Geschichte des Antisemitismus*, vol. 5, *Die Aufklärung und ihre judenfeindliche Tendenz* (1983).

Topic 4. The Absolutist State and the Jews

From the old Jewish laws to the "civic improvement of the Jews," or the "Edicts of Toleration"

31. Battenberg, Friedrich, *Judenverordnungen in Hessen-Darmstadt* (Wiesbaden: Kommission für die Geschichte der Juden in Hesse, 1987)n.
2. *Geschichte des jüd. Volkes*, vol. 2, pp. 31–42.

32. Ernst Ludwig Ehrlich, "Geschichte und Kultur der Juden in den rheinischen Territorialstaaten," in *Monumenta Judaica, Handbuch*, (Köln: Stadt Köln/Stadtmuseum, 1963), pp. 246–64.
33. Joseph Karniel, *Die Toleranzpolitik Kaiser Joseph II*. (Gerlingen: Bleicher, 1985).
34. Selma (Täubler-)Stern, *Der preuss. Staat und die Juden* (Tübingen: Mohr, 1962/75).
35. Selma (Täubler-)Stern, *Jüd Süss* (repr. München: Gotthold Müller, 1973).
36. Heinrich Schnee, *Die Hoffinanz und der moderne Staat* (Berlin: Duncker und Humblot, 1953/67).

Topic 5. Pioneers and Opponents of Emancipation 1770–1800

The Dohm–Michaelis controversy, the attitudes in France (Grégoire and Mirabeau), the French Enlightenment and the Jews, the abolition of the body tax in France, the discussions surrounding the Revolution 1790–91

Source
37. Christian K. Dohm, *Über die bürgerliche Verbesserung der Juden* (Berlin, 1781; repr. Hildesheim: Olms, 1973).

Studies
9. Simon Dubnow, *Weltgeschichte*, vol. 8, pp. 83–134.
38. Hans Liebeschütz, *Das Judentum im deutschen Geschichtsbild von Hegel bis Max Weber* (Tübingen: Mohr, 1967).

Topic 6. Emancipation 1800–1871

Germany, Belgium, Netherlands, Austria, Italy, England

4. Monika Richarz, *Jüd. Leben in Deutschland*, vol. 1, pp. 19–69.

Sources
39. Ismar Freund, *Die Emanzipation der Juden in Preussen* (Berlin: Poppelauer, 1912).
40. A. F. Pribram, *Urkunden und Regesten zur Geschichte der Juden in Wien*, 1. Abteilung, *1526–1847* (Leipzig & Wien· Braumüller, 1918).

Studies
2. *Geschichte des jüd. Volkes*, vol. 2, pp. 94–110.
41. Harm-Hinrich Brandt, "Vom aufgeklärten Absolutismus bis zur Reichs-

gründung," in *Geschichte und Kultur des Judentums*, ed. Karlheinz Müller (Würzburg: Schöningh 1988), pp. 175–200.

42. Anna Drabek, *Das österreichische Judentum* (Wien: Jugend und Volk, 1988).

9. Simon Dubnow, *Weltgeschichte*, vol. 8, pp. 194–314.

43. Karl Martin Gross et al., "Emanzipation," in *Geschichtliche Grundbegriffe* (Stuttgart: Klett 1975), vol. 2, pp. 153–97.

44. Arno Herzig, *Judentum und Emanzipation in Westfalen* (Münster: Aschendorff, 1973).

45. Helga Krohn, *Die Juden in Hamburg 1800–1850* (Frankfurt: Europäische Verlagsanstalt, 1967).

46. Helga Krohn, *Die Juden in Hamburg 1848–1918* (Hamburg: Christians, 1974).

47. Salo W. Baron, *Die Judenfrage auf dem Wiener Kongress* (Wien: Loewit, 1920).

48. *Judentum in der deutschen Umwelt 1800–1850*, ed. Hans Liebeschütz (Tübingen: Mohr, 1977); (see also derselbe unter Nr.5)

49. Sigmund Mayer, *Die Wiener Juden: Kommerz – Kultur – Politik 1700–1900* (Wien: Loewit, 1918).

50. Rina Neher-Bernheim, *Documents inédits sur l'entrée des Juifs dans la société francaise* (Tel Aviv, 1977).

51. Bernhard Post, *Judentoleranz und Judenemanzipation in Kurmainz 1774–1813* (Wiesbaden: Kommission für die Geschichte der Juden in Hessen, 1985).

52. Reinhard Rürup, *Emanzipation und Antisemitismus* (Göttingen: Vandenhoeck & Ruprecht, 1975).

53. Jacob Toury, "Die Emanzipationsgesetzgebung," in *Soziale und politische Geschichte der Juden in Deutschland 1847–1871* (Düsseldorf: Droste,   ), pp. 277–361.

54. Gerson Wolf, *Geschichte der israelitischen Cultusgemeinde in Wien 1820–1860* (Wien: Braumüller, 1861).

Topic 7. The Three Great Traditions in German-speaking Jewry 1800–1876 and Their Development in the United States

Sources

55. Articles from the *Wissenschaftliche Zeitschrift für jüd. Theologie*, ed. Abraham Geiger (1835-44).

56. The debates surrounding the Frankfurt rabbinic assembly: *Protokolle und Aktenstücke der Frankfurter Rabbinerversammlung* (Frankfurt, 1845),

and letter of Zacharias Frankel in the *Allgemeine Zeitung des Judentums*, 1845.

57. Salomon Formstecher, *Die Religion des Geistes* (Frankfurt: Hermannsche Buchhandlung, 1841).
58. Moritz Güdemann, *Sechs Predigten im Leopoldstädter Tempel (...) gehalten*, (Wien: Gerold, 1867).
59. Samuel Hirsch, *Die Religionsphilosophie der Juden, Leipzig 1842* (repr. Hildesheim: Olms, 1986).
60. Samson Raphael Hirsch, *Gesammelte Schriften* (Frankfurt: Kauffmann, 1902/04, 1921/22).
61. Samson Raphael Hirsch, *19 Briefe über das Judentum* (Berlin: Welt Verlag, 1919).
62. Markus (Mordechai) Horovitz, *Der Talmud: Drei Reden* (Frankfurt, 1883).
63. Meier Kayserling, *Bibliothek jüdischer Kanzelredner*, 2 parts (Berlin: Springer, 1870–72).
64. Jacob Löwenstein, sermons in *Treue Zionswächter* (1845–54), e.g., "An die Reformationsstürmer in Israel" (9 December 1845), pp. 193f.; "Gerechtigkeit lehrt uns die grosse Schule der Zeitereignisse" (17 April 1848), pp. 121–23, 127f., 131f.
65. Jacob Rosenheim, *Aufsätze und Ansprachen*, 2 vols. (Frankfurt: Kauffmann, 1930).
66. Gotthold Salomon & Eduard Kley, *Predigten in dem neuen israelitischen Tempel zu Hamburg gehalten* Hamburg: Amons, 1819, 1820, 1826, 1827).
67. Salomon Ludwig Steinheim, *Die Offenbarung nach dem Lehrbegriff der Synagoge* (repr. Hildesheim: Olms, 1986).

Studies
68. Ludwig Geiger, *Abraham Geiger: Leben und Lebenswerk* (Berlin, 1910).
69. Julius Guttmann, *Die Philosophie des Judentums* (München, 1933).
70. Albert Lewkowitz, *Das Judentum und die geistigen Strömungen des 19. Jahrhunderts* (Berlin, 1935; repr. Hildesheim: Olms, 1974).
71. Cäsar Seligmann, *Geschichte der jüdischen Reformbewegung* (Frankfurt: Kauffmann, 1922).
72. Max Wiener, *Jüd. Religion im Zeitalter der Emanzipation* (Berlin: Philo Verlag, 1933).

Topic 8. Wissenschaft des Judentums *(Zunz, Jost, Graetz, Luzzatto, Frankel, Steinschneider)*

Sources

73. Simon Dubnow, *Die jüd. Geschichte: Ein geschichtsphilosophischer Versuch* (Frankfurt, 1921).
74. Simon Dubnow, *Mein Leben* (Berlin, 1937).
75. Abraham Geiger, "Das erwachende Selbstgefühl und die jüdische Wissenschaft," in *Geschichte der Juden* (Leipzig, 1900), pp. 419–78.
76. *Wissenschaft des Judentums im deutschen Sprachbereich*, ed. Kurt Wilhelm, 2 vols. (Tübingen: Mohr, 1967).

Studies

77. Norbert Nahum Glatzer, *Leopold Zunz: Jude, Deutscher, Europäer* (Tübingen: Mohr, 1961).
78. Hans G. Reissner, *Eduard Gans* (Tübingen: Mohr, 1965).
79. Max Wiener, "Die religiöse Idee in der Wissenschaft des Judentums," in *Jüdische Religion im Zeitalter der Emanzipation* (Berlin, 1933), pp. 175–257.

Topic 9. Social History of the Jews in the Nineteenth Century

Professions, the Conversion movement, Jewish salons, entry into the academy, urbanization, social mobility, professional activity, political involvement of Jews in 1830 and 1848, the Jewish press from 1806 to 1837

Sources

2. *Geschichte des jüd. Volkes*, vol. 2, pp. 81–93, 126–36, 153–60, 169–81.
80. *Die Juden in Österreich*, ed. Bureau für Statistik der Juden (Berlin: Lamm, 1908).
81. Heinrich Silbergleit, *Die Bevölkerungs- und Berufsverhältnisse der Juden im deutschen Reich* (Berlin: Akademie, 1930).
82. Daniel Stauben, *Eine Reise zu den Juden auf dem Lande* (Augsburg: Ölbaum, 1986). (trans. of French original, Folk Customs and Popular Piety of Rural Jews in Alsace around 1860 [1860]).

Studies

83. Abraham Barkai, *Jüdische Minderheit und Industrialisierung: Demographie, Berufe und Einkommen der Juden in Westdeutschland 1850–1914* (Tübingen: Mohr, 1988).

84. Jacob Toury, *Soziale und politische Geschichte der Juden* (Düsseldorf: Droste, 1977).

Topic 10. *Judenhass/Antisemitism*

The controversies after the wars of liberation (1815–1820), radicalism, liberalism and Jewry 1830–1848, the riots of 1819/1848, political antisemitism, antisemitic parties, the German educated bourgeoisie and *Wissenschaft des Judentums*, debate over antisemitism in Berlin, the Dreyfus Affair in France, Blood Libels in Eastern Europe (including Hungary)

85. Hermann Bahr, *Der Antisemitismus: ein internationales Interview* (Berlin: Fischer, 1894).
86. Alex Bein, *Die Judenfrage: Biographie eines Weltproblems* (Stuttgart: Deutsche Verlagsanstalt 1980).
87. Walter Boehlich, *Der Berliner Antisemitismus-Streit* (Frankfurt: Insel, 1965).
88. Detlev Claussen, *Grenzen der Aufklärung: Zur gesellschaftlichen Geschichte des modernen Antisemitismus* (Frankfurt: Fischer, 1987).
9. Simon Dubnow, *Weltgeschichte*, vol. 10, pp. 11–73 (Deutschland), 74–188 (Österreich).
89. Norbert Kampe, *Studenten und Judenfrage im deutschen Kaiserreich: Die Entstehung einer akademischen Trägerschicht des Antisemitismus* (Göttingen: Vandenhoeck & Ruprecht, 1988).
90. Jacob Katz, *Vom Vorurteil bis zur Vernichtung: Die Geschichte des Antisemitismus 1700–1933* (München: Beck, 1989).
91. Paul Massing, *Vorgeschichte des polit. Antisemitismus* (Frankfurt: Europäische Verlagsanstalt, 1986).
92. George L. Mosse, *Ein Volk, ein Reich, ein Führer: Die völkischen Ursprünge des Nationalsozialismus* (Königstein: Athenäum, 1979).
12. Leon Poliakov, *Geschichte des Antisemitismus*, vols. 6–7 (1988).
93. Peter George Julius Pulzer, *Die Entstehung des politischen Antisemitismus in Deutschland und Österreich, 1867–1914* (Gütersloh: Mohn, 1966).
94. Eva Reichmann, *Flucht in den Hass: Die Ursachen der deutschen Judenkatastrophe* (Frankfurt: Europäische Verlagsanstalt, 1968).
95. Eleonore Sterling, *Er ist wie Du: Aus der Frühgeschichte des Antisemitismus in Deutschland 1815–1850* (München: Kaiser, 1956).
96. *Von der Judenfeindschaft zum Holocaust*, ed. Herbert A. Strauss (Frankfurt: Campus, 1985).
97. Shulamit Volkov, "Kontinuität und Diskontinuität im deutschen

Antisemitismus 1878–1945," *Vierteljahreshefte für Zeitgeschichte* 33/2 (1985).

98.   Shulamit Volkov, *Jüd. Leben und Antisemitismus im 19. und 20. Jh.* (München: Beck, 1990).

Topic 11. Jews in the Islamic Realm 1750–1948

Traditional society: "harat al-Yahud," customs and popular piety of the Sephardic Jews, the legal situation, the function of various local organizations, the reports of European travellers in the eighteenth–nineteenth centuries and the involvement of European Jews (Moses Montefiore), the operations of the Alliance Israélite Universelle (1869ff.), the origin of a secular Ladino literature, the broadening of Jewish horizons by colonialism and Arab nationalism, the Zionist movement in North Africa and Iraq, flight, expulsion, and wandering

Sources

99.   Josef Benjamin II Israel, *Acht Jahre in Asien und Afrika von 1846 bis 1855* (Hannover: Selbstverlag, 1858).

100. Ludwig Frankl, *Nach Jerusalem* (Berlin: Schocken, 1937).

101. Ludwig Frankl, *Nach Jerusalem*, part 1, *Griechenland, Kleinasien, Syrien*; part 2, *Palästina, Leipzig* (Baumgärtner, 1858).

102. *Ost und West: Illustrirte Monatsschrift für das gesamte Judentum* (Berlin, 1901–23).

103. "Berichte und Korrespondenzen" in the German-Jewish Press: *Sulamith* (1806–48), *Allgemeine Zeitung des Judentums* (1837–1922), *Der Orient* (1840–51), *Der Israelit* (1860–1938).

104. Bericht(e) der Alliance Israelite Universelle, Liegnitz, Köln, Berlin 18676–1913.

Studies

105. Jehoschuah Feldmann, *Die Jemenitischen Juden* (Köln: Selbstverlag, 1912).

106. *Festschrift anlässlich der Feier des 25-jährigen Bestehens des Hilfsvereins der deutschen Juden, gegr. am 25.5.1901* (Berlin: Selbstverlag, 1926).

107. Julius Fürst, *Kultus- und Literaturgeschichte der Juden in Asien* (Leipzig: Engelmann, 1849).

5.   Bernard Lewis, *Die Juden in der islamischen Welt* (München: Beck, 1987).

108. Bernard Lewis, *"Treibt sie ins Meer" : Die Geschichte des Antisemitismus* (Frankfurt: Ullstein, 1987).
109. Heinrich Loewe, *Juden im türkischen Orient* (Berlin: Druck Siegfried Scholem, 1915).
110. Seligmann Meyer, *Völkerrecht und Humanität in der orientalischen Frage und die Israeliten in der Türkei, Serbien und Rumänien* (Berlin, 1877).
111. Wilhelm Reich, *Berühmte Judengemeinden des osmanischen Reiches* (Frankfurt, 1913).
112. Davis Trietsch, *Die Juden in der Türkei* (Leipzig: E. Gaebler, 1915), fascicle 8, "Länder und Völker der Türkei."

Topic 12. East European Jewry 1730–1900

Inner spiritual currents (Frankists, Rabbi Israel Baal Shem Tov, the Mitnaggedim), the common battle against Enlightenment, the position of the government, reform "from above," the legal situation in Austria and the Czarist empire in the 19th century, the beginnings of a secular culture: modern Jewish literature, the reception of Zionism, Bundism, Yiddishism, the Jewish People's Party, mass migration from Eastern Europe to Western Europe and the United States

Sources
113. Michael Brocke, *Beter und Rebellen: 1000 Jahre Judentum in Polen* (Frankfurt: Deutscher Koordinierungsrat für christlich-jüdische Zusammenarbeit, 1983).
114. Michael Brocke, *Die Erzählungen des Rabbi Nachman von Bratzlaw* (München: Hauser, 1985).
115. Jakob Jaffe, *Ursachen und Verlauf der Juden-Pogrome in Russland im Oktober 1905* (Bern, 1916).
116. Berta Pappenheim, *Zur Lage der jüdischen Bevölkerung in Galizien* (Frankfurt, 1904).
117. Josef Rabinowitsch, *Schilderungen aus Russland*, trans. Isaac Marcus Jost (Leipzig, 1860).

Studies
2. *Geschichte des jüd. Volkes*, vol. 2, pp. 49–64, 111–25, 195–207.
118. Jecheskiel Caro, *Geschichte der Juden in Lemberg (bis 1792)* (Krakau: Selbstverlag, 1894).
119. Simon Dubnow, *Geschichte des Chassidismus*, 2 vols. (Berlin: Jüdischer Verlag, 1931).

9.   Simon Dubnow, *Weltgeschichte*, vol. 8, pp. 315–406.
120.   Josef Meisl, *Geschichte der Aufklärungsbewegung unter den Juden in Russland* (Berlin: Schwetschke, 1919).
121.   Josef Meisl, *Geschichte der Juden in Polen und Russland*, vols. 1–3, (Berlin: Schetschke, 1921–25).
122.   Isaac Rülf, *Die russischen Juden. Ihre Leidensgeschichte und unsere Rettungsversuche* (Memel, 1892).
13.   Gershom Scholem, *Die jüd. Mystik*, pp. 356–85, "Chassidismus."

Topic 13. The Zionist Movement, Especially German Zionism

Forerunners: Moses Hess, Herzl, the activists: Generational division in 1912, shifting of the center of gravity to the Eastern Jewish elite, the Zionist congresses, the Balfour Declaration and the British Mandate, the contribution of the German Jews to the construction of the *yishuv* until 1948

Sources
123.   *Briefe und Tagebücher Theodor Herzls*, ed. Alex Bein (Berlin: Propyläen, 1983–90).
9.   Simon Dubnow, *Weltgeschichte*, vol. 10, pp. 311–67, 438–45.
124.   Helmut Heil, *Die neuen Propheten* (Fürth: Ner Tamid, 1969).
125.   Theodor Herzl, *Altneuland* (Wien, 1902; repr. Haifa Publishing Company, 1962).
126.   Moses Hess, *Jüdische Schriften*, ed. Theodor Zlocisti (New York: Arno, 1980).
127.   Memoirs of representative German-Jewish Zionists: Kurt Blumenfeld, Martin Buber, Moses Kalvary, Franz Oppenheimer, Arthur Ruppin.

Overviews
128.   David Ben Gurion, David Kaznelson (Biographie von Anita Shapira), Golda Meir, Chaim Weizmann. Wladimir Jabotinsky, *Philister über Dir: Simson!* (novel) (Wien: E. Lichtenstein, 1935).
129.   Articles from *Die Welt* and *Der Jude*.

Studies
2.   *Geschichte des jüd. Volkes*, vol. 2, pp. 208–25, 328–62, 391–419.
130.   Adolf Böhm, *Die zionist. Bewegung (1897–1925)*, 2 vols. (Berlin: Welt Verlag; Tel Aviv: Hozaah Ivrith, 1935–37).
131.   Walter Laqueur, *Der Weg zum Staat Israel* (Wien: Europa, 1972).
132.   Yehuda Eloni, *Zionismus in Deutschland* (Gerlingen: Bleicher, 1987).

133. Richard Lichtheim, *Die Geschichte des deutschen Zionismus* (Jerusalem: Mass, 1954).
134. Erwin Roth, *Preussens Gloria im Heiligen Land* (München: Callwey, 1973).

Topic 14. Jews in America 1750–1945

The Sephardim, the contribution of the German Jews to building Jewish organizations in the United States (improvement institutions, B'nai B'rith, American Jewish Committee, etc.), the effects of the East Jewish immigration 1900–33, beginnings of Jewish lobbying

Sources
135. Chajim Bloch, *Das jüdische Amerika: Wahrnehmungen und Betrachtungen* (Wien: "Das Leben," 1926).
136. Foreign correspondent reports in the *Allgemeine Zeitung des Judentums*, e.g., No. 49, 1 December 1845: "Einwanderung in die USA," pp. 723–25; No. 27, 30 June 1845: "Gründung Tempel Emanuel," pp. 407f.
137. Robert Singerman, *Judaica Americana* (New York: Greenwood, 1990), vol. 2, pp. 410–52, "German-Jewish Periodicals printed in USA."

Studies
2. *Geschichte des jüd. Volkes*, vol. 3, pp. 322–24.
138. Michael Gold, *Juden ohne Geld* (Berlin: Neuer Deutscher Verlag 1931).
139. Karl Knortz, *Das amerikanische Judentum* (Leipzig: Engel 1914).
140. *Juden in den Vereinigten Staaten von Amerika*, ed. Joachim Rohlfes (Bonn: F.Ebert-Stiftung, 1990).
141. Achim Schrade, *Europäische Juden in Lateinamerika* (Münster, 1989).

Topic 15. Jews in Cental Europe (Poland, Czechoslovakia, Austria)
Sources
142. Gottlieb Bondy & Franz Dworsky, *Zur Geschichte der Juden in Böhmen, Mähren und Schlesien*, 2 vols. (until 1650) (Prag: Bondy, 1906).
143. Eduard Goldstücker, *Prozesse: Erfahrungen eines Mitteleuropäers* (München: Kraus, 1989).
144. Wilma Iggers, *Die Juden in Böhmen und Mähren: Ein historisches Lesebuch* (München: Beck, 1986).
145. *Urkunden und Akten zur Geschichte der Juden in Eisenstadt und den Siebengemeinden*, ed. Bernhard Wachstein (Wien: Braumüller, 1926).

Studies
2.   *Geschichte des jüd. Volkes*, vol. 2, pp. 420–34.
146.   Ruth Beckermann, *Juden in der Wiener Leopoldstadt 1918–1938* (Wien: Löcker, 1984).
147.   Anna Drabek & Mordechai Eliav, *Prag – Czernowitz – Jerusalem* (Eisenstadt: Roetzer, 1984).
148.   *Polnische Juden: Geschichte und Kultur,s.l.* ed. Marian Fuks (Interpress, 1983).
149.   *Die Juden und Judengemeinden Mährens ...*, ed. Hugo Gold (Brünn: Jüdischer Buch- und Kunstverlag, 1929).
150.   Theodor Haas, *Die Juden in Mähren* (Brönn: Jüd. Buch- und Kunstverlag, 1908).
151.   Wolfgang Häusler, *Das galizische Judentum in der Habsburgermonarchie* (München, 1979).
152.   *Deutsche – Juden – Polen*, ed. Jersch-Wenzel Stefi (Berlin: Colloquium, 1987).
153.   Ruth Kestenberg-Gladstein, *Neuere Geschichte der Juden in den böhmischen Ländern* (Tübingen: Mohr, 1969).
154.   Vladimir Lipscher, *Zwischen Kaiser, Fiskus, Adel, Zünften: Die Juden im Habsburgerreich des 17. und 18. Jh.s am Beispiel Böhmens und Mährens* (Zürich: Zentralstelle der Stundetenschaft, 1983).
155.   Helmut Teufel, "Juden im Ständestaat (Geschichte der Juden in Mähren)," in: *Die Juden in den böhmischen Ländern*, ed. Manfred Seibt (München: Oldenburg, 1983), pp. 57–72.
156.   Milada Vilimkova, *Die Prager Judenstadt* (Hanau, 1990).

Topic 16. Jews in the German Empire and the Weimar Republic (1871– 1933)

Sources
4.   Monika Richarz, *Jüd. Leben in Deutschland*, vols. 2 & 3.
157.   Gershom Scholem, *Walter Benjamin: die Geschichte einer Freundschaft* (Frankfurt: Suhrkamp, 1976).
158.   Bruno Weil, *Der Weg der deutschen Juden* (Berlin: Centralverein, 1934).

Overview
4.   Monika Richarz, *Jüd. Leben in Deutschland*, vol. 2, pp. 12–62; vol. 3, pp. 13–73.

Studies

159. Ingrid Belke, *Siegfried Kracauer (1889–1966)* (Marbach: Schiller Nationalmuseum, 1988).
160. Max Birnbaum, *Staat und Synagoge 1918–1933: Eine Geschichte des Landesverbandes jüdischer Gemeinden* (Tübingen: Mohr, 1981).
161. Mordechai Breuer, *Jüdische Orthodoxie im Deutschen Reich 1871–1918* (Frankfurt: Athenäum, 1986).
162. Peter Gay, *Freud: eine Biographie für unsere Zeit* (Frankfurt: Fischer, 1989).
163. *Juden in der Weimarer Republik*, ed. Walter Grab (Stuttgart: Burg, 1986).
164. Walter Grab, *Juden in der deutschen Wissenschaft* (Tel Aviv: Institut für deutsche Geschichte, 1986).
165. Wolf Kalz, *Gustav Landauer: Kultursozialist und Anarchist* (Meisenheim: Hain, 1967).
166. Rainer Marwedel, *Theodor Lessing 1872–1933: Eine Biographie* (Darmstadt: Luchterhand, 1987).
167. Trude Maurer, *Ostjuden in Deutschland* (Hamburg: Christians, 1986).
168. *Entscheidungsjahr 1932 ...* (Tübingen: Mohr, 1965).
169. Werner Mosse, *Deutsches Judentum in Krieg und Revolution* (Tübingen: Mohr, 1971).
170. *Juden als Träger bürgerlicher Kultur*, ed. Julius Schoeps (Stuttgart: Burg, 1989).
171. Michael Stürmer et al., *Wägen und Wagen, Salomon Oppenheimer jr. und Co.: Geschichte einer Bank und einer Familie* (München: Piper, 1989).
172. Jacob Toury, *Die politischen Orientierungen der Juden in Deutschland von Jena bis Weimar* (Tübingen: Mohr, 1966).
173. Arnold Zweig, *Bilanz der deutschen Judenheit: ein Versuch* (Köln: Melzer, 1961).
174. *Arnold Zweig – Poetik, Judentum, und Politik: Akten des internationalen Arnold Zweig-Symposiums* (Bern: Haupt, 1989).

Topic 17. Holocaust/Resistance 1933–1945

Sources

175. *Die Lage der Juden in Deutschland 1933* (Paris, 1934).
176. Helmut Eschwege, *Kennzeichen J. (Dokumente des Hitlerfaschismus 1924–1945)* (Berlin: Deutscher Verlag der Wissenschaften, 1981).

Studies

177. Uwe Dietrich Adam, *Judenpolitik im 3. Reich* (Königstein: Athenäum, 1979).
178. Uwe Dietrich Adam, *Der Judenpogrom* (Frankfurt: Fischer, 1988).
179. Hanna Arendt, *Elemente und Ursprünge totalitärer Herrschaft* (Frankfurt: Ullstein, 1955).
180. Abraham Barkai, *Vom Boykott zur Entjudung* (Frankfurt: Fischer 1988).
2. *Geschichte des jüd. Volkes*, vol. 2, pp. 363–90.
181. *Die Juden in Deutschland 1933–1945*, ed. Wolfgang Benz (München: Beck, 1988).
182. Immanuel Geiss, *Geschichte des Rassismus* (Frankfurt: Suhrkamp, 1989).
183. Eberhard Jaeckel, *Der Mord an den Juden im zweiten Weltkrieg* (Stuttgart: Deutsche Verlagsanstalt, 1985).
184. Konrad Kwiet & Helmut Eschwege, *Selbstbehauptung und Widerstand 1933–1945* (Hamburg: Christians, 1984).
185. Arnold Paucker, *Der jüd. Abwehrkampf gegen Antisemitismus und Nationalsozialismus in den letzten Jahren der Weimarer Republik* (Hamburg: Leibniz, 1969).

Topic 18. Jews in the Soviet Union 1917–1945

186. Daniela Bland-Spitz, *Die Lage der Juden und die jüdische Opposition in der Sowjetunion 1967–1977* (Diessenhofen: Rüegger, 1980).
9. Simon Dubnow, *Weltgeschichte*, vol. 11, pp. 509–34 (until 1927).
187. Abraham Heller, *Die Lage der Juden in Russland von 1917 bis zur Gegenwart* (Breslau: Marcus, 1935).

Topic 19. Jews after 1945

Europe (West Germany), Palestine/Israel, United States, South America
    The migration of Sephardim from North Africa, the migrations of 1956 from Hungary and Poland and of 1968 from Czechoslovakia, the renascence of Jewish life in Eastern Europe since 1988 (Hungary), the relationship of Diaspora Jews to Israel, reaction, the anti-Zionism debate, the "de-Zionization" of Israel (Yerida) after 1973ff., the Jewish schools movement in the Diaspora, the new "Jewish ethnicity" in the United States, the increasing significance of South America

Source
188. Alain Finkielkraut, *Der eingebildete Jude* (München: Hanser, 1982).

Studies
2.   *Geschichte des jüd. Volkes*, vol. 3, pp. 426–34.
189. Werner Bergmann, *Antisemitismus in der politischen Kultur nach 1945* (Opladen: Westdeutscher Verlag, 1990).
190. Henryk M. Broder, *Fremd im eigenen Land: Juden in der BRD* (Frankfurt: Fischer, 1979).
191. *Jüd. Leben in Deutschland seit 1945*, ed. Micha Brumlik (Frankfurt: Athenäum, 1986).
192. Kurt Grünberg, *Folgen nationalsozialistischer Verfolgung bei Kindern von Überlebenden: Juden in der BRD* (Marburg, 1983).
193. Ludolf Herbst, *Wiedergutmachung in der BRD* (München: Oldenburg, 1989).
194. Harry Maor, "Über den Wiederaufbau jüdischer Gemeinden in Deutschland seit 1945," dissertation, Mainz, 1961.
195. Jakob Josef Petuchowski, *Lexikon der jüdisch-christlichen Begegnung* (Freiburg: Herder, 1989).
196. *Antisemitismus nach dem Holocaust*, ed. Alphons Silbermann (Köln: Verlag Wissenschaft und Politik, 1986).
197. Juliane Wetzel, *Jüdisches Leben in München 1945–1951* (München: Kommissionsverlag Uni-Druck, 1987).

Addendum

198. *Neues Jüdisches Lexikon*, ed. Julius H. Schoeps (Bertelsmann-Verlag, 1992).

5. The Modern Jewish Experience

Compiled by Mark Kupovetsky for a Course Taught in Russia

Bibliography

1. E. Feldman and M. Altshuler, "Bibliografiya na russkom yazyke," in *Ocherk istorii yevreiskogo naroda*, ed. Sh. Ettinger, vol. 2 (Yerusalim, 1972), pp. 823–58.
2. B. Pinkus and A. Greenbaum, *Russian publications on Jews and Judaism in the Soviet Union, 1917–1967* (Jerusalem, 1970), pp. 37–96.
3. *Sistematicheskiy ukazatel' literatury o yevreyakh na russkom yazyke* (St.-Peterburg, 1892).

OUTLINE

Topic 1. Political Emancipation and Haskalah in the West (end of the eighteenth and beginning of the nineteenth centuries)

Studies

4. M. Davidson, *Nachalo poseleniya i emansipatsiya yevreyev v Anglii* (Odessa, 1892).
5. S. M. Dubnov, *Vsemirnaya istoriya yevreyev ot drevneyshikh vremyën do nastoyashchego: Noveyshaya istoriya* (Riga, 1937), vol. 1, pp. 60–100, 244–78.
6. H. Graetz, *Istoriya yevreyev ot drevneyshikh vremyën do nastoyashchego*, vol. 12 (Odessa, 1908).

7. M. M. Kulisher, *Velikaya frantsuzskaya revolyutsiya i yevreyskiy vopros* (Leningrad, 1924).
8. S. G. Lozinskiy, *Yevrei zapada v bor'be za pravo i svobodu, istoriko-biograficheskiye ocherki* (Moskva, 1919).
1. *Ocherk istorii yevreyskogo naroda*, vol. 2, pp. 442–47, 462–72, 482–95, 515–31.

Sources
9. *Parlamentskiye rechi po yevreyskomu voprosu*, ed. S. Pozner (St.-Peterburg, 1914).

Topic 2. Reaction and Antisemitism in the West (nineteenth and beginning of the twentieth centuries)

Studies
10. Z. Bakhrakh, *Antisemitizm v novoye vremya* (Yerusalim, 1991).
5. S. M. Dubnov, *Vsemirnaya istoriya yevreyev ot drevneyshikh vremyën do nastoyashchego: Noveyshaya istoriya* (Riga, 1938), vol. 2, pp. 5–60, 100–22; vol. 3, pp. 5–90.
11. N. Kogan, *Blagoslavleniye na genotsid: mif o vsemirnom zagovore yevreyev* (Moskva, 1990).
12. S. G. Lozinskiy, *Sotsial'nye korni antisemitizma v sredniye veka i novoye vremya* (Moskva, 1929).
1. *Ocherk istorii yevreyskogo naroda*, vol. 2, pp. 540–55.
13. L. Praysman, *Delo Dreyfusa* (Tel-Aviv, 1987).

Sources
14. A. Dreyfus, *Pyat' let moyey zhizni (1894–1899)* (St.-Peterburg, 1901).

Topic 3. Great Emigration (end of the nineteenth and beginning of the twentieth centuries)

Studies
5. S. M. Dubnov, *Vsemirnaya istoriya yevreyev ot drevneyshikh vremyën do nastoyashchego: Noveyshaya istoriya* (Riga, 1938), vol. 2, pp. 229–33, 386–89; vol. 3, pp. 215–41.
15. K. Fornberg, *Yevreyskaya emigratsiya* (Kiyev, 1908).
1. *Ocherk istorii yevreyskogo naroda*, vol. 2, pp. 532–40.
16. G. M. Prays, *Russkiye yevrei v Amerike* (St.-Peterburg, 1893).

Topic 4. The National Movement

Studies

17. Sh. Avineri, *Osnovnye techeniya v yevreyskoyu politicheskoyu mysli* (Yerusalim, 1983).
5. S. M. Dubnov, *Vsemirnaya istoriya yevreyev ot drevneyshikh vremyën do nastoyashchego: Noveyshaya istoriya* (Riga, 1938), vol. 3, pp. 242–86.
18. S. M.Dubnov and B.-Z. Dinur, *Dve kontseptsii yevreyskogo natsional'- nogo vozrozhdeniya* (Yerusalim, 1984).
19. Y. Klauzner, *Kogda natsiya boretsya za svobodu* (Yerusalim, 1978).
20. M. M. Margolin, *Natsional'noye dvizheniye v yevreystve, 1881–1913* (Petrograd, 1917).
1. *Ocherk istorii yevreyskogo naroda*, vol. 2, pp. 569–84.
21. D. S. Pasmannik, *Sud'by yevreyskogo naroda: problemy yevreyskoy obsh- chestvennosti* (Moskva, 1917).
22. A. Ruppin, *Yevrei nashego vremeni* (Petrograd, 1918).

Sources

23. Agad Gaam, *Izbrannye sochineniya* (Yerusalim, 1974).
24. B. Borokhov, *Klassovaya bor'ba i natsional'ny vopros* (Moskva, 1917).
25. T. Gerzl, *Izbrannoye* (Yerusalim, 1974).
26. M. Gess, *Rim i Yerusalim* (Tel-Aviv, 1979).
27. L. Pinsker, *Avtoemansipatsiya* (Moskva, 1917).

Topic 5. Jewish History before and after World War II

Studies

5. S. M. Dubnov, *Vsemirnaya istoriya yevreyev ot drevneyshikh vremyën do nastoyashchego: Noveyshaya istoriya* (Riga, 1938), vol. 3, pp. 412–57.
28. *Gosudarstvo Izrail'*, ed. I. Oren (Nadel), vols. 1–2 (Yerusalim, 1988).
1. *Ocherk istorii yevreyskogo naroda*, vol. 2, pp. 617–36, 652–805.
29. A. B. Volkov and P. G. Tarasov, *Gosudarstvo Izrail' i Vsemirny Yevreyskiy Kongress* (Moskva, 1991).

Topic 6. The Holocaust

Studies

30. Y. Arad, *Golokaust* (Yerusalim, 1990).
31. Y. Gutman and H. Shacker, *Katastrofa i yeyë znacheniye* (Yerusalim, 1990).
32. S. Yelisavetskiy, *Berdichevskaya tragediya* (Kiyev, 1991).

33. F. Levitas and M. Shimanovskiy, *Babiy Yar: Stranitsy tragedii* (Kiyev, 1991).
34. G. Smolyar, *Mstiteli getto* (Moskva, 1947).

Sources
35. *Chërnaya kniga*, ed. I. Erenburg and V. Grossman (Yerusalim, 1980).
36. *Dnevnik Anny Frank* (Moskva, 1960).
37. G. Hauzner, *6,000,000 obvinyayut*, 2nd ed. (Yerusalim, 1990).
38. Yu. M. Lyaknovitskiy, *Poprannaya mezuza (Kniga Drobitskogo Yara)*, vol. 1 (Kharkov, 1991).
39. *Unichtozheniye yevreyev v SSSR v gody nemetskoy okkupatsii (1941–1944): Sbornik dokumentov i materialov*, ed. Y. Arad (Yerusalim, 1991).

Topic 7. Jews in Pre-Revolutionary Russia
Studies
40. I. M. Bikerman, *Cherta yevreyskoy osedlosti* (St.-Peterburg, 1911).
41. S. Ya. Borovoy, *Yevreyskaya zemledel'cheskaya kolonizatsiya v staroy Rossii* (Moskva, 1928).
42. L. Bramson, *K istorii nachal'nogo obrazovaniya yevreyev v Rossii* (St.-Peterburg, 1896).
43. B. D. Brutskus, *Professional'ny sostav yevreyskogo naseleniya Rossii po materialam pervoy vseobshchey perepisi naseleniya* (St.-Peterburg, 1908).
44. B. D. Brutskus, *Statistika yevreyskogo naseleniya Rossii* (St.-Peterburg, 1909).
45. B. D. Brutskus and I. M. Bikerman, *Ocherki po voprosam ekonomicheskoy deyatel'nosti yevreyev v Rossii* (St.-Peterburg, 1913).
46. N. A. Bukhbinder, *Istoriya yevreyskogo rabochego dvizheniya v Rossii* (Leningrad, 1925).
5. S. N. Dubnov, *Vsemirnaya istoriya yevreyev ot drevneyshikh vremyën do nastoyashchego: Noveyshaya istoriya* (Riga, 1939), vol. 1, pp. 9–175, 287–316, 398–411.
47. Yu. M. Gessen, *Yevrei v Rossii* (St.-Peterburg, 1906).
48. Yu. M. Gessen, *Istoriya yevreyskogo naroda v Rossii*, 2nd ed., vols. 1–2 (Leningrad, 1925–27).
49. F. Kandel, *Ocherki vremyën i sobytii: Iz istorii rossiyskikh yevreyev*, vol. 2 (Yerusalim, 1990).
50. *Kniga o russkom yeveystve, 1860–1917*, ed. G. Aronson (N'yu-York, 1960).
51. P. Marek, *Ocherki po istorii prosveshcheniya yevreyev v Rossii* (Moskva, 1909).

52. I. G. Orshanskiy, *Yevrei v Rossii: Ocherki ekonomicheskogo i obshchestvennogo byta russkikh yevreyev* (St.-Peterburg, 1887).
53. I. G. Orshanskiy, *Russkoye zakonodatel'stvo o yevreyakh* (St.-Peterburg, 1887).
54. S. V. Pozner, *Yevrei v obshchey shkole* (St.-Peterburg, 1914).
55. *Sbornik materialov ob ekonomicheskom polozhenii yevreyev v Rossii*, vols. 1–2 (St.-Peterburg, 1904).
56. A. S. Tager, *Tsarskaya Rossiya i delo Beylisa* (Moskva, 1933).
57. S. L. Tsynberg, *Istoriya yevreyskoy pechati v Rossii v svyazi s obshchestvennymi techeniyami* (Petrograd, 1915).

Sources
58. S. M. Dubnov, *Kniga zhizni*, vols. 1–3 (Riga-N'yu-York, 1934–57).
59. *Materialy po istorii antiyevreyskikh pogromov v Rossii*, ed. S. M. Dubnov and G. Ya. Krasni-Almoni, vols. 1–2 (Petrograd, 1919–23).
60. *Opisaniye del byvshego arkhiva Ministerstva Narodnogo Prosveshcheniya: Kazyёnnye yevreyskiye uchilishcha*, ed. S. G. Lozinskiy, vol. 1 (Petrograd, 1920).
61. *Trudy gubernskikh komissiy po yevreyskomu voprosu* (St.-Peterburg, 1884).
62. *Iz nedavnego proshlogo: Rechi yevreyskikh deputatov v Gosudarstvennoy Dume* (Petrograd, 1917).

Topic 8. Jews in the Soviet Union

Studies

63. A. Abramovich, *V reshayushchey voyne: Uchastiye i rol' yevreyev SSSR v voyne protiv fashizma*, vols. 1–2 (Tel-Aviv, 1982).
64. S. Agurskiy, *Yevreyskiy rabochiy v kommunisticheskom dvizhenii (1917–1921)* (Minsk, 1926).
65. *Antisemitizm v Sovetskom Soyuze* (Yerusalim, 1979).
66. Yu. V. Golde, *Zemel'noye ustroystvo trudyashchikhsya-yevreyev* (Moskva, 1925).
67. I. Domalskiy, *Russkiye yevrei vchera i segodnya* (Yerusalim, 1975).
68. *Yevrei v sovetskoy Rossii (1917–1967)* (Yerusalim, 1975).
69. L. G. Zinger, *Yevreyskoye naseleniye v Sovetskom Soyuze: Statitiko-ekonomicheskiy obzor* (Moskva–Leningrad, 1932).
70. Ya. Kantor, *Natsional'noye stroitel'stvo sredi yevreyev v SSSR* (Moskva, 1934).
71. *Kniga o russkom yevreystve, 1917–1967* (N'yu-York, 1968).
72. Yu. Larin, *Yevrei i antisemitizm v SSSR* (Moskva-Leningrad, 1929).

73. Ya. L. Rappoport, *Na rubezhe dvukh epokh: Delo vrachey 1953 goda* (Moskva, 1988).
74. S. Shvarts, *Antisemitizm v Sovetskom Soyuze* (N'yu-York, 1954).
75. S. Shvarts, *Yevrei v Sovetskom Soyuze (1939–1965)* (N'yu-York, 1966).

Sources
76. *Antisemitskiye protsessy v Sovetskom Soyuze*, ed. G. Rozhanskiy, vols. 1–3 (Yerusalim, 1979–84).
77. *Yevrei i yevreyskiy narod, 1948–1953*, ed. B. Pinkus, vols. 1–7 (Yerusalim, 1973).
78. *Yevrei i yevreyskiy narod*, ed. A. Ben-Arye and Sh. Redlikh, vol 1–111 (London–Yerusalim, 1962–88).
79. *Yevreyskiy samizdat*, vols. 1–27 (Yerusalim, 1974–86).

Topic 9. Oriental Jews (Caucasus and Central Asia)
Studies
80. Z. L. Amitin-Shapiro, *Ocherk pravovogo byta sredneazyatskikh yevreyev* (Tashkent, 1931).
81. Z. L. Amitin-Shapiro, *Ocherki sotsialisticheskogo stroitel'stva sredi sredneazyatskikh yevreyev* (Tashkent, 1933).
82. I. Anisimov, *Kavkazskiye yevrei-gortsy* (Moskva, 1888).
83. M. R. Benyaminov, *Bukharskiye yevrei* (N'yu-York, 1983).
84. I. David, *Istoriya yevreyev na Kavkaze*, vols. 1–2 (Tel-Aviv, 1990).
85. B. Manoakh, *Plenniki Salmansara: Iz istorii yevreyev Vostochnogo Kavkaza* (Yerusalim, 1984).
86. M. S. Plisetskiy, *Religiya i byt gruzinskikh yevreyev* (Moskva–Leningrad, 1931).

Topic 10. Jewish Philosophy and Culture in the Nineteenth and Twentieth Centuries
Studies
87. I. Berkovich, *Vera posle Katastrofy* (Yerusalim, 1990).
88. M. Buber, *Veleniye dukha* (Tel-Aviv, 1978).
89. A. Heshel, *Zemlya Gospodnya* (Yerusalim, 1974).
90. Ivrit. yazyk vozrozhdyёnny (Yerusalim, 1984).
91. Y. Klauzner, *Novoyevreyskaya literatura* (Odessa, 1912).
92. M. Ya. Pines, *Istoriya yevreyskoy literatury na yevreysko-nemetskom yazyke* (Moskva, 1913).
93. D. Roskes, *Vopreki Apokalipsisu* (Yerusalim, 1990).

6. The Modern Jewish Experience

Compiled by Silvia Schenkolewski-Kroll for a Course Taught in Argentina

General Introduction

1. *Historia del Pueblo Judío*, ed. H. H. Ben Sasson (Madrid: Alianza, 1988).
2. M. Gilbert, *Atlas de la Historia Judía* (Jerusalén: La Semana, 1978).
3. Y. Tzur, *En una era de transición*, División C Unidad 11, *Los tiempos modernos en la investigación histórica* (Tel Aviv: Universidad Abierta, 1981), pp. 97–156.

1. The Jews in the Seventeenth and Eighteenth Centuries

   a. Jewish society: internal organization and autonomy in the Ashkenazic and Sephardic communities
   b. Emigration and Jewish participation in the economy: Mediterranean and colonial commerce (Western Europe), Court Jews (Central Europe), *arenda*, urban commerce (Eastern Europe)
   c. Behavior of European society toward the Jews in the seventeenth and eighteenth centuries (including the legal situation) and during the French Revolution

1. S. Ettinger, *Historia del Pueblo Judío*, vol. 3, *La edad moderna y contemporánea*, pp. 859–903.
3. Y. Tzur, *En una era de transición*, División B, Unidad 5, *En el umbral de los tiempos modernos*.
3. Y. Tzur, *En una era de transición*, División C, Unidad 8, *La Revolución Francesa y los judíos*.

4. E. Tcherikower, *La Revolución Francesa y los judíos* (Buenos Aires: Biblioteca Popular Judía, 1971).

2. Struggle and Change in Jewish Society of Eastern and Western Europe

a. The socioeconomic and spiritual effect of the appearance of Hasidism
b. The Baal Shem Tov and his disciples
c. Opposition to Hasidism: the Vilna Gaon
d. The Jewish Enlightenment, Haskalah, Moses Mendelssohn, the influence of the Haskalah on Jewish life: education, religious reform, lifestyle

1. *Historia del Pueblo Judío*, pp. 905–48.
3. Y. Tzur, *En una era de transición*, División C, Unidad 7, *La crisis de la ilustración*.

3. The Struggle for Emancipation; the Principle of Equal Rights

a. The legal situation of the Jews and the struggle for Emancipation in Western and Central Europe before the revolutions of 1848
b. The revolutions of 1848 and their influence on the situation of the European Jews
c. The legal situation of the Jews in Eastern Europe, forced integration, intensification of antisemitic tendencies

1. *Historia del Pueblo Judío*, pp. 949–78.
5. *La condición judía contemporánea: Génesis histórica de la condición judía contemporánea*, ed. N. Popik (Jerusalén: Organización Sionista Mundial, 1978), pp. 41–89, 146–53.
6. S. W. Baron, *Historia Social y Religiosa del Pueblo Judío*, vol. 6, *La Etapa Moderna* (Buenos Aires: Paidos, 1965), pp. 9–50.
7. S. Ettinger, "Los comienzos del cambio de actitud de la sociedad europea hacia los judíos," *La Emancipacion Judía* (Jerusalem: Monte Scopus, 1983), pp. 27-59.
8. H. D. Schmidt, "Los términos de la emancipación judía 1781–1812," *La Emancipacion Judía*, 79–106.
9. J. Katz, "El término 'Emancipación Judía'. su origen y su impacto histórico," *La Emancipacion Judía*, 107–37.
10. S. W. Baron, "El impacto de la resolución de 1848 sobre la emancipación judía," *La Emancipacion Judía*, 138–201.
11. E. Tcherikower, "Algunos aspectos de las persecuciones en Rusia en el siglo XIX," *Bases* 16 (1962): 115–25.

374 Silvia Schenkolewski-Kroll

4. Ideological Changes in Nineteenth-Century Jewish Society

a. The religious reform movement and Neo-Orthodoxy in the West, the modern Science of Judaism

b. The Haskalah in Eastern Europe; traditionalists of the East (Hasidism, the Lithuanian yeshivas, and the Musar movement)

1. *Historia del Pueblo Judío*, pp. 989–1004.
3. Y. Tzur, *En una era de transición*, División C, Unidad 9, *En una generación de transición, Josef Perl*.
6. S. W. Baron, *Historia Social*, pp. 91–146.
12. L. Trepp, *Una historia de la experiencia judía contemporánea* (Buenos Aires: Seminario Rabínico Latinoamericano, 1980), pp. 319–36.
13. J. Halpern, "El Iluminismo en Europa Oriental," *Bases* 20 (1964): 134–42.

5. Modern Antisemitism

a. The integration of the Jews into European society and the reaction of the gentile world

b. The ideological–social roots of antisemitism

c. Organization of antisemitic parties: Germany, Austria-Hungary

d. France and the Dreyfus Affair

e. Antisemitism as official government policy in Western Europe; pogroms in Russia and their consequences

1. *Historia del Pueblo Judío*, pp. 979–88, 1033–56.
14. S. Ettinger, "Las raíces del antisemitismo contemporáneo," *Dispersión y Unidad* 9 (1970): 225–48.
6. S. W. Baron, *Historia Social*, pp. 51–90.
15. J. Parkes, *Antisemitismo* (Buenos Aires: Paidos, 1965), pp. 43–120.
16. H. Zelkowicz, *El processo Dreyfus* (Buenos Aires: Biblioteca Popular Judía, 1972).

6. Beginnings of Jewish Nationalism and Independent Political Activity before World War I

a. Character of the Jewish national awakening

b. The idea of return to Zion and Hibbat Zion (Love of Zion)

c. The Autoemancipation of Pinsker

d. The nationalism of Ahad Ha-Am

e. Theodor Herzl and "The Jewish State"

f. Political Zionism and the Zionist congresses

g. The socialist movement among the Jews: the organization and development of the Bund

h. The beginnings of socialist Zionism

1. *Historia del Pueblo Judío*, pp. 1013–19, 1057–84.
17. J. Katz, "El movimento nacional judío," *Dispersión y Unidad* 9 (1970): 26–39.
18. S. Avineri, *La Idea Sionista* (Jerusalem: La Semana, 1983), pp. 13–24, 49–70, 89–98, 105–18, 131–72.
19. W. Laqueur, *Historia del Sionismo* (México: Instituto Cultural Mexicano Israelí, 1982), pp. 41–143.

7. The Great Wave of Emigration

a. Factors in emigration

b. Emigration to the United States and Anglo-Saxon countries

c. Emigration and settlement; Baron Hirsch and the ICA

d. Beginnings of the Jewish community in Latin America: the case of Argentina

1. *Historia del Pueblo Judío*, pp. 1099–1104.
6. S. W. Baron, *Historia Social*, pp. 147–200, 263–317.
20. H. Avni, *Argentina y la historia de la inmigración judía 1810–1950* (Buenos Aires: AMIA–Magnes, 1983), pp. 17–293.
21. A. Eban Legado, *La civilización y los judíos* (Madrid: Sheva, 1987), pp. 287–308.
22. V. A. Mirelman, *En búsqueda de una identidad, los inmigrantes judíos en Buenos Aires 1890–1930* (Buenos Aires: Milá, 1988), pp. 3–83, 113–38.

8. New Trends in the Evolution of the Jewish People between the Two World Wars

a. Socioeconomic changes

b. Political activity of the Jews and their rights as a national minority

c. Jewish autonomy in the Baltic nations

d. Jews in the Soviet Union: flowering and oppression of Russian Jewry

e. The Jews of Western Europe and the American continent; restriction of immigration and intensification of antisemitism

f. Consolidation of the Jewish community of the United States

1. *Historia del Pueblo Judío*, pp. 1113–60.
23. M. Altschuler, "El partido comunista soviético y la existencia nacional judía (1918–1932)," *Bases* 33–34 (1968): 21–33.

20. H. Avni, *Argentina*, pp. 295–443.
21. A. Eban Legado, *La civilización y los judíos*, pp. 308–13.
24. M. Agursky, "La controversia sobre el Sionismo en el 'Establishment' soviético: transfondo histórico," *Rumbos* 12 (1985): 83–96.
22. V. A. Mirelman, *En búsqueda de una identidad*, pp. 83–109, 139–57, 381–405.
25. S. Ettinger, "Las raíces del antisemitismo soviético," *Dispersión y Unidad* 10 (1971): 193–207.

9. The Jews and Eretz Israel since World War II

a. The Jews under Turkish dominion: the old *yishuv* and the first and second aliyahs

b. The Zionist movement and the "Nacional Homeland"; the Balfour declaration

c. Zionist ideology and politics between the wars

d. The development of the *yishuv* under the British Mandate

1. *Historia del Pueblo Judío*, pp. 1085–98, 1173–1204.
26. *Historia desde 1880*, ed. A.Comey (Jerusalem: Keter, 1980), pp. 1–122.
27. M. Gilbert, *Atlas del conflicto árabe–israelí* (Jerusalem: La Semana, 1979), pp. 4–38.
28. Y. Gorni, "Las raíces de la conciencia de confrontración judeo-árabe," *El sionismo y la cuestión palestina* (Jerusalem: Magnes, 1989), pp. 107–71.
29. J. Kolatt, "El movimento sionista y los árabes," ibid, pp. 172–213.
30. S. Schenkolewski, "Cambios en la relación de la Organización Sionista Mundial hacia la comunidad judía y el movimento sionista en la Argentina hasta 1948," *Judaica Latinoamericana* (Jerusalem: Magnes, 1988), pp. 149–66.

10. World War II and the Holocaust

a. The intensification of antisemitism in Germany and the coming to power of National Socialism

b. The "Nuremberg laws"

c. The refugees confronted with the world's indifference

d. Persecution of the Jews in the occupied countries

e. The organization of the Jews under the Nazi regime and the ghetto uprisings

f. Mass extermination

g. The behavior of the Allies with respect to the Holocaust

1. *Historia del Pueblo Judío*, pp. 1205–31.
31. D. Michman, *El Holocausto*, Unidad 1–6 (Tel Aviv: Universidad Abierta, 1986, 1987, 1989).
32. Y. Bauer, "Formas de resistencia judía durante el Holocausto," in *El Holocausto* (Jerusalén: Magnes, 1986), pp. 224–45.
33. Y. Bauer, "Reacciones de grupos líderes judíos frente a la política nazi," in *El Holocausto* (Magnes), pp. 194–223.
34. Y. Bauer, "'Hamavdil': Diferenciar el Holocausto del genocidio," *Rumbos* 6 (1982): 51–52.
35. N. Feinberg, "Actividades políticas contra el régimen nazi durante los años 1933–1939," in *El Holocausto* (Magnes), pp. 306–31.
36. W. Laqueur, "El Holocausto de Hitler: ¿quién sabia qué, cuándo y cómo?" in *El Holocausto* (Magnes), pp. 362–416.

11. The Struggle for Independence and the Establishment of the State of Israel

> a. Relations of the Zionist leadership with the British government toward the end of World War II
> b. Postwar British politics and the question of Eretz Israel
> c. Survivors of the Holocaust and illegal immigration
> d. International debate on the Palestine question; the plan for Partition
> e. The War of Independence and the creation of the State of Israel

1. *Historia del Pueblo Judío*, pp. 1233–59.
26. *Historia desde 1880*, pp. 129–34.
19. W. Laqueur, *Historia del Sionismo*, pp. 401–56.
37. J. Herzog, *Las guerras arabe-israelíes* (Jerusalen: La Semana, 1987), pp. 16–127.
27. M. Gilbert, *Atlas del conflicto*, pp. 37–49.
18. S. Avineri, *La Idea Sionista*, pp. 227–46.

12. The Diaspora since World War II

> a. Change in geographical distribution and social structure of the Jews
> b. The old centers (Western Europe, North Africa)
> c. The Jewish community in the United States
> d. The consolidation of the communities in Latin America
> e. The Jews in the Soviet Union

1. *Historia del Pueblo Judío*, pp. 1261–74.
38. R. Bachi, "La crisis demográfica del judaismo de la diáspora," *Rumbos* 10 (1984): 17–49.

39. H. Avni, "Perspectiva latinoamericana," *Rumbos* 5 (1981): 101–11.
40. N. Falbel, "Comentario a la ponecia de Jaim Avni," *Rumbos* 5 (1981): 113–16.
41. N. Lerner, "Comentario a la ponencia de Jaim Avni," *Rumbos* 5 (1981): 126–30.
42. D. Schers and H.Singer, "Las comunidades judías de Latino-América: factores internos y externos en su desarrollo," *Rumbos* 2 (1980): 47–71.
43. U.O. Schmelz and S. DellaPergola, "La demografía de los judíos en Latinoamérica," *Rumbos* 15 (1986): 17–38, 16 (1986): 155–94.
3. Y. Tzur, *En una era de transición*, División C Unidad 10, *En una generación de transición, Albert Memmi*.
44. M. Laskier, "La evolución de la actividad sionista en las comunidades de Marruecos, Túnez y Argelia 1897–1947," *Rumbos* 12 (1985): 71–82.
45. M. Laskier, "Túnez, centro de la actividad sionista en Africa del Norte," *Rumbos* 15 (1986): 179–95.
46. A. Ettinger, "El despertar judío en la Unión Soviética," *Rumbos* 16 (1986): 91–105.
47. Z. Katz, "El Kremlin y los judíos," *Dispersión y Unidad* 10 (1971): 208–16.
48. Z. Friegist, "Antisemitismo y antisionismo soviético: un nuevo ciclo," *Rumbos* 13 (1985): 167–90.

13. Israel and the Diaspora

    a. The "Reunion of Exiles" and the liquidation of Diaspora communities
    b. The problems of Israel's security
    c. Foreign relations of Israel
    d. The Sinai campaign and its consequences
    e. The Six Day War and its consequences
    f. The emigration of the Jews of the Soviet Union
    g. Socioeconomic and cultural development of Israel
    h. Changes in Israel's relations with the Diaspora

1. *Historia del Pueblo Judío*, pp. 1275–1300.
26. *Historia desde 1880*, pp. 135–323.
37. J. Herzog,*Las guerras*, pp. 129–456.
27. M. Gilbert, *Atlas del conflicto*, pp. 50–130.
21. A. Eban Legado, *La civilización y los judíos* , pp. 349–72.
49. S. Zipperstein and E. Jaffe, "Antecedentes de las relaciones étnicas judías en Israel," *Rumbos* 6 (1982): 61–84.

Index of Authors

The Index gives the chapter and note or item number in which each name is registered: 7 n. 14 means "note 14 of chapter 7." "28 b." refers to the bibliography following Chapter 28 (with the number of entries following in parentheses). The Annotated Bibliography is referenced as A; the Syllabi are referenced as 2/1 through 2/6: 2/1 no. 10 means "item 10 of Syllabus 1, U.S."